Human Rights and Empire

The political philosophy of cosmopolitanism

Is there an intrinsic relationship between human rights and the recent wars carried out in their name? Are human rights a barrier against domination and oppression, or the ideological gloss of an emerging empire? In its examination of the normative characteristics, political philosophy and metaphysical foundations of our age, *Human Rights and Empire* addresses the paradox of a contemporary humanitarianism that has abandoned politics in favour of combating evil.

Human rights continue to offer a defence against power. But as Costas Douzinas argues in the first part of this book, the Westerner is placed in the role of saviour of the victims of violence and human rights have come to operate in a divided world. The ideal, universal, position of human rights has thus been reversed. In their capacity to contribute to the creation of human identities, human rights have become a means for regulating human life, and so have become tools of public power and the expression of individual desires. The second part of the book pursues this argument in the context of recent international events, and considers how human rights have come to provide the justification for a new configuration of political, economic and military power. Cosmopolitanism is the formal ideology of the new order; the removal of violence and perpetual peace its alleged end. But insofar as wars, violence and torture are its modus operandi, human rights now codify and 'constitutionalise' the normative sources of empire.

While the sovereignty of states and the territorial principle have been weakened, no sense of world community has developed. But, Douzinas concludes, it is precisely the renewal of an ancient cosmopolitanism that may give rise to a new politics of community.

Costas Douzinas is Professor of Law and Dean of the Faculty of Arts and Humanities at Birkbeck College, University of London. His many books include *Adieu Derrida*, *Critical Jurisprudence*, *Law and Aesthetics*, *The End of Human Rights* and *Justice Miscarried*. He is Managing Editor of *Law and Critique: The International Journal of Critical Legal Thought*.

Human Rights and Empire

The political philosophy of
cosmopolitanism

Costas Douzinas

Routledge·Cavendish
Taylor & Francis Group
a GlassHouse book

First published 2007
by Routledge-Cavendish
2 Park Square, Milton Park, Abingdon, OX14 4RN, UK

Simultaneously published in the USA and Canada
by Routledge-Cavendish
270 Madison Avenue, New York, NY 10016

A Glasshouse book

*Routledge-Cavendish is an imprint of the Taylor & Francis Group,
an informa business*

Typeset in Times by
Florence Production Ltd, Stoodleigh, Devon
Printed and bound in Great Britain by
MPG Books Ltd, Bodmin, Cornwall

British Library Cataloguing in Publication Data
A catalogue record for this book is available
from the British Library

Library of Congress Cataloging in Publication Data
Douzinas, Costas, 1951–
  Human rights and empire: the political philosophy of
  cosmopolitanism/Costas Douzinas.
    p. cm.
  1. Human rights.   2. Cosmopolitanism.   I. Title
JC571.D775 2007
323.01 – dc22   2006033830

ISBN 10: 0–415–42758–4 (hbk)
ISBN 10: 0–415–42759–2 (pbk)

ISBN 13: 978–0–415–42758–6 (hbk)
ISBN 13: 978–0–415–42759–3 (pbk)

Contents

Prologue   vi

PART I
The paradoxes of human rights   I

  1 The end of human rights?   3
  2 Identity, desire, rights   34
  3 The many faces of humanitarianism   51
  4 The politics of human rights   90
  5 Freedom in a biopolitical setting   111

PART 2
The normative sources of the new world order   I3I

  6 Empire or cosmopolitanism?   133
  7 Cosmopolitanism ancient, modern, postmodern   151
  8 Human rights: values in a valueless world?   177
  9 The brief glory and the long crisis of international law 198
 10 War, violence, law   236
 11 Bare, theological and cosmopolitan sovereignty   269

 12 Epilogue: the cosmopolitanism to come   291

     Bibliography   299
     Index   313

Prologue

How can intellectuals resist the onslaught of wars, violence, religious terrorism, torture, the central characteristics of the early twenty-first century? Can 'theory' or 'philosophy' help us understand the sense of the world and develop a politics of dissent? What is the function of the academic in a culture where according to President Bush 'whoever is not with us is against us'? What is the role of critique in an environment where scholarship is judged according to managerial criteria that reward the safe, the conventional, often the banal? These questions have persistently followed and tormented critical thought in the last twenty years. I have no simple or right answers. Like many others, however, I believe that this is the time for intellectuals and academics to join the wider political and cultural debates and conflicts and bring whatever limited insights disciplinary knowledge offers to the task of imagining and working for a better world. Too often we academics have opted for a life of accommodation and non-confrontation, looking to the next promotion or book contract. Too often has the university slavishly served the demands of state, nation, ideology. And yet, the prime mission of the university remains the quest for knowledge and truth. As we know since Socrates, knowledge and truth are the inseparable partners of justice and beauty. Truth and knowledge are wedded to justice; speaking truth with justice to power is the name and honour of the European university.

Let me recount the strange story of the creation of the first European university in Bologna. Between the eleventh and twelfth centuries, the War of Investitures dominated Europe. Frederick I, the Emperor Barbarossa,

> ambitious to restore the splendour of the purple, invaded the republics of Lombardy with the arts of a statesman, the valour of a soldier and the cruelty of a tyrant. The recent discovery of Roman law, had renewed the science most favourable to despotism. And the Doctors of law of Bologna

proclaimed the emperor the absolute master of the lives and properties of his subjects.[1]

This is how Gibbon described Barbarossa's attack on the Italian cities. The reassertion of the Holy Roman Empire was a defining moment in the development of modern Europe, in the relationship between church and state and in the creation of the European University. In 1158, four eminent professors and Doctors of law, Bulgaro, Martino, Jacopo and Ugo di Porta Ravegnana – members of a School established in Bologna by the great glossator Irnerius – were invited by the Emperor to appear at the Diet of Roncaglia. They were asked to advise on the relationship between imperial law and local legal customs and political institutions, particularly those of the powerful Lombard cities. The cooperation was beneficial for both parties. The jurists, trained in the imperialism of the Justinian code, drew up a list of regalia or regulations, favouring the emperor against local claims with one dissenting voice, that of Martino. They demonstrated, with detailed commentary, that Roman Law was supreme and that its authority rested with the empire not the cities.

The emperor's gain was legal recognition. The reward for the jurists was an *Authentica Habita*, a decree or charter later accepted as the foundation act of Bologna, the oldest university in Europe. This imperial grant of privilege had three elements. Each scholar could choose to recognise the jurisdiction of his professor in all matters affecting him. Second, the charter granted everyone who travelled for the sake of study imperial protection on their way and during their stay at the place of learning, a privilege later extended to the student's return journey. Exemption from all tolls, duties and customs was also given to students and their servants (this is the beginning of the duty free concession. As it is being phased out, academics should claim that they have historical claim to it). Finally, the decree prohibited the use of reprisals against students, a common and strongly resented practice, under which if an English student, for example, left Bologna without paying his debts, the Bolognesi could recoup their money from other English students. This was a key moment in European academic history. Bologna started as a law school but developed out of the liberal arts, which flourished early in the eleventh century. Grammar, rhetoric and *dictamen*, the art of composition, were taught alongside law. The first university brought together the study of law with what we now call the humanities. Later, theology, music and mathematics were added to the

---

1   Edward Gibbon, *History of the Decline and Fall of the Roman Empire* (J.B. Bury, ed.) (London, Methuen, 1911) V.303.

curriculum. The fame of the professors drew to Bologna students from Italy and further afield. At the beginning of the thirteenth century some 10,000 attended Bologna, many coming from every part of Europe.

What lessons does the history of Bologna have for the jaded academics of the twenty-first century and for 'Bologna the Sequel', the Bologna process of European academic integration? First and foremost, academic freedom and asylum, protection of research and scholarship from all external intervention or pressure. The university is based on the absolute freedom to question publicly and to declare freely what research and knowledge tells us about truth. Thought must be unconditioned, indeed thought is the experience of the unconditional, of asking about everything, including the value of questioning itself as well as the value of truth. This is even more crucial today when truth has multiplied into many truths. The European university remains the mother of truth. The only precondition of knowledge and truth is protection from external threats and reprisals. But this protection has never been there fully de facto or *de jure*. The doctors and students of Bologna acquired their academic rights, by accepting the claims of empire and emperor. Empires call upon lawyers, philosophers and intellectuals to become their apologists for a small consideration. Cosmopolitan law has always started as a critique of the injustices of the local and has often finished as the ideology of empire.

But there was also Martino, the dissident, who did not accept the imperial claim. It is important that the university retains and reproduces this tradition at a point at which pressure from all directions is trying to turn it into a conformist punchbag for every transient and ill-thought policy initiative. The European university must oppose as much as it can power, including state, economic and media power, the power of ideology and religion, in the name of truth and justice. It must remain the place of unconditional resistance to dogmatism, moralism and conformism. To be sure, this is an almost impossible demand, as Kant himself accepted in early modernity. The very possibility of the university is based on this impossible distancing from power. But it is this impossibility that makes the university possible, as Jacques Derrida argued forcefully and repeatedly in the last ten years of his life.

These crucial questions about the role of critique and resistance have taken a specific form in legal and political philosophy. Are human rights a defensive barrier against domination and oppression or the ideological gloss of an emerging empire? Is cosmopolitanism the way to bring justice and pacify the world of late globalised capitalism? These are the kinds of questions the confusing events of the last ten years brought to the surface to see them often buried again under acres of complacent apologetics. Questioning the orthodoxies of the new world order has become almost synonymous with the exploration of sites where intellectual and academic critique could bridge the lecture hall and the town hall. This book is the result of these explorations. It brings together critical theory and recent (political and legal) history in an attempt to develop a political philosophy of resistance. It started as a series of public lectures and debates in the difficult year 2003. Its themes, hopes and, frankly, despair travelled to four continents for a period of three years and were shaped by the generous comments (and criticisms) of many academics, scholars and the general audience. The oral and passionate tone of delivery has been maintained here. This is the reason for the occasional repetition of certain themes and examples. Lectures on just wars, empire, human rights, cosmopolitanism, sovereignty and the philosophy of history were given between 2003 and 2006 at the Universities of Griffith (Brisbane), Melbourne and the Australian National University (Canberra); in Nanjing, Su Chow and Beijing; at the Universities of Dublin, Humboldt (Berlin), Bologna, Complutense (Madrid), Washington (Seattle), Haveriana (Bogota) and Pretoria; in Athens, Thessaloniki and Volos, various universitites in Britain and last, but not least, London. I owe a huge debt to the people who invited me to their universities and lecture halls and took the time to listen, agree and – often – heckle the speaker. I would like to thank in particular those who offered me various invitations and fellowships, which helped the gestation and development of the ideas of this book. They include Shaun McVeigh, Anne Orford, Hilary Charlesworth, Guo Chunfa, Shejiard Tao, Vita Fortunati, Maria Falcon, Louis Wolcher, Oscar Guardiola-Rivera, Karin von Marle, Duard Klein, Johan van der Walt, Christos Lyrintzis, Rob Walker, Costas Tsoukalas, Nicos Mouzelis, Antonis Manitakis, Rika Benveniste and Costas Hatjikyriakou. Colin Perrin has been a friend and fellow traveller in the pathways of thought for many years. It is exceptionally good fortune for me to have him as my editor at Routledge-Cavendish. I would also like to thank Lynda Watson for her meticulous editing.

Against the dictats of the intellectual property border-guards, ideas, critical ideas in particular, can only develop in the fertile hothouse of debate, argumentation and confrontation. My scholarship has been blessed with something rare: the opportunity and pleasure of collaborating and co-writing with close friends. Nothing I have ever written belongs to me exclusively. Every text is always a tissue of texts and discussions, sounds and thoughts, smells and colours many of which started with others. I cannot mention all the people, texts and influences here; I do not even know them all. But I must mention some friends whose contributions are close to the surface of the text. The most important interlocutors over a difficult period have been (and hopefully will continue to be) Patricia Tuitt, Michelle Everson, Fiona Macmillan, Maria Aristodemou, Anne Orford, Peter Rush, Alison Young, Julia Chryssostali, Patrick Hanafin, Karin von Marle, Johan van der Walt, Peter

Fitzpatrick, Thanos Zartaloudis, Bill Bowring, Tim Murphy, Nicola Lacey, Emilios Christodoulidis, Alexandra Bakalaki, Stewart Motha, Hilary Charlesworth, Alan Norrie and David Kennedy. Shaun McVeigh, Adam Geary and Piyel Haldar have been fellow travellers in the pathways of thought and resistance for decades. They will find here much they helped me understand. Any remaining mistakes are theirs, shared by me. Last but not least I should mention the students of my LLM class in the History and Philosophy of Rights at Birkbeck College and the Ph.D. researchers at the School of Law. With their commitment, enthusiasm and expertise in human rights, they keep teaching me every year much more than they can ever learn from me. Manuel Barreto, Mat Stone, Gilbert Leung and Illan Wall have been exemplary scholars and fellows in this journey.

Joanna Bourke has been an inspiration, a most wonderful partner in the hard recent winters and the best example of a public intellectual who resists the sirens of the 'common sense'. The long series of lectures and speeches, and the demonstrations and marches that went with them and the resulting book would have been impossible without her. This book is dedicated to her amazing spirit. Nicos Douzinas has been a wonderful reader and critic of these pages. Phaedra Douzina-Bakalaki is a continuous reminder of the importance of resisting (paternal) authority.

Let me finally return to Bologna's *Authentica Habita*. Our responsibility today, our responsibility to Europe, in the name of a Europe that committed atrocities, genocides, the Holocaust but has also developed the only acceptable social model against the neo-conservative neo-liberals and the neo-communist neo-liberals, our responsibility in the name of the (old) European university is to revitalise the scholar's commitment to the unconditionality of truth and justice, the intellectual's vocation of resistance. Resistance both to the powers of state, capitalism and ideology but also those of managerialism and technocracy for its own sake or for the sake of maintaining an unjust and exploitative socio-economic and a pliant political system. Beyond citizenship, nationality, belonging, the European university must remain the *oikos* (home) and *patria* (country) of the public intellectual. This is what the *Authentica* teaches us: keep open the pathways and highways the itinerant scholars took on the way to knowledge, keep opening new ones, new humanities, new laws for a cosmopolitanism to come.

Part I

The paradoxes of human rights

Chapter 1

The end of human rights?

In March 1991, President George H.W. Bush triumphantly announced that

> a new world order is coming into view . . . in which the principles of justice
> and fair play will protect the weak against the strong [and] freedom and
> humanity will find a home among nations . . . Enduring peace must be our
> mission.[1]

Eleven years later, President George W. Bush's *National Security Strategy*, in
a more subdued mood, brought the hope of enduring peace to an abrupt end:

> New deadly challenges have emerged from rogue states and terrorists. The
> nature and motivations of these new adversaries . . . make today's security
> environment more complex and dangerous [than during the cold war]
> . . . We will not hesitate to act alone, if necessary, to exercise our right of
> self-defence by acting preemptively.[2]

The war on terror, Bush Jr declared, was to be long; those 'not with us are
with the enemy'. This was *fin de siècle* stuff, depressingly doom-laden and
exuberantly millenarian. Was the twenty-first century to repeat the infamies
of the twentieth? Was the *Finis Austriae* to be followed by the *Finis
Americae*? Between the promise of perpetual peace and the threat of endless
war, a new world order has been taking shape, the normative boundaries of
which this book traces.

1 Text of address to the Congress on 6 March 2001, at the end of the Gulf War: http://
  millercenter.virginia.edu/scripps/diglibrary/prezspeeches/ghbush/ghb_1991_0306.html.
2 The *National Security Strategy* was issued by President George W. Bush on 20 September
  2002. The document can be found at www.whitehouse.gov/nsc/nss.html.

In-between those two statements, my *End of Human Rights* was published. Its last two sentences, written in the summer of 1999, were somewhat prophetic:

> When the apologists of pragmatism pronounce the end of ideology, of history or utopia, they do not mark the triumph of human rights; on the contrary, they bring human rights to an end. The end of human rights comes when they lose their end.[3]

At a period when the post-cold war optimism was at its highest, this prediction appeared at best foolhardy. It certainly landed its author into a lot of controversy. Writing less than two years later, however, after the attacks on New York and Washington, Michael Ignatieff, the liberal 'human rights warrior',[4] seemed to agree and wondered 'Is the Human Rights Era Ending?'[5] Ignatieff feared that in the wake of the terrorist attacks, security would become the prime concern of governments and the age of human rights and humanitarianism would draw to a close.

Ignatieff's worry is typical of a certain type of liberal. The lofty claims of the last decade of the twentieth century about the 'end of history' and the triumph of liberal capitalism have been replaced, since 2001, with angst-ridden debates about the 'clash of civilisations'. The new *jus cosmopoliticum*, ushered in after the triumph of the West, is now challenged, we are told, by terrorists, religious fanatics, suicide bombers and Islamic militants. Western governments responded by introducing draconian anti-terrorist measures, restricting immigration further and expanding surveillance from target and suspect groups to an ever-increasing part of the population. State practices, which had been universally condemned and had almost disappeared in the West, have become popular again. Torture returned in Western camps and prisons, most famously in Guantánamo Bay and Abu Ghraib. But torture is also extensively outsourced. 'Rendition' flights take suspects to secret camps in countries where torture takes place without embarrassment or restraint. Confessions and evidence obtained through torture are then used against others in clear violation of the legal principle that information obtained through the use of violence has no probative value, is morally reprehensible and should be legally inadmissible.

---

3 Costas Douzinas, *The End of Human Rights* (Oxford, Hart, 2000), 380; Costas Douzinas, 'The End(s) of Human Rights', 26/2 *University of Melbourne Law Review* 445 (2002).

4 I owe this apt expression to Anne Orford, *Reading Humanitarian Intervention* (Cambridge, Cambridge University Press, 2003), 186.

5 Michael Ignatieff, 'Is the Human Rights Era Ending?', *The New York Times*, 5 February 2002.

The post-Second World War Western consensus was that there are certain acts – torture prime among them – that liberal-democratic societies do not tolerate and their governments cannot do. In the West, torture was declared unacceptable and was discussed as part of a barbaric and long gone history. Torture, we were told, takes place 'elsewhere' only, in exotic and evil places, in dictatorships and totalitarian regimes. But this consensus has now broken down. Torture has become a respectable topic for conferences on practical ethics and the 'ticking bomb' hypothetical offers entertainment at dinner parties. What is particularly disturbing is the way in which lawyers, such as Alan Dershowitz, and liberal commentators, including the human rights warrior Michael Ignatieff among many, are prepared to enter into debate about the morality and legitimacy of torture and to develop detailed plans about ways of legalising it through 'torture warrants', 'sunset clauses' and judicial supervisory regimes.[6] Ignatieff is interested in the gradations of torture as part of the 'lesser evils' strategy: 'permissible duress might include forms of sleep deprivation . . . together with disinformation and disorientation (like keeping prisoners in hoods) that would produce stress'.[7] Bruce Ackerman has opposed torture but supports the use of preventive detention of suspects and the introduction of an 'emergency constitution' for limited periods.[8] The history of civil liberties in Britain and Northern Ireland teaches that while governments have few qualms in using real or imaginary emergencies to assume wide powers, they are reluctant to abandon them once the perceived threat has passed. As Lord Hoffman put it in the case examining the legality of detention without trial of terror suspects, 'the real threat to the life of the nation comes not from terrorism but from laws such as these'.[9]

6   Alan Dershowitz, *Why Terrorism Works* (New Haven, CT, Yale University Press, 2002); Michael Ignatieff, *The Lesser Evil* (Edinburgh, Edinburgh University Press, 2004); see John Gray's Swiftian satire 'Torture – A Modest Proposal' in his *Heresies* (London, Granta, 2004), 132.

7   Michael Ignatieff, 'Lesser Evils', *New York Times Magazine*, 2 May 2004, 3.

8   Bruce Ackerman, *Before the Next Attack* (New Haven, CT, Yale University Press, 2006). The 'emergency constitution' will introduce a 'sweeping revision of the emergency power provisions currently found in many of the world's constitutions' (14). The main innovation will allow the preventive detention of suspects, a provision with a long history of failure both in this country and the United States and the major object of criticism of the British government by the judiciary. Ackerman hopes to restrict the state of emergency through time limits and a political process check – the 'supermajoritarian escalator' – designed to prevent 'permanent' emergencies. It is further evidence of the loss of courage by the erstwhile liberal establishment. Giorgio Agamben's diagnosis of a current state of exception (see Chapters 5, 10 and 11) receives indirect support by someone who fundamentally disagrees with his analysis.

9   *A and Ors* v. *Secretary of State for the Home Department* [2004] UKHL 56, para. 97.

The end of last century was accompanied by excited discussions about globalisation, the subjection of the state to strict legal and moral rules on the way to its withering away and replacement by international institutions and cosmopolitan laws. Recently, however, the state has enjoyed a remarkable comeback. *Salus populi,* the paramount duty of the government, which had been forgotten in the wake of economic globalisation and the trumpeted pacification of the world, has re-entered the political lexicon. Suddenly our civilisation and way of life is in mortal danger. Extreme threats require extreme measures, something Western legal culture understood since Rome. The law and its principles must be suspended in order to be protected from lethal threats. Liberal politicians and commentators admit, a little embarrassedly, that security trumps human rights. Academics returned to the dark ruminations of Carl Schmitt and Giorgio Agamben, his contemporary disciple. The optimistic age of globalised hope has turned into the dark era of fear.[10] The state of exception, the suspension of human rights principles, even the scrapping of the whole British human rights legal arsenal through the repeal of the Human Rights Act are on the agenda. As always civil liberties are the first victim of governmental fears and public anxiety.

Our predictions about the end of human rights seem to be coming true. This is a time for good people to defend rights against attacks by fearful and fear-exploiting governments, indeed to defend them against liberals, such as Ignatieff, who have been seduced by the inducements of power and are prepared to jettison the cardinal principle of liberalism. But is the recent suspension of some civil liberties a radical departure from the legal and political order under construction after 1989? Was 9/11 a watershed in the creation of the new world order? Is Bush *fils* such a radical break from Bush *père*? It is arguable that important policies, strategies and plans introduced before the 2001 attacks have continued and intensified after the attacks. Afghanistan and Iraq were attacked partly in pursuit of the pre-emptive defence policy. But they were justified also as instances of regime change, 'just wars' to liberate Afghanis and Iraqis from warlords and dictators. They are a darker continuation of the 'Kosovo spirit' in which the West displayed a new willingness to spread human rights, freedom and democracy around the world. The failure and human misery brought about by these wars and occupations are well-documented. The *End of Human Rights* had predicted that the extravagant boasts about the dawn of a new humanitarian age would be accompanied by untold suffering.[11] The 'victories for freedom and democracy' in Afghanistan and Iraq have

---

10   Joanna Bourke, *Fear: A Cultural History* (London, Virago, 2005).
11   Douzinas op. cit., Chapter 1.

confirmed it. These victories have been drowned in a human rights disaster for the local people.

It is therefore important to continue the effort of the earlier book in the new climate, if indeed there is much 'new' around. Is there an internal relationship between the discourse and practice of human rights and our recent disastrous wars carried out partly in their name? Are human rights an effective defensive tool against domination and oppression or are they the ideological gloss of an emerging empire? To begin to answer these questions, we have to return to the tradition of human rights as developed and practised in the West over the last three centuries. Human rights have both institutional and subjective aspects. As institutional entities, they belong to constitutions, laws, court judgments, international organisations, treaties and conventions. But the prime function of rights is to construct the individual person as a subject (of law). Rights are tools and strategies for defining the meaning and powers of humanity. The human and its derivatives, humanism and humanitarianism, are all intimately linked with the work of rights. We acquire our identity in an endless struggle for recognition, in which rights are bargaining chips in our desire of others. The law and rights make a central contribution to the project of becoming subject through the reciprocal acknowledgement of self and the (mis)recognition of others.

The first part of the book links the subjective and institutional parts of human rights. The greatest achievement of rights is ontological: rights contribute to the creation of human identity. This function precedes and determines their protective role against public (and later private) power; it accompanies and colours every change in their form, content or scope. Rights have acquired ideological and legal pre-eminence precisely because they are so central in bestowing subjectivity and identity. This role has become dominant in Western postmodern societies, where human rights have become formal expressions of an insatiable and boundless desire (Chapter 2). Humanitarianism, the contemporary version of humanism, gives public expression to this role. For legal humanism, humanity has a rigid and static essence. Military humanism aims to spread it around the world. Humanitarian campaigns in the West, on the other hand, place the Westerner in the role of a saviour who rescues Third World victims from their evil compatriots (Chapter 3). The institutional importance and the accompanying problems of human rights stem from this role. When human rights become its means and object, politics is moralised, its ability to mediate conflict eroded. Post-political Western societies have abandoned – but not pacified – antagonism in favour of combating evil. People are divided into rulers, ruled and excluded. Human rights both record and uphold this hierarchy (Chapter 4). Rights offer defences against power. But they also increasingly target life and regulate parts of the body becoming major tools for the biopolitical operation of power (Chapter 5). The central concern of the first part of the book is to explore the paradoxical ways in which the ideal, transcendent position of natural law, natural and human rights has been reversed turning them into tools of public power and individual desire.

What are human rights?

In an article published in 2003, John Morss accused this author's arguments of being 'repugnant for a democratic and justice-based orientation to human rights' and sought to 'save human rights from its friends'.[12] Unlike Jürgen Habermas, whom Morss preferred, I was not particularly reverential and upbeat towards rights. At the other end, Stewart Motha and Thanos Zartaloudis concluded a careful reading of the *End* with precisely the opposite criticism. The book was too positive towards rights. Future radical politics would go 'beyond human rights' because their language distorts both difference and otherness and cannot lead to emancipation.[13] A standard rhetorical trope in situations like this is for the criticised to claim that as he is attacked both from the right and the left, he must have struck the right balance. I cannot use such a defence. First, because I do not feel comfortable in the middle of the road, the place where people get run over. But more importantly, I cannot claim to be the prudent middleman, mediator or synthesiser because both criticisms are partly correct. The apologists expect from human rights much more than is realistic and neglect their side-effects. But it is not possible to 'get rid' of rights as friendly critics have insisted. To quote a key statement from the *End*, 'human rights have only paradoxes to offer'. The paradoxical, the aporetic, the contradictory are not peripheral distractions awaiting to be ironed out by the theorist. Paradox is the organising principle of human rights for a number of reasons.

The many confusions of human rights theory stem from the semiotic and semantic openness of the term. The 'human' in rights is a 'floating signifier', 'human rights' is a thin, underdetermined concept (Chapter 2). The term has wide scope and reach, its semantic value and field of reference encompasses multiple, diverse and even conflicting practices and discourses. In terms of reach, 'human rights' denote, among others, a diverse group of constitutional, legal, judicial, academic and popular texts and commentaries; legal, political

---

12   John Morss, 'Saving Human Rights from its Friends: A Critique of the Imaginary Justice of Costas Douzinas', 27 *Melbourne University Law Review* 890 (2003).
13   Stewart Motha and Thanos Zartaloudis, 'Law, Ethics and the Utopian End of Human Rights', 12 *Social Legal Studies* (2003), 243–68 .

and cultural institutions and practices at domestic, regional and international level using human rights as their organising principle; governmental and non-governmental agencies working around human rights; the personnel working these institutions; diverse campaigns, groups and organisations at various levels; the people involved in them; multiple situations, events and people who use the term in order to describe or evaluate these situations. While the use of the term in all these texts and contexts is not inaccurate, there is no theory, doctrine or empirical description that could encompass all these and give an accurate presentation of the field. In short, there is no single field of activity called 'human rights' nor can there be a single theory describing it.

The conceptual and semantic import of the term is equally broad. Let me enumerate some of its common and often contradictory usages:

1 'Human rights' is a combined term. As *rights*, human rights are a legal category. Rights were the creation of early modern legal systems and constitute the basic building block of Western law. Broadly speaking, legal rights are relational. They involve an individual entitlement, for example, a property right, which (a) can be realised by the right-holder through the respective action of one or many duty-bearers who must act or refrain from acting in certain ways specified in the right (a property right creates a near universal duty in people not to interfere with others' property) and (b) is legally enforced against duty-bearers if they do not perform their obligations. Human rights as legal institutions involve the diverse practices, languages, institutions, remedies and personnel of the law. Initially, their sources were found in state constitutions, legislation and jurisprudence. After 1945, these sources are increasingly located in international and regional conventions, treaties and case-law. The *human* of human rights, on the other hand, refers to a more or less concrete sense of morality, which accompanies the institution of legal rights. Formally speaking, human rights are a subcategory of legal rights given special status and protection because of the importance of the goods or actions they protect and promote, typically described as dignity, freedom and equality. Their study as legal rights belongs to the doctrinal and institutional discipline of law.

2 Human rights are moral rights or claims by individuals, which may or may not have been recognised by a particular legal system. They introduce certain minimum standards of treatment to which people are entitled and create a moral framework within which state policy, administration and the law should operate. The institution of human rights therefore combines law and morality, description and prescription. This often leads

to confusion and rhetorical exaggeration. A South African during the apartheid regime or a political dissident in China today could correctly claim that they have 'the right not to be discriminated against'. No such positive, legally enforceable right exists however. 'Right' in these statements does not refer to an existing legal entitlement but to a claim about what morality (or ideology, or international law or some other higher source) demands. It is the statement of aspiration against the current state of law or a call to arms for the reform of the political and legal system. In this usage, the moral element of human rights comes into conflict with their putative legal status. This confounding of the real and the ideal is characteristic of human rights discourse. Article 1 of the Universal Declaration of Human Rights states that 'all human beings are born free and equal of right'. But as Jeremy Bentham first commented about a similar article in the French Declaration of the Rights of Man and Citizen, newborn infants are not free as they are dependent for survival on their carers, while the idea that people are born equal or enjoy equality around the world flies in the face of the huge disparities between rich and poor or the North and the South. The way out is to read the descriptive statements of the Declarations as prescriptive: people are not but ought to be free and equal. Indeed the great power of human rights lies in their rhetorical ambiguity and oscillation between the extant state of law and an absent and desired state of perfection. This ambiguity is a central characteristic of the appeal to rights, in states that violate their basic principles; it is still active, albeit in a less obvious manner, in legal systems that have incorporated lists of rights. Their study here belongs to moral and political philosophy.

3   Human rights are a topic in jurisprudence. Over their long history, the source of natural and human rights has moved from purposeful nature, to reason, to God and the Scriptures to human nature and, in their final mutation, to state constitutions and international law. What normative sources and argumentation can be used today to formulate rights and attract agreement about their principles? As moral standards, human rights derive from a group of anthropological hypotheses and moral assertions about liberty, equality, the well-being of individuals and their relationship to wider society. It would be comforting to say that human rights are recognised and given to people on account of their participation in the human race and not of any restricted or regional membership, such as citizenship, national, class or group belonging. Yet it is quite clear that the only real rights are those given by states to their citizens (Chapter 4). Aliens, refugees, the stateless, those who have no state or government to

protect them and who could have been expected to be the main beneficiaries of the rights of humanity, have very limited, if any, rights.

The change from natural to human rights marked a loss of faith in the ability to justify rights on the basis of transcendent revelation or generally acceptable truths about human nature. While arguments from human nature are still canvassed, the 'human' of human rights refers mainly to their scope (they are rights that should be given to human beings) rather than to their justification. Commonly accepted facts about human nature keep changing with scientific knowledge and, whatever their latest state, cannot generate moral commitments on their own. The main current theoretical method for the justification of rights is constructivism. Starting from the basic assumptions of liberal democracy about individual dignity, equality and tolerance, the moral philosopher builds a coherent system of rights and expectations. This approach has been criticised as excessively abstract, formal and unrealistic. An alternative detects certain value commitments in the social mores or 'deep structure' of a society, which are then raised into principles worthy of legal protection. But there is a problem; by extracting and promoting the values a society has already accepted, these theories neglect the forward looking and critical function human rights ought to have towards power and received opinion. In any case, human rights standards are today set by government representatives, diplomats and civil servants in international organisations. The normative sources are no longer to be found in divine omniscience, rational systematicity, natural or social integrity but in the interests, negotiations and compromises of states. Rights have moved away from the concerns and methods of moral and legal philosophers and towards the priorities of politicians. The attempt to embellish human rights with rational or moral coherence is doomed to fail both because of the heterogeneity of practices using the term and because even institutional and doctrinal texts cannot be rationally systematised. In pursuing the task of ironing out the inescapable ambiguities, contradictions and conflicts, liberal jurisprudence often appears as an *ex post facto* rationalisation of the workings of power.

4   Human rights are an ideology with a moral inflection. They are supposed to be above politics, a neutral, rational, natural discourse and practice and a 'moral trump card' that brings conflict to an end.[14] After 'the end of ideologies', the universal appeal of human rights has made them the

---

14 Michael Ignatieff, *Human Rights as Politics and Idolatry* (Princeton, NJ, Princeton University Press, 2001), 21.

preferred alternative to or the facade of various ideological 'isms'. The term has been used as a synonym for liberalism, market capitalism, individualism. The Soviets developed a socialist conception of human rights and many decolonisation and national independence struggles adopted 'human rights' as a less aggressive description of their aims and aspirations. In this usage, human rights lose their legal status and become a shortcut for wider ideology (or idolatry as Ignatieff puts it). They are a moral way for conducting politics but also an ideal for the organisation of the social bond. More specifically, human rights have become the official ideology of the new world order after 1989, discussed in Part 2 of this book. All recent wars and occupations have been carried wholly or partly in the name of human rights, democracy and freedom. Human rights become part of politcal philosophy and sociology.

5   In Western postmodern societies, the phrase 'I have a right to X' is used interchangeably with the expressions 'I desire or want X' or 'X should be given to me'. This linguistic inflation weakens the association of human rights claims with significant human goods and undermines their position as central principles of political and legal organisation. It indicates that the public recognition and satisfaction of individual desire have become major ways for the subjective, economic and ideological organisation of late capitalist societies (Chapter 2). The study of rights here moves to dialectics, psychology, psychoanalysis and semiotics.

6   Human rights are a major strategy for resisting the dictates of power and dissenting from the intolerance of public opinion. The end of natural law, natural and human rights has been, from their inception, to resist public and private domination and exploitation. The invention of natural law and natural right was the rebellion of philosophers and poets against the dead weight of custom and the irrational impositions of authority. The French Declaration of the Rights of Man and Citizen was drafted by revolutionary deputies and was the paradoxical manifesto of the revolution. It identified the state with the nation giving a powerful political base to nationalism, while celebrating cosmopolitanism. It declared the higher status of natural rights, while ushering in the age of the omnipotent sovereign. It celebrated the universalism of humanity, while upholding the interests of the rising bourgeoisie. Yet as the socialist leader Jean Jaures put it, there is a chance that 'history should turn [this bourgeois arsenal of weapons] against the conqueror'.[15] This was the case in the great

---

15   Quoted in Luc Ferry and Alain Renault, *From the Rights of Man to the Republican Idea* (Franklin Philip, trans.) (Chicago, IL, University of Chicago Press, 1990), 114.

revolutions of the eighteenth century, in the post-second world war 'never again' declarations, in popular uprisings against fascist and communist rule in the late twentieth century and every time the oppressed, exploited and dispossessed invoke them in their struggles. Human rights are part of a long and honourable tradition of dissent, resistance and rebellion against the oppression of power and the injustice of law. 'Natural right claimed the truth of nature against common sense and the dignity of argument and dialectic against the banality and oppression of received opinion'.[16] Natural right and its descendants enters the historical agenda directly and indirectly, disguised as religious duty, legal right or political ideology, every time people struggle 'to overthrow all relations in which man is a degraded, enslaved, abandoned or despised being'.[17]

Every exercise of right, every rearrangement of social hierarchy, opens in turn a new vista, which, if petrified, becomes itself an external limitation that must be again overcome. In a regulated world, in which little margin of action is allowed outside the parameters set by global capitalism and authoritarian state order, freedom must be redefined as resistance to 'freedom of choice', to the power to recognise and shape one's life, according to an authorised list of rights drawn by 'moral experts' and a catalogue of consumer goods approved by technocrats and policy makers (Chapter 5). The radical potential of right, both revealed and concealed in human rights, remains open to the idea of heterogeneous positions and traditions, when the emphasis moves from law's promotion of pacified obedience to that of indeterminacy and openness of self and society, the boundaries of which are always contested and never coincide with the crystallisations of power and legal entitlement. In this sense, freedom can be enhanced by the potential of rights to extend the limits of the social and to expand and redefine self and group identities. Human rights enclose both a principle of determinacy and homogenisation promoted by the military humanitarians and its radical opposite. As a recollection of old traditions, a partially institutionalised practice and an anticipation of the future, human rights have some formal authority, but they are not just products of legislation. They set limits to force, to the positivity of the law and to legislated rights that have been usurped by those against whom they were supposed to be a defence. Human rights work in the gap between ideal nature and law or, between the existent and its transcendence.

16 Douzinas op. cit., 44.
17 Ernst Bloch, *Natural Law and Human Dignity* (Dennis Schmidt, trans.) (Cambridge, MA, MIT Press, 1988), xxvii–xxix.

The multiplicity of people, texts and institutions, the variety of practices, struggles and events covered by the term means that no general theory of human rights could be developed. The only answer to the question 'what are human rights' or 'what rights do the Americans or Iraqis have' is to discuss specific instances of treatment of people in particular places and times. Rather than debating whether freedom of expression exists generally and in the abstract in the US, Britain or Iraq, we should be asking specific questions. Could communists and other left-wingers express and promote their ideological views in New York, in 1953? Were anti-Iraq war protesters allowed to put their case across in England, in 2003? Were they given adequate information and media space to refute the claims of the government? Do Iraqis have the right to life in downtown Baghdad, in 2006? To answer these specific questions, we must examine international, state and local laws at the relevant time; judicial and administrative practices; public opinion, media attitudes, workplace pressures, etc. More important than any legal, doctrinal or jurisprudential analysis, however, is the experience of the people on the ground, in New York, London and Baghdad. Human rights are protected or violated locally: at home, in the street, at school, in the workplace and the prison, in government offices and local media. For the person at the end of the policeman's boot or receiving the sacking notice from a multinational corporation, human rights treaties, conventions, commissions and reports are a gigantic irrelevance. An air of self-satisfied irrelevance is the permanent characteristic of human rights conferences. The only human rights violation most human rights experts, international lawyers and diplomats have ever experienced is being served a bad bottle of wine at their working lunches.

This is a work of general jurisprudence and political philosophy.[18] It can only be a layered presentation of different disciplinary strategies and approaches to human rights with no overall synthesis. Different insights will be offered by intellectual and political history, speculative philosophy, ontology, political philosophy, psychology, social and political theory, legal doctrine and jurisprudence. Each disciplinary approach is like the skin of an onion leading to the next again and again. There is nothing at the core of the onion, no centre or kernel that gives human rights their overall shape. No single theory can capture the multiplicity of discourses, practices, agencies, events and struggles that are using the term 'human rights'. The various skins, the successive layers, the disparate disciplinary approaches are perspectives on human rights; 'human rights' are nothing more than the various perspectives

---

18   On the meaning of general jurisprudence, see Costas Douzinas and Adam Gearey, *Critical Jurisprudence* (Oxford, Hart, 2005), Chapter 1.

on them. The next part offers an intellectual history of the term while the last tries to abandon historicism (a necessary but impossible task) and link human rights to the 'impure' histories of the genealogical method. It should be emphasised, however, that history (intellectual or political) is only one skin of the onion and has no privileged access to the essence or end of human rights. A history of human rights from Plato to NATO or from Hammurabi to Abu Ghraib (or a jurisprudence or doctrinal analysis of rights, etc.) is useful only as a single skin. It does not make the onion on its own and, if its use is overestimated, it can give a distorted view of the whole.

A short history of an idea[19]

The first reference to 'human rights' is relatively recent. It appears in legal writings of the 1920s in relation to the position of minorities in the post-imperial European states. But the main impetus for the age of rights was the adoption of the Charter of the United Nations in 1945, which made the protection of human rights one of the main aims of the organisation. Three years later, the UN General Assembly passed the Universal Declaration of Human Rights, a non-binding proclamation of minimum standards of treatment of citizens by their state authorities the world over. It paved the way for the drafting of two binding treaties: the International Covenant on Civil and Political Rights and that of Economic, Social and Cultural Rights, which after long and difficult negotiations were adopted in 1966.

The intellectual pedigree of human rights is the unlikely result of a combination of disparate events, ideas and traditions. Classical natural law, Jewish and Christian theology, the ideas of the Enlightenment, modern rationalism and postmodern multiculturalism, with their internal debates, conflicts and heresies, have all played a part. Major events such as the French Revolution and the American War of Independence, the Russian Revolution and its aftermath, the Nazi and Stalinist crimes, the Holocaust and the universal revulsion it caused join with 'less important' ones, like the preoccupations and priorities of Western (predominantly American) politicians to create what is called today 'the human rights movement'. Let us examine selectively some of these unlikely contributors. We will concentrate on the intellectual history of human rights in this part while the next will concentrate on their 'genealogy'.

The concept of nature and of natural law was first used in classical Greece and has occupied a prominent role in Western ethics, politics and law ever since. The Greeks did not distinguish between law and convention or between

---

19 This part is largely based on Chapters 1 to 6 of *The End of Human Rights*.

right and custom. Custom is a strong cement: it binds families and communities firmly, but it can also numb. Without external standards, the development of a critical approach towards traditional authority is impossible. The given goes unchallenged and the slaves stay in line. Nature as a critical concept acquired philosophical currency in the fifth century BC, when it was used by the sophists against custom and law, and by Socrates and Plato in order to combat the moral relativism of the sophists and to restore the authority of reason.[20] The discovery, or rather invention, of the concept of nature challenged the claim of the ancestral. Philosophy could now appeal from the ancestral to the good – to what is good intrinsically, according to its nature, as discovered by reason.

In Greek cosmology, the universe (*cosmos*) and every being and thing in it have their own unique nature, which provides them with their proper aim. The nature and purpose of the acorn is to become a mature oak tree providing the best shade, that of a baby boy to grow and become a just man, the purpose of a cobbler to produce the best possible sandals. A person is virtuous if he strives towards perfection according to his nature. Human perfection can be achieved only politically, in the *polis* (city in Greek) and in collaboration with other citizens. A just city provides the conditions for people to develop fully according to their nature; a city is just if its citizens can live according to their nature and perfect themselves. The universe is a moral order as every animate being and inanimate thing has a part to play in its own perfection and completion.

Turning nature into norm or into the standard of right was the greatest early step of civilisation, but it was also a cunning trick against priests and rulers. To this day, when knowledge and reason are subjected to authority, they are called 'theology' or 'legal learning' but they cannot be the philosophy practised by the Greeks.[21] Nature (the most cultured of concepts), the idea of the good and political philosophy, were all born together in an act of rebellion. Nature has remained, throughout history, a critical standard for holding power to account even when it is hijacked by religion, state or ideology. It was this natural order of things that obliged Antigone, the loving sister of Polynices, to defy the order of her uncle, King Creon, and perform burial rites for her brother. Polynices was killed while attacking his native Thebes and was left by Creon outside the city walls to be devoured by vultures, against religious

---

20   For a background discussion on this point, see generally Costas Douzinas and Ronnie Warrington, *Justice Miscarried* (Edinburgh, Edinburgh University Press, 1994), 133–7.
21   Leo Strauss, *Natural Law and History* (Chicago, IL, University of Chicago Press, 1965), 92.

law and family custom. As a punishment for her disobedience, Antigone herself was buried alive. But the divine order took revenge on the rationalist king. He was cursed for his arrogance and his family was destroyed. In this early confrontation between state law and the order of things, between male reason and calculation and female emotion and devotion to sacred and familial duties, the first and still greatest symbol of resistance against unjust law was born.

It is a short step from this natural cosmology to believe that generally shared moral principles exist. They depend on the nature of the cosmos and the interlocking purposes of beings and can be discovered by reason. In a legal dispute, the experienced judge, who knew through a long and prudent life the natural order of things, would redress the disturbed relationship and make it again harmonious. His judgment would be what was right according to the nature of things but also what the law requested. Indeed, both Greeks and Romans used the same word (*dikaion*, *jus*) to signify the lawful and the just state of affairs. For the classics, the nature of each being differed; it was flexible, it adjusted to local conditions and its discovery was subject to rational argumentation and rhetorical disputation The philosophical school of the Stoics, active in the third and second century BC, started changing that approach. The Stoics argued that all people share the ability to reason and that moral judgements have a rational foundation. Nature changed from a way of arguing to a source of rules and norms. The new natural law was universal and even divine and became the sole criterion of valid law. This God-given, eternal and absolute nature was the foundation of laws and institutions and was disclosed by reason. The Roman politician and philosopher Cicero expressed this change when he wrote that 'the true law, is the law of reason, in accordance with nature known to all, unchangeable and imperishable' (Chapter 7). Natural right used to be a matter of empirical observation, rational contemplation and dialectical confrontation. Now it became a matter of introspection and revelation. The notion of universal humanity, of a *cosmo-polites* (citizen of the world) based on the rational essence of man, was a dramatic departure from the hierarchical Greek world. It started its career as a trenchant critique of the declining civility of the Hellenistic cities. But soon the Roman Empire adjusted it to its needs. Cosmopolitanism turned from a critique of the powerful and the inequalities of late antiquity into a justification of imperial power.

But the main force moving the law towards a theory of natural rights was its gradual Christianisation. In Jewish cosmology, the universe is the creation of an omnipotent God, while Christianity places the individual and his soul at the centre of the universe. As a result, nature lost its purposeful character and became the inanimate natural world of modernity. Saint Paul's statement that

God has placed a natural law in our hearts (Rom. 11:15) replaced classical natural law. The Judeo-Christian God is a severe legislator; accordingly, the Roman idea of right or *jus* took the form of a set of commandments or rules found in the Scriptures and ingrained in the conscience. By the Middle Ages, a largely existential cosmology had been turned into a major weapon in the hands of the Church. A crucial link in the Christianisation of Roman law must be sought in the theology of Augustine and Thomas Aquinas. Aquinas distinguished four types of law: eternal, natural, divine and human. The law lost the cosmic flexibility of the classical tradition and became definite, certain and simple, its fundamental propositions formulated by God in the Decalogue. The source of natural law moved from rational morality to divine commandment: there is a higher law that consists of a small number of abstract ideals and values. These principles were declared superior to state law, which should either follow them or forfeit its claim to the loyalty of the citizens. At the same time, the idea of equality entered the historical scene. It is exemplified in St Paul's statement, that in the eyes of Christ 'there is no Greek or Jew, no freeman or slave'. Initially, equality was spiritual not political; it is given to all humans on account of the soul they possess and their participation in Christ's plan of salvation.

The early Christian confrontation between secular and higher divine law carried revolutionary potential. But once the Church's superiority over secular authorities was secured, natural law became a doctrine of justification of state power and the faithful were told to respect and obey the secular princes. Nature's revolutionary potential had to wait for the next great mutation in the history of ideas, from natural law to natural rights. This radical transformation was prepared in the writings of medieval scholastic theologians and came to fruition in the liberal political philosophers of the seventeenth and eighteenth centuries. The natural rights tradition started with the Franciscan nominalists Duns Scotus and William of Ockham. The nominalists argued, in the fourteenth century, that the supreme expression of creation is individuality, as evidenced in the historical incarnation of Christ. Its knowledge takes precedence over that of the universal forms of the classics. Abstract concepts such as law, justice or the city do not represent real entities. They owe their existence to linguistic practices and have no ontological weight or empirical value. The term 'city', for example, refers to the sum total of individual citizens and not to an ensemble of activities, aims and relations, while 'law' is just a word with no single referent or independent meaning. Society, as Mrs Thatcher, a contemporary nominalist, would say, does not exist, only individuals and families do.

William argued that the control individuals exercise over their lives and bodies is similar to that of *dominium* or property. This natural property is God's gift and a basic fact of human life.[22] Furthermore, law and morals are given by the divine legislator, whose will is absolute and obligatory per se not because it accords with nature or reason. For Duns Scotus, God's will has priority over his reason; the good exists because the omnipotent ordained it and not on account of some other independent quality. This way, the source and method of the law started changing. In a move that was to be repeated by the political philosophers of the seventeenth century, the Franciscans combined absolute legislative will with the nominalist claim that only individuals exist. The separation of God from nature and the celebration of an omnipotent and unquestionable will prepared the eventual removal of God from earthly matters and the foundation of secular sovereignty. Legal positivism and state authoritarianism found their early precursor in those devout defenders of God's power. The mutation of objective natural law into subjective individual rights was a 'Copernican moment', a cognitive, philosophical and eventually political revolution. From that point on, legal and political thought placed at the centre of its attention the sovereign and the individual, as mirror image and foil, with their respective rights and powers.

Thomas Hobbes, John Locke, Jean-Jacques Rousseau and Tom Paine argued in different ways that natural law is no longer about abstract principles of state organisation and State–Church relations but a bunch of individual rights that belong to the citizens because they pertain to their nature. The philosophers demanded that the law accords with the rational nature of man, preparing the ground for the abandonment of both classical and Christian natural law. Nature, seen as a physical universe, became radically separated from humanity, emptied of the purposes of the classics and the animism of the medievals. It stood without meaning or spirit, a frightening or pliant force to be exploited for human ends. Right, no longer objectively given in nature or the commandment of God's will, follows human reason and becomes subjective and rational. What was right according to reason or God becomes in modernity individual rights according to the law. The liberal philosophers argued that people lived in a state of nature before entering society where they enjoyed limitless freedom. However, the hazards and inconveniences of life led these noble savages to restrict their natural freedom by entering into a contract to establish society and political organisation. This social contract transferred a large part of their natural freedoms to the government in return for protection and security. But a number of important entitlements, usually listed as the rights to life, liberty and property, were retained by the contractors.

22   Michel Villey, *Le droit et les droits de l'homme* (Paris, PUF, 1983), 118–25.

The method of liberal philosophers was to observe people in their society, deduce their basic needs and desires and then postulate them as the basic characteristics of human nature. These were in accordance with reason and should be protected by the institution of rights from state power. For Hobbes, writing during the English civil war, human nature leads to conflict and, security, its greatest need, must be provided by an all-powerful state. For Locke, who lived in relative peace, man is naturally good and the state must not interfere with his natural rights. If state laws violate these natural rights they are invalid and could justify resistance against unjust power. Rousseau was the favourite author of the French revolutionaries rebelling against the socially and economically static feudal *ancien régime*. The first act of the successful Revolution was to pass a Declaration of the Rights of Man and Citizen. Similarly, Paine's *The Rights of Man* greatly influenced the American revolutionaries in their struggle against the colonial power. The American Declaration of Independence and the Bill of Rights were heavily influenced by natural rights theory.

The revolutionary potential of these principles did not escape the revolutionaries. As is often the case, victorious revolutionaries turned rulers can become more oppressive than their predecessors. The centralised Western states, which developed out of the great bourgeois revolutions, soon abandoned and condemned the theory of natural rights and adopted the doctrine of legal positivism. For the positivists, the only law worthy of the name is the law posited by the state. A clear distinction separates law from morals and appeals to a higher law, rights or the dictates of conscience have no validity in the eyes of authority. The nineteenth century was the epoch of social engineering in the metropolitan states and of empire-building and colonialism in the periphery. The law was seen as a tool in the hands of governments, institution builders and reformers; appeals to higher principles or individual rights were reactionary hurdles to progress. As the utilitarian philosopher Jeremy Bentham put it, talk of natural rights is 'nonsense, nonsense upon stilts, it is belief in witches and unicorns, for there is no right which when its abolition is advantageous to society, it should not be abolished'.

The creation of large-scale theory in sociology, economics and psychology and the rise of mass political parties accelerated the decline of the appeal of natural rights. The belief that political society was created by means of a social contract was seen as a myth while the claim that certain rights are eternal, inalienable and absolute was exploded by Emile Durkheim and Max Weber, the founders of sociology, and Karl Marx, the founder of socialism. By the first half of the twentieth century, the theory of natural rights had been discredited. It was treated as an outdated conservative tradition in academic writings as a long-gone part in the history of ideas.

The rehabilitation of natural rights under the new guise of human rights dates from the Nuremberg trial of Nazi war criminals after the war. The trial, which dramatically changed international law and politics, came close to not happening. The Nuremberg principle of arraigning state leaders for crimes against peace and humanity was unprecedented. The British Foreign Office had argued, as early as 1942, that the crimes were so grave that ordinary judicial proceedings were unable to deal with them and had suggested summary executions. The American War Department, however, was a keen supporter of the tribunal as a way of demonstrating the superiority of the rule of law. Support came unexpectedly from Stalin. The Moscow trials of the 1930s had persuaded the Russian jurists that justice should be public and popular, while ensuring that the outcome would be certain convictions and executions. The American–Soviet alliance won the argument and the tribunal was set up in 1945.

Robert Jackson, the chief American prosecutor, became the driving force of the tribunal smoothing the differences among the British, Soviet and French lawyers. The framing of the indictment was the greatest problem. The charge of war crimes existed in pre-war international law and was the easiest to prosecute. But the crime of waging an aggressive war had no proper legal definition and could not cover atrocities against the German people or the elimination of civilians on grounds of race or ideology. The first problem was dealt with by the legal device of prosecuting the defendants for conspiracy to wage war. The latter, through the creation of the novel legal category of crimes against humanity. The defence attacked the exceptional character of the trial arguing that it was a clear case of victors' justice. It challenged the jurisdiction of the tribunal, except in relation to war crimes, and attacked the retroactive application of criminal law, arguing that the concept of crimes against humanity meant that the defendants could not have known the principles they were allegedly violating. These objections were often rejected by weak legal arguments.

The tribunal made it clear that the trial was creating a new type of post-war normative order. The main defence argument was typically positivist: in following the orders and applying the laws of the Nazi state, the defendants were acting within the limits of state legality. They should not be punished for carrying out their duty under the law. To answer this objection, the court ruled that the systemic killing of Jews, communists, gays, gypsies and others by the Nazis had been against the customary law of civilised nations and could not be overridden by national laws. In doing so, the tribunal rediscovered a main tenet of natural law. Certain acts are such heinous crimes that they are banned by universal principles of humanity. Twelve defendants, including Goering and Ribbentropp, were sentenced to death. Hess was sentenced to life imprisonment, six defendants to various prison terms, while three were acquitted. The

Nuremberg trial was a turning point in international law. By introducing the individual criminal liability of political and military leaders, it paved the way for the weakening of state sovereignty and for the creation of a universal jurisdiction. The International Criminal Court that came into operation in 2002 is the child of Nuremberg. Experience indicates, however, that the law and criminal responsibility cannot prevent atrocities on their own.

The human rights revolution of the second half of the twentieth century owes much of its moral force in the arguments put forward in Nuremberg and the corresponding tribunal in Tokyo. Following these trials, a major international process was undertaken setting standards and devising procedures and institutions for the protection and promotion of human rights. Hundreds of human rights conventions, treaties, declarations and agreements have been negotiated and adopted by the United Nations, regional bodies, such as the Council of Europe and the Organisation of African Unity, and by states. Human rights diversified from 'first generation' civil and political or 'negative' rights, associated with liberalism, into second generation, economic, social and cultural or 'positive' rights, associated with the socialist tradition and, finally, into 'third generation' or group and national sovereignty rights, associated with the decolonisation process. The first generation or 'blue' rights are symbolised by individual freedom, the second, or 'red' rights by claims to equality and guarantees of a decent living standard, while the third or 'green' rights by peoples' right to self-determination and, belatedly, the protection of the environment.

The differences between 'blue' and 'red' rights became a central aspect of the ideological cold war conducted in the United Nations, international institutions, academic conferences and the world media in the second half of the twentieth century. The West claimed that the communist Gulags and lunatic asylums were logical extensions of Marxist totalitarianism. The Soviets responded that social and economic rights are superior because material survival and decent conditions of life are more important than the right to vote. 'The right to a free press is of no interest to a starving and illiterate peasant in an African village' ran the argument. For liberals, civil and political rights have priority. Their aim is to place limits around state activities. They therefore adopt a negative conception of freedom as the absence of state impositions and constraints. According to liberal theory, economic rights are not proper legal rights. They are claimed by groups, not individuals; they are 'positive' in their action, in other words, they call for state intervention in economy and society, for heavy taxation and central planning, in order to deliver the necessary levels of employment presupposed by the right to work or the revenues necessary for welfare provision and free health care or education. Finally, economic and social rights are not 'justiciable': they cannot be guaranteed by legislation in a liberal state and, moreover, courts cannot enforce them. The appalling oppression of dissidents in the communist countries was seen as proof of the correctness of the Western arguments. The claim that the market is the superior, if not the only, mechanism of distribution was the Western mantra in response to the communist allegations about capitalism-induced squalor, unemployment and racism.

These ideological conflicts made it impossible for the United Nations to draft a common international bill of rights. The attempt to produce an inclusive and binding UN treaty was abandoned under American pressure and two separate covenants were drawn and eventually adopted. The ideological conflict was reflected in the text of the treaties. Following Western priorities, human rights were hierarchised. The civil and political rights covenant creates a state duty 'to respect and ensure to all' the listed rights. The economic and social rights treaty is much more flexible and equivocal: member states under-take 'to take steps, individually and through international assistance and co-operation . . . with a view to achieving progressively the full realisation' of the covenant rights. A second approach to standard-setting led to the creation of treaties with more limited scope. Certain categories of person, such as refugees and stateless persons, migrant workers, children and women, may need special protection. Specific instruments were also drafted to eliminate particular forms of human rights violations such as genocide, torture, racial and gender discrimination.

What lies behind this apparently unstoppable proliferation of human rights? At the level of international law and institutions, the main justifica-tion for this incessant codification has been the brutal treatment of people by their own governments. The horrors of the Second World War and the Holo-caust made it clear that democracy and national legal and constitutional traditions cannot always prevent large-scale violations of rights. As Hannah Arendt put it, 'it is quite conceivable that one fine day, a highly organised and mechanised humanity will conclude quite democratically – namely by majority decision – that for humanity as a whole it would be better to liquidate certain parts thereof'.[23] The Germans voted Adolph Hitler into power, later Slobodan Milosevic was repeatedly elected President of Yugoslavia. International human rights were conceived as a type of higher law that should prevail over national policies. They are supposed to impose restrictions upon governments to pre-vent them from being beastly to their own citizens. An endless process of inter-national and humanitarian law-making has been put into operation, aimed at protecting people from the putative expressions of their own sovereignty.

23 Hannah Arendt, *The Origins of Totalitarianism* (San Diego, CA, Harvest Books, 1977), 299.

To paraphrase Nietzsche, if God, the source of natural law, is dead, he has been replaced by international law.

Law-making in the huge business of human rights has been undertaken by government representatives, diplomats, policy advisers, international civil servants and human rights experts. Indeed the proliferation of treaties and codes has made human rights a new type of positive law. Codification, from Justinian to the *Code Napoléon,* has been the ultimate exercise of legislative sovereignty, the supreme expression of state power. Governments were the enemy against whom human rights were conceived as a defence. Undoubtedly, the atrocities of this century shook and shocked some governments and politicians as much as ordinary people. But the business of government is to govern not to follow moral principles. Governmental actions in the international arena are dictated by national interest and political considerations, and morality enters the stage always late, when the principle invoked happens to condemn the actions of a political adversary. When human rights and national interest coincide, governments become their greatest champions. But this is the exception. The government-operated international human rights law is the best illustration of the poacher turned gamekeeper.

The higher status of human rights is seen as the result of their legal globalisation. The law addresses all states and all humans qua human and declares their entitlements to be part of humanity's patrimony, which has replaced human nature as the rhetorical ground of rights. Every state and power comes under the mantle of the international law of human rights, every government becomes civilised as the 'law of the princes' has finally become the 'universal' law of human dignity. But this is an empirical universality, based on the competitive solidarity of sovereign governments and on the pragmatic concerns and calculations of international politics. A state that adopts the international treaties can claim to be a human rights state, turning human rights into a ploy for state legitimacy. Natural and human rights were conceived as a tool against the despotism of power and the arrogance of wealth. Their co-optation by governments means that they have lost much of their critical force and their initial aim and role has been reversed.

Problems in law-making are confounded by difficulties in interpretation and implementation. The international mechanisms are rudimentary and can scarcely improve, while national sovereignty remains the paramount principle in law. The main method is the drawing of periodic or ad hoc reports about human rights violations; the main weapon, adverse publicity and the doubtful force that shame carries in international relations. There are various types of reporting: monitoring, the most common, is carried out usually by volunteers and experts around the world under the auspices of the UN Human Rights Commission. 'Special rapporteurs' appointed by the Commission draw up reports about specific areas of concern, like torture, or about individual countries with a poor human rights record. Under another model, states are invited to submit periodic reports about their compliance with certain treaty obligations to committees created for that purpose (the most famous being the Human Rights Committee under the International Covenant on Civil and Political Rights). Weak implementation mechanisms ensure that the shield of national sovereignty is not seriously pierced, unless the interest of the great powers dictates otherwise, as events in the Balkans and Iraq have shown. Finally, in a few instances international courts or commissions investigate complaints by victims of human rights abuses and conduct quasi-judicial proceedings against states. But the jurisprudence of human rights courts is extremely restricted and dubious and its rapid changes in direction confirm some of the worst fears of legal realism: barristers appearing before international bodies such as the European Court of Human Rights quickly learn that it is better preparation to research the political affiliations of the government-appointed judges rather than to read the Court's case-law. Changes in the political orientation of the appointing governments are soon reflected in the personnel and case-law of international human rights courts and commissions.

The most effective international system of implementation has been that under the European Convention on Human Rights (ECHR). The Convention protects the main civil and political rights and no concession towards the socialist tradition was made at its inception in 1950. But the Convention introduced a radical innovation that has changed legal civilisation. Traditional international law was the law of the 'civilised princes', a states-based law with no place for individuals. But under the ECHR, aggrieved Europeans (as well as residents in member-states) after exhausting the remedies offered in their national legal systems can submit an application to the European Court based in Strasbourg alleging that their rights have been violated by the actions of their state. The Court conducts a full judicial investigation of the claim during which the citizen plaintiff is put on an equal footing with the defendant state. At the end of the process, the state is obliged to comply with any adverse findings of the Court. Britain has changed its laws on telephone tapping, contempt of court and the treatment of transsexuals, Germany gave non-German speaking defendants the right to an interpreter, Austria abolished state monopoly on cable and satellite television and Ireland decriminalised homosexuality. States can also bring applications alleging violations by their co-signatories against their citizens. When a number of governments brought an inter-state application against the then Greek dictatorship in 1968 they acted uniquely as their brothers' keepers. After it was found that every right in the Convention was violated by the Colonels who were not prepared to end the emergency measures, Greece had to withdraw from the organisation on the eve of its expulsion. But that was the exception. Inter-state cases are usually politically motivated. They have been brought by Ireland against the United Kingdom over British policies in Northern Ireland and by Cyprus against Turkey over the invasion and occupation of the island. This attitude represents the way that most governments approach human rights. They are happy to invoke them when their application happens to condemn an enemy.

But, despite the various international agreements and mechanisms, it must be emphasised that human rights are violated or protected at the local level. Human rights were created as a superior or additional protection from the state, its military and police, its political and public authorities, its judges, businesses and media. These are still the culprits or – rarely – the angels. Irrespective of what international institutions say or how many treaties foreign secretaries sign, human rights are violated or upheld in the street, the workplace and the local police station. Local legal, political initiatives and campaigns are more effective than any number of international treaties, committees and reports. Non-governmental organisations (NGOs), such as the Red Cross, Amnesty International and Oxfam have been important participants in human rights campaigns in recent years. When not seen as tools of governmental policy, NGOs are able to mobilise public opinion for the promotion of rights because they can defend themselves from the accusation of double standards and ulterior motives. This type of humanitarianism represents the radical potential of human rights and links to the spirit of popular organisation and activism of the revolutionary natural rights tradition (Chapter 3).

Genealogical complications

Human rights have been presented so far as a noble creation of the history of ideas. While this approach is indispensable for an understanding of their intellectual provenance, it often suffers from the philosophical and historical defects of historicism. History is presented as the forward march of all-conquering reason, which erases mistakes and combats prejudices. For historicism, the seed of a value was sown at some point in the past, it grew through generations and inspired people who fought for its realisation. After many trials and tribulations, the philosophical potentiality becomes finally historical actuality. History moves one way, values unravel inexorably towards their perfection in a linear process of gradual disclosure of essences and values, like freedom, equality or rights. The present is always and necessarily superior over the past because of the forward march of history.

This is the kind of history Friedrich Nietzsche and Michel Foucault attacked as a particularly sycophantic type of storytelling. They replaced it with the 'genealogical' methodology. The term 'genealogy', used by Nietzsche in his attack on the morality of Christianity, alludes to a 'dirty' and uneven view of the historical process. History is created in a clash of forces and a succession of dominations, in which fortunate and unlucky events, coincidences and bad turns combine in unexpected ways to create (or unpick) some of our most hallowed institutions and values. Abandoning the Kantian insistence on a priori conditions of understanding, on eternal and universally valid norms, Nietzsche developed a new type of history, which does not progress triumphantly towards the present in a march that gradually replaces ignorance, arbitrariness and conflict with science, law and peace. The job of the historian is to examine not the ethereal sources and linear paths but the contingent conditions and unforeseen circumstances out of which values grow. This method takes personal genealogy as its model. Each individual has come to life through a series of contingent events. They include the unpredictable encounter of our parents and a chance act of procreation, which led to this particular individual but would have led to someone else had it happened at a different time and place. But despite the centrality of randomness in life (the secular term for *moira* or *fata*), rationalist philosophers and social engineers have combined in a long missionary campaign to delete contingency and emotion in favour of reason, planning and control.

Once we adopt the genealogical method, political intrigue, personal antipathies and conflicts, domestic priorities, the backroom gossip of national and international institutions and contingent events become as important in the development and understanding of human rights as intellectual history, political philosophy and jurisprudence. In the United States, in particular, government officials, legislators, NGO leaders and media celebrities adopted human rights as the ideological banner under which 'culture wars' and international political battles have been fought. The United States, the superpower of the cold war and the global hegemon in its aftermath, has been the only country with the necessary power and sufficient interest to pursue an international campaign in the name of humanity. But this interest does not stem solely from the solid commitment of American administrations to the ideals of freedom and equality (Chapters 6, 9 and 10). More mundane and less easily visible reasons lie behind the inexorable ascendancy of morality. On the international stage, human rights have been an invaluable American weapon in the ideological battles of the day.

After the end of the Second World War (and again of the cold war), the international order had come unstuck. Pre-war principles and institutions had failed; and the gap at the centre of the world order was filled by human rights. They provided a high moral ground for the new order and the United Nations, its prime institutional expression. But the commitment to morality and rights was schizophrenically accompanied by the principle of non-intervention in the internal affairs of states. The promotion of morality and the defence of sovereignty, two allegedly antagonistic principles, served two separate agendas of the great powers: the need to legitimise the new world order through its commitment to rights, without exposing the victorious states to scrutiny and criticism about their own flagrant violations. While the major powers fought tooth and nail over the definitions and priorities of human rights, they unanimously agreed that these rights could not be used to pierce the shield of national sovereignty. Their uneasy alliance allowed governments and NGOs to criticise states they disapproved ideologically on human rights grounds, while protecting the great powers and their client states from attacks on their own abuses.

An early example is illuminating. The newly established UN Human Rights Commission, chaired by Eleanor Roosevelt, in an unparalleled feat of self-abnegation decided not even to read individual complaints of human rights abuses submitted to it, thus becoming the most elaborate and expensive wastepaper basket ever invented. One of the discarded petitions was drafted by W.E.B. Du Bois on behalf of the National Association for the Advancement of Colored People (NAACP) and detailed lynching, Jim Crow and extensive racial discrimination in the United States. Mrs Roosevelt met Du Bois, who wanted to place the appeal on the agenda of the General Assembly. She threatened to resign from the American delegation if that was done and argued forcefully that 'it would be better to look for and work for results within this country without exposing the US to distorted accusations by other countries'.[24] The Soviet delegate, to whom Du Bois turned next, happily adopted the grievances of the American blacks. Throughout the cold war, Western condemnations of the Gulags and political repression were ritually followed by Soviet denunciations of American racism (and British behaviour in Northern Ireland). The stage had been set for turning human rights into a football for ideological point-scoring, a rhetorical supplement and support for the geo-political priorities of the superpowers.

Indeed, the signing of the Universal Declaration, on 10 December 1948, and the execution of the seven defendants condemned to death by the Tokyo war crime tribunals, on 23 December, brought the two parts of the post-war project together. Constitutional moments in the national and international order contain both backward and forward-looking elements. The trials gave an account of the past, while the Declarations and Conventions aspired to regulate the future. They were both parts of the same project. The trials and

---

24   Kirsten Sellars, *The Rise and Rise of Human Rights* (Stroud, Sutton, 2000), 20.

the treaties started a long process, which aims to downgrade political and social conflict and replace it with a series of legal-technical disputes that can be resolved by lawyers and judges. This aspect was particularly evident in the desire of the Western powers to de-legitimise war and freeze world boundaries in their late 1940s state. For the colonial powers, Japan's crime was that it had disrupted and even overturned pre-existing colonial arrangements. After their victory, the allies started reoccupying their old colonies in an endgame before decolonisation. The trials were used to introduce legal principles that could outlaw the coming anti-colonial struggles. Radhabinod Pal, the Indian judge on the Tokyo bench, forcefully articulated this objection in his dissenting view when he stated that 'the dominated nations of the present day status quo cannot be made to submit to eternal domination only in the name of peace'.[25]

If human rights provided the perfect replacement for the exhausted principles of the world order, the impetus behind specific initiatives and campaigns has not always been repression in far-flung parts of the world but domestic priorities and conflicts in the great powers. Governments judge human rights by their usefulness and success on the home front. President Roosevelt, for example, used human rights rhetoric to confront American detachment from the war. If, for political philosophers human rights belong to moral discourse and reasoned argumentation, pragmatic calculation dominates their application and enforcement in domestic and international politics. Already at the end of the first round of institutional creation and standard-setting, in the late 1940s, two lies had taken hold: first, that the war was fought for the protection of human rights and, second, that traditional American rights and freedoms had been exported to the rest of the world. While the former idea still colours the way we appreciate our 'good wars', the latter has come good only in the last ten years (Chapter 10).

The ascendancy of human rights in the late 1940s was succeeded by a long period in which they were subordinated to the priorities of anti-communism. The attitudes of the great powers followed domestic political priorities. In the early 1950s, the American right saw human rights as a communist conspiracy internationally and as a seditious weapon of the civil rights movement internally. The Bricker amendment, a legislative measure aimed largely at human rights provisions, failed to be adopted by the American Congress in 1953 by a whisker. It would have given the Senate ultimate power over international treaties and allowed it to invalidate those which allegedly conflicted with the Constitution. Following this constitutional scare, the US government announced that it would not ratify the two UN Covenants (for

25   Ibid. 52.

which it had fought as a way of downgrading social and economic rights) setting a continuing trend of non-ratification of important human rights treaties.[26] It took twenty-six years for the US to ratify the civil and political rights covenant, forty years for the genocide convention and twenty-eight for the convention against racial discrimination. Congress has not ratified, however, the economic and social rights covenant, the convention banning discrimination against women and, the US is the only country, with Somalia, that has not ratified the convention on the rights of children.

The ideological struggles of the cold war, which had split human rights between civil and political in the blue corner and economic and social in the red, started receding during the period of détente. By the time of the Carter administration, human rights had acquired broad appeal in Capitol Hill. The dictatorial client states which had profited from the American protective umbrella during the cold war started coming in for some mild criticism from the government and much stronger from human rights NGOs. The new foreign policy human rights rhetoric was the perfect post-Vietnam, post-cold war, recession-era antidote to the American malaise. Human rights were an idea whose time had come, unifying, morally satisfying and also cheap into the bargain. President Carter stumbled on the issue during the presidential campaign but, once he realised its usefulness, made the most of it. As an administration insider put it, 'fate intervened – happenstance, things, letters – that blew the issue up unexpectedly'.[27] Ideological controversies, utilitarian calculations and random events seem to have influenced the history of human rights more than principles and idealism.

The Carter administration signalled a radical reorientation of American policy. The continuous appeal to human rights, the Annual Country Reports issued by the State Department and the economic and eventually military sanctions imposed on 'rogue' regimes placed rights at the heart of American foreign policy.[28] 'Human rights are suddenly chic. For years we were preachers, idealists, busybodies and now we are respectable' wrote an NGO official in 1977.[29] Congress passed legislation in the mid-1970s linking foreign

---

26 Natalie Hoffman, *Human Rights Treaties and the Senate: A History of Opposition* (Chapel Hill, NC, University of North Carolina Press, 1990).

27 Quoted in Sellars, op. cit., 119.

28 A much more modest British annual report on human rights was published for the first time by the Department for International Development, in April 1998. Part of New Labour's 'ethical' foreign policy, it was compared 'in style and format [to] a big public company announcing its results', with 'upbeat' tone and 'corporate and glossy' mood (*The Guardian*, 22 April 1998, 11).

29 Kenneth Cmiel, 'The Emergence of Human Rights in the United States', 86 *Journal of American History* 1248 (1999).

aid to human rights performance.[30] The new approach facilitated access to opposition parties and movements around the world thus offering information previously unavailable and creating the right political atmosphere for American interests once democratic forces had removed their US-sponsored oppressors. At the same time, democrats and activists raised the commitment to human rights to 'a form of patriotism, reaffirming the best traditions of the American nation'.[31] The new vista restored the *esprit de corps* and appetite for leadership of the demoralised American elite.

The interest in human rights waned somehow after the Carter presidency. It returned with the Manichean policies of the Reagan administration. In the war against the 'evil empire' (a war conducted in alliance with some of the most oppressive regimes in the world), the defence of human rights was identified with the promotion of democracy defined in terms of elections that are not demonstrably and brutally fraudulent.[32] The United States issues detailed country reports about human rights abuses around the world and uses them as bargaining chips in trade, aid and diplomatic negotiations. Their accuracy was disputed. Robert Bernstein, the founder of Human Rights Watch, claimed that the American branch was established in 1981 to 'correct "all the lies" of the early State Department reports'.[33] While these reports may have become more objective recently, human rights groups point to a consistent pattern of human rights violations by the American state. They include unchallenged police brutality, the treatment of asylum seekers, prison conditions and the death sentence and explain that these and other violations 'disproportionately affect racial minorities'.[34] But the general direction of the post-cold war order had already been established. Human rights had proved

---

30 Ibid. 1235.

31 Ibid. 1239.

32 Robert Johnson, 'Misguided Morality: Ethics and the Reagan Doctrine', 103 *Political Science Quarterly* 509 (1988).

33 Smiel, op. cit., 1236.

34 'Amnesty urges curb on US "human rights abuse"', *The Guardian*, 14 April 1999, 9. 'When we use international human rights standards, then clearly the US is failing the test daily' stated Amnesty director Andre Sané launching an appeal to the UN Human Rights Commission about human rights abuses in the United States. The Amnesty International 2005 report condemning various human rights violations was derided by Vice President Cheney in the following terms: 'For Amnesty International to suggest that somehow the United States is a violator of human rights, I frankly don't take them seriously' ('Cheney Offended by Amnesty criticism', CNN.com). It is noticeable that the European Court of Human Rights has ruled that the condition of detention of prisoners awaiting execution in American death rows amount to a violation of Article 3 of the Convention, which prohibits torture, inhuman and degrading treatment. *Soering* v. *United Kingdom* Series A, No. 161, 11 EHRR 439, Judgment of 7 July 1989.

their value to its practitioners, with the benefactors often profiting more than the beneficiaries.

Human rights finally triumphed in 1989. The humanitarian wars of the Clinton years were a logical extension of a long American policy of active involvement in the domestic affairs of countries around the world, which had stopped short of direct intervention in the face of the countervailing power of the Soviet Union. After its demise, the latent hegemony of the Clinton years could become real. Human rights have moved from being a weapon ensuring that states pursue anti-communist and pro-Western policies to the status of the lingua franca of the new world order. Europe adopted Christianity after the victory of Emperor Constantine over the three other claimants to the imperial throne and his conversion in the fourth century AD. Similarly, today the American victory over its communist adversaries has made human rights, the West's ideology, the credo of the new world order (Chapter 8). They are no longer critical tools in global conflict or in local disputes between satellite states but the main way of doing business and acquiring friends in the globalised marketplace.

Today, the cachet of human rights has become both bigger and smaller. It is bigger, because notional and nominal acceptance of their norms and regulatory organs is the necessary prerequisite, the entry ticket to the world dispensation. Flouting these rules, or rather their interpretation by the great powers, means no longer diplomatic denunciation at international fora and theatrical attacks for the sake of the media but bombardment, invasion and occupation. In the 1990s, President Bush Sr used the language of human rights and democracy as justification for wars and interventions. After 2001, Bush Jr combined the rhetoric of freedom and democracy with the darker language of mortal danger and home (in)security. On the other hand, their import-ance has diminished. They are seen as an indispensable and natural part of the Western landscape, something that one owns automatically, like TV sets and mobile phones. Because we produce abundantly and have so many human rights in the West, we must find markets to export them. But as with our butter mountains and wine lakes, we must also ensure that the recipients of our generosity pay the right market price, lest the value of the produce gets undermined. As Tom Farer puts it, the recent wars are 'between believers in free peoples and markets, on the one hand, and infidels on the other; it is a war between democratic capitalism and its enemies'.[35] The imposition of an impoverished type of democracy on the occupied lands seems to be a higher

---

35 Tom Farer, 'The Interplay of Domestic Politics, Human Rights and US Foreign Policy' (forthcoming, on file with author).

priority than the protection of human rights. Indeed, 'if democracy alone is the end, then as long as we are confident that some will survive to hold free and fair elections what matters more than civilian deaths other than the lives of our own troops?'[36] Iraq has shown that human rights may be paramount but the humans are not.

The rhetoric of human rights seems to have triumphed because it can be adopted by left and right, the north and the south, the state and the pulpit, the minister and the rebel. This is the characteristic that makes them the only ideology in town, the ideology after the end of ideologies, the ideology at the end of history. But this 'broad church' allure of rights is also their weakness. It was argued above that natural and, later, human rights were conceived as a defence against the dominations of power and the arrogance and oppression of wealth. After their institutional inauguration, they were hijacked by governments that understood the benefits of a moral-sounding policy. This trend has now moved to its final stage. Human rights are the way people speak about the world and their aspirations, the expression of what is universally good in life. They have become ingrained in the new world order, their claims adopted, absorbed and reflexively insured against challenge. Assent and critique, approbation and censure are part of the same game, both contributing to the endless proliferation and to the colonialism of rights. Human rights have become the credo of the middle classes. In this sense, the greatest achievement of rights discourse is not that it narrows the distance between East and West, left and right or the rich and the poor, but that it has imposed the ideology of the rich on the poor. Yet, paradoxically, a residue of transcendence remains. Every time a poor, oppressed, tortured person uses the language of rights – because no other is currently available – to protest, resist, fight, she draws from and connects with the most honourable metaphysics, morality and politics of the Western world. Human rights have only paradoxes to offer.

36 Ibid.

Chapter 2

Identity, desire, rights

The classical world believed that man perfects himself in community, in the Greek *polis,* the Roman city, the medieval *civitas.* A life of virtue can be lived with others in a just city. Ethical life can be developed only politically, in a *polis.* A city-state is just if it provides its citizens with the necessary conditions for a life of virtue. No distinction exists between the duties and entitlements of the citizen and the good of the city. For the ethics of virtue, to act morally is to perform one's duties. But all this changed radically in modernity. The individual, freed from tradition, history and community, became the foundation and principle of social and political organisation. The natural hierarchy of the classical world was replaced by a mobile and dynamic social order in which, in Marx's felicitous phrase, 'everything that is solid melts in the air'. Duty was replaced by individual rights, the good was separated from morality. While the classical world defined first what is good and derived moral and legal duties from this definition, for the moderns the good follows the right. To be in the right means to act freely, obeying the – moral, state – law in pursuit of self-interest.

What does not melt, what becomes the motivating force of modernity is individual desire. Modernity does not just enthrone the individual. It is the epoch of the free reign of will and its darker companion – desire. Thomas Hobbes, the greatest early modern philosopher, identified the change with great clarity: 'The desires and other passions of man, are in themselves no sin. No more are the actions which proceed from them till they know a law that forbids them.'[1] The quest for the public good, the *res publica*, which characterised the premodern world from Plato to Augustine and Aquinas was replaced now by the pursuit of individual interest and pleasure:

---

1 Thomas Hobbes, *Leviathan* (Richard Tuck, ed.) (Cambridge, Cambridge University Press, 1996), Chapter 6, 39.

> Whatsoever is the object of any mans Appetite or Desire; that is it, which for his part calleth *Good:* And the object of his Hate and Aversion, Evill . . . *Good* and *Evill,* are names that signifie our Appetites, and Aversions; which in different tempers, customes, and doctrines of men, are different.[2]

Good and bad are no longer ethical categories located in the design of the cosmos or in a transcendent religious realm. They are just words, conventional signs used to express what 'different men' love and hate. Good is to follow your desire and evil what conflicts with or deters desire. And in a final blow of demystification, Hobbes presents the love of good or of God, the classical foundations of the social bond, as so many masks for desire: 'men Desire, they are also sayd to LOVE: and to HATE those things, for which they have Aversion. So that Desire, and Love, are the same thing.'[3]

The medieval natural hierarchy of cosmic spheres and social classes becomes internalised and is replicated in the organisation of human nature. For Hobbes, desire drives people; it finds its limit in what negates desire. Desire must face the desires of others who want the same things as self and, death, the absolute denial of desire. Death, the negation of nature, is at the same time the most natural of facts. Death's fear, the most powerful of passions, leads men to abandon unrestricted freedom in return for the security offered by their contractual subjection to the Sovereign.[4] In Hobbes 'death takes the place of the *telos*'.[5] Because the strength of people pursuing their desire is broadly equal, because desire is unlimited and uncontrollable, sovereign power must be total and illimitable. The sovereign is the mirror image of the individual; his absolute power, the expression of desire unbound. His subjects, on the other hand, forfeit the right to resistance and are subjected to severe laws and strict sanctions because desire has no immanent limits and needs external controls. Harsh laws rigidly enforced – modern positivism – are the outcome of desire's emancipation. Well before Freud's discovery, Hobbes's anthropology had made desire and death the cause and effect of law.

The interweaving of desire and law, first identified by Hobbes, has shadowed the course of modernity. The law has treated desire under the heading of free will. People are free to choose how to act. As a result, they are liable if they act unlawfully and cause harm to others. Modern law attaches to

---

2 Ibid. Chapter 16, 110.
3 Ibid. Chapter 6, 38.
4 Ibid. Chapter 13, 90.
5 Leo Strauss, *Natural Law and History* (Chicago, IL, University of Chicago Press, 1965), 181.

conscious, knowing, rational acts. It is not interested in motives but in intentions. Motives are the springboards of action; they are responses to individual needs, desires, aims, to conscious purposes and unconscious urges. Intentions, on the other hand, are artificial legal constructs used to attribute liability for willed acts without much examination of the motivation for action. As Alan Norrie put it, by neglecting motives, criminal law does not go 'beyond the standpoint of the small child'.[6] Free will is the domain of law; desire that of individual and social pathology. But despite law's denials, desire has been the backstreet artist who, hidden from view, has moved the social and legal system along. It is now receiving its proper recognition for the first time. The pursuit of desire is becoming the organising principle of Western postmodern societies. Its name, human rights.

The American Declaration of Independence placed the rights to 'life, liberty and the pursuit of happiness' at the heart of the modern polity. Life and liberty are the institutional expressions of emancipation, the principal aim of the Enlightenment. The right to happiness was not found in other early declarations. The 'American dream' was introduced early into the ideology of the United States. Today it is turning into the main principle of Western human rights. The struggle against tyranny, prejudice and oppression is still the first priority in many parts of the world and, despite advances, it has not been fully won in the West either. But Western postmodern societies have turned the 'pursuit of happiness' and 'self-realisation' into the central aspirations of self and polity. Every individual or group wish can be turned into a political claim and eventually into a legal right. Examples of this inflation of rights-talk are everywhere. The resistance against laws regulating raves in the 1990s was organised under the slogan 'the right to the night' or the 'right to party'. A British minister stated that we all have the human right to properly functioning home appliances. Smoking is a violation of the human rights of non-smokers and the ban on smoking in public places is an attack on the rights of smokers. Criminal acts are seen as attacks on the human rights of their victims. The Pope's criticism of Islam, in September 2006, was defended as an exercise of his right to free speech. In colloquial speech, 'I have a right to X' has become synonymous with 'I want X' or 'X should be given to me'. Human rights have migrated from street protests to self-help manuals and from political campaigns to solipsistic claims to self-realisation and self-fulfilment. Alongside resistance to oppression and domination (the prime end of human rights) stand the postmodern slogans 'be you', 'express yourself', 'do as you wish', 'never give up on your desires'. In a society in which every desire is a potential right, it

---

6   Alan Norrie, *Crime, Reason and History* (London, Weidenfeld & Nicolson, 1993), 37.

is forbidden to forbid. To understand how we reached this position, we must examine closer the connection between law, identity and desire.

Rights and identity

The human self is not a stable and isolated entity, which, once formed, goes into the world and acts according to pre-arranged motives and intentions. Self is created in constant relations with others, the subject is always inter-subjective. My identity is constructed in an ongoing dialogue and struggle for recognition, in which others (both people and institutions) acknowledge certain characteristics, attributes and traits as mine, helping create my own sense of self. Identity emerges out of this conversation and struggle with others which follows the dialectic of desire. Law is a tool and effect of this dialectic; human rights acknowledge the constitutive role of desire. This is the basic truth behind identity politics and multiculturalism.

Our quest for the contribution rights make to the constitution of self starts with the philosophy of Hegel and moves to its radicalisation and updating by psychoanalytical theory. Hegel's basic idea can be put simply. The starting point is that the self is both separate from and dependent upon the external world. Dependence on the not-I, both the object and the other person, makes the self realise that he is not complete but lacking and that he is constantly driven by desire. Life is a continuous struggle to overcome the foreignness of the other person or object. Survival depends on overcoming this radical split from the not-I, while maintaining the sense of uniqueness of self. A first strategy of the desiring self, faced with the need to heal the split between subject and object, is to negate the object. The desire for food, for example, negates the otherness of the object by eating the foodstuff. It fails. Desire as the motor for the recognition of identity can be met only by another human's desire. A first type of recognition keeps the relationship with the other person external, treating him as inferior. In a master and slave relationship, the slave's recognition is forced. The service he offers is not reciprocated by the master who treats him as an object. But this type of one-way recognition is deficient for the master too, as it comes from someone not considered a worthy or equal partner. Only mutual recognition works. I must be recognised by someone I recognise as admirable, intelligent and good to acquire these characteristics. I must reciprocally know myself in another. I can only become a certain type of person, if I recognise in the other the characteristics of that type, which are then reflected back onto me in her desire. I cannot change myself, therefore, without changing the other and changes in the other, who stands in recognition of me, change me too. The self-conscious subject, created through the other's desire can never be self-identical: he is an amalgam of selfhood and otherness, of sameness and difference.

Identity is therefore dynamic, always on the move. It is an ongoing dialogue with others that keeps changing others and redrawing my own self-image. Significant others are the primary interlocutors. The lover identifies himself through the characteristics and idiosyncrasies of the loved one, finds the other in himself and finds in the lover, both himself and the other. Love makes me see myself through the eyes of my lover; it makes me understand her identity through the same ideas and emotions I use to reflect on my own motives, desires and actions. But the struggle for recognition never stops. Our identity is always under negotiation in encounters with others, from acquaintances and colleagues to total strangers in the street. Often, this recognition is distorted. When aspects of my self-image and esteem are not recognised by others, the dialogue can turn into violent conflict. This is the case with hate speech, which turns key components of my self-understanding, such as race or sexuality, into objects of derision and attack. Furthermore, while identity is a negotiation with other people, it is mediated by objects and by legal and social institutions. Legal rights are important weapons in our struggle for recognition, bargaining chips for negotiating identity.

Legal rights were the creation of early modern legal systems and are the basic building block of Western law. Rights are individual entitlements but their action is relational. They are realised through the acts or omissions of others. If the duty-bearer fails to perform his obligations, the right can be enforced through legal remedies. A property right, for example, gives exclusive use and enjoyment of an object to its owner by excluding all others from interfering with it. But property offers more than that. When I take possession of an object, I externalise myself by placing my will onto that object and through it into the world. Property brings me into contact with others and becomes a necessary moment in the dialectics of identity. Desiring the object and taking hold of it is a way of negotiating my desire for (the recognition of) others. Here the law comes in. The simple possession of an object is always under threat. Property becomes safe only through the operation of law. Property rights give legal recognition to the fact of possession. Other people now recognise my ownership on condition that I recognise theirs. Property rights lead to a form of interpersonal recognition in which others respect me through the incarnation of my will in the object protected by law.

Property and legal rights more generally give the self recognition for qualities one shares with everyone else. Legal rights acknowledge all as free and formally equal. When I say to a policeman or an employer 'you cannot do this, it is against my rights', I implicitly make three related claims. First, in a rule of law system, the law creates and protects equal rights for all and does not allow discriminating on irrelevant or spurious grounds. Second, legal rights make me worthy of respect; they confirm that, like all others, I have free will, moral autonomy and responsibility. Finally, legal recognition gives me self-respect, when I realise that I too am capable of moral action and that, like others, I am an end in myself. Human dignity, respect for others and self-respect are linked with the ability to make moral decisions and to raise legal claims. Legal rights are the way through which I acquire the recognition given to everyone and anyone, irrespective of individual characteristics. If according to Bob Dylan, to be outside the law you must be honest, legal recognition tells us that to be a person you must be in the law, you must have rights.

Legal rights offer the minimum recognition of abstract humanity. They become tools for negotiating more concrete recognition in contracts, sales and other deals. The exchange of contractual offer and acceptance brings the wills of the contractors together shaping them into a common will. Recognition now moves from the universal humanity of property rights to the contractual object, the concrete embodiment of will. Possession and enjoyment of property had identified the subject and the object for another subject. The alienation of the object, the third element of the contract, turns the contractor into a concrete individual through his recognition as an autonomous agent by someone else. In this sense, the contract of sale makes the minimum recognition of legal relations real and symbolises the birth of the subject. In conveyancing, the contractors not only exchange objects but they also recognise each other as separate, free and as possessors of rights and duties – in and through the contract they constitute each other as subjects. We desire objects not for their own sake but as means to the desire of and for other persons. Subjectivity is therefore constructed symbolically (*syn-bolon* means coming together, agreement) and the property contract has a little bit of magic. The contractors get their love object but on top they receive something more than they bargained for: they become recognised as free and equal through the desire of the other.[7] Property rights and contract help constitute subjectivity as inter-subjectivity through the mediation of objectivity.

Still, however, even the more concrete recognition resulting from conveyancing remains rudimentary and defective. The reciprocity of the acknowledgement is partial, contingent and transient. Property rights embody the self in things that, in turn, become attributes of personality. Recognition is not extended to a unique individual but to a property-owner externalised in his property. It is as if people exist in their property. Similarly, with contract:

---

7 Jeanne Shroeder, *The Vestal and the Fasces* (Berkeley, CA, University of California Press, 1998).

once it has been signed and the exchange completed, the contractors return to their previous stage of non-recognition; their fleeting and superficial reciprocity disappears. Contract's greatest achievement is to organise relations among strangers. It facilitates respect for their dignity, the universal attribute of humanity. The legal mentality teaches us to respect others as right-holders whose legitimate claims will be honoured as much as ours. But this is also their greatest limitation. Private rights lead to the external convergence of people based on self-interest. They keep the two selves separate, the relationship superficial, temporary, they offer an inadequate type of identity. The legal person is far too abstract, the law far too formal. The real human person becomes an abstraction – a point of locating a bundle of rights and duties. His concrete traits and needs are irrelevant to the law.

Poverty offers a good example of the underlying problem. Lack of assets in the midst of a society of riches based on property rights makes the poor feel 'excluded, shunned, scorned, by everyone'.[8] The recognition offered by the abstract right to property, by the potential to hold property, is clearly inadequate. As Anatole France put it, the law in its majesty punishes both the rich and the poor for stealing bread and sleeping under bridges. Hegel agrees: 'If life can be preserved by stealing a loaf, this certainly constitutes an infringement of someone's property, but it would be wrong to regard such an action as common theft.'[9] While the poor have full legal rights and the dignity and respect legal recognition offers, they cannot make them real. The only way the law helps a person in need is by recognising his rights without giving him, however, the means for satisfying them or the resources necessary for turning potential right into actual satisfaction of needs. Caught between law's recognition of abstract equality and its indifference towards their material inequality and concrete needs, the poor are the best examples of the failings of legal rights as a tool for identity recognition and construction.

The law tries to remedy the failings of legal rights through the creation of human rights. Human rights extend recognition from the private to the public domain. Civil and political rights, the first generation of human rights, express the universal dignity bestowed to a person on account of their humanity. People given the rights of citizenship are recognised as equal not only in formal legal relations but also as regards political power. Political rights express the mutual recognition of citizens as citizens, they recognise the constitutive role of recognition itself. New political rights aim at creating new ways of being in

8   Georg Hegel, *Vorlesung über die Philosophe des Rechts* (Frankfurt, Suhrkamp, 1983), 194–5.

9   Georg Hegel, *Philosophy of Right* (T.M. Knox, trans.) (Oxford, Oxford University Press), para. 127.

common and at reducing domination. The political history of the last two centuries is marked by the struggles to extend the recognition of citizenship to excluded groups from poor men to women to various minorities and non-nationals.

If the formal freedom of legal rights has been accompanied closely by domination, formal equality has been shadowed by various types of oppression such as economic exploitation, social marginalisation and cultural worthlessness.[10] Economic exploitation of the metropolitan poor through unemployment, breadline wages, poor health and casualisation, or of the developing world through colonialism, unequal trade and crippling debt undermines and eventually destroys the possibility of self-development. When daily survival is the order of the day, all aspirations for social improvement or cultural expression are extinguished. The oppressed cannot enjoy or even aspire to a fulfilled life which would allow their personality to flourish and be recognised in its complex integrity. Oppression undermines people's ability to decide what is the best life-plan for them and deprives them of the necessary means to carry it out. It does not allow its victims to be recognised as concrete and unique selves and prevents the fulfilment of their aspirations and capacities.[11]

The formalism and abstraction of law make the legal person an empty vessel or cipher and hinder the recognition of his concrete, unique characteristics (Chapter 3). This is what social, economic and cultural rights are meant to change: they add gender, colour, sexuality, desires and needs to the abstract outline of the legal person. Legal rights give recognition to the sameness of humanity, to the attributes that make us all similar. Social and economic rights, on the other hand, acknowledge the differences, which give self concrete identity and make it a rich, complicated, 'thick' personality. Gender, ethnicity or sexuality, the differentiating characteristics, make the person real. The distance between abstract human nature and concrete group characteristics justifies the demand for differential treatment, which respects the specific aspects of identity. But here we reach the crux of the matter. Even when group claims are accepted, the individual struggle for recognition is not over. In the continuous conversation with other people and institutions that constructs our identity, the law will always fall short. It may recognise aspects of my gender, sexuality or ethnicity through socio-economic rights. It may ban discrimination of these grounds. These are major achievements but their scope is limited. The

---

10 Iris Marion Young, *Justice and the Politics of Difference* (Princeton, NJ, Princeton University Press, 1990), 56.

11 See generally, Alan Gewirth, *Self-Fulfilment* (Princeton, NJ, Princeton University Press, 1998).

law classifies people according to universal categories and general concepts. Multiculturalism and the politics of difference do not diverge from the strategy of generalisation. Concrete identities, on the other hand, are constructed through the contingent and highly mutable combination of many positions, the outcome of a highly specific group of characteristics, only some of which are generalisable and shared with others. The law may try to stop discrimination against women or gays, but it cannot give full recognition to this woman or that gay. This is the reason why the success of anti-discrimination legislation is necessarily limited.

Most elements of identity remain immersed in our personal histories, trajectories and narratives with their defining moments, turns and traumas. I may be English or Greek, straight or gay, Labour, Tory or communist, a lawyer, plumber or unemployed, a fan of Tottenham or Arsenal, Christian, Moslem or atheist, and so on. More importantly, the self is a world: a unique mixture of past events, encounters with others, beliefs, feelings and commitments, conscious and unconscious desires and drives. This unique and unshareable combination is daily tested and recognised or not as what is singularly myself in an infinite number of encounters with others: a creature of shared dignity and rights but also of total idiosyncrasy and absolute difference inescapably caught in desire for others and exemplified by the uniqueness and unrepeatable epiphany of a face. Here the universalising logic of the law necessarily fails the singularity of self.

The uniqueness of the face defies the dialectic of same and different, self and other. The main elements of my identity, the building blocks of what I consider the 'real me' refer to a huge variety of positions, beliefs and traits that have very little relationship with the shared dignity of legal rights and cannot be captured by the difference-promoting extensions of human rights. My identity is the shifting articulation of all these disparate elements or 'subject positions', which combine in various ways, occasionally and transiently under the direction of one particular dominant element, other times without any clear hierarchy. Concrete identities are constructed in psychological, social and political contexts, in psychoanalytical terms, they are the outcome of a situated desire of the other. The stakes of the struggle for recognition and the politics of identity are the creation of self as a unique individual. The psychological need for differentiation and individuation cannot be met by the equalising logic of the law.

Negotiating with others the potential or real conflicts of the diverse subject positions is a main part of the individual politics of identity. In following my football team to an away game, for example, membership of the tribe of Tottenham supporters becomes the dominant characteristic. But when my fellow supporters start goading a player for his race or sexuality, which happens also to be my race or sexuality, if their behaviour offends my ideological allegiances, then my two commitments come into conflict. In these cases, my loyalty to Tottenham or to the Tories becomes strained, if my party publicly and vociferously attacks my sexuality. I may try to forget the conflict by either rationalising the behaviour of my fellows or by accepting that somehow my race or sexuality is problematic and by replacing self-respect with shame. In all cases, my identity is being constantly (re)created through the recognition of others involved in actual or silent conversations with me. Any relevant laws or rights, such as those created by anti-discrimination, hate speech or public order law, become important tools in negotiating my self-image and my response to others. But often these conversations fail. According to Charles Taylor, what characterises modernity is not so much the need for recognition but the multiplicity of 'conditions in which the attempt to be recognised can fail'.[12] This failure may result from the withholding of recognition by our closest and most intimate. In many cases, however, it is the outcome of inevitable and avoidable misrecognitions by the big Other of legal and social institutions.

These are the successes and failures of the operation of identity-building through human rights. There are wider political problems, however. By recognising the general categories of difference, rights promote the sense that differences are natural, inevitable, of equal and rather insignificant value. They are contingent surface characteristics, while what is important is the underlying 'common humanity', Fukuyama's 'factor X'.[13] An influential strand of liberalism argues that by achieving a multicultural society and a non-discriminatory legal system, dignity and formal equality have been broadly protected and there is not much point in fighting the effects of those 'superficial' differences further, since deep down we are all the same. A politics of recognition through human rights aspires to give identities equal formal protection, to reproduce in law the patchwork of colours, shapes and types of postmodern society.

But the formal recognition of hybridisation evident in postcolonial multiculturalism and political correctness offers no serious alternative to the apathy and politics of consensus of Western societies. The ideology of the new world order fully accepts the multicultural aesthetic of exotic foods, art and culture of the domesticated others, while denouncing at the same time the evil of their unreconstructed counterparts. The inclusion of difference, otherness and diversity at the margins of the dominant culture indicates that the ideology of

12 Charles Taylor, *Hegel* (Cambridge, Cambridge University Press, 1997), 35.
13 Francis Fukuyama, *Our Postmodern Future* (London, Profile, 2002), 149. See Chapter 3 in this volume.

'natural' superiority is no longer necessary as long as the 'others' do not challenge social hierarchies and accept their role as enriching cultural curiosities.
The acceptance and formal recognition of horizontal – cultural – differences
and the recognition of plural identities forgets that, throughout Western history,
perceived 'differences' have been interpreted as markers of inferiority and
used as justification for oppression and domination. It is true that in a purely
descriptive way we are all different and unique in our difference from all
others. But the dominant usage of 'difference' has always been normative.
When colour is defined as racial inferiority and leads to the enslavement or
oppression of blacks; when gender confines some to unpaid work and gives
others public and domestic power; when uncommon sexualities are defined
as immoral and criminal; in these and many more instances, difference is not
just an innocent 'natural' contingency but the social and cultural ground
for the subjugation and exploitation of those defined as 'different' from the
dominant norm. Difference has helped classify traits and characteristics as right
and wrong, normal and abnormal, and distribute people accordingly on a
spectrum of power, domination and oppression. A patchwork society, a society
where differences have been domesticated inhibits the development of political
resistance. Separated in their ghettoes, which will soon be listed by English
Heritage, resplendent in their colourful costumes and soulful rhythms, the
recipients of multicultural recognition and largesse are asked to forget that
alongside approved horizontal differences, a vertical fault-line common to
all minorities places them on the opposite corner from the dominant powers.
The politics of liberal multiculturalism reaches its limits, once people start
demanding the world and not just a corner in Brick Lane.[14]

---

14   Richard Mullender in his thoughtful 'Hegel. Human Rights and Particularism', 30 *Journal
of Law and Society* 554 (2003) has criticised my argument in Costas Douzinas, 'Identity,
Recognition, Rights or What Can Hegel Teach us About Human Rights', 29 *Journal of Law
and Society* 379 (2002). His main criticism is that human rights law does not 'respond to
people in all their particularity' but establishes 'a framework within which individual
particularity can find expression in a wide variety of ways' since it is an 'open-ended project
in process', at 558. This is not a critique but a repetition of my position, which is faithful
to Hegel's concept of the struggle for recognition. Identity construction and recognition
through legal and human rights cannot deliver what it promises, namely what Mullender
calls 'individual particularity' and I 'uniqueness'. Whether this is a welcome result of its
design (Mullender's position) or, an inevitable failure despite its claims (my position) depends
on the anthropology and political philosophy one adopts. Mine derives from left-Hegelian
and (neo) Marxist positions rather than from Carl Schmitt: domination, oppression and the
ensuing conflict are main characteristics of late capitalism and its emerging imperial phase.
The liberal claims about universal interests represented in human rights law or about the
'reflective equilibrium' between universal morality and particular cultures both conceal (in

Human rights do not belong to humans and do not follow the dictates of humanity; they construct humans. A human being is someone who can successfully claim human rights and the group of rights we have determines how 'human' we are; our identity depends on the bunch of rights we can successfully mobilise in relations with others. If this is the case, rights must be linked with deep-seated psychological functions and needs. From the heights of Hegelian dialectics, we now move to the much darker territory of Freudian psychoanalysis.

Rights and desire

Human rights acknowledge the radical intersubjectivity of human identity, they involve the other and the law in the construction of self. The Hegelian tradition explains how rights are key tools in the struggle for recognition. Psychoanalysis adds that such recognition passes through the desire of the other, as the big Other of the symbolic order or as the other person.[15] The desire for integrity projects the other as non-lacking, but this gesture misfires: the other is as lacking as self and this is what creates the endless proliferation of human rights. Let us examine this dialectic of lack as expressed in rights.

Psychoanalytical theory explains in great detail the process through which the human self comes into existence. According to Jacques Lacan, Freud's disciple, the infant is separated from the maternal body and becomes independent by entering the symbolic order, a combination of language and law. Language acquisition and social interdictions act as a social third that intervenes and breaks the original mother–infant dyad inscribing loss, absence and lack in the midst of the emerging self. Lack is partially addressed through the child's identification with signifiers, words and images. In the famous 'mirror stage', the infant between six and eighteen months experiences a sense of jubilation when she first recognises her image in the mirror or in the gaze of her mother and, through the reflection, comes to identify with a whole and complete body and a sense of being one, separate, complete. But this image of wholeness differs from the child's sensual experience of disobedient limbs

---

their reference to universal interests or values) and reveal (in their consistent failure to deliver anything of the kind) the basic anthropological facts of domination and conflict. The answer to the failure of the recognition offered by the ideology of liberal universalism however is not to turn to 'particularism', communitarianism or some compromise between the two. These too are versions of humanism and suffer from the same defects. When broad equilibrium between two sides is impossible, because of their huge power asymmetry, rational reflection cannot remedy the problem. Conflict is not an anthropological given but the result of socio-economic domination and political oppression.

15 See generally Douzinas, *The End of Human Rights* (Oxford, Hart, 2000), 297–318.

and a disjointed body. The biological reason for this disjuncture is that perceptual aptitudes develop well before motility and other motor functions.

The first sense of identity is external to the ego, an image of the ego, which becomes available visually. The ego does not precede the image but is made in the image of the image. Its unity is imaginary, in a double sense: it is visual and illusionary, the result of an anticipated wholeness and completeness imagined through the projection of the uncoordinated body into an adorable visual other.[16] Similarly, with words. Language creates arbitrary links between signifiers and signifieds and between words and things. But again the power of the signifier is creative. The bodily unity and temporal consistency of self is organised around the proper name, Joanna or Phaedra given to us or the pronoun 'you' addressed to the infant. I come into being by being called Costas and, similarly, all other entities become images and words, first, and then emerge into consciousness. The name gives me identity and continuity over time, makes me recognizable to others. The subject speaks and comes to existence by being spoken in language, in other words by being alienated once more from bodily and sensory experience into the cold world of signs. Identity and bodily integrity are not given but are constructed through the internalisation of external images and words and the repeated recognition of self by the other, who by appearing complete to the self becomes the cause of a hoped and anticipated integrity.

The process of separation and differentiation of self is completed through the law of the father. The Oedipal double interdiction on incest and parricide prohibits the infant's return to the primal union and leads the child to identify with the father.[17] Going back to the undifferentiated womb, becoming the symbolic phallus (the mother's presumed object of desire) would be catastrophic. For psychoanalysis, therefore, the basic law that creates humanity as a speaking species is that of division and separation: from the maternal body, through the Oedipal law of the Father, from one's one body through the narcissistic identification with its image, from the other as subject and object through their negation in the sign. I must identify with my image in the mirror and with my name, those disembodied and meaningless signs, those instances of otherness to become an ego. I must accept division and negativity, I must

---

16 Costas Douzinas, '*Prosopon and Antiprosopon*: Prolegomena for a Legal Iconology' in Costas Douzinas and Lynda Nead, eds, *Law and the Image: The Authority of Art and the Aesthetics of Law*, University of Chicago Press, IL, 1999, 36–67.

17 For Lacan, access to the symbolic order is much easier for the girl-child who, in not having the penis, accepts with less difficulty the interdiction on becoming the mother's imaginary phallus. In this sense, men who harbour the ridiculous hope that the physical organ is identical with the symbolic position are failed women.

accept that I am what I am not, in Rimbaud's felicitous phrase that 'Je est un autre'. The ego from the start is alter, an other; it is born in its encounter with the big Other, the linguistic-legal universe symbolised by a sign that Lacan calls the master signifier or the Name of the Father.

A residue of the primal union with the maternal body survives however the entry into the symbolic order. This residue, called by Lacan the Real, the phallus or the *petit objet a* (the little other object), symbolises the desired integrity or wholeness that is both impossible (since the self created only after the separation has no access to the primal union) and prohibited (through the action of language and law). This little other, the remnant of the Real after its ban by the symbolic, is the inner secret or 'kernel' of the subject. It creates a ceaseless and destructive pressure to return to the primal union (the death drive), which at the same time gives rise to an awesome, obscene enjoyment or *jouissance*. While desire has an always deferred object, the death drive circles pure lack and is energised by the failures of subjectivity. The Oedipal interdictions attempt to shield the subject from this abysmal desire. It is preferable to identify symbolically with the social other who bars enjoyment than be handed over to the abyss of the Real. At the same time, the banned desire for nothingness organises and pictures itself in objects, the *petit objet a*, which acts as cause, object and effect of desire. This little object, the remainder and reminder of the primal union which was not experienced, however, takes different forms that trigger the awe of *jouissance*: the (lost) breast, a gaze, a particular voice can distress us in ways the conscious self can neither understand nor accommodate.

To protect himself from this disturbance of the Real, the subject builds imaginary scenaria, which displace *jouissance* towards ordinary objects and set off ordinary desires. We attach ourselves to various fetishes such as a sports car, a better job, more money or success. But the attainment of the fantasy does not satiate desire, which immediately attaches itself to a new object, an even faster car or further promotion ad infinitum. The cause of desire is always deferred because return to the Real is impossible and barred. Desire is the excess of demand over need, something in every demand that cannot be reduced to a need. The little object 'fills the lack, the split that traverses the subject after castration, but, on the other hand, the *objet a* prevents any object from really filling the lack'.[18] Because the real object of desire cannot be present, it is displaced into inadequate identifications and imaginary constructions raised on the ground of repressed desire. These imaginary identifications with objects and ideals are failing attempts to deny death. They both mis-recognise desire

18   Renata Salecl, *The Spoils of Freedom* (London, Routledge, 1994), 126.

and defend the self from the spectre of its morbidity. The little object is always deferred because it does not refer to a specific need or request but to the wish to become again complete, to be fully loved by the other in a way that would fill the lack. But this is impossible; the little object, the remainder of the Real, makes all substitute objects inadequate, deferring and differing pleasure, always in search of something else or more or elsewhere.

Human rights as a function for the subject act like the little object. Rights allow us to express our needs in language by formulating them as a demand. When we make a demand, we not only ask the other to fulfil a need but also to offer us unreserved love. An infant, who asks for his mother's breast, needs food but also asks for the mother's attention and love. Desire is always the desire of the other and signifies precisely the excess of demand over need. Each time my need for an object enters language and addresses the other it is a request for recognition and love. But this demand for wholeness and unqualified recognition cannot be met by the other, either the big Other of the symbolic order (language, law, the state) or the other person. The big Other is the cause and symbol of lack. No master-signifier exists outside the symbolic universe to help turn it into a unified, complete and transparent order. Similarly, the other person, whose love we crave, is subjected to the same separation (the symbolic castration) and lack as ourselves. The other cannot offer what the subject lacks, because he is also lacking. In our appeal to the other, we confront lack, a lack that can neither be filled nor fully symbolised.

A human rights claim involves two demands addressed to the other: a specific request in relation to one aspect of the claimant's personality or status (to be left alone, not to suffer in one's bodily integrity, to be treated equally), but, second, a much wider demand to have one's whole identity recognised in its specific characteristics. In demanding recognition and love from the other person, we also ask the big Other, the symbolic order represented by the law, to recognise us in our identity through the other. When a person of colour claims, for example, that the rejection of a job application amounted to a denial of her human right to non-discrimination, she makes two related but relatively independent claims: that the rejection amounts both to an unfair denial of the applicant's need for a job but also to the denigration of her wider identity with its integral racial component. Every right, therefore, links a need of a part of the body or personality with what exceeds need, the desire that the claimant be recognised and loved as a whole and complete person.

But the attainment of identity through the desire and recognition of the other fails even in those cases in which human rights are successful on the surface and succeed in legalising desire. The subject of rights tries incessantly to find in the desire of the other the missing object that will fill lack and turn him into a complete integral being. But this object does not exist and cannot be possessed. The impossibility of fulfilling desire leads into ever-increasing demands for recognition and every acknowledgement of right leads to a spiralling escalation of further claims. In this sense, the promise of self-realisation becomes the impossible demand to be recognised by others as non-lacking. Human rights become expressions of the unattainable 'right to be loved'.

Rights are the substitute given to the subject, the little pleasure or reward offered for his socio-legal subjection. As a remainder of desired social integrity and as substitutes for lack, rights are the cause and object of desire. At the same time, rights signify lack and prevent it from being filled. They give the impression that the subject and society can become whole: if only my attributes and characteristics were given legal recognition, I would be happy; if only the demands of human dignity and equality were fully enforced by the law, society would be just. But, like the little object, rights both displace and fill the lack and make the desired wholeness impossible. The other's desire escapes the subject, always seeking something else. The little that remains allows the self to exist as a desiring being. Rights become a phantasmatic supplement that arouses but never satiates the subject's desire.

> The discourse of universal human rights thus presents a fantasy scenario in which society and the individual are perceived as whole, as non-split. In this fantasy, society is understood as something that can be rationally organised, as a community that can become non-conflictual if only it respects 'human rights'.[19]

But rights always agitate for more rights: they create ever new areas of claim and entitlement that again and again prove insufficient. We keep demanding and inventing new rights in an endless attempt to fill the lack, but desire is endlessly deferred.

Human rights keep desire going. Every success in the struggle for new rights leads to new and further claims in a spiral of demands that cannot be fulfilled. Rights may meet real or imaginary needs and may extend recognition to people. But their main task is to keep the legal subject in the position of desiring, in other words, to help maintain it as subject. Following our desire, we keep fighting for more and more effective rights. But the ensuing progressive legalisation of existence, in which many aspects of life become rights, keeps undermining the unity of self. Each new and specialised right, the right to same-sex marriage, for example, exposes the artificiality of the ego by increasingly

19 Ibid. 127.

colonising its intimate parts. New rights remove activities and relations from their intimate and communal habitat and make them calculable, exchangeable, cheap. While rights are a compensation for the lack of wholeness, the more rights I get, the more I need to claim, and, paradoxically, the greater the sense of disjointure of self. Rights to happiness and self-fulfilment are self-devouring; the 'rights culture' turns everything into a legal claim and leaves nothing to its 'natural' integrity. As endless desire and escalating fears increasingly dominate relationships, community starts fragmenting. What used to be the site of commonality turns into a collection of atomised beings defending themselves. There is a great paradox at the heart of rights culture. The more rights I have, the smaller my protection from harms; the more rights I have, the greater my desire for even more but the weaker the pleasure they offer. The ideological triumph of human rights is paradoxically consistent with the empirical observation that our age has witnessed their greatest violations.

Political power acknowledges and codifies the insight that rights make us human. In the Western world, their protection has become the mark of civility of a society. But their success is limited. No right can earn me the full recognition and love of the other and no Bill of Rights can complete the struggle for a just society. Indeed, the more rights we introduce, the greater the pressure to legislate for more, to enforce them better, to turn the person into an infinite collector of rights, and humanity into an endlessly proliferating mosaic of laws. The law keeps colonising life and the social world, while the endless spiral of more rights, acquisitions and possessions fuels the subject's imagination and dominates the symbolic world. Rights become the reward not only for psychological lack but also for political impotence. The acceleration of this process in postmodern societies means that some people are able to assert their absolute power, while others are reduced to the status of the permanently oppressed underclass. Fully positivised rights and legalised desire extinguish the self-creating potential of human rights. They become the symptom of all-devouring desire – a sign of the sovereignty or the individual – and at the same time its partial cure. In a strange and paradoxical twist, postmodern societies follow what one could call 'Foucault's law': the more rights we have the more insecure and unfree we feel.

Chapter 3

The many faces of humanitarianism

Humanism and human rights

Who or what is the 'human' of human rights and the 'humanity' of humanitarianism? The question sounds naive, silly even. Yet, important philosophical and ontological questions are involved. If rights are given to beings on account of their humanity, 'human' nature with its needs, characteristics and desires is the normative source of rights. The definition of the human will determine the substance and scope of rights. Even if we knew who is the 'human', when does its existence and the associated rights begin and when do they end? Are foetuses, designer babies, clones, those in permanent vegetative state fully human? What about animals? The animal rights movement, from deep ecology and anti-vivisection militancy to its gentler green versions, has placed the legal differentiation between human and animal firmly on the political agenda and has drafted a number of bills of animal entitlements. The previous chapter explored ways in which legal and human rights help construct subjectivity and identity. This chapter examines the ideology of humanism in its various transformations and permutations. It starts with the history of the concepts of 'humanity' and human nature.

Humanity is an invention of modernity. Both Athens and Rome had citizens but not 'men', in the sense of members of the human species. Free men were Athenians or Spartans, Romans or Carthaginians, but not persons; they were Greeks or barbarians but not humans. The word *humanitas* appeared in the Roman Republic. It was a translation of *paideia,* the Greek word for culture and education, and was defined as *eruditio et institutio in bonas artes.*[1] The Romans inherited the idea of humanity from Hellenistic philosophy, in particular Stoicism, and used it to distinguish between the *homo humanus,* the educated Roman, and the *homo barbarus.* The 'human man'

---

1 Erudition and training in morals and the arts.

was regulated by the *jus civile*, had some knowledge of Greek culture and philosophy and spoke in a cultivated language – he was like a graduate who read Greats at Oxford and speaks with a slightly posh accent. The *homo barbarus* was subjected to the *jus gentium*, lacked the sophistication of the real man and lived in the periphery of the empire. The first humanism was the result of the encounter between Greek and Roman civilisation and was used by the Romans to impress their superiority upon the world. Similarly, the early modern humanism of the Italian Renaissance retained a nostalgia for a lost past and the exclusion of those who are not equal to that Edenic period. It was presented as a return to Greek and Roman prototypes and targeted the barbarism of medieval scholasticism and the Gothic north.

A different conception of *humanitas* emerged in Christian theology, superbly captured in the Pauline statement that there is no Greek or Jew, free man or slave. All men are equally part of spiritual humanity, which is juxtaposed to the deity and the inanimate world of nature. They can all be saved through God's plan of salvation. Universal equality – albeit of a spiritual character – a concept unknown to the classics, entered the world stage. But the religious grounding of humanity was undermined by the liberal political philosophies of the eighteenth century. The foundation of humanity was transferred from God to (human) nature, initially perceived in a deistic and today a scientific manner. By the end of the eighteenth century, the concept of 'man' came into existence and soon became the absolute and inalienable value around which the whole world revolved. Humanity, man as species existence, entered the historical stage as the peculiar combination of classical and Christian metaphysics.

For humanism, there is a universal essence of man and this essence is the attribute of each individual who is the real subject.[2] Michael Ignatieff is typical when he writes that 'our species is one, and each of the individuals who compose it is entitled to equal moral consideration'.[3] As species existence, man appears without differentiation or distinction in his nakedness and simplicity, united with all others in an empty nature deprived of substantive characteristics except for his free will, reason and soul – the universal elements of human essence. This is the man of the rights of man, someone without

---

2   Louis Althusser, *For Marx* (Ben Brewster, trans., ed.) (London, Verso, 1969), 228: 'If the essence of man is to be a universal attribute, it is essential that *concrete subjects* exist as absolute givens; this implies an empiricism of the subject. If these empirical individuals are to be men, it is essential that each carries in himself the whole human essence, if not in fact, at least in principle; this implies an idealism of the *essence*. So empiricism of the subject implies idealism of the essence and vice versa' (emphasis in original).

3   Michael Ignatieff, *Human Rights as Politics and Idolatry* (Princeton, NJ, Princeton University Press, 2001).

history, desires or needs, an abstraction that has as little humanity as possible, since he has jettisoned all those traits and qualities that build human identity. If according to Heidegger, subjectivity is the metaphysical principle of modernity, it is legal personality, the 'man' of the rights of man and subject of rights who exemplifies and drives the new epoch. A minimum of humanity is what allows man to claim autonomy, moral responsibility and legal subjectivity.

The idea that the essence of humanity is to be found in a human cipher lacking the characteristics that make each person a unique being is bizarre. It is still the dominant ideology of liberalism. Francis Fukuyama recently repeated the eighteenth-century orthodoxies in the context of genetic engineering:

> [W]hen we strip all of a person's contingent and accidental characteristics away, there remains some essential human quality underneath that is worthy of a certain minimal level of respect – call it Factor X. Skin, color, looks, social class and wealth, gender, cultural background, and even one's natural talents are all accidents of birth relegated to the class of nonessential characteristics . . . But in the political realm we are required to respect people equally on the basis of their possession of Factor X.[4]

For Fukuyama, the differences that create our identity are superficial and accidental, contingent characteristics of no major importance. In this, he repeats Rawls's claim that the principles of justice can only be agreed by people who have no knowledge of their specific talents, needs and desires, which are concealed under a veil of ignorance.[5] But unlike Rawls and Habermas, who discover the elusive factor defining the essence of humanity in transcendental

---

4   Francis Fukuyama, *Our Postmodern Future* (London, Profile, 2002), 149.
5   At the other end of the liberal spectrum, Jürgen Habermas in *The Future of Human Nature* (Cambridge, Polity, 2003) detects the 'X factor' in the 'integrity of human nature'. Integrity is the basis of rationality and, in turn, of the universal ethics of human species, upon which human rights are based. The universal morality of human rights and the principles of freedom and equality are part of the 'species ethics'. Genetic intervention and custom-made designer babies are unacceptable because they violate this integrity and our moral self-understanding. Moral agency, Habermas argues, builds on a distinction between the 'man-made' and the 'grown' of human bodies given to us by nature. This distinction has allowed the development of autonomous morality and democracy, the highest achievements of universal rationality, but is now threatened by genetic intervention. While cultures differ, moral self-recognition is the result of the 'vision different cultures have of "man" who - in his anthropological universality – is everywhere the same', at 39. Since for Habermas, this self-understanding is not culturally determined, it must be an anthropological given. The liberal conceit is evident. Western moral humanism, the most local of traditions, is declared a universal anthropological category. Fukuyama's 'Factor X', by avoiding to give content to the anthropological constant looks more credible than the 'species ethics' of Habermas.

characteristics and species ethics, Fukuyama seeks it in our genetic inheritance. We may all be different, but behind the accidental idiosyncrasies a universal equivalence lurks, a certain *je ne sais quoi* that endows us with our human dignity.

Yet, if we look at the empirical person who enjoys the 'rights of man', he is and remains a 'man all too man' – a well-off citizen, a heterosexual, white, urban male. This 'man of rights' condenses in his identity the abstract dignity of humanity and the real prerogatives of belonging to the community of the powerful. In other words, the accidental surface differences of race, colour, gender, ethnicity have been consistently defined as inequalities supporting the domination of some and subjection of others, despite the common underlying factor X. One could write the history of human rights as the ongoing and always failing struggle to close the gap between the abstract man and the concrete citizen; to add flesh, blood and sex to the pale outline of the 'human'. The persistence throughout history of barbarians, inhuman humans, the 'vermin', 'dogs' and 'cockroaches' of our older and more recent concentration camps, such as Guantánamo Bay and Abu Ghraib, the potential of world annihilation by humanity's creations as well as recent developments in genetic technology and robotics indicate that no definition of humanity is definite or conclusive. Humanity's mastery, like God's omnipotence, includes the ability to redefine who or what counts as human and even to destroy itself. From Aristotle's slaves to designer babies, clones and cyborgs, the boundaries of humanity have been shifting. What history has taught us is that there is nothing sacred about any definition of humanity and nothing eternal about its scope. No common 'factor X' exists.

The meaning of humanity, as the ground normative source, is fought over today by the universalists and relativists, the two more prominent expressions of postmodern humanism. The universalist claims that cultural values and moral norms should pass a test of universal applicability and logical consistency and often concludes that if there is one moral truth but many errors, it is incumbent upon its agents to impose it on others. The relativists and the communitarians (since relativism is a meta-ethical position) start from the obvious observation that values are context-bound and try to impose them on those who disagree with the oppressiveness of tradition. In Kosovo, Serbs massacred in the name of threatened community (the Serb nation should keep Kosovo its 'cradle' in perpetuity and oppress Albanians who lived there in a large majority). The allies bombed in the name of threatened humanity and in support of universal rights, even though the link between the rights of Kosovar Albanians and the bombing of civilians in Belgrade is not immediately apparent. Both positions, when they define the meaning and value of humanity fully and without remainder find everything that resists them expendable. They exemplify, perhaps in different ways, the contemporary metaphysical urge: they have made an axiomatic decision as to what constitutes the essence of humanity and follow it with a stubborn disregard for opposing arguments.

The individualism of universal principles forgets that every person is a world and comes into existence in common with others, that we are all in community. Being in common is an integral part of being self: self is exposed to the other, it is posed in exteriority, the other is part of the intimacy of self. Before me comes the (m)other. I am because the other and language has called me 'you', 'Costas'. My face is always exposed to others, always turned toward an other and faced by him or her never facing myself. On the other hand, being in community with others is the opposite of the communitarian common being or belonging to an essential community. Most communitarians define community through the commonality of tradition, history and culture, the various past crystallisations whose inescapable weight determines present possibilities. The essence of the communitarian community is often to compel or 'allow' people to find their 'essence', common 'humanity' now defined as the spirit of tradition, or the nation, religion, the people, the leader. We have to follow traditional values and exclude what is alien and other. Community as communion accepts human rights only to the extent that they help submerge the *I* into the *We*, all the way till death, the point of 'absolute communion' with dead tradition.[6]

If we abandon the essentialism of humanity, human rights appear as highly artificial constructs, a historical accident of European intellectual and political history. The concept of rights belongs to the symbolic order of language and law, which determines their scope and reach with scant regard for ontologically solid categories, like those of man, human nature or dignity. The 'human' of rights or the 'humanity' of humanitarianism can be called a 'floating signifier'. As a signifier, it is just a word, a discursive element, neither automatically nor necessarily linked to any particular signified or meaning. On the contrary, the word 'human' is empty of all meaning and can be attached to an infinite number of signifieds. As a result, it cannot be fully and finally pinned down to any particular conception because it transcends and over-determines them all.[7] But the 'humanity' of human rights is not just an empty signifier; it carries an enormous symbolic capital, a surplus of value and dignity endowed by the

---

6   Jean-Luc Nancy, *The Inoperative Community* (Minneapolis, MN, University of Minnesota Press, 1991), Introduction.

7   For a use of the psychoanalytic concept of 'overdetermination' in political theory, see Ernesto Laclau and Chantal Mouffe, *Hegemony and Socialist Strategy: Towards a Radical Democratic Politics* (Winston Moore and Paul Cammack, trans.) (London, Verso 1985), 97–105.

revolutions and the declarations and augmented by every new struggle that adopts the rhetoric of human rights. This symbolic excess turns the 'human' into a floating signifier, into something that combatants in political, social and legal struggles want to co-opt to their cause, and explains its importance for political campaigns.

From a semiotic perspective, rights do not refer to things or other material entities in the world but are pure combinations of legal and linguistic signs, words and images, symbols and fantasies. No person, thing or relation is in principle closed to the logic of rights. Any entity open to semiotic substitution can become the subject or object of rights; any right can be extended to new areas and persons, or, conversely, withdrawn from existing ones. Civil and political rights have been extended to social and economic rights, and then to rights in culture and the environment. Individual rights have been supplemented by group, national or animal rights. The Spanish MP Francisco Garido moved a resolution in Parliament to create human rights for great apes, the animals genetically closest to humans.[8] The right to free speech or to annual holidays can be accompanied by a right to love, to party or to have back episodes of Star Trek shown daily. Or, as a British minister put it, we all have a human right to properly functioning kitchen appliances. If something can be put into language, it may acquire rights and can certainly become the object of rights.

The only limits to the ceaseless expansion or contraction of rights are conventional: the effectiveness of political struggles and the limited and limiting logic of the law. Human rights struggles are symbolic and political: their immediate battleground is the meaning of words, such as 'difference' and 'similarity' or 'equality' and 'otherness', but if successful, they have ontological consequences – they radically change the constitution of the legal subject and affect peoples' lives. A refugee whose claim to enter the recipient country has been constructed in human rights terms is a more privileged subject – more 'human' – than someone else, whose claim is seen as simply economic turning him into a 'bogus' subject. Similarly, the claim of gay and lesbians to be admitted to the army has a greater chance of success if presented as a rights claim about discrimination than if it attacks the irrationality of the exclusion

8   Peter Singer, 'Great Apes Deserve Life, Liberty and the Prohibition of Torture', *The Guardian*, 27 May 2006, 32.

9   Compare *R.* v. *Ministry of Defence, ex parte Smith* [1996] 1 All ER 257 CA with *Smith* v. *Grady* v. *UK*, ECHR Application No. 33985 and 33986/96, Judgment of 27 September 1999. The English courts found that discharge from the army was not unreasonable but the European Court of Human Rights ruled that it amounted to a violation of the right to privacy in Article 8 of the Convention.

on administrative law grounds.[9] Its success has wider repercussions than the protection of army employment. The claimants' position changes as a result, their identity becomes fuller and more nuanced through the official recognition of their sexuality. If we accept the psychoanalytic insight that people have no essential identities outside of those constructed in symbolic discourses and practices,[10] a key aim of politics and of law is to fix meanings and to close identities by making the contingent, historical links between signifiers and signifieds permanent and necessary. But such attempts can succeed only partially because the work of desire never stops. If human rights are the cause and effect of desire, they do not belong to humans; human rights construct humans.[11]

We can conclude that 'humanity' cannot act as the a priori normative source and is mute in the matter of legal and moral rules. Humanity is not a property shared, it has no foundation and no ends, it is the definition of groundlessness. It is discernible in the incessant surprising of the human condition and its exposure to an undecided open future. Its function lies not in a philosophical essence but in its non-essence, in the endless process of redefinition and the continuous but impossible attempt to escape fate and external determination. In this ontology, what links me to the other is not common membership of humanity, common ethnicity or even common citizenship. Each one is a unique world, the point of knotting of singular memories, desires, fantasies, needs, planned and random encounters. This infinite and ever changing set of events, people and thoughts is unrepeated and unrepeatable, unique for each of us like our face, unexpected and surprising like a *coup de foudre*. Each one is unique but this uniqueness is always created with others, the other is part of me and I am part of the other. But my being – always a being together – is on the move, created and recreated in the infinite number of encounters with the unique worlds of other singular beings. This is the ontology of the cosmopolitanism to come (Chapter 11).

Humanity has no intrinsic normative value. It is continuously mobilised, however, in political, military and, recently, humanitarian campaigns. Humanitarianism started its career as a limited regulation of war but has now expanded and affects all aspects of culture and politics. The next part examines the military humanitarianism of our recent wars while the last will explore the effects of humanitarianism on the citizens of the Western world.

10   The seminal text is Jaques Lacan, 'The Mirror Stage As Formative of the Function of the *I* As Revealed in Psychoanalytic Experience' in Jaques Lacan, *écrits: a selection* (Alan Sheridan, trans.) (London, Routledge, 2001).

11   See Chapter 2.

Military humanitarianism

The humanitarian movement started in the nineteenth century. According to received opinion, the key event was the foundation of the International Committee of the Red Cross by Jean-Henri Dunant, in 1859, after he witnessed the widespread slaughter of combatants at the battle of Solferino between France and Austria. Dunant spearheaded the adoption of the Geneva Convention of 1864 under which governments agreed to allow access to battlefields for neutral field hospitals, ambulances and medical staff. By the First World War, the Red Cross had established itself as the largest humanitarian organisation responsible for monitoring the Geneva Conventions, which codified the laws of war and established rules for the humane treatment of prisoners of war. Traditional humanitarian law is the body of international law which attempts to regulate the use of force during armed conflict, the modern version of the *jus in bello*. Its core principles have developed from just war theory and are rather basic and broad: the use of force must be a last resort; a distinction must be maintained during hostilities between military personnel and civilians; all efforts must be made to minimise non-combatant casualties; finally, the use of force must be proportional to its objective.

A less technical use of the term humanitarianism refers to the efforts by organisations and governments to alleviate mass suffering after major natural catastrophes and to aid populations caught in war or civil strife. Combining both types of humanitarianism and enjoying the strongest reputation, the Red Cross adopted, in 1965, seven fundamental principles that became the rulebook of humanitarian action: humanity, impartiality, neutrality, independence, voluntary service, unity and universality. The main characteristic of the Red Cross and of humanitarianism more generally was supposed to be, as these principles indicate, its non-political character and its neutrality towards the protagonists of wars and natural disasters. Other charities and NGOs such as Oxfam, Save the Children and Christian Aid have adopted the same non-political posture. Amnesty International, for example, campaigns for prisoners of conscience without regard for their political views.

Early humanitarianism did not make distinctions between good and bad wars, just and unjust causes or, even, between aggressors and innocents. It was committed to the direct and immediate reduction of human suffering through the protection of prisoners of war and civilians involved in conflict or through famine relief and medical aid. As interest in development and human rights grew in the 1970s and 1980s, NGOs adopted these concerns and promoted policies of popular appeal. A high point of NGO humanitarianism was the Live Aid campaign in 1984–5 to raise funds for relief of the Ethiopian famine. Carried out in the face of governmental indifference, humanitarian aid had few political conditions attached and avoided association with Western foreign or defence objectives. Indeed, up to 1989, the division between state-led development aid with strategic ends and ideological priorities and politically neutral needs-based humanitariarism was clear.

But this clear distinction has been blurred after the end of the cold war. The roots of the new humanitarianism lie in the growing Western involvement in the internal affairs of the developing world and the use of economic sanctions and force for humanitarian purposes. The move beyond the aims of saving lives and reducing suffering to the more muscular recent humanitarianism has two strands. The first grew out of conflict situations. It extended involvement from the provision of immediate assistance to victims, to a commitment to solidarity and advocacy and a concern for the long-term protection and security of groups at risk. The second strand, which deals with national catastrophes such as famines, droughts or tsunami, expressed an interest in the long-term development of poor countries beyond the failing aid policies of governments. This broader and deeper humanitarianism was obliged to make strategic choices about aims to be prioritised and groups to be assisted. Once the neutrality principle was broken, the road was opened, in the 1990s, for various NGOs to advocate Western military intervention for humanitarian purposes.

This politicisation of aid work is in conflict with the apolitical profile on which the public appreciation for NGOs depends. As a result, NGOs have become extremely concerned to reassert their traditional neutrality and non-political reputation. One way of reconciling conflicting priorities and justifying policy choices was to present them in the language of morality and ethics instead of that of politics. Human rights have become the preferred vocabulary of this new type of humanitarianism and are often used to disguise complex and contentious decisions. In some conflicts, the justice of the cause is clear; in most, it is not. The blurring of the line dividing human rights and humanitarianism has led to disturbing consequences. Some policies and regulatory regimes have been translated into the language of rights, others have not. The treatments of war prisoners, for example, has been largely displaced from the international law language of regulation and limits on state action into that of prisoners' rights. The effects of this change are evident in the American assertion that the Guantánamo Bay prisoners have no rights because they are evil murderers and a threat to Western security. This is a clear violation of the Geneva Conventions but can be justified in the language of human rights. Human rights with their principles and counter-principles and their concern to create an equilibrium of entitlements are much easier to manipulate than clear proscriptions of state action.

Something similar has happened with anti-terrorist legislation. The emphasis placed by the British government on the protection of the rights of the majority from terrorism, after the July 2005 London bombings, is consistent with human rights legislation. Most substantive rights under the European Convention on Human Rights can be limited or restricted in the interests of national security or for the protection of the rights of others. When national security becomes human security, when 'the others' are defined as anyone who may be affected by a terrorist act (potentially everyone), there is very little these overbroad qualifications disallow. In this sense, the annoyance of the British government with judges who found detention without trial and the control orders imposed on terrorist suspects in violation of human rights, was justified. As the scope of the human rights language expands and most political and social claims and counter-claims are expressed in it, the protection afforded by clearly formulated prohibitions of international law becomes weakened. When everything becomes actually or potentially a right, nothing attracts the full or special protection of a superior or absolute right.

These developments have led to a convergence between humanitarian work and governmental rhetoric and policies. As David Kennedy, an influential Harvard international lawyer, has argued, contemporary humanitarianism is no longer the cry of dissidents, campaigners and protesters but a common vocabulary that brings together the government, the army and erstwhile radicals and human rights activists.[12] The dissidents have stopped marching and protesting. Instead they have become bit players in governmental policy-making and even in military planning. Kennedy approves this development and reserves his strongest criticisms for the remaining radicals, idealists and activists. The indictment is long: radical humanitarians believe in abstract generalisations, they do not accept responsibility for the long-term consequences of their actions and are happy to criticise governments from the margins; unlike governments and policy-makers, they do not carry out cost-benefit analyses of their activities; their commitment to broad principles of improving humanity to be carried out through constitutional reform, legal measures and institution-building blinds them both to the inadequacy of the tools and the adverse effects of their activities; they see themselves as outsiders and avert their eyes from power generally and their own power specifically.[13] Kennedy concludes that humanitarians believe hubristically that history will

---

12   David Kennedy, *The Dark Side of Virtue* (Princeton, NJ, Princeton University Press, 2004), Chapter 8.

13   Ibid. 327–9.

progress through the adoption of their principles and recipes. These 'do-gooder' relics of a previous era judge power extrinsically 'from religious conviction, natural right, positive law' and pathetically try to preserve their 'ethical vision'.

But this has been changing. Since at least the end of the cold war 'many humanitarian voices have become more comfortable speaking about the completion of their realist project'.[14] People who have spent a lifetime feeling marginal to power often find it difficult to imagine that they could inherit the earth in quite this way. They have been admitted into the corridors and back rooms of power and this unnatural coupling paves the way for the future. This development may be shocking news to Amnesty International members stuffing envelopes to support political prisoners. There is ample evidence to support it, however. Colin Powell stated before the Afghanistan war that ' "NGOs are such a force multiplier for us, such an important part of our combat team . . . [We are] all committed to the same, singular purpose to help humankind . . ." We share the same values and objectives so let us combine forces on the side of civilisation.'[15] Before the Iraq war, aid organisations were offered grants by the American government to join the coalition. They had to show attachment to American moral values and concern for civilians. The Red Cross and Oxfam argued against that war, rightly anticipating a humanitarian catastrophe, while Médecins Sans Frontières, an organisation that campaigned actively for the Kosovo war, remained neutral. Bernard Kouchner, its founder, has been credited with coining the term *droit d'ingérance humanitaire* and became the UN-appointed viceroy of Kosovo.

Most NGOs, however, accepted government funding and joined the war effort. They became subcontractors competing with private companies for market share. As the director of the US Agency of International Development (USAID) put it, NGOs under US contracts 'are an arm of the US government and should do a better job highlighting their ties to the Bush administration if they want to continue receiving money'.[16] The head of programmes for USAID in Afghanistan agreed: 'We're not here because of the drought and the famine and the condition of women. We're here because of 9/11. We're here because of Osama bin Laden.'[17] Aid NGOs now work with the military in post-conflict

---

14 Ibid. 277.
15 Rony Brauman and Pierre Salignon, 'Iraq: In Search of a Humanitarian Crisis' in Fabrice Weissman, ed., *In the Shadow of 'Just Wars'* (London, Hurst, 2004), 269–70.
16 Ibid. 284. In a bizarre story that exemplifies how Western governments exploit the work of NGOs, the Russians exposed, in 2006, two spies working for British intelligence who used fake rocks to conceal receivers for gathering and passing on secret data. The spies' contacts and aid recipients were various Russian human rights NGOs.
17 Quoted in Michael Ignatieff, *Empire Lite* (London, Vintage, 2003), 90–1.

zones assuming responsibility as public service subcontractors for the provision of health and education. Humanitarian governance is 'imperial because it requires imperial means: garrison of troops and foreign civilian administrators, and because it serves imperial interests'.[18] As a result of the perception that NGOs are no longer impartial, aid officers have been under continuous attack in Afghanistan where 'the humanitarian emblems designed to protect them now identify them as legitimate targets,'[19] while international NGOs have largely pulled out of Iraq after lethal attacks on the UN compound, the Red Cross headquarters and NGO officers. Michael Hardt and Antonio Negri compare NGOs with the Dominicans and the Jesuits of colonialism, arguing that they act 'as the charitable campaigns and mendicant order of Empire'.[20] It is not wrong to say that the media campaigns of NGOs have prepared public opinion for 'humanitarian wars' and are willingly or inadvertently integral parts of the new order supporting and promoting its moral claims.

According to David Kennedy, humanitarian policy-makers working for governments, international institutions and international NGOs have adapted much better than their activist counterparts to the needs of 'ruleship'. The humanitarians dealing with the use of force in close collaboration with the army are a prime example. The military has given up its exclusive claim to power and the radicals their traditional attraction to pacifism in order to participate fully in military policy-making and post-conflict governance. Humanitarian lawyers and NGO officers are fully involved in the planning and conduct of wars. Like their newly found military comrades, they see force as a tool towards ends and they balance legal and moral rules in instrumental terms. The common language unites humanitarians and military in balancing acts, tradeoffs and calculation of consequences. The vocabulary has 'drifted free of legal roots and has become the mark of civilisation and participation in a shared ethical and professional common sense community'. This pragmatic merger of military and humanitarian roles has allegedly led the military to 'best practice' and has 'civilised warfare'. In the lead to the Iraq war, we are told, humanitarians and military spoke exactly the same language, with the reformed former radicals apparently interpreting legal limitations on the conduct of war more permissively than the military.[21]

The military on their part realising the cachet of humanitarianism has adopted

---

18   Ibid. 59. Ignatieff refers to Kosovo but his statement is even more applicable to Afghanistan or Iraq.

19   Conor Foley, 'Caught in the Crossfire', *The Guardian*, 7 May 2004, 23.

20   Michael Hardt and Antonio Negri, *Empire* (Cambridge, MA, Harvard University Press, 2000), 36.

21   Kennedy, op. cit., 271 and Chapter 8 *passim*.

a not dissimilar rhetoric. A few examples can illustrate the point. According to Michael Ignatieff, the Kosovo air raids were decided in the NATO Brussels headquarters with military planners and lawyers peering over screens with the lawyers advising on the legalities before a bombing raid was ordered.[22] While this elaborate procedure did not limit civilian casualties, it meets the definition of a 'humane war'.[23] Colonel Tim Collins, the commander of the Irish Guards during the Iraq war, was an exemplary humanitarian soldier when telling his troops before crossing into Iraq to join the campaign:

> We are going to Iraq to liberate and not to conquer. We will not fly our flags in their country . . . The only flag that will be flown in that ancient land is their own . . . Iraq is steeped in history; it is the site of the Garden of Eden, of the Great Flood and the birthplace of Abraham. Tread lightly there.[24]

Collins soon realised that occupation *lite* is not an option and changed his views. Another telling example was the practice of American aircraft to drop aid packages in Afghanistan in-between bombing raids. 'Cruise missiles and corned beef' could be the motto of military humanitarianism.

David Kennedy concludes after a visit to an aircraft carrier that humanitarian norms have been 'metabolised into the routines of the US Navy'.[25] The military is the world's 'largest human rights training institution' and the vocabulary of humanitarianism is nowhere 'as effective as it seemed to be abroad the USS *Independence*'.[26] As Michael Walzer, another reformed radical puts it:

> I am inclined to say that justice has become, in all Western countries, one of the tests that any proposed military strategy or action has to meet . . . moral theory has been incorporated into war-making as a real constraint on when and how wars are fought.[27]

22 Michael Ignatieff, *Virtual War* (London, Vintage, 2001), 111.
23 Christopher Coker, *Humane Warfare* (London, Routledge, 2001).
24 Two years later, Collins despaired. No weapons of mass destruction were found, the occupation had acted as the 'best recruiting agent for Al-Qaeda ever' and 'if freedom and a chance to live a dignified, stable life free from terror was the motive, then I think of more than 170 families last week who would have settled for what they had under Saddam' [reference to occupation casualties] (*The Observer*, 18 September 2005, 17).
25 Kennedy, op. cit., 287, 289.
26 Ibid. 294, 296.
27 Michael Walzer, *Arguing about War* (New Haven, CT, Yale University Press, 2004), 12.

But we should take such bravura statements with a dose of salt. General Wesley Clark, the commander of the Kosovo operation, complained that Europe's 'legal issues' were 'obstacles to properly planning and preparing' the war and adversely affected its operational effectiveness. 'We never want to do this again' he concluded and Iraq confirmed his prediction. Only lip service was paid to the legal concerns.[28]

Even if we discount the exaggerations and excessive missionary zeal of the military–humanitarian complex, it looks as if an imperial officer corps and bureaucracy is emerging. The unnatural coupling of ultimate power and its erstwhile critics appears to be well under way. Disciplines, professions and tasks have been cross-pollinated and created a new professional class, the 'humanitarians' or 'internationals'. The term applies to 'people who aspire to make the worlds more just, to the projects they have launched over the past century in pursuit of that goal, and to the professional vocabularies which have sprung up to defend and elaborate those projects'.[29] The group includes the usual suspects: human rights activists, lawyers, international civil servants, NGO operators and assorted do-gooders and extends to politicians, military strategists and ordinary soldiers and all those whose task is to spread the principles of the new world order, if necessary, by force. Whatever the ideology, humanitarianism has become a job opportunity. Ignatieff concludes that the 'internationals' 'run everything' in Kosovo:

> Pristina's streets are clogged with the tell-tale white Land Cruisers of the international administrators, and all the fashionable, hillside villas have been snapped up by the Western aid agencies. The earnest aid workers, with their laptops, modems, sneakers and T-shirts, all preach the mantra of 'building local capacity', while the only discernible capacity being created is the scores of young people who serve as drivers, translators and fixers for the international community.[30]

It looks as if the most discernible effect of 'nation-building' is the creation of a body of colonial administrators. 'Kabul . . . is one of the few places where a bright spark just out of college can end up in a job that comes with a servant and a driver'.[31] It is not surprising; most of the states following the Americans in their wars and occupations are former imperial powers, well-versed in the job of running colonial outposts.

28   Wesley Clark, *Waging Modern War* (Oxford, Public Affairs, 2002), 421, 426.
29   Kennedy, op. cit., 236–7.
30   Ignatieff, *Empire Lite*, 73–4.
31   Ibid. 94.

The earlier 'naive' humanitarians of the Vietnam war judged the actions of power from an external perspective such as religion, natural or positive human rights law and claimed to speak 'truth or virtue to power'. Their descendants have realised that if they want to restrain power they must adopt its aims and mindset, become full participants in power's games and try to influence it from the inside. In more prosaic terms, humanitarians have understood that responsibility involves engagement with power and have abandoned the infantile appeal of pacifism, 'the radicalism of people who do not expect to exercise power or use force, ever and who are not prepared to make the judgments that this exercise and use require'.[32] They have become part of the leading elite, the priests and missionaries of the new world order. For the pragmatist ideologist, the task now is to consolidate and generalise this project of osmosis between humanitarians, the military and politicians and turn it into a world ideology:

> We must promote the vocabulary among civilian populations, or we must strengthen the legitimacy of professional humanitarians as the voice of a universal ethics ... harmonic convergence between the military and humanitarian sensibility will only be achieved once the humanitarian vocabulary becomes a dominant global ideology of legitimacy.[33]

This is an amazing claim. The purpose of natural law, human rights and humanitarianism has been, from their inception, to resist public and private domination and oppression. When Kennedy deplores radical humanitarians who speak 'truth to power' from a position of religious conviction, natural right or positive law, he acknowledges some of the main formalisations of dissent and opposition. For those who have nothing else to fall back upon, human rights becomes a kind of imaginary or exceptional law.[34] Human rights work in the gap between ideal nature and law, or between real people and universal abstractions. The perspective of the future does not belong to governments, accountants and lawyers. It certainly does not belong to international organ-isations, diplomats and professional humanitarians. Governments were the enemy against whom human rights were invented. The 'universal ethics' of professional humanitarians on the other hand is a misnomer. Its universalism turns the priorities of the American elite into global principle; its ethics upgrade the deontology of a small coterie into a universal moral code. To claim that

---

32 Walzer, op. cit., 14.
33 Kennedy, op. cit., 277.
34 Costas Douzinas, *The End of Human Rights* (Oxford, Hart, 2000), Chapter 12.

human rights are today a main weapon for generating governmental legitimacy is to turn the thief into the prison-guard. At this point, human rights lose their end and their role comes to an end.

We must defend, therefore, the radical do-gooders, the marginal pacifists, the anti-war and anti-globalisation protesters and all those who, Bartleby-like, 'would prefer not to' become scriveners for the elites and accountants of power. They represent the most important European moral and political legacy while military humanitarians represent the abandonment of politics by the liberal nomenclature for a few slivers of power. One could call this, the postmodern *trahison des clercs*. Hilary Charlesworth, in a hilarious retort to Kennedy, doubts that many principled radicals are left in the humanitarian community anyway: 'The international human rights movement already largely operates in the pragmatic mode.'[35] She may be right, in which case the principle of hope that human rights feebly represent today will have been extinguished in the quest for government grants and junior partner role in military campaigns. Professionalism will have won by abolishing the *raison d'être* of humanitarianism. Following Alex de Waal, we can call this enterprise and its officers 'Global Ethics Inc'.[36]

We should, however, insist against realists, pragmatists and the ideologues of power that the energy necessary for the protection, horizontal proliferation and vertical expansion of human rights comes from below, from those whose lives have been blighted by oppression or exploitation and who have not been offered or have not accepted the blandishments and rewards of political apathy. Human rights professionals, whether radical or pragmatic, are at best ancillary to this task, which cannot be delegated. This question of delegation and substitution is crucial for the politics of humanitarianism within the Western world, to which we now turn.

The stakes of humanitarianism

'Thanks for coming to support the greatest thing in the history of the world', Chris Martin, the lead singer of pop band Coldplay told the crowd at the Live8 concert in Hyde Park, London, in July 2005. 'We are not looking for charity, we are looking for justice' was how U2 lead singer and event co-organiser Bono expressed the purpose of the series of concerts organised to coincide

---

35 Hilary Charlesworth, 'Author, Author!: A Response to David Kennedy', 15 *Harvard Human Rights Journal* 127 (2002), 130.
36 Alex de Waal, 'The Moral Solipsism of Global Ethics Inc.' *London Review of Books*, 23 August 2001, 15.

with the meeting of the G8 leaders in Scotland. In repeated appeals to the leaders of the eight richest nations of the world, Live8 demanded that African debt should be written off and aid levels substantially increased. Human rights should be put at the centre of the agenda of the Western leaders.

There is no doubt that the many hundreds of thousands who followed the eight concerts around the world agreed with these sentiments. Tears and sympathy for African suffering and pain dominated the acres of space dedicated to the concert in the British newspapers. The crowds had a great time listening to Madonna, Pink Floyd and Paul McCartney, participating in the 'biggest thing ever organised' and protesting against African poverty and disease. Justice 'was the simplest and most pervasive theme ... Everyone is, suddenly, globally, politicised'.[37] As a combination of hedonism and good conscience, Live8 will not be easily overtaken in size or hyperbole. This was partying as politics, drinking and dancing as moral calling.

Public protest involves an element of publicity acknowledged in the law of public order. Marches, demonstrations, rallies, picketing and sit-ins have always involved some violence or at least inconvenience for protesters and the public at large. Marches and demonstrations take place in public; they also bring people together and create out of isolated monads a public concerned with issues that transcend limited self-interest. The classical agora and forum were re-enacted metaphorically in the public sphere of newspapers and debating societies of early capitalism and, physically, in the streets, squares and other public places of modern protesting. But publicity, sharing ideas or actions, marching together is scarcely the point of the politics of the new type of humanitarianism. In the global politics of protest, inconvenience has been replaced by partying, publicity by TV campaigns, empathy by private donations. Indeed, to the extent that the main tactic of humanitarian campaigns is to have people donate money while watching celebrity-filled shows on TV, the public character has been lost. We participate in human rights struggles from our front room not as *polites*, publicly minded citizens, but as *idiotes*, private persons, committed to personal interest. No wonder that the G8 leaders and targets of Live8 stated, according to Chancellor Gordon Brown, that they would be happy to participate in the 'action' against them.

Humanitarianism has turned into the ultimate political ideology bringing together the well-being of the West with the hardships of the global South. But what does it mean for politics to become TV campaigns? What type of humanity does humanitarianism project? The idea of humanity that Band Aid, Live8 and Amnesty International letter-writing campaigns propose and

---

37 Euan Ferguson, *The Observer*, 3 July 2005, 2.

promote dominates our imagination and our institutions and determines the way we see ourselves and others. In theory, humanity brings together and transcends regional characteristics such as nationality, citizenship, class, gender, race or sexuality. Michael Ignatieff is on sure ground when he claims that human rights embody the idea that 'our species is one'.[38] We should be able to recognise the same human person, despite empirical differences, all over the world, in the City of London and the slums of Bombay, in the country houses of Berkshire and the town houses of Baghdad. The ideology of humanitarianism: the human has the same needs, desires and traits everywhere and these (ought to) determine the rights we have. Rights follow our nature. As natural, they are evident, they are agreed by everyone; there is no person of good faith who does not accept their universality or political efficacy. They are the entitlements of common humanity, they belong to us on account of our membership of the species human rather than of narrower categories.

But then doubts start creeping up. We would not need legal enforcement of these 'obvious' entitlements if they were that obvious. Their institutional proclamation and protection indicates that humanity is not one, that human nature is not common to all, that nature cannot protect its own. Live8 is part of the sad recognition that, despite the claims of humanism, humanity is split, the 'human' breaks up into distinct parts. One part is the humanity that suffers, the human as victim; the other is the humanity that saves, the human as rescuer. Humanity's goodness depends on its suffering but without goodness suffering would not be recognised. The two parts call each other to existence as the two sides of the same coin. You cannot have a rescuer without a victim and there is no victim unless a rescuer recognises him as such. But there is a second split. Humanity suffers because parts of it are evil, degenerate, cruel and inflict indescribable horrors upon the rest. There can be no redemption without sin, no gift without deprivation, no Band Aid without famine.

This second separation is officially acknowledged in the important concept of 'crimes against humanity'. The Nuremberg trial, which first introduced this legal novelty, is seen as a symbolic moment in the creation of the human rights movement. Human rights emerged when humanity acknowledged that one of its parts commits despicable atrocities against another, while a third, the saviour and redeemer, uses law, reason and occasionally force to punish the perpetrators and remedy pain and harm. Humanity suffers as a result of evil and crime, or through the effects of avoidable human error or unavoidable bad luck. If humanity suffers because of its own evil and must be rescued,

---

38   Michael Ignatieff, *Human Rights as Politics and Idolatry* (Princeton, NJ, Princeton University Press, 2001), 3.

evil and its consequences, vulnerability suffering pain, are its universal characteristics.

Religious traditions and political ideologies attribute suffering to evil. For Christian, particularly Protestant theology, suffering is a permanent existential characteristic, the unavoidable effect of original sin. Suffering and pain are the result of transgression, of lack or deprivation of goodness but also the sinner's opportunity for salvation by imitating Christ's passion. Indeed, the word pain derives from the Latin *poena*, punishment. The human rights movement agrees. It aims to put cruelty first, to stop 'unmerited suffering and gross physical cruelty'.[39] In the dialectic of good and evil, evil comes first; the good is defined negatively as *steresis kakou*, as the removal, remedy or absence of evil. Human rights and humanitarianism bring the different parts of humanity together, they try to suture a common human essence out of the deeply cut body. Let us examine briefly the three masks of the human: the suffering victim, the atrocious evil-doer and the moral rescuer.

First, man as victim. The victim is someone whose dignity and worth has been violated. Powerless, helpless and innocent, her basic nature and needs have been denied. But there is more: victims are part of an indistinct mass or horde of despairing, dispirited people. They are faceless and nameless, the massacred Tutsis, the trafficked refugees, the gassed Kurds, the raped Bosnians. Victims are kept in camps, they are incarcerated in prisons, banned into exitless territories en masse. Losing humanity, becoming less than human; losing individuality, becoming part of a horde, crowd or mob; losing self-determination, becoming enslaved; these are the results of evil, otherwise known as human rights violations. Indeed here we may have the best example of what Giorgio Agamben calls 'bare or sacred life'[40] or Bernard Ogilvie, the 'one use human':[41] biological life abandoned by the juridical and political order of the nation-state, valueless life that can be killed with impunity. The publicity campaigns with the 'imploring eyes' of dying children and mourning mothers are 'the most telling contemporary cipher of the bare life that humanitarian organisations, in perfect symmetry with state power, need'.[42] The target of our charity is an amorphous mass of people. It populates our TV screens, newspapers and NGO fund-raising campaigns. The victims are paraded exhausted, tortured, starving but always nameless, a crowd, a mob that inhabits

39   Ibid. 173.
40   See Chapters 4 and 5.
41   Bernard Ogilvie quoted by Etienne Balibar, *Politics and Truth* (Athens, Nissos, 2005), 43.
42   Giorgio Agamben, *Homo Sacer. Sovereign Power and Bare Life* (Daniel Heller-Roazen, trans.) (Stanford, CA, Stanford University Press, 1998), 133–4.

the exotic parts of the world. As a former president of Médecins Sans Frontières put it,

> he to whom humanitarian actions is addressed is not defined by his skills or potential, but above all, by his deficiencies and disempowerment. It is his fundamental vulnerability and dependency, rather than his agency and ability to surmount difficulty that is foregrounded by humanitarianism.[43]

The victim is only one side of the Other. The reverse side represents the evil abroad in those scary parts of the world. This second half, the cause of the fall and the suffering, the Mr Jeckyll or the wolf-man, is absolute evil. Its names legion: the African dictator, the Slav torturer, the Balkan rapist, the Moslem butcher, the corrupt bureaucrat, the Levantine conman, the monstrous sacrificer. The beast of Baghdad, the butcher of Belgrade, the warlord, the rogue and the bandit are the single cause and inescapable companion of suffering. As Jacques Derrida puts it, 'the beast is not simply an animal but the very incarnation of evil, of the satanic, the diabolical, the demonic – a beast of the Apocalypse'.[44] Or, according to Connor Gearty, these representatives of evil 'are not only different, but worse, worse even than animals who are, after all, incapable of evil'.[45] This excess of evil means that the victims are victimised by their own; to that extent their suffering is not undeserved. Famine, malnutrition, disease and lack of medicines result from the intrinsic corruption of the evil Other, signs of divine punishment or of appropriate fate in the form of acts of God or *force majeure*. The Other of the West combines the suffering mass and the radical evil-doer, the subhuman and the inhuman rolled into one.

In this moral universe, the claim that there is a single essence to humanity to be discovered in evil, suffering and its relief, for which debt relief stands as a metaphor, is foundational. Whoever is below the standard is not fully up to the status of human. Indeed, every human rights campaign or humanitarian intervention presupposes an element of contempt for the situation and the victims. Human rights are part of an attitude of the postcolonial world in which the 'misery' of Africa is the result of its failings and corruption, its traditional attitudes and lack of modernisation, its nepotism and inefficiency,

---

43 Rony Brennan, 'Contradictions of Humanitarianism', 7 *Alphabet City* 140 (2000).
44 Jacques Derrida, *Rogues* (Pascale-Anne Brault and Michael Naas, trans.) (Stanford, CA, Stanford University Press 2005), 97.
45 Connor Gearty, 'With a Little Help From Our Friends', 34/1 *Index on Censorship* 47 (2005).

in a word of its sub-humanity. We can feel great pity for the victims of human rights abuses; but pity is tinged with a little contempt for their fickleness and passivity and huge aversion towards the bestiality of their compatriots and tormentors. We do not like these others, but we love pitying them. They, the savages/victims, make us civilised.

This brings us to the rescuer. The human rights campaigner, the Western philanthropist and the humanitarian partygoer are there to save the victims. Participation and contributions to the humanitarian movement may be resulting in some 'collateral benefit'. There is a kernel of nobility in joining letter-writing campaigns or giving money to 'good causes' to alleviate suffering. Such campaigns have given help to political prisoners and to victims of torture, civil war and natural catastrophe. But a strange paradox accompanies increased humanitarian activism. Our era has witnessed more violations of human rights than any previous less 'enlightened' one. Ours is the epoch of massacre, genocide, ethnic cleansing, the age of the Holocaust. At no point in human history has there been a greater gap between the North and the South, between the poor and the rich in the developed world or between the 'seduced' and the excluded globally. The results of massive humanitarian campaigns are rather meager. In 2006, an audit of G8 promises made to Live8 a year earlier found that rich countries are failing badly to meet the targets they themselves set.[46] No degree of progress allows us to ignore that never before in absolute figures, have so many men, women, and children been subjugated, starved, or exterminated on earth. The triumph of humanitarianism is drowned in human disaster. The 'best' and the 'worst' come together, prompting and feeding off each other. But if we approach the rescue missions of humanitarianism as part of a wider project on intervention both in the South and in the North, some of the apparent contradictions start disappearing.

Liberal theory understands rights as an expression and protection of individual desire, albeit indirectly. Amidst the proliferation of theorists on human rights, few have argued that human suffering is their common foundation or theme. One is Klaus Gunther, for whom all major European institutional innovations and protections, from the Magna Carta, to the French Declaration of the Rights of Man, to the various Bills of Rights across the continent, to the European Convention on Human Rights, have been reactions to different types of atrocity. European history is replete with wars, oppression, annihilation of others and, as a result, the history of human rights is written in blood. In Gunther's analysis, negative historical experiences and the development of the human rights movement are closely linked:

---

46 *The Guardian*, 3 July 2006, 13.

> If you want to know what is meant by 'human dignity' or 'equal concern and respect' for every human being, you can either look at various kinds of legal definitions, or you can think of the German Gestapo torturing a political opponent or the Holocaust of the European Jews.[47]

For Gunther, Europeans share memories of injustice and fear, a resource that should be used to promote a human rights culture. We must listen to our past pain and wrongs, everyone who has a story to tell must be heard. Gunther concludes that

> the most important effect of human rights . . . is the recognition of every individual as an equal participant in the political process which leads to a decision on primary rules . . . One has the power and ability to criticise and amend the rules of justice.[48]

Gunther offers a postmodern theoretical foundation for human rights that goes well beyond Rorty's pragmatism and meek attempts at 'sentimental education'. According to Rorty, this means educating people to listen to strangers and understand their ways of life. By bringing out similarities in our respective ways of life, the feeling that strangers are 'people like us' will be strengthened and the sense of moral community widened. The main strategy for spreading human rights and democracy is to narrate stories of pain, suffering and humiliation happening all over the world.[49] This pedagogy of pity will put people 'in the shoes of those despised and oppressed' and make them more empathetic and less prone to killing and torching others.[50] The assumed premise of Rorty's argument is that 'our' culture, society and politics are the ideal others (should) aspire to achieve. The pragmatist's emphasis on efficiency and results means that a standard of civilisation must be set as the blueprint and aim. For Rorty, this is American liberal culture. In a postmodern repetition of the methods of early social anthropology, Rorty believes that we must understand the ways and travails of others in order to help them efficiently become like us. Gunther's variation is more honest. Sentimental education must emphasise our own suffering. Past European woes and humiliations should be used to

---

47   Klaus Gunther, 'Human Rights and Political Culture' in Philip Alston, ed., *The EU and Human Rights* (Oxford, Oxford University Press, 1999), 126.
48   Ibid. 132.
49   Richard Rorty, 'Human Rights, Rationality and Sentimentality' in Stephen Shute and Susan Hurley, eds, *On Human Rights* (New York, Basic Books, 1993), 117; Rorty, *Contingency, Irony and Solidarity* (Cambridge, Cambridge University Press, 1989), xvi.
50   Ibid. 126–7.

raise public awareness. Because we suffered in the past and may do so again in the future, we should refrain from visiting similar woes on others and try to ameliorate their pain. *La noblesse oblige* has become in our post-aristocratic world *la souffrance oblige*.

The liberal tradition therefore distinguishes between human rights and the weak moral obligation to rescue. Rescue is based on a feeling of superiority and the principle of substitution. I am duty-bound to help the suffering other because I am well-off, lucky, unaffected by the atrocities I read about in my newspapers and see on TV screens.[51] But I could have been born in one of those hard places or life may still reduce me to the victim's predicament. We should act morally towards suffering others because we could imagine being in their position. As Michael Ignatieff puts it, 'the ground we share may actually be . . . not much more than the basic intuition that what is pain and humiliation for you is bound to be pain and humiliation for me'.[52] Charity is part of a risk-aversion strategy, an insurance policy against bad luck or an offering to the gods for our great fortune. But as Richard Rorty has convincingly argued, in his deconstructive mood, neo-Kantian philosophy's obsessions with epistemology and metaphysics reduces the sense of solidarity and weakens the ability to listen to strangers and respond to their suffering.[53]

Gunther's theory is a variation of the morality of substitution. Our past suffering becomes the foundation of our moral action. It is because we Europeans have been there, because we have been beastly to each other and suffered as a result, that we should now promote human rights. The memory of 'collective trauma' should be recovered and put to good effect. Morality moves back where the liberals place it: the self, the ego and its mishaps. Human rights have been constructed as defences of the self against the incursions of powerful others, initially the state increasingly now other people. Gunther tries to make them more attuned to the pity the public is made to feel in humanitarian campaigns. But is the best way of doing this to try and link human rights with European atrocities against Europeans? Europeans suffered in the

---

51 This is a position Emmanuel Levinas attacked. Levinas insisted that there can be no reciprocity or substitution between the person making the ethical demand and its addressee. The encounter with the other is painful, disturbing and traumatic. In Levinasian ethics, the ego is caught by the other, it becomes literally hostage to the other's request. The other's demand torments and decentres me but only I can respond. This has nothing to do with the pity philanthropic campaigns generate nor with the moral superiority the charitable donator receives. See Douzinas, *End*, Chapter 13.

52 Ignatieff, *Politics*, 95.

53 Richard Rorty, *Philosophy and Social Hope* (London, Penguin, 1999), xv; 'Introduction' in *Philosophical Papers* (Cambridge, Cambridge University Press, 1991), 13.

past at the hands of other Europeans as parts of European humanity. But our greatest atrocities then and now are committed against 'aliens' considered less than human. The treatment of the Jews in the Holocaust or of the Muslims in Bosnia are recent examples. Slaves, Indians, aboriginals and indigenous people, on the other hand, have been consistently placed in the non-human part of humanity. Some ten million Congolese died in the early twentieth century as a result of Belgian forced labour and mass murder. Millions died of avoidable famines in India under colonial rule. Up to one million Algerians died during their war of independence. These were crimes by humanity but not against humanity. We shed tears for these out of sense of superiority and charity rather than out of shared history, community or humanity. If we have a shared history, humanitarianism in its celebration of our goodness erases it. European campaigns of extermination, slavery, colonial subjugation, capitalist exploitation and imperial domination are forgotten or glorified, as shown in recent revisionist celebrations of the British Empire. These atrocities are what psychoanalysis calls the real or traumatic kernel of the West, the cause and effect of economic affluence and personal enjoyment. The horrors visited by the West on its 'others' are conveniently forgotten and displaced. Horrible, atrocious acts are only committed by the evil inhuman other.

Indeed, the human rights movement came into life late, after the Second World War. Humanity started committing crimes against itself in the 1930s when the Germans, this philosophical embodiment of humanity, acted atrociously against its own. The German crimes were appropriately called crimes against humanity because only the West is endowed with full humanity and can become the proper victim of atrocity. Humanity offends against herself in the West and against sub-humans in the South. During the recent wars in Bosnia and Kosovo, commentators were shocked that atrocities could take place right in the 'heart of Europe'. We, Europeans, had supposedly learned the lesson after our rare, 'exceptional' misdeeds and it was inconceivable that we could become criminals again. To be sure, the Balkans are approached as peripheral parts of the civilised world, placed in Europe by accident of geography rather than achievement of history or culture. The Balkan wars confirmed again the principle that we, the Europeans, are the chosen people, the essence of humanity in its three facets.

Gunther's proposal cannot be implemented for precisely the reasons that have turned the pain of others into a powerful ideology and suffering into the main characteristic of humanity. The premise and appeal of humanitarianism is distance and alienation. We must participate in campaigns and fine-tune our morality because we, Western liberals, have *not* suffered in the past, because we cannot share the torments of those unfortunate and exotic parts of the world now. Because we have always been human, we must now extend our generosity to those less than human. This is confirmed by Gunther's understanding of the principal achievement of human rights culture and main recipe for their violation, namely participation in democratic procedures and legislation. It is not very different from the claim that the aim of our recent wars was to spread formal democracy and neo-liberal capitalism to backward parts of the world. They are inescapably part of the egocentric and ethnocentric approach to the suffering of others. Gunther's claim that democratic participation is the greatest achievement of human rights is a rather extreme and sad case of Eurocentrism refuted by the growing political apathy around the world. Indeed, the historical trajectories of civil liberties, human rights and democracy diverged wildly from the start and often came into conflict.[54] Furthermore, as Michael Mann has recently shown, the idea that democracies do not commit genocide is utterly wrong.[55]

Giving money to alleviate the suffering of others is both an insurance policy against the risks of life and as the ultimate moral duty. Live8 interspersed images of starving children and of Aids sufferers at the end of their life with those of beautiful, healthy superstars and fans and the wonderful costumes of dancers and accompanying choirs. On the part of the victims the haggard animal on TV screens, on the other side good conscience and the imperative to intervene. It is a short step from that to define violations of human rights as the supreme form of suffering and to portray the human rights movement as the redemptive practice of our age. A simple equation has taken hold of our political imagination. Human rights are entitlements to be free from evil. As the preamble of the Universal Declaration of Human Rights puts it, it is disregard and contempt for human rights that have led to barbarous acts.

Pity and a sense of superiority unite the humanitarians. The massive pity engineered by humanitarian campaigns supports Western superiority, increases distantiation from its targets and breeds disdain. Pity is addressed by a superior to an inferior, it is the patronising emotion of looking down at the person pitied. The human rights campaigner as rescuer can become deeply egotistical: he is the one who keeps the world together and, as a bonus, he receives full recognition for his goodness by others from close and afar. Individual pity is not sympathy. *Syn* connotes being with, being together with others; *pathos* means feeling, emotion and, in another sense, suffering. The Greek verb *sym-pascho* and noun *sym-patheia* mean to suffer with others, to feel with and for

---

54 C.B. McPherson, *The Life and Times of Liberal Democracy* (Oxford, Oxford University Press, 1991).
55 Michael Mann, *The Dark Side of Democracy: Explaining Ethnic Cleansing* (Cambridge, Cambridge University Press, 2005).

others, to be affected by the same thing and to link emotions in public. For the human rights world, however, feelings towards the suffering are the result of the absence of togetherness. Because we do not suffer, because there is no possible link between us and the victims, our good luck turns into a modicum of guilt, shame and a few pound coins. If political and historical events can be measured according to the amount of pain they produce, if indeed this is the only calculus through which we can judge history, humanity is one after all: it is united through inevitable suffering and the pity it generates.

Let me open here a historical parenthesis. Contemporary humanitarianism repeats and exaggerates many aspects of the humanitarian campaigns and reforms of the eighteenth and nineteenth centuries. Humanitarian reformers of that period detailed the pain and suffering endured by people in slavery, or caught up in the criminal justice system, in crammed and unsafe work-places, in cruel and impoverished domestic conditions, etc. The brutalities of life in England were depicted through explicit imagery as well as graphic novels and journalism. This strategy, part of the epoch's concern to raise sensibility and launch the bourgeois civilising process, aimed at turning public opinion against cruel practices and improving the life of the poor.

Images of suffering of the distant poor and oppressed form the core strategy of contemporary humanitarian campaigns, too, alongside public relations, advertising, film and video. The young man before the Tiananmen Square tanks, the Amnesty International candle surrounded by barbed wire, the burned girl running away from the fire-bombed Vietnamese village have iconic status and represent human rights much more than a thousand speeches, learned articles and books. As a sympathetic commentator puts it, human rights politics is 'a politics of images spun from one side of the globe to the other, typically with little local history or context'.[56] The search for images of victims, especially children, and for a 'good story' dominated the media over the Yugoslav wars. According to one relief agency worker 'almost every journalist who came to see her in Kosovo asked one thing: could she give them a rape victim to interview'.[57]

Yet, while our culture is saturated with imagery and theories of visuality, very little has been written about the visual politics of humanitarianism. In contrast, the visual nature of sympathy and its side-effects were fully discussed in the eighteenth and nineteenth centuries. Following the tenets of the Scottish moral enlightenment, Adam Smith argued that ethics is a matter

---

56   Kenneth Cmiel, 'The Emergence of Human Rights Politics in the United States', 86/3 *Journal of American History* (1999), 1233.

57   Quoted in David Chandler, *From Kosovo to Kabul* (London, Pluto Press, 2002), 36.

of sentiments aroused by sympathy. Sympathy in turn is the result of seeing the suffering of others. 'By the imagination we place ourselves in his situation, we conceive ourselves enduring all the same torments, we enter as it were into his body, and become in some measure the same person with him.'[58] But Smith was also prepared to acknowledge the limitations of sympathy. An earthquake destroying China, he admitted, would not match for real disturbance the 'most frivolous disaster that could befall [a man of humanity in Europe]'. Losing a little finger is more important than the 'ruin of a hundred millions of his brethren'.[59] Edmund Burke agreed: immediately felt pain or danger is terrible but 'at certain distances, and with certain modifications, they may be, and they are delightful'.[60] The proliferating attempts at arousing humanitarian sensibility evident in sentimental, sensationalist and gothic fiction and journalism were subjected to relentless criticism. John Keats and William Hazlitt accused sentimental poetry of exploring 'not the feelings of the imagined sufferer but the feelings of the spectator watching that sufferer and was geared to demonstrating the spectator's/reader's own exquisite sensibility'.[61]

The troublesome aspects of humanitarianism were fully discussed in the earlier period. The critics understood that the practice of arousing sympathy through the display of the suffering of others in scenes of execution, torture, public punishment and humiliation could go terribly wrong. It could blunt the moral fibre of the viewer and turn him into a savage by aligning him with the cruelty of the perpetrator rather than the pain of the victim. The humanitarian '"civilised" virtue requires a shocked spectatorial sympathy in response to pain scenarios both real and wilfully imagined . . . the cult of sensibility had proclaimed pain unacceptable but simultaneously discovered it to be alluring "delicious"'.[62] Images and tales of suffering have great voyeuristic and pornographic potential. Suffering was often eroticised in humanitarian campaigns. Overt sexual references about the 'sexual coercion and rape of slave women, the rape of war victims, and to the genital mutilation and torture of both male and female slaves' were accompanied more commonly with the indirect humanitarian eroticisation of pain through 'the illicit excitement

---

58 Adam Smith, *The Theory of Moral Sentiments* (Knud Haakonssen, ed.) (Cambridge, Cambridge University Press, 2002), 9.
59 Ibid. 157.
60 Edmund Burke, *A Philosophical Enquiry into the Origin of Our Ideas of the Sublime and Beautiful* (J.T. Boulton, ed.) (London, Routledge & Kegan Paul, 1958), 14.
61 Karen Halttunen, 'Humanitarianism and the Pornography of Pain in Anglo-American Culture', 100/2 *American Historical Review* 303 (1995), 308.
62 Ibid. 331, 332.

generated by the infliction of pain'.[63] Sigmund Freud reported that *Uncle Tom's Cabin*, a book celebrated by Richard Rorty for spreading sympathy for slaves among white Americans in the nineteenth century, was mentioned by many of his patients as the original stimulus of the common fantasy that a child is being beaten.[64]

The historical record causes a nauseous feeling of déjà vu. The examples of extreme suffering of the earlier period are very close to our own imagery of cruelty. If anything, the images of pain and suffering are more horrible today. They have permeated all aspects of contemporary culture and define music, lifestyle, fashion, the media and many areas of art alongside politics and humanitarian campaigns. But their voyeuristic or pornographic side was not discussed until the Abu Ghraib torture photographs emerged and even then in an embarrassed and apologetic way that did not address the politics of humanitarian imagery. It may be that we are more aware about human cruelty, that we have become more humanitarian than our ancestors. But we appear to know less about the causes of cruelty and atrocity and to understand very little about the way that images of suffering work on our emotional and psychological life.

The politics of humanitarianism

The effects of humanitarianism on politics are profound. If evil and suffering lie at the foundation of humanity, if an inescapable original sin determines its fate, ethics becomes a barrier against beastliness and the main aim of politics is to restrain evil and relieve suffering. In this ethics, the idea of freedom is primarily negative: it is a defence against the various malevolent interventions of public power. Politics adopts an ethical posturing as a result. Its judgements become moral diagnoses about the evil of others, its action takes the form of rescuing people. As Wendy Brown puts it, human rights activism becomes an 'antipolitics – a pure defence of the innocent and the powerless against power, a pure defence of the individual against immense and potentially cruel or despotic machineries'.[65] At the liberal end of the political spectrum, Michael Ignatieff agrees with the conclusion but not the analysis:

---

63   Ibid. 325.
64   Sigmund Freud, 'A Child is Being Beaten' in James Strachey, ed., *Collected Papers* (London, Hogarth Press, 1934), vol. 2, 173.
65   Wendy Brown, 'Human Rights and the Politics of Fatalism' in 103 2/3 *South Atlantic Quarterly* 453 (2004).

Human rights activism likes to portray itself as an anti-politics, in defence of universal moral claims designed to delegitimise 'political' (i.e., ideological or sectarian) justifications for the abuse of human beings. In practice, impartiality and neutrality are just as impossible as universal and equal concern for everyone's human rights.[66]

The specific political situation that led to the abuses, the colonial history and the conflicts that matured into civil war, the economics that allowed the famine to develop, all these are irrelevant from the perspective of the moralist. For the Kantian deontologist, the moral attitude should not be contaminated by the specifics of the situation. The moral action is a disinterested response to the demands of the law; moral duty is addressed first and foremost towards the actor and his rational commitment to morality and only secondarily towards the other, the target of its action. But as Alasdair McIntyre objected, acting morally is not acting as Kant thought 'against inclination; it is to act from inclination formed by the cultivation of virtues. Moral education is an '*education sentimentale*'' which however, unlike Rorty's, respects local communities and discovers in them the sources of virtue.[67] Human rights moralism, on the other hand, has it both ways. Following Kantian absolutism, it claims that acts are right or wrong, no grey zones exist, there are yes and no answers to every ethical dilemma. Paying too much attention to past events, to local politics and cultural sensitivities risks conceding principle to calculation and compromise. At the same time, pragmatic humanitarians follow the most extreme form of utilitarian calculation. Humanitarianism's inescapable contradiction allows its proponents to attack perceived evil in the most uncompromising moral terms while doing deals with the devil.

Second, since our campaigns are moral in essence, doubting the rightness or appropriateness of the solution cannot be done in good faith. People may be mobilised in a common cause but the solutions to the problem are given and unchallenged. 'Eight men in a room can change the world' was the main slogan of Live8. The millions of people participating in the event around the world were presented as a lobby group addressing the eight heads of state. There was no mention, however, of a simple and undoubted fact: these states are the main cause, through colonialism, imperialism and exported neoliberal capitalism, of the huge disparities between the North and the South. Similarly, with human rights. We in the West have developed rights as a response to the unavoidable failures of human nature, its propensity to sin.

---

66 Ignatieff, fn. 38, 9.
67 Alasdair McIntyre, *After Virtue* (London, Duckworth, 1981), 140.

Because we have understood the centrality of suffering and sin and have built defences against it, we have the obligation to send them to the less fortunate. Because we produce abundantly and have so many rights in the West, we must find markets to export them. In the same way that we give our secondhand clothes to Oxfam to be sent to Africa, we also send human rights and democracy. If however the less civilised do not accept our charity we will have to impose it on them with fighter bombers and tanks.

The global humanitarian sees victims of misfortune everywhere. Undifferentiated pain and suffering has become the universal currency of the South, and pity the global response of the North. Pity is misanthropic. It is the closest we get today to the Hegelian master and slave dialectic; the slave's recognition of the master in his position of mastery is not reciprocated, the relationship remains one directional. The identity of both remains defective because it lacks the mutuality of full recognition. If subjectivity is the outcome of inter-subjectivity mediated by objectivity,[68] the gift is the object that guarantees the (superiority of the) identity of the giver by turning the recipient, who is unable to reciprocate, into the passive support of the Westerner's self. In this sense, donations have a malevolent aspect: they bestow identity to some at the expense of others who, by receiving material goods without consideration, become the effective givers of recognition without return. Individual empathy in the face of suffering may be a noble characteristic. The good Samaritan, the person who gives himself to the other in a non-calculating act is a great moral example. In extreme situations, helping the other becomes an act of heroism and even of martyrdom.

The good Samaritan was a rich government functionary. His role is now performed by the humanitarian militarist and the ethical capitalist. There are many business opportunities in suffering and increased profit margins in promoting human rights. Advice about 'ethical' investment options and 'ethical consumerism' is routinely published in most serious newspapers in Britain and the United States. It usually includes references to the human rights record of the country or company involved. A few examples indicate the close relationship between the 'best' and the 'worst'. George Soros, the financial speculator and venture capitalist, was one of the main contributors to the collapse of the British currency in 1987. This led to thousands of small businesses going bankrupt and people losing their homes. The Soros foundation, largely funded by the gains of such parasitical if not piratical activities, however, promotes democracy and human rights in Eastern Europe and the Balkans. Bill Gates, having monopolised through Microsoft the computing

---

68   Douzinas op. cit., Chapter 10.

industry, is generously giving millions away to good causes around the world. The oil giant Shell does not have a reputation for human rights campaigns. Indeed, in 1995, Shell was involved in the execution of nine Ogoni activists, including the renowned author Ken Saro-Wiwa, who fought for the land rights of their people brutally violated by the Nigerian government with the connivance of Shell. However after protests against its activities, Shell now proclaims its commitment to human rights. Its website has an introduction to Nigerian literature, in which Saro-Wiwa is presented as a martyr. Similarly, the Chinese government, never slow in realising a business opportunity allows a few high profile dissidents to emigrate to the West as a sop to human rights campaigns while continuing its repression. This way it sets itself up 'as a business enterprise that deals in politicised human persons as precious commodities'.[69] As Joseph Slaughter puts it, human rights has now become a large corporation and should be renamed 'Human Rights Inc'.

The great modern philosophies of history promised progress through reason. Napoleon, the first modern emperor, was the 'spirit [that is freedom] on horse-back' for Hegel. The communists preached 'soviets and electricity'; humanity would be united in future equality through the marvels of technology and common ownership of the means of production. The Nazis tried to purify humanity by eliminating the Jews and the gypsies as inferior races, the Stalinists by purging those who disagreed or obstructed the ideology of violently accelerating the historical process. All great ideologies of the last century ended in violence, atrocities and disaster. These great rationalisms justified their atrocities against race, class, ideology or ethnicity with the argument that a few million dead were the necessary price to pay for the future unity of humanity. Ideologies are systems of thought, ways of understanding and explaining the world drawn from a particular perspective, that of class, nation or religion.

Today, we have abandoned both ideology and the attempt to understand the world. Post-communist humanitarianism, scared by the atrocities of twentieth-century ideology, prefers a suffering humanity and replaces the grand narratives of history with the misfortune of the species. This accords fully with the neo-liberal claim that history has ended, that all history-moving political conflict has been resolved and ideology no longer has any value. The young people who join NGOs would have joined left-wing groups and campaigns a few years earlier. The quest for justice, the great motivating force of politics has become anti-political. Care for the victims, defence of rights, promotion

---

69 Rey Chow, *The Protestant Ethnic and the Spirit of Capitalism* (New York, Columbia University Press, 2002), 21.

of free choices is the indisputable ideology of our post-political world. Humanity has been united not through the plans of revolutionaries, but through universal pain, pity and the market. Political events are not analysed concretely or examined for their historical roots; they are judged by the amount of suffering they generate. It is a comforting vision. We are guided exclusively by moral feelings. United in our pity, we call for soothing interventions and care little for the pre- or post-intervention situation as long as they reduce the amount of pain. As a result, the complexity of history, the thick political context and the plurality of possible responses to each new 'humanitarian tragedy' is lost.

Ideologies sacrificed individuals for the future of humanity; for humanitarians, individuals count only as ciphers for suffering humanity. The uniqueness of every person and situation is replaced by a grey, monolithic humanity, the very opposite of the infinite diversity of human experience. According to Alain Finkielkraut, 'the humanitarian generation does not like men – they are too disconcerting – but enjoys taking care of them. Free men scare it. Eager to express tenderness fully while making sure that men do not get away, it prefers handicapped people.'[70] Moreover, as the value of pity and of the resulting intervention is determined in a virtual stock exchange of suffering, the 'price' of calamities is endlessly pushed upwards. The Holocaust has become the universal standard of comparison, and the measure of evil of each new real or imagined atrocity, each Rwanda, Bosnia, Kosovo, is judged against that. As Paul Ricoeur put it, 'the victims of Auschwitz are the representatives, par excellence, in our memory of all history's victims. Victimisation is the other side of history that no trick of reason can ever justify.'[71] Pity has replaced politics, morality reason, suffering progress. The universal exchange of suffering and market capitalism have finally become global currency.

Religion is inherently a discourse of truth. It must proclaim the superiority of its doctrines. Universal morality follows the same route. It is impossible to claim the universality of a moral code or principle and accept that others may legitimately disagree with it. If there are many views but one right answer, it is incumbent upon the person, the state or the alliance who has it to pass it on and eventually impose it on others. Morality, like religion, arranges people in hierarchy of superiority. The 'globalisation of human rights fits a historical

---

70 Alain Finkielkraut, *In the Name of Humanity* (New York, Columbia University Press, 2000), 91.

71 Paul Ricoeur, *Time and Narrative*, Vol. 3 (Chicago, IL, University of Chicago Press, 1988), 187.

pattern in which all high morality comes from the West as a civilising agent against lower forms of civilisation in the rest of the world'.[72] Despite differences in content, colonialism and the human rights movement form a continuum, episodes in the same drama, which started with the great discoveries of the new world and is now carried out in the streets of Iraq: bringing civilisation to the barbarians. The claim to spread Reason and Christianity gave the Western empires their sense of superiority and their universalising impetus. The urge is still there; the ideas have been redefined but the belief in the universality of our world-view remains as strong as that of the colonialists. Human rights 'are secularising the Last Judgment' admits Ulrich Beck.[73] There is little difference between imposing reason and good governance or between proselytising for Christianity and human rights. They are both part of the cultural package of the West, aggressive and redemptive at the same time. As Immanuel Wallerstein put it, 'the intervenors, when challenged, always resort to a moral justification – natural law and Christianity in the sixteenth century, the civilising mission in the nineteenth century, and human rights and democracy in the late twentieth and twenty-first centuries'.[74]

The Westerner used to carry the white man's burden, the obligation to spread civilisation, reason, religion and law to the barbaric part of the world. If the colonial prototypes were the missionary and the colonial administrator, the postcolonial are the human rights campaigner and the NGO operative.[75] Humanity has replaced civilisation. 'The humanitarian empire is the new face of an old figure' one of its supporters admits. 'It is held together by common elements of rhetoric and self-belief: the idea, if not the practice, of democracy; the idea, if not the practice, of human rights; the idea, if not the practice, of equality before the law.'[76] The postmodern philanthropist, on the other hand, does not need to go to far-flung places to build clinics and missions. Globalisation has ensured that he can do that from his front room, watching TV images of desolation and atrocity and paying with his credit card.

---

72 Ibid. 210.
73 Ulrich Beck, *Cosmopolitan Vision* (Cambridge, Polity, 2006), 142.
74 Immanuel Wallerstein, *European Universalism: The Rhetoric of Power* (New York, The New Press, 2006), 27.
75 David Rieff, *A Bed for the Night* (London, Vintage, 2002); Barbara Harlow, 'From the Civilising Mission to Humanitarian Intervention' in Peter Pfeiffer ed., *Text and Nation* (New York, Camden House, 1996); Alex de Waal, *Famine Crimes. Politics and the Disaster Relief Industry in Africa* (Oxford, James Currey, 2002); for a hilarious portrayal of the pleasures and woes of peacekeepers, NGO officers and other 'internationals' see Kenneth Cain, Heidi Postlewait and Andrew Thomson, *Emergency Sex* (London, Ebury Press, 2004).
76 Ignatieff, *Empire Lite*, op. cit., 17.

As Upendra Baxi puts it, 'human rights movements organise themselves in the image of markets' turning 'human suffering and human rights' into commodities, profit and career opportunities.[77]

But, despite the structural differences between victim and rescuer, the vision of politics projected in human rights campaigns is common to both. The donor is as much a passive recipient of messages and solutions as the victim and aid-recipient. His contribution is restricted to accepting the alternatives offered by governments and the media. If the victim is the witless plaything of powers beyond his control, the donor equally accepts that this part of the world is beyond redemption and philanthropy is a transient palliative. Unlike the missionary, the humanitarian does not need to believe in any particular religion or ideology, except the global ideology that people suffer and we have an obligation to relieve their woes. Pain and suffering has replaced ideology and moral sentiments have replaced politics, as Richard Rorty advised us to do. But this type of humanitarian activism ends as an anti-politics, as the defence of 'innocents' without any understanding of the operations of power and without the slightest interest in the collective action that would change the causes of poverty, disease or war.

The 'Other' of humanitarianism

The massive character of humanitarian campaigns despite their relatively meagre returns indicates that the stakes go beyond the immediate action. On the surface, the characteristics of the victims stand in stark contrast to those of their saviours. By joining the humanitarian drive we create our own selves. Standing against the faceless mass, the saviour is individualised. Standing against the evil, the donor becomes virtuous. Standing against inhumanity, the campaigner is elevated to full humanity. And as human rights are not given easily to community building and political collaboration, the main sentiment connecting donors and letter writers is their relief that they do not find themselves in the position of the recipients of their generosity.

Human rights campaigns construct the post-political Western subjectivity: they promise the development of a non-traumatised self (and society) supported by our reflection into our suffering mirror-images and by the displacement of the evil in our midst onto their barbaric inhumanity. Using psychoanalytical terms, we can distinguish three types of otherness that support our selfhood

---

77   Upendra Baxi, *The Future of Human Rights* (New Delhi, Oxford University Press, 2000), 121, 122.

and identity, the imaginary, the symbolic and the real. When defined as victim, as the extreme example of universal suffering, the Other is seen as an inferior I, someone who aspires (or should aspire) to reach the same level of civilisation or governance we have. Their inferiority turns them into our imaginary Other in reverse, our narcissistic mirror-image and potential double. These unfortunates are the infants of humanity, ourselves in a state of nascency. In their dark skins and incomprehensible languages, in their colourful and 'lazy' lives, in their suffering and perseverance, we see the beautiful people we are. They must be helped to grow up, to develop and become like us. Because the victim is our likeness in reverse, we know his interests and impose them 'for his own good'.

The cures we offer to this imaginary other follows our own desires and recipes. The humanitarian movement is full of these priority cures: liberalisation of trade and opening the local markets is more important than guaranteeing minimum standards of living; imposing a system of elections is more important than survival. Lack of voting rights in one-party states, censorship of the press or lack of judicial guarantees in China or Zimbabwe are the prime examples of beastliness; death from hunger or debilitating disease, high infant mortality or low life expectancy are not equally important. In the 1980s, the European Community built wine lakes and butter mountains and preferred to stock uselessly and even destroy the produce to avoid flooding the marketplace and driving prices down. Similarly today, democracy and good governance, our greatest exports must be sold at the right price: they must follow our rules and should not be used against our interests. As an American official put it complaining about Venezuelan policies challenging American hegemony and redistributing the oil wealth of the country, 'the government's actions and frequent statements contribute to regional instability . . . despite being democratically elected, the government of President Hugo Chavez has systematically undermined democratic institutions'.[78]

The second type of otherness is symbolic. We enter the world through our introduction to the symbolic order, as speaking beings subjected to the law.[79] The others, the unfortunate victims of dictators and tsunamis, have not learned as yet to speak (our) language and accept (our) laws, they are non-proper speakers or in-fants. Consumption of Western goods and civil and political rights are signs of progress. If the Chinese have Big Macs and Hollywood movies, democracy and freedom will eventually follow. Learning the

---

78   *The Guardian,* 14 January 2006, 17.
79   Douzinas, op. cit., Chapter 11.

importance of consumerism and human rights may take some time as all education and socialisation does. But it takes precedence over economic redistribution and cultural recognition. Our legal culture promotes equality and dignity by turning concrete people to abstract persons, bearers of formal rights. According to Zen Bankowski,

> it is as legal persons, the abstract bearers of rights and duties under the law, that we treat concrete people equally. Thus the real human person becomes an abstraction – a point at which is located a bundle of rights and duties. Other concrete facts about them are irrelevant to the law . . . You do not help a person but give them their rights.[80]

This is the West's considered answer: give these unfortunates human rights and second-hand clothes and they will, in time, attain full humanity.

Finally, we have the evil inhuman, the irrational, cruel, brutal, disgusting Other. This is the other of the unconscious. As Slavoj Zizek puts it, 'there is a kind of passive exposure to an overwhelming Otherness, which is the very basis of being human . . . [the inhuman] is marked by a terrifying excess which, although it negates what we understand as "humanity" is inherent to being human'.[81] We have called this abysmal other that lurks in the psyche and unsettles the ego various names: God or Satan, barbarian or foreigner, in psychoanalysis death drive or the Real. Individually and socially we are hostages to this irreducible untameable otherness. Becoming human is possible only against this impenetrable inhuman background. Split into two, according to a simple moral calculus, this Other has both a tormenting and a tormented part, both radical evil and radical passivity. He represents our narcissistic self in its infancy (civilisation as potentia, possibility or risk), civilisation in its cradle; but also what is most frightening and horrific in us, the death drive, the evil persona that lurks in our midst. We present the Other as radically different, precisely because he is what we both love and hate about ourselves, the childhood and the beast of humanity. The racial connotations of this hierarchy are not far from the surface. As Makau Mutua has argued, 'Savages and victims are generally non-white and non-Western, while the saviours are white. This old truism has found new life in the metaphor of human rights'.[82]

80 Zenon Bankowski, *Living Lawfully: Love in Law and Law in Love* (London: Kluwer Academic, 2001), 56, 57.

81 Slavoj Zizek, 'Against Human Rights', *New Left Review*, 34, July–August 2005.

82 Makau Mutua, 'Savages, Victims Saviours', 42/1 *Harvard International Law Journal* 201 (2001), 207.

A similar residue, a 'nonlinked thing'[83] beyond control and constitutive faultline haunts community and its law. It is analogous to an 'unconscious affect', encountered in the 'sharp and vague feeling that the civilians are not civilised and that something is ill-disposed towards civility' that 'betrays the recurrence of the shameful sickness within what passes for health and betrays the "presence" of the unmanageable'.[84] The original separation from other people and societies, the break that lies at the foundation of the modern nation-state cannot be fully represented or managed but keeps coming back as social sickness and personal malady. The unnameable other returns in xenophobia and racism, in hatred and discrimination and remains intractable to politics. Politics becomes a 'politics of forgetting', a forgetting of past injustices and current symptoms, a considered strategy that tries to ban what questions the legitimacy of institutions by turning the threatening imponderable powers into memory and myth or into celebration of fictitious unity.

Psychoanalysis reminds us that lack and desire leads to symptoms, often violent and repetitive, the cause of which is forgotten because it never entered consciousness. One could claim that the perennial and perennially failing quest for justice is the result of these symptoms, a trace that signifies a past trauma or a future union, always deferred and different. Justice is the name of social desire for unity and wholeness and the series of symptoms created by the lack of this foundational and unattainable condition. Injustice, on the other hand, is the way through which people construct this sense of lack, incompleteness or disorder, the name given to the symptoms of social exclusion, domination or oppression.[85] This approach could help us understand the psychic and social investment in human rights campaigns. The absolute and inhuman otherness that lurks in us leads to repression, cruelty and returns in symptoms. We call evil the effects of what we are unable to control in our psychic or social selves, the uncanny fears and symptoms the inhuman part of humanity causes. Absolute evil begins with the attempt to tame this untameable, to dismiss the inhuman in the human in order to master humanity completely.[86] We try to silence the terror of the inhuman thing within us by turning it into a question of morality, into evil and obscenity and displacing it into the savage and suffering others. The victims we try to rescue are stand-ins for our own

---

83 Jean-François Lyotard, 'A l'Insy (Unbeknownst), in Miami Theory Collective, ed. *Community at Loose Ends* (Minneapolis, MN, University of Minnesota Press, 1991), 42–8 at 46.

84 Ibid. at 44, 43.

85 Costas Douzinas and Adam Gearey, *Critical Jurisprudence. The Political Philosophy of Justice* (Oxford, Hart, 2005).

86 Jean-François Lyotard, 'The Other's Rights' in Stephen Shute and Susan Hurley, eds, *On Human Rights* (New York, Basic Books, 1993).

malady. We hope to become whole, to integrate our conscious, rational self and domesticate our unconscious, traumatic, affective part by projecting it into those others upon whom we export our pathetic and atrocious traits. To become fully human, to become whole, our inhuman part is wholly projected onto the other. The internal divide becomes a symmetrical external separation as humanity is neatly split into two: barbarian and kinsman, victim and rescuer, the (evil) inhuman and the (moral) human. The legal category of crimes against humanity expresses well this split. It is humanity that commits atrocities against itself, it is humanity that acts inhumanely, in denial of its dependency on the inhuman other that lurks within us. As Jean-François Lyotard put it, the Holocaust was the completion of the dream to exterminate those people (the Jews, the gypsies) who in their otherness bear witness to the absolute other. The rights of the other are about speaking new, the immemorial power of the other and our inability to announce it.[87]

The stakes of humanitarian campaigns are high. Positing the victim and/or savage other of humanitarianism we create humanity. The perpetrator/victim is a reminder and revenant from our disavowed past. He is the West's imaginary double, someone who carries our own characteristics and fears albeit in a reversed impoverished sense. If the moral universe revolves around the recognition of evil, every project to combine people in the name of the good is itself condemned as evil. Willing and pursuing the good inevitably turns into the nightmare of totalitarianism. This is the reason why the price of human rights politics is conservatism. The moralist conception both makes impossible and bars positive political visions and possibilities. Human rights ethics legitimise what the West already possesses; evil is what we do not possess or enjoy. But as Alain Badiou puts it, while the human is partly inhuman, she is also more than human. There is a superhuman or immortal dimension in the human. We become human to the extent that we attest to a nature that, while fully mortal, is not expendable and does not conform to the rules of the game. The status of victim, on the other hand, 'of suffering beast, of emaciated dying individual, reduces man to his animal substructure, to his pure and simple identity as dying . . . neither mortality nor cruelty can define the singularity of the human within the world of the living'.[88]

We should reverse our ethical approach: it is not suffering and evil that define the good as the defence humanity puts up against its bad part. It is our positive ability to do good, our welcoming of the potential to act and change the world

87 Jean-François Lyotard, *Heidegger and the 'Jews'* (A. Michel and M. Roberts, trans.) (Minneapolis, University of Minnesota Press, 1990), *passim.*
88 Alain Badiou, quoted in Peter Halward, *Badiou: A Subject to Truth* (Minneapolis, MN, University of Minnesota Press, 2003), 257.

that comes first and must denounce evil as the toleration or promotion of the existent, not the other way around. In this sense, human rights are not what protects from suffering and inhumanity. Radical humanitarianism aims to confront the existent with a transcendence found in history, to make the human, constantly told that suffering is humanity's inescapable destiny, more than human. We must discover or invent a transcendence in immanence. We may need to sidestep rights in favour of right.

Chapter 4

The politics of human rights

Rights and metaphysics

Natural and human rights were the outcome of a long historical process, which led to the destruction of premodern communities of virtue and religious ethics and amounted, according to Alasdair McIntyre, to a moral catastrophe.[1] Premodern man had a stable and secure place in the social order with specific duties and a determined social identity. In the classical world, domination was based on a strict social hierarchy that carried a gradation of dignity and honour and allowed some to participate in public affairs, while others, women, children, slaves, were ruled by those above them on the social ladder. Christianity added a new type of self-subjection, willing obedience to an inner voice. In the interstices of the confessional and the assizes, the body was attached to the soul and an economy of salvation emerged. The Christian self is called to account by a transcendent law that speaks to him directly. The big Other oscillates, in modernity, between visible and invisible powers or between the physical and metaphysical. The new mechanism of subjection takes the form of the

> inner voice . . . that of a transcendent authority which everyone is bound to obey, which always already compels everyone to obey, including the rebels (they certainly do not escape the voice of the Law, even if they do not surrender to it) – because the foundation of authority is not located outside the individual, in some natural inequality or dependency, but within him, in his very being as creature of the verb, and as faithful to it.[2]

1 Alasdair McIntyre, *After Virtue* (London, Duckworth, 1981), 2–5.
2 Etienne Balibar, 'Subjection and Subjectivation' in Joan Copjec, ed., *Supposing the Subject* (London, Verso, 1994), 10.

Whether it comes from god or sovereign, lord or the subject's own conscience, the voice that calls from outside or incessantly murmurs within in sleepless nights always takes the same form, that of law.

Modernity keeps the earlier forms of domination and subjection but develops them in a new direction. The secularisation of the universalist claims of Christianity led to the birth of the free individual. Freedom and the accompanying rights became the guiding principle of the new age. Restraints on action must be willingly accepted by the emancipated subject. Modern man can no longer be subjected to a law exclusively set by a 'natural' hierarchy or God. He is free to the extent that he makes his own law and he is responsible for the law he has made. Gathering and adding to the premodern forms of subjection, modern autonomous man obeys a law (*nomos*) he gives to himself (*autos*). In Kantian morality, the categorical imperative combines man's reason and freedom in an act of self-legislation. State law, on the other hand, is legislated in his name by his political superiors, now called his representatives. The three forms of subjection to God, rulers and inner self become condensed in the modern *nomophilia* (love of the law): I become free – a subject – by being subjected to a law legislated (by me or) in my name. This is modernity's law.

Orthodox Christianity led the way into modernity by becoming the institution of mediation between the transcendent and the secular. The Church preaches that all humans possess an inalienable soul which makes them part of Christ's plan of salvation. Only those who believe in Christ's incarnation and sacrifice, however, will be fully admitted to the Kingdom of Heaven. Non-Christians have few, if any, privileges in the providential plan. Their exclusion creates the missionary duty of the Church militant to reach out and proselytise them. Their ignorant and sinful sectarianism must be abandoned for the universal truth of Christ. The mission of the Church is to guide every person in the world away from false gods and customs and help them develop the universal human potential that lies in every soul. The Church pronounced its ecumenical mission precisely because a radical gap separates reality from the ideal. Christ's message does not describe or define the world; it aims to change it. In the hands of St Paul, Christ's command to abandon parents and families and follow him becomes an axiom, a prescription and battle cry.[3] Let us turn all people into Christians, let us make the singular event of Christ universal, let us impose the message of truth and love upon everyone in the world. As Alain Badiou puts it, Paul shows 'how a universal thought,

---

3 Alain Badiou, *Saint Paul: The Foundation of Universalism* (Ray Brassier, trans.) (Stanford, CA, Stanford University Press, 2003).

proceeding on the basis of the worldly proliferation of alterities (the Jew, the Greek, women, men, slaves, free men and so on) produces a Sameness and Equality (there is no longer either Jew, or Greek, and so on). The production of equality and the casting off, in thought, of differences are the material signs of the universal'.[4]

The religious divide between human and divine survives in disenchanted modernity, displaced onto the equally non-negotiable split between the universal and the particular. The metaphysical principle of modernity is situated in an irreconcilable separation between the secular version of the ideal and the real. The discourse of natural rights presents the clearest expression of this split in which the pole of the universal inherits the structural characteristics of divinity, while the particular carries elements of fallen humanity. Let us follow briefly this logic in the Declarations of Rights that followed the great revolutions of the eighteenth century and pronounced the universal and eternal entitlements of man. These rights are absolute and inalienable, independent of governments, social or political systems, they belong to the whole humanity. Article 1 of the French Declaration of the Rights of Man and Citizen states 'men are born and remain free and equal in their rights'. Yet, the Declaration is quite categorical about the real source of universal rights. According to Article 2, 'the final end of every political institution is the preservation of the natural and imprescriptible rights of man' and Article 3 proceeds to define this association: 'The source of all sovereignty lies essentially in the Nation. No corporation or individual may exercise any authority not expressly derived therefrom.' We can call the idea of equal freedom in Article 1 modernity's metaphysical principle, while that of national sovereignty of Article 3, its reality principle.

The act of declaring gives the impression that rights pre-date the declaration, legislated by God, nature or some other transcendent source. And yet, the declaration rather than announcing pre-existing entitlements brings them into existence. Furthermore, it is the declaration of these natural rights against their perversion by the *ancien régime* that gives the constitutional assembly the power to introduce these far-reaching new arrangements. The declaration initiates what it claims only to describe. But the creative power of these declarations did not stop there. They brought into life a new of type of political association, the nation-state and, a new type of 'man', the national citizen, who becomes the beneficiary of these rights. The modern subject is split into two, the universal man and the national citizen, soul and body, member of ecumenical humanism and citizen.

---

4 Ibid. 109.

Natural rights designated what is right and due to each according to his nature. But nature, too, is divided into a universal component, belonging in theory to all members of the species human and a local one, given only to the citizens of the state. Rights are declared on behalf of the universal 'man', humanity is the notional beneficiary of these statements of principle. But their real recipients were the members of the newly emerging nation-states. This is one of many expressions of the radical split inaugurated in modernity which, repeated throughout our legal and political life, determines modern subjectivity. The subject of natural rights appears as someone who is born in freedom and equality and enjoys a list of abstract entitlements. He is a person without history or tradition, gender, colour or religion, needs and desires. This is what made Hegel call the legal person an 'empty vessel'. For Marx, the person who enjoyed these 'rights' was an 'egotistic man, man separated from other men and community'.[5] Finally, the conservative Joseph de Maistre ironically proclaimed that 'I have met Italians, Russians, Spaniards, Englishmen, Frenchmen, but I do not know man in general'.[6] Modernity stripped man of all his characteristics and turned him into an autonomous person, a non-social moral being. Moral obligations have been vacated, relations with others are based either on self-interest or legal obligation. Emancipated from history, religion, culture and ethics, the varied sources of normativity of the previous era, modern man encounters real law in one source only, the law of the state. 'Modern society aimed at the creation of a social space in which there was to be *no moral proximity* . . . Between the self and the other, there was to be distance bridged only by legal rules . . . obeyed in as far as they appealed to self interest.'[7]

Natural rights fit this picture perfectly. They are the legal entitlements of the isolated individual, whose social relations and moral rights and obligations are so many routes to the achievement of the unencumbered self. When man replaces nature or God as the metaphysical ground of modernity, he is split into an abstract subject, whose ghostly features are outlined in the declarations of rights, and into the empirical real individual. Rights both acknowledge and conceal the distance between justice and law or between the ideal world of equality and the empirical world of domination, oppression and inequality. The metaphysical provenance of this anthropology means that there can be no reconciliation between the two parts, even though in Wendy Brown's

---

5 Karl Marx, 'On the Jewish Question' in *Early Texts* (D. McLellan, trans.) (Oxford, Blackwell, 1971), 102.
6 Quoted in Claude Lefort, *The Political Forms of Modern Society* (Cambridge, Polity, 1986), 257.
7 Zygmunt Bauman, *Postmodern Ethics* (Oxford, Blackwell, 1993), 83.

felicitous phrase liberalism achieved a 'détente between universal and particular'.[8] It is brutal to define humanity by blood and soil, to make it a universal celebration of parochial traditions and authoritarian communities. But it is equally atrocious and unrealistic to deprive the human of his links with his historical and cultural roots. In modernity, we need both the freedom of the unencumbered self to resist communal bonds and impositions and the recognition given by community and tradition necessary for the development of a real, rich self. We must negotiate a route through the universal and the particular, but the religious inheritance places the two in constant combat.

The philosophical presuppositions and anthropological visions animating the secular tradition of natural/human rights indicate their strong links with Christianity. If all humans are created free and share certain rights, humanity has a common core. This is the language of Christianity glossed over by Enlightenment philosophy. Reason, soul and freedom, the common human attributes, must be combined in harmony to create the institutional and personal supports of modern man. Moral constraints must be freely accepted by the subject acting in accordance to the dictates of reason, in the same way that the Christian followed freely the whispering voice of conscience. This almost impossible enterprise was carried out in Kant's moral and legal philosophy that turns religious transcendence into the transcendental preconditions of reason. Kant's categorical imperative brings together reason and free will in an act of self-legislation. Rights recognise man as an autonomous moral person, a free dignified agent worthy of respect. On the high plane of Kantian morality, people act towards others disinterestedly in the way they would like others to act towards them and conflicts of interest are downplayed. Civil and political rights give institutional expression to morality and freedom, citizenship and its rights are the local instantiations of the universal attributes of humanity. But metaphysics cannot legislate for the world. It is the national assembly that does so. The Kantian tradition, keeping its idealist core claims that general state law, irrespective of who legislates it, must be obeyed, as if it was made by the citizens themselves. This is the hypothetical process that Rawls revived with his idea of an original position from which people negotiate and legislate the principles of justice. The law is given by higher authority but is willed by us, isn't this the secular version of Christianity? It is not so much that rights traditions divide into universalist and relative or communitarian versions, as much of contemporary human rights theory claims. On the contrary, the

---

8 Wendy Brown, *States of Injury* (Princeton, NJ, Princeton University Press, 1995), 57.

modern declarations of rights incorporated the Christian *civitas dei* into society, incarnated the spirit into the letter of the law and inaugurated their historical separation. The message of the great declarations could be read as the axiom of a secular gospel: let us make everyone, despite their differences and disparities, equal. Such would be their revolutionary interpretation.

In the same way that the catholic message of Christianity was turned into modern imperialism (let us impose the authority of the Church upon non-believers) and postmodern multiculturalism (let us accept all differences as equally valid), secularised grace has been turned into the global saviour of human rights and religious transcendence into the universalism of international law. As a result, a degree of sacredness has been bestowed on the universal pole of human rights, religion's heir, making what is presented as particular somewhat suspect. Admittedly, the universal can only exist against the particular, the real is the indispensable foil for the ideal. The gap between man and citizen or between ideal and real has been posited in terms that prevent its closure. Sociologically, the premodern conditions, which had allowed an alliance or antagonistic cohabitation between ideal and real, have departed for good. Philosophically, it was the opposition exemplified in St Paul's message that brought the two terms into existence and made them parasitic into each other. The ideal, the universal, appears as a stain in the world of reality, what is always lacking from its empirical instantiations, which, however, crave and tend towards it. The partial conclusion of the war between law and fact would have to await the end of modernity.

The democratic and socialist traditions, on the other hand, move the ground of legal authority from the obscure tergiversations of reason to the collective expression of political will. Rights and legislation are no longer the outcome of rational operations but the concrete result of deliberations and decisions by the citizens, their beneficiaries. The law-making power belongs to the people. Birth into humanity creates certain strong entitlements under the principle of autonomy, but it is the privilege of citizenship and its expression in popular sovereignty that makes them real. Again, however, a gap between the universal attribute of humanity and its local instantiation appears. Rights were denied to those who do not possess or enjoy the universal attributes of reason. Women, slaves, foreigners and colonials are not fully rational; they cannot act rationally and become morally autonomous, nor are they included in the body exercising popular sovereignty. In the same way that the ecumenical mission approached the heathen, its secular successors accept that some people suffer from moral depravity or defective reason. It is the obligation of the beneficiaries of reason, modernity and morality, to take it to them. People may not be forced to be free, but at least they should be forced to be modern.

One could conclude, that while human rights institutionally define the present they are never given fully to presence. As legal rights or constitutional entitlements, they construct the human subject. But as expressions of the ideal, they either recall a long gone Edenic past or they promise a future cosmopolitanism, in which the gap between ideal and real will be closed. Human rights are condemned to nostalgia or to prophesy. In a world in which justice (the ideal, the universal) and law are radically de-linked, the claims of human rights remain radically incomplete. Our lived lie, the hope for those without hope, human rights have become the metaphysical principle in an aggressively secular society. As a description of the existent, they become the modern legitimacy of power. As an axiom of action they retain a certain revolutionary energy. This is their great weakness and their greatest strength.

Rights and exclusion

If we move from the metaphysical ground of modernity towards its political instantiations, the split between the ideal and the real, between man and citizen or universal and particular becomes a threshold or zone in which claims to universality are founded on a number of exclusions. The first and constitutive exclusion of modern politics is apparent when we move from the abstract 'man' of the declarations to the real beneficiaries of rights. As first Jeremy Bentham sarcastically observed, nothing is further from the truth than the claim of Article 1 of the French (and now Universal Declaration of Rights) according to which we are all born free and equal. People are born dependent for survival on their parents and carers and equality is a concept unknown to the infant. Bentham, by deliberately confusing the constative aspect of the statement (it is a fact that people are born free and equal) with its normative/ performative and axiomatic mode (this is what ought to happen), indicated that these statements of principle are naive at best and hypocritical at worst. Indeed, if we look at the composition of the real beneficiaries of rights, they have some distinct but not surprising characteristics. As Chapters 2 and 3 argued, the privileged subject of rights of man has been a white, well-off, heterosexual male, who condenses in his person the abstract dignity of humanity and the real prerogatives of belonging to the community of the powerful.

Those in the pole of the ruled, on the other hand, while part of 'universal humanity', have been consistently deprived of many of its notional entitlements. Their subjection takes two main forms. First, domination: this is either the denial of self-determination to large numbers of people who are deprived of basic civil and political liberties or the denial of the resources necessary for exercising these rights in a meaningful way. Second, oppression: the denial of equality through economic, social or cultural dependence and exploitation. Women, minorities, blacks, colonials, migrants, aliens to name just a few have had for the greatest part of the last 200 years limited if any rights. But the denial of basic political rights or the deprivation of the economic, social and cultural resources necessary for self-determination has always been glossed over in the name of freedom and equality.

Civil rights have been denied to people (women, blacks, ethnic and other minorities) because they have not been raised to the dignity of full humanity. Minorities have been routinely portrayed as uneducated, uncivilised or simply unworthy of the privileges of the fully human. Economic rights have been denied because interventions in the economy to provide a minimum redistribution in favour of the poor would lead to a violation of freedom – admittedly only for the rich. The exclusion from basic rights of non-proper people, that is of people with no property, the right colour, race, religion or ideology has been the main characteristic of modernity. Conversely, the ongoing struggle to add gender, race, colour and sexuality to the abstract cipher of the legal subject has been the most honourable use of human rights. Many political struggles have mobilised the language of rights, which has now become a main form of political protest and action. However, adding a new right or right-bearer to the existing group does not eliminate exclusion; it only alters its shape and scope.

A second type of exclusion pits the universal against the particular. In early modernity, the prime expression of particularity was the nation-state, the national a perfect foil for the universality of humanity. The early declarations of rights established the power of a particular political association, the nation-state, to become the sovereign, of the constitutional assembly to assume the role of the law-maker and of a particular 'man', the national citizen, to become the beneficiary of rights. As Keith Baker puts it, the deputies

> entrusted with legislative power, will seize constituent power on behalf of the nation even in the absence of any explicit charge to do so, in this revolutionary usurpation of power, the gap in legitimacy will be filled by 'presenting the people with the tables of the essential rights, under the title of *Declaration of Rights*'.[9]

Let us consider national sovereignty, first. The declarations set out the universality of rights but their immediate effect was to establish the boundless power of the national state and its law. In a paradoxical fashion, these

9 Keith Baker, 'The Idea of a Declaration of Rights' in Dale van Kley, ed., *The French Idea of Freedom* (Stanford, CA, Stanford University Press, 1992), 169.

declarations of universal principle founded local sovereignty. If the declarations ushered in the epoch of the individual, they also launched the age of the nation – the mirror-image of the individual. Human rights and national sovereignty – the two antithetical principles of international law – were born together, their contradiction more apparent than real.

The legislator of the proclaimed universal community was none other than the historical legislator of the French or American nation. One could argue that the French National Assembly notionally split itself into two parts: a philosophical and a historical. The first legislated on behalf of 'man' for the whole world, the second for the only territory and people it could, France and its dependencies. The gap between the two is also the distance between the universality of the law (eventually of human rights) and the generality of state legislation. From that point onwards, it remains unknown, as Lyotard put it,

> whether the law thereby declared is French or human, whether the war conducted in the name of rights is one of conquest or one of liberation, . . . whether those nations which are not French ought to become French or become human by endowing themselves with Constitutions that conform to the Declaration.[10]

Statehood, sovereignty and territory are bound to a national principle. If the declarations inaugurated modernity, they also started nationalism and its consequences: genocide, ethnic and civil wars, ethnic cleansing, minorities, refugees, the stateless. This national principle of universality has become absolute in the new world order, at a point when we are told that the nation-state is on the retreat: every nation should have its own state and every state should have one (dominant) nation. Kosovo, Chechnya, Scotland, Kyrgistan, the Basque country, Quebec, Corsica should all become independent states in order to confirm the paradoxical principle that the national is the only persistent universal.

If we return to the subjective side of early modernity, citizenship introduced a new type of privilege that was protected for some by excluding others. Nation-states are defined by territorial boundaries that have shifted exclusion from class to nation, the modern formal line of belonging. The modern subject reaches his humanity by acquiring political rights of citizenship. Citizenship confers privilege and is given selectively, according to criteria of blood and birth. Aliens are not citizens. They do not have rights because they are not

---

10 Jean-François Lyotard, *The Differend* (Georges Van Den Abbeele, trans.) (Manchester, Manchester University Press, 1998), 147.

part of the state and they are lesser human beings because they are not citizens. One is a human to greater or lesser degree because one is a citizen to a greater or lesser degree. The alien is the gap between human and citizen. We become human through citizenship, and subjectivity is based on the gap, the difference between universal man and state citizen. Modern subjectivity is based on those others whose existence is evidence of the universality of human nature but whose exclusion is absolutely crucial for concrete personhood, in other words, for citizenship. Citizenship 'shifts exclusion from an open class barrier to a national, or hidden class, barrier'.[11]

Hannah Arendt wrote that stateless persons and refugees have no rights because no one wants to oppress them. There are people who have been abandoned in a limbo state beyond oppression and whose rightlessness and desolation is greater than that of the slaves in classical Greece towards whom their masters had important specific duties. For Arendt, citizen rights are the only rights worthy of the name, while the rights of man either do not exist or are a misnomer for some other type of rights. Arendt was right to state that 'a man who is nothing but a man has lost the very qualities which make it possible for other people to treat him as a man'.[12] If human rights are entitlements given to people on account of their humanity and not their membership of some narrower group such as nations, class or party, then those people who have no law or group to protect them, the refugees, the stateless, the prisoners in Guantánamo Bay, should have at least the protection offered to humans qua human. And yet, these are the people who have no or very few rights. In this sense, one could claim that human rights as described by liberal philosophy do not exist, because birth and basic humanity does not come with any attached rights. Politics creates rights and only civil rights created politically and enforced legally by domestic legal systems give protection to political actors, in other words citizens.

This second type of brutal and total exclusion involves an important symbolic moment. The rejection and persecution of foreigners downplays national divisions and conflicts and promotes the imaginary vision of a happy and unified community. The symbolic identification with nationalist ideologies and the resultant exclusion of those who do not belong creates a fantasy of common interests, which transcends the divide between rulers and ruled. These identifications foster a sense of belonging and common destiny, by creating a clear divide between 'us' (the English, the Germans, the West) and 'the rest'. Nationalism, (anti-)communism, today human rights have all played this

---

11   Immanuel Wallerstein, *Utopistics* (New York, The New Press, 1998), 21.
12   Hannah Arendt, *The Origins of Totalitarianism* (San Diego, CA, Harvest Books, 1979), 300.

cementing role. Outsiders are banned from the communion of the select and are seen as inferior and *ad extremis* subhuman. This hidden class barrier continues the religious legacy of the 'elected people' with its missionary zeal and secularises spiritual universality. The colonial French, the imperial English, the Americans today stand for the universal. Imperialism, colonialism, foreign conquest and occupation are all part of the mission to export and instil universal values as understood by the chosen nation on the heathen. Hegel famously said that Napoleon leading his armies in the battle of Jena represented the spirit on horseback. Today, the spirit rides on high altitude bombers and promotes American consumer brands rather than enlightenment reason. But the logic remains the same.

We can conclude that power arranges the 'sovereign people' into rulers, ruled and excluded. The rulers are the beneficiaries of the power structure and enjoy the full gamut of rights. The ruled are given the dignity and respect that civil and political rights bestow but they do not enjoy real, material equality beyond the formal equality of law. The ruled are the seduced majority of the postmodern world. Rights are inducements or rewards offered to them for their acceptance of the balance of power. The excluded are the outsiders. Exemplified by the 'bogus refugee' and the inmate of the concentration camp, they represent absolute otherness. They join the 'one use humans':[13] people, groups and populations considered surplus to the needs of capitalism and left to their 'natural' or 'man-made' fate from earthquakes and tsunamis, Aids and famines or, ethnic cleansing and small-scale genocides. They resemble the inhuman or non-human, they deserve no dignity and receive no respect. But while they have no possible contact with the insiders, being totally alien, their presence disturbs them. Like the psychoanalytical real, discussed in Chapters 2 and 3, the excluded are an uncanny presence, they cause a disturbance to self and community.

Rights are both the expression and the terrain on which the distribution of people into positions of domination and subjugation operates. Conversely, we can examine power's mode of operation, by witnessing what people are given or deprived which rights at a particular place or point in time. In this sense, again, human rights have only paradoxes to offer. Rights both express the split between ideal and real or abstract man and concrete citizen and attempt to heal it. The various struggles for social, economic, people's, women's and gay rights have added some flesh, blood and sex to the pale outline of the 'human'. Human rights have been equally crucial in the recent attacks on national sovereignty

---

13 Bernard Ogilvie, quoted by Etienne Balibar, 'Trois Concepts de la Politique: Emancipation, Transformation, Civilité', in *Truth and Politics* (Athens, Nissos, 2005), 43.

and in the move towards a cosmopolitan order. Rights are not opposed to the exercise of power; they are one way through which the effects of power are distributed across the social body. As Giorgio Agamben put it,

> the spaces, the liberties and the rights won by individuals in their conflicts with certain powers always simultaneously prepared a tacit but increasing inscription of individuals' lives within the state order, thus offering a new and more dreadful foundation for the very sovereign power from which they wanted to liberate themselves.[14]

Rights as politics

In the new world order, the form and scope of power, domination and exclusion is changing. Human rights have become both the object of political struggles ('we demand the right to this or that' is a typical battle-cry of social movements and one issue campaigns) and a mode of political action (democracy is seen as the exercise of a multiplicity of rights, such as free speech, association, assembly, information, etc.). But what is the nature of politics conducted through and for human rights?

To understand the parallel processes through which natural/human rights became a tool and target of politics we must return to Marx. Marx gave an exemplary and unsurpassed presentation of the paradoxical nature of natural rights. In feudal society, political power, economic wealth and social status coincided in the same person. Feudal lords composed the dominant political and economic class. But the political predominance of the rising bourgeoisie could be ensured precisely through the apparent loss of direct political power. The main innovation of natural rights was to remove politics from society and bring to an end the automatic identification of the economically dominant class with political leadership. Politics became confined into the separate domain of the state. Property and religion, on the other hand, the main safeguards of class dominance, were turned into social institutions belonging to the private sphere and protected from state intervention through the operation of legal rights. This 'demotion' to the private realm made property more secure and effective, and guaranteed its continued dominance better than the medieval fusion of political and economic power. In this dialectical formulation, the main aim of natural rights was to remove politics from society and depoliticise the economy. After the separation, the state is presented as (politically) dominant, while real (economic) power lies in capitalist society. The bourgeois abandonment of the direct political power of feudal lords and kings was the

---

14   Giorgio Agamben, *Homo Sacer* (Stanford, CA, Stanford University Press, 1998), 121.

precondition for the ascendancy of bourgeois society and the triumph of its capitalist principles.

In this bourgeois hall of mirrors, natural rights support selfishness and private profit. Politics and the state, on the other hand, replace religion and the church and become a terrestrial quasi-heaven in which social divisions are temporarily forgotten as the citizens participate in limited formal democracy. The liberal subject lives a double life: a daily life of strife in pursuit of personal economic interest and a second which, like a metaphorical Sabbath, is devoted to political activity and the 'common good'. In reality, a clear hierarchy subordinates the political rights of the ethereal citizen to the concrete interests of the capitalist, which have taken the form of natural rights. Equality and liberty act as ideo-logical fictions emanating from the state and sustaining a society of inequality, oppression and exploitation. Marx was the first to realise this paradox. While natural rights emerged as a symbol of universal emancipation, they were at the same time a powerful weapon in the hands of the rising capitalist class. Rights were seen, from the beginning, as a potential means of protection from arbitrary power. But at the same time, they were the institutions securing and naturalising dominant economic and social relations. Rights were used to take out of political challenge and social struggles the central institutions of capital-ism, such as property, contractual relations, the family, religion. Ideologies, private interests and egotistical concerns appear natural, normal, in the public good when glossed over by the rights vocabulary.

Today, human rights have expanded and touch almost every part of daily existence and politics. While classical natural rights protected prop-erty and religion by making them 'apolitical', the main contemporary effect of human rights is to depoliticise politics itself. To understand this effect of human rights, let us introduce a key distinction in recent political philos-ophy between 'politics' (*la politique*) and 'the political' (*le politique*). This distinction was initially drawn by the French Heideggerians Philippe Lacoue-Labarthe and Jean-Luc Nancy.[15] It builds on insights of the Frankfurt School about the managerial and anti-ideological turn of parliamentary politics in the West. It has been used, recently, in different contexts by a number of post-structuralist and post-Marxist theorists such as Claude Lefort, Alain Badiou, Ernesto Laclau, Slavoj Zizek, Antonio Negri and Etienne Balibar. According to Chantal Mouffe, 'politics' refers to the manifold practices of conventional politics. It is the terrain of routine political life, the activity of debating, lobbying and horse-trading that takes places around Westminster and Whitehall. The

15   Philippe Lacoue-Labarthe and Jean-Luc Nancy, *Retreating the Political* (Simon Sparks, ed.) (London, Routledge, 1997).

'political', on the other hand, refers to the way in which the social bond is instituted and concerns the deep rifts in society. Politics organises the practices and institutions through which order is created, normalising social co-existence in the context of conflict provided by the political.[16]

The definition of the political as the dimension of antagonism constitutive of society follows Carl Schmitt's definition of politics as the relationship between friend and enemy. Following Schmitt, William Rasch sees the political, 'as the ineliminable antagonism serv[ing] as the condition of possibility for the limited and channelled struggles of both domestic and international politics'.[17] Alain Badiou argues, similarly, that two possibilities of action exist in each political situation: ordinary politics is the realm where established interests, accepted differences and approved knowledges give formal recognition to consolidated identities and sanction existing distributions and hierarchies. But every situation includes the possibility of radical break.[18] Badiou calls such breaks or singular innovations, events. An event persists in history and changes its route through the militant proclamation and fidelity to its 'truth' by rare individuals who, through their commitment, become its subjects. Indeed, truth is precisely the loyal commitment by people to the possibility of radical break of the event. St Paul created the 'event of Jesus' by confirming his truth through his action, Lenin the event of Marx.[19] The sites where these truths might emerge are close to the most anonymous and vulnerable of the people, places considered as empty or void by the dominant forces.

The French philosopher Jacques Rancière, drawing a similar distinction, defines normal politics (or 'policing' as he calls it) as a process of argumentation and negotiation among the various parts of the social whole.[20] It aims at (re)distributing benefits, rewards and positions without challenging the overall balance. In this consensual politics, which dominates the West, the ruled, the subordinate classes and groups, accept the position and role assigned to them in the social edifice. Politics becomes preoccupied with questions of

16   Chantal Mouffe, *On the Political* (London, Routledge, 2005), 8–9.
17   Rasch, op. cit., 6.
18   Alain Badiou, *Ethics* (Peter Halward, trans.) (London, Verso, 2001); *Being and Event* (Oliver Feltham, trans.) (New York, Continuum, 2005).
19   Alain Badiou, *Saint Paul: The Foundation of Universalism* (Ray Brassier, trans.) (Stanford, CA, Stanford University Press, 2003).
20   Jacques Rancière, *Disagreement* (Julie Rose, trans.) (Minneapolis, MN, University of Minnesota Press, 1998); *On the Shores of Politics* (Liz Heron, trans.) (London, Verso, 1995); 'Who is the Subject of the Rights of Man?' in Ian Balfour and Eduardo Cadava, *And Justice for All?*, 103: 2/3 *South Atlantic Quarterly* (2004), 297.

distribution and rational agreement, its dominant approaches, the economic and deliberative. In the former, politics is presented as an economic operation, the field where negotiation and compromises between competing forces are worked out, accounted and aggregated. Individuals and groups act as rationally driven pursuers of interest and politics turns into an activity resembling the marketplace. In the deliberative model, instrumental rationality is replaced by argumentative and communicative ethics and politics becomes the field where rational consensus about public goods can be reached. Political arguments and debate follow the procedures and protocols of deliberative action. They become an approximation of the Habermasian 'ideal speech situation' and facilitate rational agreements and consensus-building.

In both approaches, groups accept their position in the social hierarchy. Each part of the social body, every group, class or person is attached to their given identity. Power's predominant form is that of *auctoritas* or legitimate authority. Parties, governments and leaders represent and express legitimate sectional interests but, at the same time, they accept the overriding character of the common good and use economic or deliberative methods in order to promote both particular interests and common concerns. Rights play a key role here: they recognise, finesse and adjudicate the claims of groups and people and adjust them to changes in social life. In this vision, law aims to become identical with the natural life of society, to map the social landscape by replicating accurately within itself the 'facts' of social life and helping reproduce the existing order.

Economic and deliberative approaches to politics underplay conflict and antagonism, the central reality of the political. They discount or neglect *potestas* or domination, the second form of power. This type of power is exercised by some over others and takes a variety of forms such as domination, oppression or exclusion. As Carl Schmitt famously put it in the *Concept of the Political*, 'every religious, moral, economic, ethical, or other anthithesis transforms into a political one if it is sufficiently strong to group human beings effectively according to friend and enemy'.[21] If conflict and strife are an inescapable condition of human existence, any attempt to subject politics to moral principles and ethical values or to determine them purely according to instrumental rationality is both descriptively inaccurate and politically naive, if not suspect. In the current post-political suspension of politics, in particular, the attempt to replace conflict by a collaboration of enlightened bureaucrats and liberal multiculturalists has dire effects. As Slavoj Zizek has argued, when the political

---

21 Carl Schmitt, *The Concept of the Political* (G.Schwab trans.) (New Brunswick, NJ, Rutgers University Press, 1976), 37.

is foreclosed from the symbolic realm and departs politics, it returns in the real as radical evil, racism, extreme and destructive fundamentalism.[22] The state becomes reduced to the muscleman for the market internally and a superficially tolerant enforcer of humanitarianism externally.

But conflict does not disappear. The alternative view of politics or the 'political' returns to Marx and unavoidable conflict. Politics proper is a form of disruption of the established social order by a group or class that has no place in it. Antagonism is the result of the tension between the structured social body, where every group has its role, function and place, and what Rancière calls 'the part of no part' or the 'supernumenary' part. Such groups have been radically excluded from the social order; they are invisible, outside the established sense of what exists and is acceptable and their irruption upsets the overall established equilibrium. The excluded may try to claim political recognition by adopting the existing rules of the game and turning their demands into regional expressions of the established order. This is the case with reformist social movements. There is another scene however in which the excluded group or the banned ideology challenges the social hierarchy. This kind of antagonism or 'dissensus', 'is not a conflict of interests, opinions or, values; it is a division put in the "common sense": a dispute about what is given, about the frame within which we see something as given'.[23] Politics proper erupts only when an excluded part demands to be included and must change the rules of inclusion to achieve that. In this process, a new political subject is constituted, in excess to the hierarchised and visible group of groups, places and functions in society.

The creation of the Athenian *demos* is an early example of this process. The people as a body had no fixed place in the social edifice but demanded to be included, to be heard on an equal footing with the rulers. In doing so, the *demos* emerged as a group and was recognised as a partner in political dialogue and the exercise of power. The *demos* was the people who had no qualification for exercising power. Democracy is the 'power of those who have no specific qualification for ruling, except the fact of having no qualification'.[24] Something similar happened when Olympe de Gouges and other women protested, after the French revolution, that if they were political enough to be sent to the scaffold for anti-revolutionary activities, they should also be given political rights. Women were both included in the political process as targets of repression and excluded from the rights of man. By mobilising this contradiction they

22 Slavoj Zizek, *Tarrying with the Negative: Kant, Hegel and the Critique of Ideology* (Durham, NC, Duke University Press, 1993), 209–210.

23 Rancière, *Subject*, op. cit., 304.

24 Ibid. 305.

realised the potential of revolutionary rights. According to Rancière, these women

> acted as subjects that did not have the rights that they had [the rights given to all humans by the Declaration of Rights] and had the rights that they had not [through their public action they enacted the political rights not given to them].[25]

Another example is the proletariat in Marxist theory. The working class has no place within bourgeois political society, it does not exist politically.[26] But in organising and pursuing its own sectional interests, the proletariat acts for the whole society: its emancipation will free the whole of humanity, including its capitalist enemies. Normal politics is exercised when a community is limited to its recognised parts. When politics breaks out, a supplement is added and the uncounted are counted for the first time by changing the rules of counting.

When the radically excluded protest the wrong they suffer, they present themselves as representatives of the whole society, as stand-ins for the universal. We, the nobodies, they proclaim, are everything against those who stand only for their particular interests. Political conflict brings together the structured whole and the excluded representative of the universal into one place and rewrites the rules of inclusion and exclusion. The inclusion of the invisible part overthrows the rules of the game and interrupts the natural order of domination. A new order is precipitated and transforms social visibility. The irruption of the excluded is the political event par excellence: it changes the political scene and then disappears. Before the transformation, political change is a matter of policing and consensus. After the change, politics returns to normality; its terrain has been modified, however, through the inclusion of the new group or subject and the redefinition of the rules of political legitimacy.

Based on this analysis, Rancière offers a radical re-interpretation of the politics of human rights. Human rights do not belong to humans, rights constitute the subject of modernity. But if rights do not belong to definite subjects, citizens or other groups, those without rights can invoke them. The strength of human rights, according to Rancière, is this back and forth movement between the abstract statement of principles in Constitutions and Bills of Rights and their denial in legal and political practice. The dissonance creates the conditions for the excluded to put the statements of principle to the test

---

25 Ibid.
26 Alain Badiou, 'Homage to Jacques Derrida', in Costas Douzinas, ed., *Adieu Derrida* (London, Palgrave Macmillan, 2006), 34–46.

and demand their verification. This process of struggle defines human rights through a double negation. Declarations of rights prescribe formal equality and limited freedom. But these abstract principles stand alongside terrible inequalities. Freedom and equality are not qualities of people; they are political predicates, the meaning and scope of which is the object of political struggles. Abstract principles are put to the test and the social order is asked to confirm or deny interpretations that would extend their scope.

Rancière's theoretical distinction between the depoliticised politics of consent and dissent is extremely useful. But its application to human rights is problematic. He wants to reclaim the radical potential of human rights against the claim that only citizens enjoy them. Yet, this is the dominant situation in advanced Western societies. The legal quest for the creation of new rights or for the extension of existing ones to new groups or individuals has become a prime example of the politics of consensus. Rights stabilise inter-subjective relations by giving minimum recognition to identity; they codify the liberal ideology of limited freedom and formal equality; they express and promote individual desire. The enforcement of rights is entrusted in the individual right-holder who initiates the process by using the available legal remedies to claim redress for the non-recognition of identity.

A rights-claim typically requests the admission of the claimant to the position of the subject of a widely available benefit or position. In this action, contra Rancière, it reinforces rather than challenges the established ways. First, it accepts the established power and distribution orders and aims to admit the new claimant in a peripheral position in them. Second, the legal system is assigned as the gatekeeper and protector of the order and the social and political claim is transformed into a demand for admission to the law. The role of law is to transform social and political tensions into a set of solvable problems regulated by rules and hand them over to rule experts. This is how rights work in their daily routine operation. They are tools for expressing and promoting established political arrangements and socio-economic distributions. In this sense, legal rights belong to the consensual domain of politics. They are entitlements of those who have accepted the established distributions. The rights claimant is the opposite of the revolutionaries of the early Declarations, whose task was to change the overall design of the law. To this extent, his actions abandon the original commitment of rights to resist and oppose oppression and domination. In this process, Rancière's 'excessive' subjects, who stand for the universal from a position of exclusion, have been replaced by social and identity groups seeking basic recognition and limited redistribution.

In the new world order, the excluded have no access to rights and none is possible. They are outside Rancière's regime of visibility and access is foreclosed by political, legal and military means. Economic migrants, refugees, prisoners in the war on terror, torture victims, inhabitants of African camps, these 'one use humans' attest to total and irreversible exclusion. These people cannot be a part within or outside the political space nor can they represent the universal in whose name inclusion can be asserted. They are just no part; they are the indispensable precondition of human rights but at the same time the living, dying rather, proof of their impossibility. The law not only cannot understand the surplus subject, its very operation prevents the emergence of such subjects. On the way to the new world order, human rights as the ideology at the 'end of history' plugs the interval between man and citizen, universal and particular, law and fact, appearance and reality, the spaces that generated exclusions and created the hope of their transcendence. This type of human rights politics leads to the acceptance of the given distribution of power and fuller and more committed participation in it. The space between abstract rights and the struggle for their verification that characterised earlier periods has been reduced, rights have become rewards for accepting the dominant order, but they are empty, of little use for anyone who challenges it. At that point we send them abroad 'along medicines and clothes, to people deprived of medicine, clothes and rights'.[27]

Successful human rights struggles have undoubtedly improved the lives of people by marginal rearrangements of social hierarchies and non-threatening redistributions of the social product. But their effect is to de-politicise conflict, to remove any possibility of radical change, in a way similar to that argued by Marx in the nineteenth century about the role of the rights to property and religious freedom. Human rights operate in a dual manner: they both conceal and affirm the dominant structure but they can also reveal inequality and oppression and help challenge them. This double operation refers us back to the distinction between politics and the political. As Claude Lefort put it:

> the political is revealed not in what we call political activity, but in the double movements whereby the institution of society appears and is obscured. It appears in the sense that the process whereby society is ordered and unified across its divisions becomes visible, it is obscured in the sense that the locus of politics (the locus in which parties compete . . .) becomes defined as particular, while the principle that generates the overall configuration is concealed.[28]

---

27   Rancière, *Subject*, op. cit., 307.
28   Claude Lefort, *Democracy and Political Theory* (David Macey, trans.) (Minneapolis, MN, University of Minnesota Press, 1988), 11.

The Heideggerian echoes of the distinction between the ontological level (the political) and the ontic (routine politics) are striking. Following Jean-Luc Nancy, the most political heir of Heidegger, the political is where Being opens and reveals itself, 'the site where what it means to *be* in common is open to definition'.[29] In this sense, the political is another name for the ontological togetherness of people, the being together in community (to come). Politics, on the other hand, is the 'play of forces and interests engaged in a conflict over the representation and governance of social existence'.[30] Politics both opens a gap and builds a bridge; it is where representations conceal and reveal Being in the dealings, negotiations and justifications of routine daily transactions. This approach allows us to understand the error of Carl Schmitt and his followers. His emphasis on the relationship between friend and enemy is extremely perceptive as regards the international stage. International politics was characterised until recently by a plurality of actors and controlled instances of conflict between sovereign states. But the price for this broadly accurate presentation of monolithic sovereigns facing each other on the world stage is a largely incorrect picture of domestic politics. In order to be one among equals externally, the sovereign is presented as all-powerful internally. However, this underplays and even misunderstands the importance of internal social and political conflict. The overwhelming emphasis placed on the relationship to the external enemy prevents an understanding of domination and permanent struggle within the social body. But if the constitution of the political as an independent realm is linked to the reproduction of domination and exploitation, located primarily at the level of the economy, the priorities should be reversed. The modern sovereign asserts and tries to acquire omnipotence (the power to suspend the law) precisely because the domination it represents and supports is under permanent threat from internal social forces. The constitution of the political is involved with inherent antagonisms, both revealed and concealed in daily politics.

Isn't this precisely the operation of human rights too? Human rights claims and struggles bring to the surface the exclusion, domination and exploitation and the inescapable strife that permeates social and political life. But at the same time, they conceal the deep roots of conflict and domination by framing struggle and resistance in the terms of legal and individual remedies, which, if successful, lead to small individual improvements and a marginal

29 Christopher Fynsk, 'Foreword', in Jean-Luc Nancy, *The Inoperative Community* (Peter Connor, ed.) (Minneapolis, MN, University of Minnesota Press, 1991), x. This discussion has been influenced by conversations on the political with Emilios Christodoulidis.
30 Ibid.

rearrangement of the social edifice. Can human rights become again a politics of *dissensus* in Rancière's sense? Can the politics of human rights open the particular to the claims of the empty universal? Can politics escape the limitations of representation and rights towards a politics of right? This would be, to use a rather problematic neologism, a politics of 'righting Being', of re-articulating the meaning of the world around the elimination of domination and exploitation.[31] The intrinsic link of early natural rights with (religious) transcendence opened the possibility. It is still active in parts of the world not fully incorporated in the biopolitical operations of power. But only just. The metaphysics of the age is that of the deconstruction of essence and meaning, the closing of the divide between ideal and real, the subjection of the universal to the dominant particular. Economic globalisation and semiotic monolingualism are carrying out this task in practice; its intellectual apologists do it in theory. The political and moral duty of the critic is to keep the rift open, to discover and fight for transcendence in immanence.

---

31 Costas Douzinas, *The End of Human Rights* (Oxford, Hart, 2000), 209–16.

Chapter 5

Freedom in a biopolitical setting

From the society of discipline to the society of control

Rights were the noblest institutional innovation of modernity, the 'man' of rights, the best crystallisation of Enlightenment principles. And yet, endless exclusions have accompanied every statement of right. Rights are both protections used by people against a voracious state or intractable powers and, tools in the modern arsenal for creating and disciplining the subject. Premodern exclusion, based on the inequalities of social hierarchy and divine order, was too obvious, repellent and uneconomical to the modern eye. Similarly, the few rights the absolute rulers of early modernity gave to their subjects were seen as part of royal nature. Right was an attribute of sovereignty and restricted the sovereign only as a revocable grant from the king to his subjects.[1] Modern domination is much harder to detect. Freedom and equality are the ostensive foundations of the political system, autonomy and popular sovereignty their institutional applications. At the same time, exclusions, exceptions and separations have been the inescapable companions of freedom and equality. An exploration of this intertwining of freedom and subordination calls for a change of perspective and an abandonment of liberal political philosophy.

According to Michel Foucault, a new type of power and new methods for acquiring knowledge emerged at around the time natural rights entered the world stage. Let us examine briefly its main characteristics, as they relate to law and rights. In a number of specialised institutions, such as factories and workshops, hospitals and schools, barracks and prisons, people were subjected to continuous observation, classification and disciplining aimed at shaping

---

1 Etienne Balibar, 'Citizen Subject', in Eduardo Cadava *et al.*, eds, *Who Comes After the Subject?* (New York, Routledge, 1991), 33; 'Subjection and Subjectivation', in Joan Copjek, ed., *Supposing the Subject* (London, Verso, 1994), 4.

bodies and making them economically productive and socially pliant. In the nineteenth century, subjection operated as 'subjectification': a process of creating individuals in ways that serve the functional needs of economic, military and administrative systems of power. These institutions led to the creation of the human sciences. When the administrative machinery of the great monarchies started measuring the wealth, fertility, death rates and movements of populations for the purpose of its own aggrandisement, it inaugurated the sciences of demography and epidemiology. Statistics, the method that allowed the development of scientific approaches to social policy, acknowledges its debt by calling itself the science of state. The great incarceration of delinquents and criminals in the nineteenth century led to the creation of criminology. In these new 'disciplinary societies', knowledge cannot be gained prior to or independently of the uses to which it will be put as a function of power relations. Knowledge and science are both the cause and effect of power relations and cannot be distinguished from them.

For this theory, power operates through a positive and creative arrangement of forces. Power produces reality; it creates new objects of cognition, intervention and investment, such as sexuality and delinquency. It gives birth to the individual and to the knowledge we have of him. Power, knowledge and the law are not external to each other. Theories of power are usually built around the great subjects, the king, the state, the ruling class, capital. But power is a multiplicity of shifting relations rather than an object of possession. It is exercised from innumerable points, 'furrowed across individuals, cutting them up and remoulding them, marking off irreducible regions in them, in their bodies and minds'.[2] Political and legal philosophy have remained preoccupied with the premodern themes of sovereignty and right, focusing on the mechanisms that make power appear rational and legitimate while neglecting its operation as the 'conduct of others' conduct'.[3] Legal forms, procedures and rules were seen as external to power, as the foundations of systems of rights and constitutions which restrained the state. But their protective action was supported by tiny everyday physical mechanisms, a myriad micro-powers of supervision and bodily manipulation, which distributed the subjects across the social spectrum in positions of inequality. This ill-fitting but productive machine worked in the shadows shaping the bodies and souls of the modern subject, while theories of sovereignty and right glossed over the disciplinary technologies and concealed the way in which domination was reproduced.

2 Michel Foucault, *The History of Sexuality* (Harmondsworth, Penguin, 1981), 96.
3 'Preface' in Michel Foucault, *The Uses of Pleasure: The History of Sexuality, Vol. 2* (London, Penguin, 1989), 203.

Sovereign right was transferred from king to subject-citizens, who became the 'collective' sovereign of democracy. But as the disciplines were constituted and propagated by legal and administrative practices, rights offered limited protections against the power of the machinery of the state.

Legal rights promised protection against domination and subjection but they themselves came to existence and were supported by the very disciplinary technologies, which acted as the dark side of the brilliant pronouncements of freedom, equality and the rule of law. The techniques of coercion and subjection of bodies and through them of souls were the underside of societies proclaiming the rule of law, constitutionalism and civil liberties and helped legitimise a new form of power. From this perspective, natural and human rights are not just restraints on power; they are tools of the new society of control. This paradox can be stated in simple terms: rights help emancipate and protect people but they are also instruments of power used to discipline, exclude and dominate. Social orders establish and perpetuate themselves by rejecting, silencing, and banning certain 'others' as mad, foreign, criminal, inhuman. People are excluded because their existence is inimical to the systematic nature and political claims of dominant power relations or because they are cognitively unthinkable, beyond the ability of current knowledge to comprehend their difference.[4]

In a further mutation, disciplinary power has now been superseded by 'bio-power', a combination of power and life. The early modern sovereign had the right to take life or to let subjects live. In the age of bio-power, the very existence of man as a living being is put into question and the sovereign's power becomes to make live and let die.[5] Power in close collaboration with knowledge and law is now exercised on the body and on life processes. Over the last thirty years, this process has accelerated. The disciplinary society has morphed into a society of intense control and power has been increasingly adopting what Foucault called a 'bio-political' form. According to Michael Hardt and Antonio Negri, the practices and institutions of normalisation identified by Michel Foucault have proliferated and intensified to such an extent that every aspect of social relations is now subjected to the operations of power.[6] Disciplinary technologies defined some behaviour as normal and other as

4 For the place of the other in Western thought and the implications for law and jurisprudence see Costas Douzinas and Ronnie Warrington *Justice Miscarried: Ethics and Aesthetics in Law* (Edinburgh, Edinburgh University Press, 1994) and Douzinas, *End*, Chapter 13.

5 Michel Foucault, *Society Must be Defended* (London, Allen Lane, 2003), Chapter 11.

6 Michael Hardt and Antonio Negri, *Empire* (Cambridge, MA, Harvard University Press, 2000), 12.

deviant. They marked the boundaries of acceptable thought and practice and, through the exclusion of the abnormal and alien, policed bodies and souls. But the disciplinary institutions are now on the retreat and disciplining expands throughout the smooth social surface of Western societies. Global communications, new media, extreme consumerism, total surveillance through CCTV, detailed personal information held in ID cards, passports, public and private databanks all combine in the new form of biopolitical power that extends its hold to the whole of life.

The identity cards law passed in the UK in early 2006, for example, will allow the British government to compile a national identity register database that will record the biometric data of the population, including fingerprints, digitised facial scans and iris scans, with chip and pin technology and the possibility of adding DNA profiling. The security reasons for these policies have been ridiculed by critics, including Liberal and Tory politicians, who have argued that no terrorist attack will be prevented by the introduction of the cards. While the ID card is nominally introduced to help in the 'war on terror', its implications are much wider. People will be obliged to produce the card in most transactions with state institutions and private companies. The cards will be swiped when people apply for jobs or for a driving or a fishing licence, when they withdraw money from banks, set up Internet accounts or take out insurance policies. 'Every time the card is swiped, the central database logs the transaction so that an accurate plot of your life is drawn.'[7] Similar biometric data are collected by American immigration authorities on all foreign citizens travelling to the USA.

Surveillance of telephone and electronic communications has been a standard state practice for many years. Civil libertarians justifiably complain that emergency measures adopted in restricted areas or for limited purposes were soon expanded to the whole population. In the United Kingdom, new policing measures in Northern Ireland were treated as dress rehearsals for export to the mainland. This was the case, for example, in relation to prevention of terrorism and police powers legislation, which was tried out in the province, because of its 'special circumstances', and then imported into Britain. Fingerprinting accompanied arrest and conviction for serious criminal offences as punishment and in order to facilitate future identification. The ID cards, however, allegedly a measure in the war on terror, move in a radical new direction. They will appropriate and register the most intimate and exposed elements of personal life. In the past, the targets of espionage and surveillance

---

7   Henry Porter, 'This ID Project is Even More Sinister Than We First Thought' *The Observer*, 19 March 2006, 27.

were clearly defined political enemies (the IRA, communists, anarchists) or criminals. Privacy-based objections to this avalanche of surveillance, registration and classification measures are important but limited. Privacy defends personal confidences and intimate aspects of people's lives. Biopolitical control, on the other hand, is integrated in reach and undifferentiated in scope. It does not distinguish between sensitive and indifferent parts of personal life; everything is relevant in charting a life and subjecting it to the demands of power. Furthermore, it does not separate certain groups out as targets of special attention. We are all suspects and potential criminals now, 'mankind has been declared the most dangerous of classes'.[8] Registration of our bodies is the price we have to pay for the increased 'freedom of choice' we have been granted. 'Power is thus expressed as a control that extends throughout the depths of the consciousnesses and bodies of the population – and at the same time across the entirety of social relations.'[9] People are both autonomous and alienated as the working population has internalised the priorities of system reproduction and experiences them as an exercise of freedom.

The implications of these changes for jurisprudence are momentous. Legal philosophy is still preoccupied with the validity, extent and scope of legal controls over state power. This anachronistic approach is confounded by the even greater unreality of liberal jurisprudence, for which social reality is a kind of computer game simulation emptied of all social content. 'Virtual world' jurisprudence still dominates the teaching and research curriculum. One obvious symptom is its total neglect of the process through which norms are created. Following changes in Western capitalism, which is no longer dependent on economic production but on circulation and consumption, jurisprudence has abandoned the study of law creation and the actual operation and effects of rights and focuses 'on the circulation of norms and rights throughout the juridical system, as normative discourse is raised to a level of total abstraction'.[10] Michael Hardt and Antonio Negri describe liberal jurisprudence accurately as an extreme abstraction from social concerns. But their conclusion that John Rawls's theory of justice or Ronald Dworkin's concept of rights anticipate and describe the legal system of the new world order is wide of the mark. The coherent and principled legal system Rawls and Dworkin evangelise bears no relationship to the way the law actually operates. Both in its biopolitical form and in its sovereign expression, the law

---

8   Giorgio Agamben, 'Bodies Without Words: Against the Biopolitical Tatoo', 5/2 *German Law Journal* (2004).
9   Hardt and Negri, op. cit., 24.
10 Paul Passavant, 'From Empire's Law to the Multitude's Rights' in J. Dean and P. Passavant, eds, *Empire's New Clothes* (New York, Routledge, 2004), 98.

replicates social relations losing all remnants of consistency and coherence and openly violating the principles of justice and rights that gave it a modicum of completeness and integrity. To paraphrase Foucault, jurisprudence needs to 'cut off the head of the King', to change its focus from the great topics of sovereignty and right to the everyday mundane structures of domination. This is what the Italian philosopher Giorgo Agamben has been doing for some time.

Agamben has radicalised Foucault's approach by arguing that power has always operated on bare biological life. He rejects the classical distinction between *potestas* (power based on force and domination) and *auctoritas* (authority, legitimate power) and argues that politics is constituted through an original exclusion of certain people who are abandoned by power, in the sense that power has no interest in them. Agamben uses the Roman institution of *homo sacer* as the best example of this abandonment.[11] The *homo sacer*, both the sacred and the cursed man under Roman law, is someone who may be killed with impunity, but whose death cannot be raised to the honour of a sacrifice to the gods. The *homo sacer* lives beyond the reach or interest of law, he inhabits a limbo state or zone of indistinction between public life (*bios* – a life narrativised in the public sphere and worthy of respecting and remembering) and private life (*zoe* – mere biological existence). Politics exists, argues Agamben, 'because man is a living being who, in language, separates and opposes himself to his own bare life and, at the same time, maintains himself in relation to bare life in an inclusive exclusion'.[12]

Classical politics was born in the opposition between these two orders of life. Bare life, a life without meaning or purpose, is the hinge and threshold of politics, an undifferentiated zone in which meaningful political and abandoned life constitute each other by their mutual exclusion and inclusion. In modernity, bios and zoe have been confused and natural life has become a strategic consideration of the mechanisms and calculations of power. As zoe becomes the source and the target of the rights of man, birth is the principle of operation of the sovereign. One is born into a nation-state, birth identifies nativity with nationality and offers biological life to the investments of power. 'Nation-state means a state that makes nativity or birth [*nascita*] (that is naked human life) the foundation of its sovereignty.'[13] But while Foucault had argued that bio-power takes hold in the wake of the sovereign, Agamben retains the

---

11 Giorgio Agamben, *Homo Sacer* (Stanford, CA, Stanford University Press, 1998)
12 Ibid. 8.
13 Giorgio Agamben, *Means without Ends* (Vincenzo Binetti and Cesare Casarino trans.) (Minneapolis, MN, University of Minnesota Press, 2000), 20.

sovereign as the key to the political drama and, structurally, as the mirror image of the *homo sacer*. The total and constant control over life is an attribute of the sovereign's omnipotence. Following Carl Schmitt, Agamben defines the sovereign through the power to institute a state of exception and suspend normal legality in order to save the law from radical threats (Chapters 10 and 11).[14] The decision to suspend the law, which marks out the sovereign, is both outside law's procedures and within the law as a precondition of its operation.

Giorgio Agamben's limbo state between zoe and bios is exemplified by camps and prisons, such as Guantánamo Bay, Abu Ghraib, Belmarsh, the secret prisons and dark sites of CIA. In these camps, the legal exception becomes the rule. They symbolise the spatial arrangement of the new world order, Schmitt's *nomos* of empire. In the camp, power confronts life without the mediation of law or rights and directly takes over its management. Guantánamo Bay, the most notorious camp, appears both as a topographical location and as a non-space. Situated in Cuba, it is outside Cuban sovereignty. But according to the American government, it is extra-territorial for the purposes of American law too, at least as far as the prisoners held there are concerned.[15] Its location places it inside (Cuba, American jurisdiction) and at the same time outside, symbolising the topographical principle of empire. We could imagine a

14 Giorgio Agamben, *State of Exception* (Kevin Attell, trans.) (Chicago, IL, University of Chicago Press, 2005).

15 In *Rasul and Odah* v. *Bush* 215 F Supp 2d 55 (DDS 2002), the application of the writ of habeas corpus and other civil liberties to the Guantánamo detainees was discussed as a question of the jurisdiction American courts have over the treatment of prisoners and Guantánamo Bay detainees. The district court examined the 1903 Lease agreement between the United States and Cuba, which gave 'jurisdiction and control' over Guantánamo Bay to the former, but left 'ultimate sovereignty' with Cuba. The court held that only one sovereign has power over a certain territory and, in this instance, ultimate sovereignty lies with Cuba. As a result, the American courts have no jurisdiction and the writ of habeas corpus does not run in Guantánamo Bay. The Supreme Court in *Rasul* v. *Bush* (Judgment of 28 June 2004) changed the basis of the decision and argued that since the prison guards are under American jurisdiction, habeas corpus could challenge the legality of the detention. In the later case of *Hamdi* v. *Rumsfeld* (Judgment of 28 June 2004), the Supreme Court accepted that some due process protections should be given to detainees. In all these cases, the key arguement was about the legal position of the custodians and not the human rights of the prisoners. In late September 2006, Congress passed a bill setting up military tribunals to try suspects, complying with a Supreme Court ruling (*Hamdan* v. *Rumsfeld,* Judgment of 29 June 2006) according to which such tribunals must be approved by Congress and not imposed by the Pentagon, as was the case with the tribunals set up at Guantánamo Bay. But defendants' rights will fall well short of those guaranteed by civilian and most military courts. The Bill claims that the Geneva Conventions in relation to the treatment of detainees will be followed and defines war crimes. But it gives the president absolute power to interpret them and decide which interrogation techniques are legal and which not.

Borgesian map with a Magrittean twist. An arrow would point to the place in Cuba saying 'this is not Guantánamo Bay'. Every person, event and situation is inside the global dispensation of empire but everything can be equally abandoned to the state of total exteriority, of non-humanity. The camp is a threshold zone; 'humanity', the threshold concept around which the imperial project is organised.

Observing the legal limbo of the detainees, it is difficult to disagree with Hannah Arendt who, commenting on nineteenth-century rights campaigns, wrote that those jurists and philanthropists who tried to create rights to protect minorities 'showed an uncanny similarity in language and composition to that of societies for the prevention of cruelty to animals'.[16] Arendt's link of humanitarianism with the treatment of animals goes further back. The eighteenth-century culture of sensibility that led to the bourgeois 'civilising process' and humanitarian reforms 'steadily broadened the arena within which humanitarian feeling was encouraged to operate, extending compassion to animals and to previously despised types of persons including slaves, criminals and the insane'.[17] Jamal Al-Harith, a British former detainee of Guantánamo Bay, gives a twenty-first-century version:

> After a while we stopped asking for human rights – we wanted animal rights. In Camp X-Ray my cage was right next to a kennel housing an Alsatian dog. He had a wooden house with air conditioning and green grass to exercise on. I said to the guards, 'I want his rights', and they replied, 'That dog is a member of the US army.'[18]

In a biopolitical setting, the question is no longer moral (the restriction of cruelty) but ontological (who becomes human out of the state of animality). Just as the exception sustains the norm, humanity is created against the figure of the non-human.

We can follow power's anthropogenetic strategies in the operations of Abu Ghraib, the space described as a legal limbo or no-man's-land. A first can be called the strategy of abandonment. According to Nori Samir Gunbar Al-Yasseri, an Abu Ghraib prisoner, the American soldiers

---

16 Hannah Arendt, *The Origins of Totalitarianism* (San Diego, CA, Harvest Books, 1979), 292.

17 Karen Halttunen, 'Humanitarianism and the Pornography of Pain in Anglo-American Culture', 100/2 *American Historical Review* 303 (1995).

18 http://www.mirror.co.uk/news/allnews/content_objectid=14042696_method=full_siteid=50143_headline=-MY-HELL-IN-CAMP-X-RAY-name_page.html.

stripped us naked as a newborn baby. Then they ordered us to hold our penises and stroke it . . . . They started to take photographs as if it was a porn movie. And they treated us like animals not humans . . . . No one showed us mercy. Nothing but cursing and beating. Then they started to write words on our buttocks, which we didn't know what it means. After that they left us for the next two days naked with no clothes, with no mattress, as if we were dogs.[19]

Ameen Sa'eed Al-Sheikh, another prisoner, tells of an exchange with an American interrogator: 'Do you believe in anything?' 'I believe in Allah', 'But I believe in torture and I will torture you.'[20] According to Jay Bybee, American Assistant Attorney-General, torture is defined as 'extreme acts', which

> must be of an intensity akin to that which accompanies serious physical injury such as death or organ failure . . . . because the acts inflicting torture are extreme, there is [a] significant range of acts that, though they might constitute cruel, inhuman, or degrading treatment or punishment, fail to rise to the level of torture.[21]

Al-Yasseri, Al-Sheikh and Al-Harith, who could not have the rights of an American dog, indicate the one extreme of biopolitics, what Joanna Bourke has elegantly called the 'threshold of the human'.[22]

According to the American definition, inhuman acts not leading to 'death or organ failure' do not constitute torture. Torture is not to inflict inhumanity on the victim, but to treat him as non-human, a dog, bare life. The response of liberals to this theatre of cruelty has been mixed, condemnatory but muted. Pragmatist commentators and lawyers, such as Michael Ignatieff, and Alan Dershowitz,[23] who 'understand' the security concerns have tried to develop legal and regulatory mechanisms, which could normalise torture. At the other end, the House of Lords and High Court in London have been quite critical. 'America's idea of what is torture is not the same as ours and does not appear to coincide with that of most civilised nations', Justice

19 Mark Danner, *Torture and Truth. America, Abu Ghraib and the War on Terror* (London: Granta Books, 2005), 228.

20 Ibid. 219.

21 Elizabeth Eaves, 'Defining Deviancy Down', *Harper's*, September 2004, 6.

22 Joanna Bourke, 'The Theshold of the Human. Sexual Violence in the War on Terror', Oxford Amnesty lecture, 7 February 2006 (forthcoming).

23 Michael Ignatieff, *The Lesser Evil* (Edinburgh, Edinburgh University Press, 2004); Alan Dershowitz, *Why Terrorism Works* (New Haven, CT, Yale University Press, 2002).

Collins stated in 2006.[24] On the same day, the world's media were deluged with a huge new tranche of torture photographs from Abu Ghraib. They include pornographic images, simulated sex acts and photos of dead bodies. Many have an air of normality, with soldiers filling in forms or clipping their fingernails in front of hooded, naked detainees. The website Salon.com, which published some of the pictures, commented that 'the DVD also includes photographs of guards threatening Iraqi prisoners with dogs . . . hooded prisoners being forced to masturbate, a video showing a mentally disturbed prisoner smashing his head against a door [and] oddly . . . numerous photographs of slaughtered animals'.[25]

The public reaction to the torture pictures was highly significant. The early photographs shocked and titillated. In particular the pictures of women, most notably Lynndie England, perpetrating sexual abuse, evoked the dominatrix figure of American cartoons.[26] The inhuman was a woman, doing what women are not supposed to do. Lynndie's pleasure created a vicarious sense of titillation. Soon, however, the shock was domesticated. The Internet became crowded with pictures of men and women 'doing a Lynndie' and detailed instructions on how to 'do a Lynndie'. It was not surprising, therefore, that the publication of the 2006 photographs did not create a similar response. Most newspapers published short articles in the inside pages, while the American government found the possible reaction of Arabs to American interests in the Middle East the main problem and stated that they should not have been published because they violate the 'privacy' of the protagonists!

Simone de Beauvoir, referring to torture in Algeria, wrote that 'in 1957, the burns in the face, on the sexual organs, the nails torn out, the impalements, the shrieks, the convulsions, outraged me'. But, by the 'sinister month of December 1961, like many of my fellow men, I suppose, I suffer from a kind of tetanus of the imagination . . . . One gets used to it'.[27] The normality of the pictures, their continuous references to animals and dead bodies indicate that the stakes go well beyond the prison and torture chamber walls. The legitimation of torture by liberals, the animalisation of prisoners, the proliferation of pornographic pictures, the initial titillation and later boredom

24   *The Guardian*, 17 February 2006, 1.
25   *The Guardian*, 17 February 2006, 17.
26   Richard Goldstein, 'Bitch Bites Man!', in *Village Voice*, 10 May 2004, in http://www. villagevoice.com/generic/show_print.php?id=53375&page=goldstein2&issue.
27   Simone de Beauvoir, *La Force des Choses*, Tome 2 (Paris, Gallimard, 1963), 125–265.

of the public's response make us all participants in these events. But what have we become used to? The insistence of the American government that these acts are carried out for humanity's protection from terrorists may be of help. The Americans are not wrong. But the benefit is not so much the protection of our security but the public display of what it means to be human. It takes inhumanity to define humanity by separating out the non-human. The extreme strategy of bio-power is precisely to demarcate the human through extreme acts of inhumanity inflicted on bare animal life. One could call it the 'shock and awe' strategy and its banalisation. It reverses Arendt's thesis on the banality of evil: evil must be both radical, immense and banal in order to work. The acts were carried out and the photos disseminated for our sake as part of the strategy of imaginary empire, discussed at length in Chapter 10. Lynndie may be a great American scapegoat and martyr after all.

A similar analysis can be applied to recent British anti-terrorist legislation and litigation. In the wake of 9/11, the Home Secretary was given the power to detain foreign terror suspects indefinitely. Seventeen people were held under these powers. In December 2004, the House of Lords quashed these powers as discriminatory, not proportionate to the terrorist threat and a violation of international obligations. 'The real threat to the life of the nation comes not from terrorism but from laws such as these', thundered Lord Hoffman.[28] In January 2006, the government replaced the internment powers with a regime of 'control orders' intended to 'contain and disrupt those we cannot prosecute or deport'. These new orders allowed the imposition of a strict surveillance regime on suspects up to but not including house arrest. On 1 August 2006, the Court of Appeal upheld an earlier High Court decision by Mr Justice Sullivan quashing control orders against six Iraqis, which included a daily eighteen-hour curfew. The three judges ruled unanimously that the orders amounted to imprisonment by other means. These 'virtual house arrest' powers were incompatible with Article 5 of the European Convention of Human Rights, which bans indefinite detention without trial. The Home Secretary immediately stated that he would try to appeal the decision,

> because I am concerned about its effects on public safety. We are at a sustained high level of threat from a terrorist attack . . . Our security services are at full stretch and control orders form an essential part of our fight against terrorism.[29]

---

28 *A and others* v. *Secretary of State for the Home Department*, Appellate Committee of the House of Lords (16 December 2004), at 97.

29 *The Guardian*, 2 August 2006, 3.

It can be argued that the public part of the government's anti-terrorist strategy has been to work on popular imagination promoting the terrorist threats to Western security against the perceived symbolic coherence of legal principles in national and international law. The small number of the people considered a sufficient security threat to have detention or control orders issued against them indicates that their main function is 'theatrical'. It advertises the threat facing the nation and reminds people of the extraordinary arsenal of powers and sanctions available to the state. We are asked to identify with these measures and the wider concerns they advertise precisely because so few suspects worthy of their draconian reach have been found. In a logic that recalls the Moscow trials, the threat is at its greatest when its evidence is at the weakest.

Law and rights in the age of bio-power

At the other end of biopolitics, the normal humanity alluded in the torture pictures is replete with the rights and liberties so brutally deprived from the victims. Early human rights were historical victories of groups and individuals against state power; but they also 'simultaneously prepared a tacit but increasing inscription of individuals' lives within the state order, thus offering a new and more dreadful foundation for the very sovereign power from which they wanted to liberate themselves'.[30] With the proliferation of biopolitical regulation, the endlessly multiplying rights paradoxically increase power's investment on bodies.[31] These developments are reflected in the operation of the legal system. In a complementary process, areas of private activity are increasingly legalised, while public services and utilities are released from their redistributive aims and given over to the stricter disciplines of private profit and the market. As

---

30 Agamben, *Homo Sacer* op. cit., 121.

31 Andrew Norris, 'The Exemplary Exception' and Andreas Kalyvas, 'The Sovereign Weaver' both in Andrew Norris, ed., *Politics, Metaphysics and Death* (Durham, NC, Duke University Press, 2005) accuse Agamben for being either contradictory or wrong by defining the camp inmates as people without rights and then going on to criticise rights as foundations and tools of the biopolitical organisation of power. But there is nothing contradictory in this position. Rights 'have only paradoxes to offer'. Their effects are closely linked with power in its various modi operandi. Their absence constructs the (non) human as abandoned by power while their abundant presence invests the human with the effects of power. Indeed Foucault, in a late lecture series, saw sovereign power and biopolitics as complementary in the context of Nazism. 'The two mechanisms – the classic, archaic mechanism that gave the State the right of life and death over its citizens, and the new mechanism organised around discipline and regulation, or in other words, the new mechanism of biopower – coincide exactly' (Michel Foucault, *Society Must Be Defended* (David Macey, trans.) (London, Allen Lane, 2003), 260).

a result, the modern legal system abandons the unrealistic claim that it forms a consistent system of norms and starts resembling an experimental machine 'full of parts that came from elsewhere, strange couplings, chance relations, cogs and levers that aren't connected, that don't work, and yet somehow produce judgements, prisoners, sanctions and so on'.[32]

More specifically, administrative law keeps extending its scope to an increasing number of areas. Indeed, in a remarkable imitation of communist legal systems, most new law is introduced as part of a hugely expanded and variegated administrative domain. This regulatory colonisation does not represent or pursue any inherent logic, overarching policy direction or coherent value system. Policy direction changes violently from one day to the next and from one field to the other. Detailed regulation distributes benefits, facilities and positions; it constructs small-scale institutions, assigning variable roles, planning local micro-relations and disciplining people by arranging them along lines of normal behaviour. Legislative and regulatory systems are adopted to promote transient, provisional and local policy objectives with no immediate or obvious link with wider social policy, other than the overall control of life. Indeed, governance appears as an aimless and endless process of negotiation among 'stake-holders' in public goods. Policy has become visible throughout the operation of law-making and administration; in many instances policy and rule-making are delegated to experts, who fill the gaps according to the latest claims of scientific knowledge.

Every policy area or regulatory regime is a way of defining a field or problem and the available solutions. Family law, planning, criminal justice and policing as much as official secrecy, privacy and data protection are parts of a regulatory palimpsest, a patchwork of rarely connected priorities. To use recent examples, is the paedophiles register and its publicisation a matter of criminal sanctions, of policing and prevention, of data protection and freedom of information or of privacy rights? Is immigration policy a matter of economic,security or human rights considerations? Depending on the resource implications, the bargaining power of the respective 'stake-holders' and the pressure of the media (or of 'public opinion'), policies emerge and create their 'compliance mechanisms'. Privatisation and deregulation, on the other hand, hive off parts of state regulation and hand them over to formally private concerns acting in a public capacity. Here the 'logic of the market' imposes its discipline on life. Consumerism and a ubiquitous but joyless sexuality exercise a much more extensive control on life than any public power. In the age of deregulation,

---

32 Michel Foucault quoted in Colin Gordon, 'Afterword' in *Power/Knowledge* (Brighton, Harvester, 1980), 257.

the state complements the market and acts as its enforcer. This is why the prophesied withering away of the state will remain premature for as long as politics is separate from economic activity in order to provide the coercion and security needs of capitalism.

The parallel processes of juridification and deregulation mean that the formal sources of normativity are no longer of great importance. Whether they originate in private managers or state bureaucrats, rules are no longer the democratic expression of sovereignty or the liberal formalization of morality. They are treated both by legislators and citizens in a purely utilitarian way. As the proceduralists do not tire of reminding us, laws are frameworks for organising private activities, reducing market uncertainties and lowering transaction costs. Even Jürgen Habermas, the major theorist of normative cosmopolitanism, despairs:

> In this *postpolitical* world the multinational corporation becomes the model for all conduct. The *impotence of a normatively guided politics* . . . is only a special case of a more general development. Its vanishing point is a completely decentered world society that splinters into a disordered mass of self-reproducing and self-steering functional systems.[33]

The World Bank, on the other hand, welcomes the prospect. In its *Governance and Development* report, it states that the rule of law is necessary in developing states

> to create a sufficient stable setting for economic actors – entrepreneurs, farmers and workers – to assess economic opportunities and risks, to make investments of capital and labour, to transact business with each other, and to have reasonable assurance or recourse against arbitrary interference or expropriation.[34]

This is a sad remnant of the honourable tradition of the rule of law. From one of the great achievements of the European legal tradition, it is now 'reduced to an ensemble of rules and no other basis than the daily proof of its smooth functioning'.[35]

---

33 Jürgen Habermas, *The Inclusion of the Other* (Cambridge, Polity, 1998), 125 (first italicisation in original, the second mine).

34 The World Bank, *Governance and Development* (1992).

35 Jean-Marie Guehenno, *The End of the Nation-state* (Victoria Elliott, trans.) (Minneapolis, MN, University of Minnesota Press, 1995), 99.

As law is disseminated throughout society, its form becomes detailed and full of discretion, its sources multiple and diffused, its aims unclear, unknown or contradictory, its effects unpredictable, variable and uneven. All the key themes of legality are weakened. Rule and normativity are replaced by normalisation, value by discretion and the legal subject by administratively assigned roles and competencies. The law is expanding but at the price of assuming the characteristics of contemporary society, thus becoming open, decentred, fragmented, nebulous and multiform. Outside the trappings of central power, beyond Whitehall, Westminster and the superior courts, law is increasingly law because it calls itself law. Its legitimacy at street level is based on its ability to mobilise the icons of legality and the force of the police. Detailed regulation emanating from local, national, supranational and international sources penetrates all areas and aspects of life. From the most intimate and domestic relations to global economics and communication processes, no area is immune from state or market intervention. Everything, from the composition of tinned food to great atrocities has found its way in (public or private) 'law'. But this is no longer law in the *rechsstaat* tradition.

This state of affairs is particularly evident in international economic law. As Adam Gearey notes, the work of international economic institutions displays the 'breaking down of the certainties of conventional jurisprudence. In the place of the old order are regulatory regimes that operate along political and economic lines rather than in conformity with the logic of law'.[36] Anne Orford has detailed the way in which the World Bank has used human rights for biopolitical intervention in the former communist states and the Third World. 'Education packages' aim to teach the 'cultural, political, national values' of market capitalism and to train in the skills of efficiency and compliance. Reproduction, health and sanitation, nutrition, youth development, population control, HIV/Aids bring together international economic institutions, NGOs and human rights activists in a huge operation of biopolitical control of the poor. In Third World states, 'whole populations are policed, the criterion of selection being whether one's community or demographic group has been targeted for an aid project'.[37] According to Orford, human rights reinforce the process of normalisation by subjecting all aspects of bodies to political control, from private and intimate to public life and work, in order to produce the 'human capital necessary to reproduce markets'.[38]

36 Adam Gearey, *Globalisation and Law* (Lanham, MD, Rowman & Littlefield, 2005), 80.
37 Patricia Stamp, 'Foucault and the New Imperial Order', *Arena Journal,* 119 (1994), 17.
38 Anne Orford, 'Beyond Harmonisation: Trade, Human Rights and the Economy of Sacrifice' 18 *Leiden Journal of International Law*, 179 (2005).

This omnivorous – public or private – regulatory activity means that some legal statements take a normative – 'ought' – form; most are just descriptive. In its imperial mode and mood, law is well on the way to replicating life in its annals. If modern law claims to regulate the world, postmodern just mimics it. In Borges' story of the cartographers of empire, the mythical cartographers, asked to produce the most accurate possible map, ended with one the same size as the territory it mapped. The law repeats the enterprise; it has undertaken the most accurate mapping of society, a process that will end up with law and the natural life of society or, with order and desire becoming co-extensive and in perfect synchrony. The dynamic of modern law (and of the metaphysics of modernity) was to open a distance, occasionally imperceptible, between law and the order of the world. Now this distance is fast disappearing in the vast expanse of law-life. But this is a law with force but without value or normative weight, a law that constitutes and constraints but does not signify. In the great legal positivist edifices of the twentieth century, validity was considered the hallmark of law, with efficiency a secondary and external addition. Today, only efficiency matters. Validity, modern law's mark of identification, has disappeared and is discussed in law textbooks as a relic from the past not dissimilar to natural law. Contemporary rights increasingly assume the characteristics of society, reproducing society's 'natural' order but no longer acting as correction of the order. 'Nothing is more dismal', writes Agamben 'than this unconditional being-in-force of juridical categories in a world in which they no longer mirror any comprehensive ethical content: their being-in-force is truly meaningless'.[39]

We are thus faced with a new paradox: power relations and practices proliferate and penetrate deep into the social, often taking a loose and variable legal form. Their common characteristics are few: an often extremely tenuous derivation from the legislative power, more importantly their link with the increasingly empty referent 'law', which bestows upon them a symbolic weight. If, for positivism, the 'law is the law', the underlying idea becomes now fully radicalised. Power relations seek legitimacy by attaching to themselves the predication 'legal'. Law is everything that succeeds in calling itself law, law and society are becoming increasingly co-extensive. If, as Mrs Thatcher argued, society no longer exists, law has contributed to its demise by shifting its boundaries towards an endlessly malleable network of relationships following the complimentary logic of regulation and rights.

---

39   Agamben, *Means,* op. cit., 133.

Despite the illusions of cosmopolitans, both citizenship and autonomy are on the retreat and no alternative global vision appears on the horizon. Citizenship was defined in the context of the nation-state through limited participation in the exercise of sovereignty. Autonomy had a moral element that linked the person to the public *sensus communis* of similar rational and moral beings. Today, people are increasingly detached from the solidarity national democracies offered and autonomy has become a-moral, a synonym for private freedom of choice. Law appears at its most imperialistic at the precise moment when it starts losing its specificity. Rights as much as regulatory norms abandon their normativity in order to normalise. The legal rule of empire: everything that happens is potentially legal; if nothing happened that would be legal too.

On freedom in a biopolitical world

'A pigeon would die of hunger near a basin filled with the best meats', writes Jean-Jacques Rousseau. 'And a cat upon heaps of fruits or grain, although each could very well nourish itself on the food it disdains if it made up its mind to try some.' Compare the pigeon and the cat with the hunger striker, the martyr or even the suicide bomber:

> [The beast] chooses or rejects by instinct and [man] by an act of freedom, so that a beast cannot deviate from the rule that is prescribed to it even when it would be advantageous for it to do so, and a man deviates from it often to his detriment . . . Thus dissolute men abandon themselves to excesses which cause them fever and death, because the mind depraves the senses and because the will still speaks when the nature is silent.[40]

For Rousseau, animals follow nature, they follow a law set for them, they cannot choose to break it. Man on the contrary is free enough to die of freedom. Freedom is precisely to choose to go against the nature of need, desire or custom that tells the hunger striker to stop suffering, to eat, drink, survive. Moral anti-naturalism has been a persistent undercurrent of modern philosophy. For Kant, moral action is motivated exclusively by respect for a law which demands that needs, passions and interests are set aside. Freud argued that civilisation is an attempt to negate sexual desires. Both Freud and his follower Lacan discover a typical expression of modernity in Kant's sadistic renunciation of

---

40 Jean-Jacques Rousseau, *The First and Second Discourse* (R. and J. Masters, trans.) (New York, St Martin's Press, 1964), 5.

the flesh.[41] In the Jewish tradition, the law sustains the community, often against the demands of nature or reason. For Martin Buber, Jews act in order to understand while Emmanuel Levinas denounces the Greek or Western 'temptation of temptation', the demand to subordinate action to knowledge and thus overcome the 'purity' of obedience to the law.[42] Man's essence is not to have an essence, his nature the capacity to distance himself from natural or social codes (the 'second nature') and start *ex nihilo* time and again. Humanity resides in freedom, which means that man is free to choose suffering. This is precisely what autonomy means, freedom as the highest moral achievement of modernity. What distinguishes humanity is the Bartleby principle: 'I would prefer not to.'

Freedom has now been replaced by 'choice', freedom to choose is the way of late capitalism. The Labour government in particular is keen to offer as many choices as possible: we can choose our child's school and his meals, our doctor and our university, our hospital and our cemetery. In the near future, we will be able to choose the physical looks, genetic information and behavioural traits of our offspring. But what kind of freedom this proliferation of choices gives? Slavoj Zizek has discussed recently the institution of *rumspringa* (from the German *herumspringen*, to jump around) practised by Amish communities in the United States. Amish teenagers are allowed and even encouraged to leave their cloistered communities behind for a couple of years and experience the normal American way of life. After that they have to decide how to live their lives. The teenagers are known to indulge in wild life for a period but 90 per cent return to their community. 'Far from allowing the youngsters a truly free choice – that is, giving them a chance to decide based on the full knowledge and experience of both sides of the choice – such a solution is a fake choice if there ever was one' concludes Zizek.[43]

Zizek is right. These teenagers are offered a formal choice but they are not informed or educated about their options. They are thrown into normal American life totally unprepared. Indeed, the only way to prepare them would have been to remove them from the Amish community at a young age and have them lead a normal life, something that would not have prepared them, of course, for the austere life of the Amish. Both ways of preparing people to

---

41 Jacques Lacan, 'Kant avec Sade', 51 *October* (Winter 1989), 55–75; Costas Douzinas, 'Antigone Death and Law's Birth: on Ontology and Psychoanalytical Ethics', 16 *Cardozo Law Review* 1325 (1995); Douzinas, 'Eros and Thanatos' in D. Manderson, ed., *Courting Death* (London, Pluto Press, 1999).

42 Costas Douzinas and Ronnie Warrington, *Justice Miscarried* (Edinburgh, Edinburgh University Press, 1994), Chapter 4.

43 Slavoj Zizek, *The Parallax View* (Cambridge MA, MIT Press, 2006), 331.

exercise freedom lead to forced choices. Choice is turned into the handmaiden of necessity: you are free when you choose what is already in your nature. Free choice comes with a dose of compulsion. To be free is to choose (freely in principle but inescapably in practice) what has conditioned you. While market capitalism perpetuates enormous inequalities, it has organised its domination around the appearance of freedom and equality. We are free to the extent that we can shop in the same shops everywhere in the world; we are equal to the extent that all the brands are equally available, even though not equally affordable. We are free and equal if we are able to buy as a matter of right anything being sold. Free man is shopping man. But this type of choice designates the deterioration, decline, if not total abolition, of freedom as understood by modernity. If humanity was the freedom to choose against nature, man has now become 'free' to choose to follow nature or the 'second nature' of social conformity, free to choose between different types of fake happiness. Humanity has been redefined as the freedom to follow slavishly the limited set of choices offered to us.

Postmodern rights promote 'choice' contra freedom, conformism versus imagination. Children are given rights against their parents; patients, students and welfare recipients are termed 'customers' and are offered consumer rights and fake 'choices'. In Western capitalist societies, it is forbidden to forbid, and rights, freedom and choice have become the mantras of politics. The politics of choice tends to turn the expression of wish, the 'I want X' into 'I have a right to X' (Chapter 2). But as Wendy Brown put it, rights not only 'mask by depoliticising the social power of institutions such as private property or the family, they organise mass populations for exploitation and regulation'.[44] The dark side of rights is the inexorable rise of registration, classification and control of individuals and populations. Rights act both as a defensive wall and a modality of bio-power.

Rights were the metaphysical principle, which opened the distance between the ideal and the real and introduced the demands of justice in legal operations. But as we move to the age of non-political politics, the split between ideal and real, which sustained the metaphysics of modernity and gave human rights their paradoxical vitality, has been radically transformed. Bio-power abolishes the line of separation between universal and particular, human and citizen, ought and is. The two sides of the divide are collapsing into one another. They are becoming a zone of indifference, where passage from one to the other retains a certain rhetorical force but no axiological significance. Man and citizen are no longer separate, the ideal and reality are two sides of the same coin.

---

44 Wendy Brown, *States of Injury* (Princeton, NJ, Princeton University Press, 1995), 99.

The cosmopolitan extension of the nation-state promises to turn nationality into citizenship of a world state, making the particular ecumenical. Conversely, imperial expansion imbues local traditions with the normative peaks of the universal. The postmodern body has become the ubiquitous site where bio-power invests universal consumption and local sexuality. We argued above that in modernity one could be neither a consistent relativist nor a realistic universalist. In the age of empire, one is perforce both.

Part 2

The normative sources of the new world order

Chapter 6

Empire or cosmopolitanism?

Having dual identity – Greek and British – leads often to a schizophrenic life. Enough has been written about the differences in eating and drinking habits, distinct ways of work and play, the idiosyncracies of love intimacies and courtesies to strangers. But, in my case, what has really made me feel split in my loyalties has been politics. As a 'Briton' in Athens, I had a difficult time trying to persuade Greek friends about the atrocities, murders and mass expulsions committed by Serb allies and co-religionists in Bosnia and Kosovo. As a 'Greek' in London, I was mortified and angry at crass, ignorant, often racist remarks about the Serbs. Around that time, I realised that, in matters of politics, I would remain forever a Briton in Athens and a Greek in London. This is a condition I cannot rationally define but which has dominated my emotional experience and the discussion of politics (something that happens all the time in Athens and more rarely in London).

This disorientating identity dislocation has become recently quite pronounced. Ever since the unprecedented anti-war demonstrations in February 2003, Athens has been almost permanently on the march. Weekly demonstrations and rallies against the war and occupation take place in central Athens and routinely end up outside the American Embassy proudly – and one feels unhappily – situated in a main artery, having bypassed the British Embassy, which is rather coyly located off the main route. The common theme of these demonstrations has been the denunciation of imperialism and empire. Some of the arguments and the conspiracy theories circulating are quite outrageous but nobody doubts that we live in a new imperial world with the United States as the global hegemon. In London, the E-word had not been part of daily discourse. Postcolonialism and multiculturalism (concepts little known to the Greeks) have made discussion about empire something one does not do in civilised company. A rather muted but conspicuous sense of shame, even guilt, means that the imperial past has been confined to the academic conference hall and the history journal. Imperial and postcolonial life has been explored mainly in the novel, where the experiences of immigrants to Britain have become a main and well-trodden theme.

Until recently. Suddenly, newspapers and TV have been involved in a strange revisionism. The British empire has been rediscovered as a civilising and certainly economically progressive historical force at a point when an emerging global hegemon has revived interest both in imperial history and its future. The timing is significant. A British viceroy ran Bosnia until recently, British generals commanded wars in Bosnia and Kosovo, and control Sierra Leone and parts of Iraq and Afghanistan, while British bureaucrats are involved in nation-building in all the above and more. But, unlike Greece, powerful voices in the British and American media have been welcoming this development and encouraging the United States (and Britain as the minority partner at best or America's 'lapdog' at worst) to own up to its true nature and fulfil empire's historical mission. Dozens of books, academic and popular have been published in the last few years with empire on the title. Empire has been declared to be 'lite', incoherent, new, humanitarian, liberal, overstretched, a colossus, a rogue or just plain American.[1]

The recent scholarship on empire breaks down along political lines. Commentators on the right welcome its emergence as the logical culmination of economic and cultural globalisation and as a protection against the neo-barbarians at the gates of civilisation. Those on the left denounce it on symmetrically reversed grounds. The two sides rarely engage each other, however. As in earlier times, the normative import of the terms 'empire' and 'imperialism' is contested and their use indicates political commitment to one or the other camp rather than a disinterested historical or theoretical outlook. 'Empire' splits those who debate it in the metropolis as much as those who experience it in the periphery.

Somewhere in the middle of these positions, a new camp has recently emerged that did not exist in earlier discussions: the cosmopolitans. They position themselves as enemies of patriotism and nationalism, as promoters of global social processes, institutions and world citizenship and as critics of hegemonic and imperial designs. One could call cosmopolitanism, globalisation

---

1 Michael Hardt and Antonio Negri, *Empire* (Cambridge, MA, Harvard University Press, 2000); Michael Ignatieff, *Empire Lite* (London, Vintage, 2003); Michael Mann, *Incoherent Empire,* (London, Verso, 2005); David Harvey, *The New Imperialism* (Oxford, Oxford University Press, 2005); Roger Burbach and Jim Tarbell, *Imperial Overstretch* (London, Zed Books, 2004); Niall Ferguson, *Colossus* (London, Penguin, 2004); Jacques Derrida, *Rogues* (Pascale-Anne Brault and Michael Naas, trans.) (Stanford, CA, Stanford University Press, 2005); Andrew Bacevich, *American Empire* (Cambridge, MA, Harvard University Press, 2002).

with a human face. In the words of an ardent proponent, 'cosmopolitanization' (*sic*) is a

> multidimensional process which has irreversibly changed the historical nature of social worlds and the standing of states . . . it comprises the development of multiple loyalties . . . diverse transnational forms of life, the emergence of non-state political actors (from Amnesty International to the WTO), the development of global protest movements . . . When the Security Council makes a resolution it is received as though it speaks for the whole of humanity.[2]

The cosmopolitans have a long and varied shopping list which, like much of the scholarship on imperialism, has included many interesting discussions of recent developments. If there is a problem it lies with the mix of the disparate parts and the overall direction. 'Empire' has a long and well-known, if disputed, history that allows people to align themselves with well-understood positions of support or rejection. Cosmopolitanism is harder in this sense; no polity has ever used the term or anything similar to define itself. Indeed cosmopolitanism has often been a term of abuse (in the attacks of Hitler and Stalin against 'cosmopolitan' Jews, communists and homosexuals) or ridicule. A philosophical ally captures the ambiguity well when he describes a common understanding of the cosmopolitan as a 'Comme des Garçons-clad sophisticate with a platinum frequent-flyer card regarding, with kindly condescension, a ruddy-faced farmer in workman's overalls' to which we can only add that our cosmopolitan clutches the eponymous glossy magazine.[3]

There is no doubt that these strands of scholarship respond to recent socio-economic and political developments. They form the background against which this book has been written. It is useful, therefore, to start with a brief summary of the five broad categories of scholarship on empire, imperialism and cosmopolitanism currently on offer:

1   *Aggressive imperialism.* The latter-day imperialists argue that the United States have developed into the strongest empire in the history of the world. The US should stop being in denial and accept its responsibilities and burdens fully, openly and without reservations. The main concern among its proponents is that, while the Americans have the resources, they may

---

2   Ulrick Beck, *Cosmopolitan Vision* (Cambridge, Polity, 2006), 9.
3   Kwame Antony Appiah, *Cosmopolitanism. Ethics in a World of Strangers* (London, Allen Lane, 2006), xiii.

not 'have the guts to act as a global hegemon and make the world a more stable place'. Indeed for historian Niall Ferguson, the West should accept its new civilising and stabilising mission and honestly admit that 'globalisation is a fancy word for imperialism, imposing your values and institutions on others'.[4] As the military historian Michael Howerd put it,

> if the Americans do not badge themselves as sheriff and hunt down the bad guys, who will? If this means the assertion of hegemonical or imperial rule, so be it. There are worse things than empires. After half a century the white man's burden must be taken up again.[5]

Similarly, Robert Cooper, a British foreign policy adviser, has called for a return to old imperial principles:

> The challenge to the postmodern world is to get used to the idea of double standards. Among ourselves [in the West], we operate on the basis of laws and open cooperative security. But when dealing with more old-fashioned kinds of states outside the postmodern continent of Europe, we need to revert to the rougher methods of an earlier era – force, pre-emptive attack, deception, whatever is necessary to deal with those who still live in the nineteenth century world of every state for itself. Among ourselves, we keep the law but when we are operating in the jungle, we must also use the laws of the jungle.[6]

The main – but not the only – motive for the imperialist party is the problem of security in a post-9/11 world of failed and rogue states. A strong empire is the answer to the anarchy of the world after the collapse of the 'evil empire'. War, violence and direct rule over the outposts of empire are the immediate response, power and force its organising concepts. Niall Ferguson has argued that the Iraqi occupation should last between forty and seventy years.

These positions are reflected in a mirror image by (most) scholars on the left. The leftists agree with their opponents on the diagnosis of an emerging empire but denounce American imperialism as both powerful

---

4   Niall Ferguson, 'Welcome the New Imperialism', *The Guardian*, 31 October 2001, 13.
5   Michael Howerd, 'Smoke on the Horizon', *Financial Times*, 7 September 2002, Weekend section, 1.
6   Robert Cooper, 'The New Liberal Imperialism', *The Observer*, 1 April 2002, 3.

without precedent and terrifyingly dangerous.[7] America had imperialist tendencies, they argue, from the beginning. Expansionism is built in the American constitution but has been always accompanied with the claim that conquest spreads freedom.[8] Jefferson's promise of an 'empire of liberty' helped rationalise expansion and the conquest of the West. The 'go west' mentality of the early Republic had to cross the seas, once the western frontiers were conquered and the Indians, Mexicans and other indigenous people were eliminated or subjugated. President William McKinley asserted, during the Spanish–American war of 1898, that the American imperialism was 'benevolent'. But the policies of openness and expansion displaced the inhabitants of these lands. Their claims were discounted and their lands were treated as *terra nullius*, land belonging to nobody. Freedom, unlike equality, is an ambiguous and contested concept, which can be easily co-opted and used for the most antagonistic purposes. For left-wing historians, American freedom was achieved through the sacrifice of indigenous people, legally sanctioned by the Supreme Court in the so-called Indian cases at the end of the nineteenth century.[9] As Peter Fitzpatrick puts it, the '"momentous" national settlement depended upon an explicitly counterrevolutionary and explicitly antidemocratic exclusion and sacrifice of Indian peoples, and in so doing they created the racial un-Constitution of the United States'.[10]

Woodrow Wilson, a key influence on twentieth-century American foreign policy, claimed that only the United States had the military power and moral authority to bring self-determination and democracy to the world. But the rhetoric of the benevolent back-seat driver was regularly accompanied by direct conquest and occupation of foreign lands. Areas of Mexico, Haiti, the Dominican Republic, Panama, Nicaragua and Cuba were occupied during the nineteenth century. In the most audacious act of imperialism, the Philippines alongside Puerto Rico were annexed in 1899. The Americans hailed the occupation as an advance in global freedom. But the Filipinos resisted for a decade after the Spanish–American war. They were subjected to extreme torture practices and many

---

7 See among others, Noam Chomsky, *Military Humanism* (London, Pluto, 1999); Burbach and Tarbell, op. cit.

8 For Michael Hardt and Antonio Negri, freedom and expansion are the characteristics of the Constitution of the United States. These give it a great advantage over the more formalistic and less mobile European ones.

9 *Downes* v. *Bidwell* (1901) 182 US 244.

10 Peter Fitzpatrick, 'The Immanence of Empire' in Jodi Dean and Paul Passavant, *Empire's New Clothes* (New York, Routledge 2004), 50–1.

civilians were killed in anti-insurgency operations.[11] According to some estimates up to one million people died, but no official count was kept of casualties. 'Only by denying reality and characterising the Filipinos as "niggers, barbarians and savages" could the Americans rationalise the horror of the Philippines'.[12] As Bernard Porter, a friendly historian of empire puts it, 'these do not seem to be the actions of a standard-bearer of "freedom"'.[13]

For its contemporary critics, the United States is the greatest 'rogue state', far more powerful and dangerous than the ever-changing components of the 'axis of evil'.[14] As Eric Hobsbawm, put it, 'previous empires did not aim at global domination and none believed themselves to be invulnerable'.[15] The usually restrained Richard Falk goes further. He asks rhetorically whether empire is turning to fascism and concludes that 'the dangers of global fascism cannot be discounted as imaginary or alarmist'.[16] While they disagree on almost everything else, both promoters and critics of empire concur that its colours are American.

2   The *humanitarian imperialists* or 'muscular liberals'. They are exemplified by Michael Ignatieff, who has consistently tried to pull America from its state of denial:

> What word but empire describes the awesome thing that America is becoming? It is the only nation that polices the world through five global military commands; maintains more than a million men and women at arms on four continents; deploys carrier battle groups on watch in every ocean; guarantees the survival of countries from Israel to South Korea; drives the wheels of global trade and commerce; and fills the hearts and minds of an entire planet with its dreams and desires.[17]

Ignatieff was responding to Donald Rumsfeld's famous statement that 'we don't do empire' and to President Bush's 'America has no empire to extend

---

11   For recent histories of American imperialism see Bernard Porter, *Empire and Superempire* (New Haven, CT, Yale University Press, 2006), Chapter 2; Fred Anderson and Andrew Cayton, *The Dominion of War* (London, Atlantic Books, 2005), Chapters 2, 4, 5 and 7.
12   Burbach and Tarbell op. cit., 41.
13   Bernard Porter, op.cit., 90.
14   Derrida, op. cit.; Noam Chomsky, *Rogue States* (London, Pluto, 2002).
15   Eric Hobsbawm, 'After the Winning of the War', *Le Monde Diplomatique*, June 2003, 6.
16   Richard Falk, *The Declining World Order* (New York, Routledge, 2004), 251.
17   Michael Ignatieff, 'The Burden', *New York Times Magazine*, 5 January 2003.

or utopia to establish'.[18] America, claim its officials, rather than subjugating people and states, liberates from tyranny, spreads freedom and democracy and enforces the human rights of the downtrodden of the earth. Compelling evidence shows, however, that the United States has been involved in expansionist projects of one or the other type throughout its history. The rather incredible denials reflect a wider tendency in American ideology. The United States was the first country to declare independence from the British Empire, the first modern state to build its identity on revolution and liberation from colonial rule rather than on a pre-existing or invented national or ethnic tradition. Anti-colonial and anti-imperialist credentials have always had a place in the ideology of the Republic and inspired the American left. But at the same time, American history is full of violence, war and persistent excursions into imperial adventures. As a historian of empire recently put it, 'the idea of America as an "anti-imperialist" power, in fact, is a fairly recent construction, and has everything to do with the bad odour that came to surround the word in the twentieth century'.[19]

Ignatieff's answer to the historical and ideological problems of imperialism is 'empire *lite*', the only way of protecting human rights and humanitarian values in a brutal world. A '*lite*' or informal empire, unlike previous examples, involves a hegemonic centre without colonies, 'a global sphere of influence without the burden of direct administration and the risks of daily policing'.[20] Empire *lite* is benevolent. Benign imperialism started in the 'humanitarian interventions' in Bosnia, Kosovo and East Timor at the end of the twentieth century. Its *raison d'être* is to save people from tyranny, to prevent and stop atrocities and to spread freedom and democracy all over the world.

Priorities changed, however, after the 9/11 attacks and security became the main concern of the great powers. The United States must consolidate its global hegemony in order to quell the 'menace of the barbarians', who no longer content to attack their own have turned against the metropolis. 'Barbarians' are everywhere. According to Ignatieff, they are the outcome of the rise and partial failure of human rights, the semi-official ideology of the Western world. Human rights introduced the principle of self-determination and promoted decolonisation. But this process largely failed and led to the proliferation of failed and rogue states and assorted barbarians. These threats create the need to impose order and rule on

18 Rumsfeld quoted in Porter, op. cit., 1; Bush quoted in Falk, op. cit., 198.
19 Porter, 64.
20 Michael Ignatieff, *Empire Lite* (London, Vintage, 2003).

empire's borders (this is an *imperium* à la Rome) through muscular and effective responses. But as human rights and self-determination do not allow the long occupation of failed states or zones, the humanitarian empire *lite* opts for a new form of tutelage called 'nation-building'. 'Nation-building is the kind of imperialism you get in a human rights era, a time when great powers believe simultaneously in the rights of small nations to govern themselves and in their own right to rule the world.'[21] The idea is straightforward. After the occupation force has restored order and stabilised the security situation, international institutions and NGOs (known as the 'internationals')[22] are called in to run the country and tutor a local elite in the ways of decent rule. Once this has been achieved, elections will be called and the local elite, now with full democratic legitimacy, will guarantee the interests of the imperial centre and prevent the place from erupting into anarchy and violence again. Empire *lite* is empire on the cheap 'ruling the world without putting in place any new imperial architecture – new military alliances, new legal institutions, new international development organisms'.[23]

Moral righteousness is central to the actions of the humanitarian empire. The Americans, because of their colonial past, need, more than others, good motives and a moral vocation to accompany imperial adventures. The millenarian aspirations of the nascent union started early. John Winthrop wrote in 1630 that the Puritan settlements of New England were a 'Citty upon a Hill with the eies of all people . . . upon us'.[24] America acquired right from the start the mythology of the 'elect nation', a megalomaniac delusion that has followed closely and bolstered all kinds of nationalism, despite the obvious contradiction of every nation believing to be God's (or spirit's, history's, etc.) only choice. But while the Jews, the Greeks or the French can draw succour and (real or imagined) inspiration from tales of old glories and disasters, the claim to fame for a new and panspermic nation like the United States could only be conceptual. Its glory does not hail from its long historical provenance, its ancient marvels and sorrows or its genetic line but from its ideas and creations:

---

21   Ibid. 106.
22   See the insightful presentation of the 'internationals' in David Rieff, *A Bed for the Night* (London, Vintage, 2002); Alex de Waal, *Famine Crimes. Politics and the Disaster Relief Industry in Africa* (Oxford, James Currey, 2002) For a hilarious portrayal of the pleasures and woes of peacekeepers, NGO officers and other 'internationals', see Kenneth Cain, Heidi Postlewait and Andrew Thomson, *Emergency Sex* (London, Ebury Press, 2004).
23   Ignatieff, op. cit., 13.
24   Quoted in Porter, op. cit., 102.

the constitution that mummifies for ever its foundational myth and principles, the flag that brings together its many ethnicities that have little in common. More importantly, its organisational principles: liberty ('we are a free country'), capitalist dynamism and prosperity, the 'American way'. Such extravagant claims may be a way of concealing the deep rifts in American society and creating meaning and value where none exists; but they can be easily turned into universal axioms.[25] For Benjamin Franklin, the American cause was 'the cause of all mankind';[26] for Woodrow Wilson, 'American principles and policies are those of forward-looking men and women everywhere, of every modern nation, of every enlightened community. They are the principles of mankind and must prevail'.[27] But as the American historians Fred Anderson and Andrew Cayton put it, the 'equation of freedom with the nation – this image of the United States as liberator rather than conqueror – justified interventionism without losing any of its racist, ethnocentric edge when twentieth-century Americans abandoned empire-building by territorial acquisition in favour of hegemonic imperialism'.[28]

Kosovo, Afghanistan, Iraq are the contemporary descendants of both noble principles and imperial destiny. For Michael Ignatieff, empire is the 'last hope for democracy and stability alike' in Iraq and the rest of the region.[29] Humanitarian invasions spread democracy, freedom and human rights and introduce failed and rogue states (forcibly if necessary) to the benefits of modernisation, international trade and technological innovation. Moral good and national interests are fortunately in synch. This is what distinguishes the American from previous empires: it provides global security without oppression or exploitation. Joining rescue and security, empire *lite* faces the ongoing brutality and cruelty of the barbarian part of humanity in a morally acceptable way. From sanctions to limited wars, from occupations to nation-building and the international administration of culprit and failed states, the aim is to protect (us) and save and correct (the others).

3   A different conclusion, however, which shares many of the premises of humanitarian imperialism, is found in postmodern *cosmopolitanism*. Cosmopolitanism, the preferred concept and institutional blueprint of

---

25   Greil Marcus, *The Shape of Thngs to Come: Prophecy and the American Voice* (London, Faber, 2006).

26   Quoted in Kagan, op. cit., 88.

27   Quoted in Bacevich, op. cit., 225.

28   Fred Anderson and Andrew Cayton, *The Dominion of War: Empire and Conflict in America, 1500–2000* (London, Atlantic, 2005), 423.

29   Michael Ignatieff, 'The Burden', *New York Times Magazine*, 5 January 2003, 24.

contemporary liberalism, accepts the need for a morally guided global legal and institutional framework, while categorically rejecting the hegemonic claims of imperial power. Earlier versions motivated by the fear of world catastrophe unleashed by nuclear weapons called for the establishment of global political institutions with a constitutional framework. A strengthened United Nations in the role of a limited world government was a step in this direction.[30] A world government was seen as the natural next step after the passing of the epoch of the nation-state with its powerful sovereign claims. The hegemonic centre will be replaced in this approach by a benign world government, which will benefit from the weakening of national sovereignty.

A more realistic cosmopolitan approach has developed recently.[31] Under the headings of global democracy, the rule of law and justice, it advocates the weakening but not abolition of the state form and the strengthening of international and transnational institutions short of a world government. State sovereignty should be further weakened and subjected to moral and legal norms. Suggested measures include strengthening the UN and other international institutions; international criminal liability for the actions of political and military leaders; improved standards of accountability and democracy to judge state policies; the extension of the rule of law to international relations; developing globalisation from below, involving NGOs and civil society in state and international decision making; promoting cosmopolitan, normative or substantive democracy.[32] Regional institutions and federations should ensure compliance with constitutional arrangements and defend and promote the role of public services. As Richard Falk puts it, the world order of liberal cosmopolitanism is 'no longer state-centric, although the role of states remains crucial, even if reconfigured in light of legal and ethical norms'.[33]

The cosmopolitans supported the early humanitarian wars of the new world order. But the rise of the neo-conservatives in Washington, the aggressive American posture after 9/11 and the war in Iraq led many to change sides. Cosmopolitans emphasise the radical nature of the break

---

30 Grenville Clark and Louis Sohn, *World Peace Through Law* (Cambridge, MA, Harvard University Press, 3rd edn, 1966); James Yunker, *World Union on the Horizon* (Lanham, MD, University Press of America, 1993); D. Heater, *World Citizenship and Government* (London, Palgrave, 1996).

31 See Daniele Archibugi and Daniel Held, eds., *Cosmopolitan Democracy* (Cambridge, Polity, 1995); David Held, *Democracy and Global Order* (Cambridge, Polity, 1995); Daniele Archibugi, ed., *Debating Cosmopolitics* (London, Verso, 2003).

32 Falk, Chapters 3 and 4; Held, op. cit.

33 Falk, op. cit, 28.

from previous policies and lament the missed opportunity of strengthening international institutions and developing civil society, which had started in the 1990s. The election of President Bush Jr and his response to the terrorist attacks was the turning point. Two separate phases of the new world order can therefore be distinguished. The humanitarian cosmopolitan stage under Presidents Bush Sr and Clinton started morphing into a second imperialist stage. Richard Falk goes furthest by admitting that 'the idealism of the benevolent school has been incorporated into the refashioning of the imperial project by the Bush leadership'.[34] But the more 'muscular' liberals, represented by Christopher Hitchens and the so-called 'Euston Manifesto', do not distinguish between the two. Kosovo and Iraq are part of the same project of security and freedom. The admittedly short distance between imperialists and cosmopolitans is almost totally eliminated.

4   The *imperialism of globalisation*. The first sustained critique of imperialism was the offspring of Marxist political economy at the beginning of the twentieth century. Lenin's influential essay *Imperialism, the Highest Stage of Capitalism* argued that imperialism becomes the dominant political form when capitalism enters its monopoly stage. At this point, market competition gives way to monopolies controlled by finance capital, which need to expand outwards once their domestic markets are saturated. Their insatiable hunger for profit makes them want to control foreign markets in order to secure outlets for investment in raw materials, manufacturing and finance. As a result, imperialist wars for the domination of regions, countries and markets break out among the main metropolitan powers. Endless conflict and colonialism make imperialism a particularly aggressive and intensely exploitative historical stage. Lenin's hope was that world revolution would bring imperialism to an end. Revolution missed its rendezvous with history, however. Old style imperialism and colonialism came to a pause in the second part of the twentieth century. Decolonisation, the rise of the Third World and of international institutions put imperialism and its critique out of fashion alongside the other 'grand narratives' of historical progress.

The main aim of American foreign policy, in the second half of the twentieth century, was to protect its political and commercial hegemony. During the cold war, intervention in the affairs of satellite countries became endemic. As the self-proclaimed leader of the free world, the United States used both covert operations and military force to impose anti-communist regimes and obedience to its policy priorities around the world. Without

34   Ibid. 248.

directly occupying foreign countries, the Americans asserted the power to decide who was fit to rule countries within its informal empire's sphere of influence. This period is characterised by Henry Kissinger's statement on the eve of Salvador Allende's electoral victory in Chile: 'I don't see why we need to stand idly by and watch a country go communist due to the irresponsibility of its own people.'[35] Kissinger represented a conservative realism prepared to make deals with all types of regimes and brutality as long as they served perceived national interests. It is general knowledge that the United States plotted covertly to remove democratically elected governments who were not sufficiently pro-American, supported dictators (they did both in the case of Greece), backed terrorist activities against its enemies, violated many norms of international law and became involved in many local and two major wars in Korea and Vietnam, which left millions dead.

The centrality of political economy, albeit in a looser postmodern form, was reasserted in the 1990s when 'globalization' became the ubiquitous economic-cultural companion of the 'end of history' thesis. According to the leftist critique of the political economy of globalisation, the neo-liberal policies of the 'Washington consensus' adopted by the World Bank and the IMF have weakened the moral and political factors, which had mitigated the harshness of capitalism.[36] Socialism had offered capitalism the motive to develop a human face at the cost of narrowing profit margins. After 1989, however, global capitalism abandoned its earlier moral pretensions associated with state responsibility and returned to a virtually unregulated form. International financial institutions, totally committed to the dominant neo-liberal ideology, have imposed a package of measures on developing countries which include strict fiscal austerity, monetary controls, unencumbered capital flows, privatisation, deregulation and unlimited openness to Western investment. Income inequalities have increased, as a result, further impoverishing the poor in the developing world and cutting expenditure in public services. State action has been replaced by exclusive reliance on the profit motive, the promotion of efficiency and productivity and unbending hostility towards socialist measures and labour protections.

The Marxist-inspired left has understandably emphasised the economic and cultural aspects of the new world order. The recent militarist turn is

---

35   Roger Burbach, *The Pinochet Affair* (London, Zed Books, 2003), 10.
36   Adam Gearey, *Globalisation and Law* (Lanham, MD, Rowman & Littlefield, 2005), Chapter 3 and *passim.*

often diagnosed as a brief and even unnecessary episode associated with the strange priorities of the neo-conservative clique in Washington, which are not always compatible with the interests of multinational corporations and finance capital. In an extremely interesting reinterpretation of the theory of imperialism, David Harvey has revived the Marxist separa-tion of the political from the economic realm, distinguishing between the logic of state and territory and the logic of capital accumulation. Harvey interprets recent history as a dialectical interplay between capital and state, two logics that often diverge and even come into conflict. While the logic of capital tends to dominate the imperialist phase of capitalism, in certain circumstances state priorities take precedence. According to Harvey, this is the case with the current neoconservative geopolitical vision. Occupation of Iraq and control of the Middle East secures a bridgehead on the Eurasian landmass separating Europe from Russia and China and placing the US in 'military and geostrategic position to control the whole globe militarily and, through oil, economically'.[37] However, the importance of political economy remains central and acts as a useful correction for the state-centric approach of most theorists of empire. 'A plausible case can be made that [the Vietnam and Iraq wars] inhibit rather than enhance the fortunes of capital', argues Harvey.[38] Empires are vulnerable to overstretch, as Paul Kennedy predicted, and are overdetermined by the priorities of the dominant economic forces. Even the all-powerful American empire may soon become counter-productive for the imperialists, in which case we may go back to a more peaceful order of capitalist exploitation.

5   According to Michael Hardt and Antonio Negri, the failure of the revolution, against Lenin's prediction, led to Empire, 'the last instance of a successful restructuring of capitalism under the impact of war and rebellion'.[39] The left has always had its utopias. Hardt and Negri's *Empire* is a strange blueprint for a *cosmopolitan communism*.[40] *Empire* was a publishing and cultural phenomenon at the beginning of the twenty-first century and marked the return of grand political theory. It has been extravagantly compared with the *Communist Manifesto* and revived a sense of excitement and vigour sorely lacking in recent political theory of the cosmopolitan type. Hardt and Negri have documented and denounced the emergence of a new type of empire which, unlike European imperialism,

37   David Harvey, *The New Imperialism* (Oxford, Oxford University Press, 2005), 199.
38   Ibid. 30.
39   Gopal Balakrishnan, 'Introduction' in Gopal Balakrishnan ed., *Debating Empire* (London, Verso, 2003), x.
40   Hardt and Negri, op. cit.

extends a decentred and deterritorialising apparatus of rule that incorporates the entire globe within its open frontiers. While empire does not have a metropolitan centre or capital, its constitution follows the expansionist and democratic constitutionalism of the United States.

It is true that the American nation is united more by concepts than by its past glories and disasters. Liberty, despite its notorious ambiguity, is globally a more marketable brand than Athena's duel with Poseidon, the story of Romulus and Remus or God's covenant with Israel. The Americans are the 'universal' nation because their foundational myth is not predominantly narrative but conceptual and open-ended. They are not just chosen by God, history or destiny like every other nation and nationalist in the world. They have elected themselves, in an act of will that does not describe a moment of divine choice or providence but proscribes: its motto is a command and promise, first to itself (the autonomy of the moderns) and then to the rest of the world (the postmodern imperialism): let us go out there (the West, Mexico, the Philippines, Iraq, etc.) and make everyone free, make them little Americans. American conquests are seen as 'a collective sacrifice in the service of human liberty . . . any rejection of their nation as a rejection of liberty itself'.[41] It is a vision that unites the political spectrum. Jeanne Kirkpatrick claimed that 'the US is not simply a great power but also a cluster of ideals. And by a marvellous even divine coincidence, pursuit of these ideals can only enhance the country's power, wealth and security'.[42] Madeleine Albright thought that America is 'the indispensable nation'.[43] For Condoleezza Rice, 'American values are universal'. When President Bush Jr finally introduced God into the act, combining divine calling and earthly mission in the claim that America is 'chosen by God and commissioned by history to be the model to the world', dominant American ideology reached maturity.[44] These hubristic claims do not seem to worry Hardt and Negri. Unlike other leftists, they argue that empire is not an imposition from above, but the result of the reaction of dominant economic and political forces to the actions of the world proletariat or citizenry, called the multitude. They rather implausibly hope that the same multitude can transform the imperial dispensation into a cosmopolitan communism, utilising the positive aspects of globalisation and turning them to the cause of liberation.

41   Anderson and Cayton, 423.
42   Tom Farer, 'The interplay of Domestic Politics, human Rights and US Foreign Policy' (forthcoming, on file with author).
43   Quoted in Porter, op. cit., 103.
44   Ibid. 102, 103.

This brief review of the expanding bibliography indicates that empire, imperialism and cosmopolitanism dominate debates in contemporary history and politics. Whether approved or denounced, empire is a key organising concept in academic discussions about our current travails. The theories briefly reviewed here place the current state of the world on a line between benign cosmopolitanism and aggressive imperialism. Most belong methodologically to the realist or pragmatic school of politics, an approach that occasionally resembles a sophisticated type of journalism. Most, however, agree on certain minimum facts. It is an indisputable fact that a new world order was ushered after the end of the cold war. It is undeniable that the United States is the sole superpower and the hegemonic centre in the new order. It is also true that resistance to the hegemon's actions has been developing in many forms and places, including the academy, albeit in a rather modest form. Most commentators agree that the American refusal to admit its past and present imperialism is an acute case of being in denial. It is finally true that many of the current trends have been around in some form or other for a very long time. The provenance of empire and cosmopolitanism is firmly located in political history and the history of ideas to warrant the claim that they are radical innovations. Empire is as old as Persia and China and, cosmopolitanism has been around since the Cynics and the Stoics in the fourth century BC.

Continuing the argument about the nationality and nature of empire does not add much to the extensive literature. The geopolitical concerns of the new world order, its economic policies, comparisons with previous empires and imperialisms form part of its background. But the interest of this book in empire is different. This is not a further addition to the burgeoning literature of *empirology* but a contribution to the history of ideas, political philosophy and jurisprudence in an *age of emerging empire*.

The choice of names or epithets to describe phenomena (empire, imperialism, cosmopolitanism) is not innocent. All nomination carries strong normative and political choices, all name-giving determines in part the trajectory of the thing or being that comes into existence in the act of naming.[45] Rather than denoting an objective reality, the name chosen and the associated – contested – concept indicate a political decision and a normative preference. The political judgement of this book is that the differences and distinctions between empire, imperialism and cosmopolitanism are smaller, the continuities greater, than some of their advocates admit. Major historical breaks, life-turning events become such only if people act on that basis, if they read back into them an

---

45 Costas Douzinas, 'Derrida's Eulogy' in Douzinas, ed., *Adieu Derrida* (London, Palgrave Macmillan, 2007), 1.

epoch-making character. There is energy behind the project of an American empire, while cosmopolitanism is still the concern of a few European intellectuals. I do not want to contribute to the extravagant claims or normative designs of current intellectual fashions. As a result, this book uses the terms 'empire' (a contested normative account), 'new world order' (a neutral description, if the 'new' is ever neutral or new), hegemony (a somewhat sophisticated imperialism, deriving from hegemon or ruler in Greek) and the 'new times' (a chronological periodisation for the post-1989 world with all the ambiguities of historicism) interchangeably, unless otherwise indicated, to indicate that they refer both a historical period and the socio-political arrangements of our age. Cosmopolitanism is different. It belongs to one of the noblest Western traditions, that of utopia. To acquire its imaginary power and rediscover its classical radical urge, it must be freed from its contemporary champions, who have turned it into a rather dull institutional blueprint.

The aim of this book is to examine the normative characteristics, the political philosophy and the metaphysics of our age. What conception of community and of self do political developments at the international level reflect? Have new legal institutions, practices and norms developed? Is a humanitarian norm the core principle of international law? Have these institutions contributed to the imperial configuration of the new times? Has the new order created its own concepts of right and wrong, of truth and falsity, of sovereignty and right? Can violence and war be put at the service of moral ends? Is sovereignty retreating from the world stage to be replaced by the normative demands of humanity? The overarching concern is with the sense of the new world order. What are the sources of meaning and value of our age? Do they indicate the rise of a global cosmopolitan community? Let me indicate six central characteristics of the emerging order, which are explored in the second part of the book both in terms of their history (cosmopolitanism, just war) and in their present transformations:

1   The new world order is moral-legal. Human rights, freedom and democracy provide the justification for the new configuration of political, economic and military power and the just cause for war. The idea that empires are benevolent, that they follow moral imperatives, that they spread the good (Christianity, civilisation, freedom, human rights or whatever particular ideology is supposed to represent goodness in a period) is an integral part of their history. The Spaniards freed the Indians from superstition and brought Christianity, rational government and modernity. The French were the tool of the universal spirit, Napoleon reason on horseback, according to Hegel. The British claimed that the African conquest was partly motivated by a desire to abolish slavery and to promote good governance

and Christianity. The Americans too, 'like all imperialists', writes Michael Mann, 'are self-righteous. The politicians utter impeccable ideals of freedom, democracy and human rights for the world, and they promise it material plenty'[46] (Chapters 7 and 8).

2   Modern and postmodern cosmopolitanism is presented as the evolving institutional structure (at least at its first stage) and the formal ideology of the world order. It promises the end of wars and the dawn of an age of perpetual peace. But its classical history invests cosmopolitanism with the radical energy of utopia (Chapters 7 and 12).

3   International law, despite its existential crisis and the apparent disagreements of its practitioners, has undertaken the role of codifying and 'constitutionalising' the normative foundations of empire (Chapter 9).

4   While the removal of force and violence and a just peace are its alleged ends, the new order is drowned in the endless violence of a 'long war' presented as a just war. Force and violence are the main tools of imperial operations and, at the same time, the symbolic and imaginary principles of the new order (Chapter 10).

5   The hegemonic power concentrates overwhelming material force (economic, military and technological). The new order is built on a principle of imperial omnipotence and structural asymmetry between imperial centre and the rest of the world (Chapter 10).

6   The sovereignty of states and the territorial principle, which characterised the international order of modernity, are gradually weakened. But sovereignty is not withering away as the cosmopolitans and Hardt and Negri claim. No sense of world community (imperial or cosmopolitan) has developed; instead lost sovereignty becomes condensed in a hegemonic centre. We may be witnessing the historical novelty of the emergence of an emperor in search of a fully fledged empire (Chapter 11).

In J.M. Coetzee's wonderful novel *Waiting for the Barbarians*, a local magistrate in a remote town at empire's frontier becomes gradually disenchanted by the heavy-handed measures taken by the security forces against the 'barbarians' on the other side of the border. These nomadic and peaceful people pose no threat, but the colonel in charge of security presents them as a mortal danger to empire. He persecutes them and brutally tortures and kills those he arrests in the public square. The distressed magistrate hides a 'barbarian' girl mutilated from torture and eventually returns her to her kin. When his nemesis, the colonel, finds out, he tortures and humiliates the magistrate in

---

46   Michael Mann, *Incoherent Empire* (London, Verso, 2005), 100.

the most atrocious way. Removed from office, emptied of identity, full of a gradually receding hatred and close to death, the humane magistrate, like Kafka's man from the country, finally realises the truth:

> I was not, as I like to think, the indulgent pleasure-loving opposite of the cold, rigid colonel. I was the lie that empire tells itself when times are easy, he the truth the empire tells when the harsh winds blow. Two sides of imperial rule, no more, no less.[47]

---

47   J.M. Coetzee, *Waiting for the Barbarians* (London, Secker & Warburg, 1980), 135.

Chapter 7

Cosmopolitanism ancient, modern, postmodern

The advocates of the new world order cannot match its characteristics with any of the set blueprints of political theory. Empire and imperialism in particular have too many negative connotations and, despite clear similarities with the present dispensation, cannot be sufficiently purified for use in a nominally postcolonial world. Cosmopolitanism, an ancient philosophical tradition, has therefore been revived and turned into a shorthand for the (partly actual partly hoped for) institutional and constitutional design of the new order. Its post-modern promoters promise and prophesise the end of wars and the dawn of an age of perpetual peace, if the cosmopolitan constitution is fully implemented. A main difference between (emerging) cosmopolitanism and the post-Second World War order is the elevation of a strong moral component with a weak legal gloss – human rights – into the ruling ideology. At the same time, the last twenty years have witnessed continuous violence, war and conquest. As in most millenarianism, extensive destruction and pillage precedes the promised land of peace and plenty. This and the next chapter turn to the main ideological components of the emerging empire, first cosmopolitanism then human rights.

Ancient cosmopolitanism

'The important fact now is that the human condition has itself become cosmopolitan'.[1] As a statement of fact, Ulrich Beck's assertion must count as audacious and counter-intuitive. Is cosmopolitanism the next step in the inexorable rise of globalisation and the decline of the nation-state? Is it the only alternative to developing Empire? The *cosmo-polites* is the citizen of the world; cosmopolitanism a world federation, a world state or a global

1 Ulrich Beck, *Cosmopolitan Vision* (Cambridge, Polity, 2006), 2.

'cosmopolitical democracy' that controls the use of force, polices the peace among its constituents members and guarantees human rights to all. Can cosmopolitan law and institutions lead a better, more just and humane arrangement for our globalised world? Let us have a look at the history of cosmopolitanism.

Cosmos and *polis* are the two key concepts in Greek political philosophy. The classical Greek cosmos was the arrangement of the *dike* (order) of the world. It included the *physis* (nature) of all beings, the *ethos* of social mores, the *nomos* of customs and laws and, most importantly, the *logos* or rational foundation of all that exists. The cosmos was a closed but harmonious and ordered universe. Entities were arranged in a hierarchical way, each holding its unique and differential place within the overall scheme according to its proper degree of perfection, 'at the top the incorruptible imponderable luminous spheres, at the bottom, the heavy, opaque material bodies'.[2] The purpose of a being determined its nature and its place in the order of things. The aims, purposes and ends of the cosmos and of things and beings could be achieved politically, in the *polis*, the city-state, always in conjunction with others. The citizens acquired their natural (which was also moral) perfection only in the company of others, in the *agora* of Athens and Corinth. Conversely, a city was just if it created the conditions for its citizens to attain their full nature and achieve their purpose. *Cosmos* and *polis* or *physis* and *nomos* were intricately linked but variable. Cities became just and citizens virtuous by following their individual purpose and realising their unique nature. No common law linked the city-states and no common humanity their citizens.

The dramatic mutation introduced by the Stoics changed the variable nature of *physis* and *nomos*. *Nomos* (law) was expanded and became the bond bringing the universe together. Universal and even divine *logos* (reason) united the wise and virtuous; its sacred character communed to its followers a sublime pathos. The Stoics believed in a golden age, governed by unwritten laws whose content promoted the innate equality and unity of all in a rational empire of love. 'An extremely anthropocentric, yet divinely sublime, nature governed by necessity was held over positive society and became the sole criterion of valid law.'[3] Admittedly, this early universalism was not predominantly political. The Stoics preached the superiority of a private life of

---

2 Blandine Barret-Kriegel, *Les Droits de l'homme et le droit naturel* (Paris, PUF, 1989), 46. It should be emphasised here that this cosmology is intrinsically linked with the inegalitarian nature of classical natural right and ancient societies. For Aristotle, slavery was natural and therefore not an affront to natural right.
3 Ernst Bloch, *Natural Law and Human Dignity* (Dennis Schmidt, trans.) (Cambridge, MA, MIT Press, 1988),13.

tranquillity and reflection and practised *ataraxia* (imperturbability), the supreme duty of self-control over passions and irrationality. Their passion against passions even transgressed class divides. One major early Stoic philosopher was a slave (Epictetus), another an emperor (Marcus Aurelius).

While the Stoics were not particularly interested in state constitutions, they made a lasting contribution to political thought. Zeno, the founder of the *Stoa* (a brightly coloured arcade where he taught), a Cypriot who taught in Athens in the first half of the third century, is considered as the inventor of cosmopolitanism. His *Republic* is the only sustained work of Stoic political philosophy. It has survived in fragments quoted by later writers intent in either revising or attacking the master. The main concern of later philosophers, when referring to Zeno's *Republic,* was the apparent affinity between Zeno's theories and those of the Cynics, as expressed in particular by the natural philosophy of Diogenes. The *Republic* is the most complete discussion of the Stoic theory of the *polis*. Zeno, following Plato, presented a quasi-constitution for his ideal city. He suggested, among other radical ideas, the abolition of formal education, marriage, temples, court houses and gymnasia, the rejection of money and other conventional institutions, the holding of property in common and the adoption of a simple common dress for men and women. Eros was the republic's God; citizens were encouraged to form strong erotic relationships and sexual attraction was accorded a moral element.[4] As Malcolm Schofield has shown persuasively, Zeno's *Republic* was seriously censored by the later Stoics Cassius and Athenodorus, through whose writings we have partial knowledge of the book. They intensely disliked and tried to remove any 'trace of Cynicism' from the key text of a major Stoic because it was regarded as 'antinomian'.[5] The worry of the latecomers is understandable. Zeno attacked the key institutions and conventions of the city, including religion, law and money, but made no detailed positive suggestions.[6] He argued that customs, conventions and institutions should be replaced by eros and the exercise of virtue. Poverty, frugality and 'incivility to kings and their ambassadors in particular' was Zeno's way.[7] Only the wise and virtuous are real men, free citizens, good friends and passionate lovers. They transcend 'the tawdry demi-monde of the many parochial cities with their ethnic divisions and prejudices, wars, slavery, traditional families and conventional private property'.[8]

---

4   Malcolm Schofield, 'The City of Love', in *The Stoic Idea of the City* (Cambridge, Cambridge University Press, 1999), Chapter 2.

5   Ibid. 10.

6   M.I. Finley, 'Utopianism Ancient and Modern' in *The Use and Abuse of History* (London, Chatto & Windus, 1975), 188.

7   Schofield, op. cit., 149.

8   Finley, 241–2.

Zeno's *Republic*, while not explicitly cosmopolitan, was the first extensive discussion of the *polis* in the context of *cosmopolis*. The influence of Diogenes of Sinopi, the infamous Cynic, is evident. Diogenes was reputedly the first to describe himself as a *cosmopolites*, when he famously stated that he does not feel at home anywhere except in the cosmos itself. Stoic beliefs about the city developed as an interpretation of Diogenes' phrase.[9] For Diogenes, no actually existing city or law is real; the only correct Republic is that of the cosmos. Following these ideas, Diogenes described himself as 'cityless, homeless, without a country, poor, a wanderer, living life from day to day'.[10] As Moses Hadas put it, Diogenes' cosmopolitanism was 'the proud assertion of a ragged exile's consciousness of his own worth in the face of a bourgeois society which scorned him'.[11] Crates, his disciple and successor with the staff and ragged cloak, gave a clearer description of the cosmopolis: '[Crates] said that ignominy and poverty were his country, which Fortune could not take captive, and Diogenes was his city, which envy could not plot against.'[12]

Plutarch, writing some four centuries after Zeno at the height of the Roman Empire, is full of praise for the cosmopolitan outlook. According to Plutarch, Zeno preached:

> that all inhabitants of this world of ours should not live differentiated by their respective rules of justice in separate cities and communities, but that we should consider all men to be of one community and one polity, and that we should have a common life and an order common to us all, even as a herd that feeds together and shares the pasturage of a common field. This Zeno wrote, giving shape to a dream or, as it were, a shadowy picture of a well-ordered and philanthropic commonwealth.[13]

Plutarch's enthusiasm for Zeno, despite his dislike of Stoicism, appears in a chapter of *Moralia* praising Alexander the Great, presented as the man who brought together all men everywhere into one body and made them consider the whole earth as their fatherland. Most contemporary commentators, however, consider these passages unreliable. 'The League of Nations Alexander'

9   Schofield, op. cit., 64.
10 Diogenes Laertius, *Lives of Eminent Philosophers* (2 vols, H.S. Long, ed.) (Oxford, Oxford University Press, 1961), VI. 38.
11 Moses Hadas, 'From Nationalism to Cosmopolitanism in the Greco-Roman World' 4/1 *Journal of the History of Ideas* 105 (1943), 108.
12 Diogenes Laertius, *Lives*, VI, 93.
13 Plutarch, 'On the Fortune or Virtue of Alexander' in *Moralia*, vol. IV (A de Selincourt trans.) (London, Heinemann, 1957), 329 (6).

is a figment of Plutarch and of contemporary scholars' imagination serving political agendas of their respective periods.[14] The Macedonian empire was the first however to bring together imperial designs and cosmopolitan ideals, even if the latter could be seen as post facto rationalisations of conquest and imperialism.

The late Stoics repeated and modified Diogenes' and Zeno's ideas and, as a result, the cosmopolitan outlook started taking philosophical root. In various fragments, the earthly cities are described as not real because they are not ruled by justice and law. Only the *cosmopolis* will allow its citizens to develop the necessary sophistication of wisdom and virtue. Zeno's emphasis on virtue and love, his attack on laws, customs and institutions led Clemes to state that the only real city is the cosmos:

> The Stoics say that the universe (*ouranos* or *oikoumene* in Greek) is in the proper sense a *polis*, but that those here on earth are not – they are called cities, but they are not really. For a city or a *demos* (people) is something morally good, an organisation or group of men administered by law and of great refinement (or urban sophistication – *asteion*).[15]

Cosmopolitanism was critical and even antinomian precisely because the *nomoi* and institutions of the age were falling far short of the ideals of justice and law. The Stoics taught that 'just and virtuous conduct cannot be defined by the laws and mores of the state of which one happens to be a citizen'.[16] In this sense, they are the first legal critics but also the first utopian thinkers of the Western world. As Schofield remarks, 'Zeno's *Republic* was already regarded as incorrigibly utopian in classical antiquity'.[17] The alternative to the polis is the cosmos, not as a better arrangement of institutions but as the place where gods and men gather together and laws express the natural integrity of the relationship between human and divine. There is a city of Cecrops (the founder of Athens) and a city of Zeus. The polis of Zeus, the city in the sky, is not situated in any particular place; it can be everywhere and nowhere. Logos and

---

14 Peter Green, *Alexander of Macedon* (Oxford, University of California Press, 1991), 484. Green attacks Sir William Tarn, who declared that Alexander was 'the first man known who contemplated the brotherhood of man or the unity of mankind' ('Alexander the Great and the Unity of Mankind' in G.T. Griffith, ed., *Alexander the Great: The Main Problems* (Cambridge, Heffer, 1966), 266. Green argues that Tarn tried to present Alexander as a benign cosmopolitan because he disliked his homosexuality and imperialism.

15 Clement of Alexandria, *Opera* (4 vols, W. Dindorf, ed.) (Oxford, 1869), IV 26, SVF III 327.

16 Derek Heater, *World Citizenship and Government* (London, Palgrave, 1996), 26.

17 Schofield, op. cit., 147.

eros are its foundation against the artifice of customs, corrupt laws and institutions. Its citizens are errant, nomadic, today they would be refugees, outsiders, migrants. They dislike power, distrust the powerful and suspect institutions not based on justice and virtue. Diogenes, the dog-philosopher, famously told Alexander the Great, who came to visit him at his barrel of a home in Athens, to move aside because he was blocking the sun.

But there was a second institutional route along which Stoic universal humanity developed further. The rational unity of the human race became the foundation of ideas of equality. This was a dramatic departure from the Greek world of free and slaves, of Hellenes and barbarians and put them in touch with a different tradition:

> The contact with the ancient prophets of Israel, who were the first to lay claim to an analogous position, was a singular event full of conse-quence. The unity of the human race, the natural right to peace, formal democracy, mutual aid . . . came to be the beginnings of a more or less definite concept.[18]

These revolutionary ideas were initially confined to the austere gaze of the philosopher or promised the idealised perfection of the Hellenistic world. The synthesis of the two great traditions of Athens and Jerusalem, and the concrete application of ideas of political equality would have to wait the political declarations of early modernity.

As the Greek city-states started dissolving, first in the Macedonian and later in the Roman Empire, the idea of a law common to all imperial subjects, of a *jus gentium*, started to take hold. The Stoics had avoided direct political involvement, but the universal morality they espoused and deduced from rational human nature was of great use to the builders of the Roman Empire as a restraint on ethnic and local nationalisms and individual passions. The late Stoic Chryssipus, for example, described universal humanity as a nation, while for Posidonius, the world was 'the commonwealth of gods and men'.[19] But the Greek Stoics kept their distance from power in the main and imagined the cosmopolis as an ontological and ethical correction of the polis. As a commentator on Chrysippos put it, the Stoic cosmic polis was 'not comparable to the empire Alexander extended to the ends of the earth; it is a question for them of human relationships, free of political form'.[20]

18　Bloch, op. cit., 16.
19　Ibid. 14.
20　E. Brehier quoted in Heater, op. cit., 15.

This changed with the Romans. The Stoic influence was greatest among people of power, office and affairs. Cicero was a populist orator, pragmatic lawyer and politician, Seneca, Nero's closest confidant, while Marcus Aurelius, an emperor and general. Cosmopolitanism turned, accordingly, from Cynic philosophy and Stoic ontology into an instrument of rule, no longer the philosophy of an ideal world but a strategy for world power. Cicero started the process. He mis-digested and eclectically revised the main tenets of Stoic thought, turning its rational universality into the ideology of Rome.[21] He rationalised Roman law and claimed that many of its central tenents could be traced back to universal rational norms. The Stoics were the first pagans to believe that natural law is the expression of a divine reason, which pervades the world and makes human law one of its aspects. Cicero popularised this idea:

> The true law, is the law of reason, in accordance with nature known to all, unchangeable and imperishable should call men to their duties by its precepts and deter them from wrongdoing with its prohibitions ... nor will it be one law in Rome and a different one in Athens, nor otherwise tomorrow than it is today; but one and the same law, eternal and unchangeable will bind all people and all ages; and God, its designer, expounder and enacter, will be the sole and universal ruler and governor of all things.[22]

For Cicero, gods and men share the same *logos* or *ratio* (reason), which finds its best expression in the *nomos* (*lex*) of nature and city. But if gods and men share reason and law they also share a *civitas*. The common logos, an abstract almost mystical idea for the Greek Stoics, now becomes the law of the city. Cicero still clings to some of the earlier notions and sees the city as the place that brings together the divine and secular. But soon, law and the city became fully secularised. Marcus Aurelius became an emperor in AD 161 and spent a large part of his office successfully defending the northern and eastern frontiers and expanding the Empire. In his late *Meditations*, Marcus argues for a close, almost logical link between reason and cosmopolitanism and, at the same time, makes the gods disappear:

---

21 Pangle, op. cit., gives a detailed description of Cicero's criticisms and revisions of Greek stoicism. More generally, see Michel Villey, *Histoire de la Philosophie du Droit* (Paris, PUF, 4th edn, 1975), 428–80.

22 Cicero, *Republic* (N. Rudd, trans.) (Oxford, Oxford University Press, 1998), III, 22.

> If the intellectual capacity is common to all, common too is the reason, which makes us rational beings. If so, we share reason which tells us what ought and ought not to happen in common. If so, the law is common. If so, we are citizens. If so, we are fellow-members of a republic. If so, the cosmos is like a city – for in what other single polity can the whole human race belong in common?[23]

The antinomian positions of the Cynics and Zeno have been finally reversed, the *logos spermatikos* turned from a critique into an apology of the law of the city. The *cosmopolis,* which had started its career as an ideal polis, ended as the servant and extension of a very earthly and imperial city.

In a parallel development, the Stoic 'common notions', through which men partook of universal reason and became aware of its dictates, were psychologised. The *orthos logos* (right reason) of the Greeks, which united natural necessity with the laws of reason, was turned into the *recta ratio* of 'a common sense that has become the supreme source of law'.[24] The pragmatic Roman jurists identified *jus naturale* with the Roman law: 'For "natural" was to them . . . the normal and reasonable order of human interests and, for this reason, not in need of further evidence'.[25] *Natura initium juris*:[26] nature turned from a variable and dynamic purposeful order into the source of a legal code. Nature commands and its moral prescriptions can be found in the soul. Gradually natural right became a matter of introspection and legislation rather than of rational contemplation and dialectical confrontation. The philosophical universalism of the Stoics became a global law applying to the territory demarcated and controlled by the Roman garrisons. The Romans perceived their empire as natural, eternal and limitless. 'To establish an empire is an essay in world creation' writes Eric Vogelin and this task was facilitated by the mutation of cosmopolis from a state of mind into a limitless territorial space and of natural law from a moral and ontological order into a set of precepts emanating from a legislating centre.[27] As Alex Colas notes, 'imperial self-representation from the very beginning sought to emphasise Rome's all

---

23   Marcus Aurelius Antoninus, *Meditations* (C.R. Haines, trans.) (London, Heinemann, 1959), IV. 4.

24   Cicero, op. cit., III, 20.

25   Erns Levy, 'Natural Law in Roman Thought', 15 *Studia et Documenta Historiae et Juris* (1949), 7.

26   Cicero, *De inventione* (H.M. Hubbell, trans.) (London, Heinemann, 1949), II, 22, 65

27   Eric Voegelin, 'World-Empire and the Unity of Mankind', 38/2 *International Affairs* 171 (April 1966),179.

encompassing, all-embracing nature'.[28] Rome was created out of 'successive incorporations, of new arrivals and additions to the Roman people'.[29] Empires aspire to absorb the known world into their own rule and turn the law of the imperial centre into universal law.

Classical political philosophy revolved around the confrontation between *physis* or *cosmos* and *nomos* or *polis*. Its Roman simplification opened two possible lines, which have since dominated political history and philosophy. According to the original Cynic philosophy, nature and cosmos, with their principles of dignity and equality deduced by reason or given by God, are tools of resistance against the injustices of the city. In this version, the spirit of the cosmos is mobilised against the order of the polis. Both utopianism and radical movements for social justice belong to this tradition. The second eventually dominant version elevates the law of the polis to the status of the law of the cosmos, extending its writ to the globe and giving it metaphysical *gravitas*. This is the cosmopolitanism of empire. It sanctions institutions, social hierarchies and inequalities with the imprimatur of reason and nature (nowadays universalism and human rights). Cosmopolitanism starts as a moral universalism but often degenerates into imperial globalism. The transformation of pagan Rome into the Christian Roman Empire repeated the same dialectic. Augustine's *City of God*, a relentless critique of the sins and failings of secular power, became a justification of imperial aspirations once they were subjected to the demands of the Church. The continuous slide of cosmopolitan ideas towards empire is one of the dominant motifs of modernity.

Modern cosmopolitanism

Modern cosmopolitanism returns to these tensions. It is the offspring of that great philosophical nation, Germany. A combination of metaphysics and *nomophilia*,[30] cosmopolitanism is a kind of constitutional patriotism and the child of three generations defeated in war. Its patriarchs are Kant, Kelsen, Habermas as well as Goethe, Herder, Humboldt, Nietzsche, Marx and Simmel. They all 'construed the modern period as a transition from early conditions of

---

28   Alex Colas, *Open Doors and Closed Frontiers: the Limits of American Empire* (forthcoming, copy with author).

29   Greg Woolf, 'Inventing Empire in Ancient Rome' in S.A. Alcock *et al.*, eds, *Empires. Perspectives from Archaeology and History* (Cambridge, Cambridge University Press, 1999), 317.

30   *Nomophilia* is the intellectual and sexual condition of experiencing extreme pleasure from contact with the law.

relatively closed societies to "universal eras" [*univeresellen Epochen*] (Goethe) of interdependent societies'.[31] The modern idea of cosmopolitanism originated in a series of essays written by Kant over a twelve-year period before and after the French Revolution.[32] Kant's utopia included two legal elements: binding international law and cosmopolitan law. The creation of a consensual and fully binding international law and institutions would lead to lawful external relations and turn states into legal subjects with reciprocal rights and duties. The cosmopolitan law of universal civic society, on the other hand, would guarantee the rights of all irrespective of the state of their domestic law. People have entered, argued Kant 'into a universal community, and it has developed to the point where a violations of rights in *one* part of the world is felt *everywhere*'.[33] The task was to formalise and generalise this feeling. The cosmopolitan order would come about through a contract among states creating a league or 'pacific federation' of nations. It would be a voluntary coalition without a constitution. The people have no role to play in Kant's republic. The 'majesty of the people [popular sovereignty] is an absurd expression' wrote Kant.[34] Kant's cosmopolitanism was a league of states and definitely not a world republic of the people. A combination of reason and self-interest, Kant believed, would make states keep to their agreements. The collective power of the league would guarantee the independent existence and security of states and individuals but also ensure that states exist in a power equilibrium. A state would have no legal obligation to remain in the league, if it acted against its interests. Its duty to remain within the federation would be self-imposed and moral.

For Kantian metaphysics, cosmopolitan right was a pure idea deriving from the requirements of practical reason, from right and duty. Everyone must hold it sacred, however great the sacrifice the ruling powers would have to make for its achievement. Kant insisted that we must act according to the principle of perpetual peace even if there is no possibility of realising it. All politics, declared Kant, must bend the knee before right. Kant's utopianism was underpinned by his belief that the cunning of reason was working beneath the great battles of history and was leading to its universal end, the perfect civil union of humankind. The league was the first step for the abolition of war and the emergence of a state of perpetual peace. This hope was metaphysically

31   Beck, op. cit., 9.
32   'Idea for a Universal History from a Cosmopolitan Point of View' and 'Towards Perpetual Peace: A Philosophical Sketch' in *Kant's Political Writings* (H. Reiss, ed.) (Cambridge, Cambridge University Press, 1986).
33   Ibid. 107–8.
34   Ibid. 16.

guaranteed 'by no less authority than the great artist Nature herself which would lead to a community of nations from which there would be no return'. The 'purpose of nature' would eventually lead to the coincidence of politics and morality. Admittedly, before the achievement of this state of grace justified wars would still take place but they would be strictly limited. The spread of democracy and the consequent need to have popular assent for a declaration of war would provide an important constraint as would the introduction of strict legal rules for the initiation and conduct of war.[35] Wars of annihilation and enslavement would be outlawed, although colonisation could be justified for bringing culture to uncivilised people and cleansing the colonising nation of its depraved characters.

Kant's dream started taking shape in the great revolutions and constitutions of the eighteenth century. The relationship between the universal (cosmos) and the national (polis) became the political horizon of modernity. The American and French revolutions pronounced natural rights inalienable because they were independent of governments, temporal and local factors, and expressed in legal form the natural rights of man. Rights were declared to belong to all humanity. Yet, the legislator of this universalism was the French or American assembly, and the beneficiaries of these universal rights were the citizens of the two nations. From that point, sovereignty follows a national principle and belongs to a dual time. The constitutions introduced a historical teleology, which promised the future unification of nation and humanity. The variations opened at the time of the Roman Empire were again evident: imperialism in the Napoleonic wars, in which the French nation claimed to be the expression of humanity and to spread through conquest and occupation its civilising influence to the world; and the beginnings of a modern cosmopolitanism, in which slavery was abolished and colonial people were given political rights for a limited time after the French Revolution. The cosmopolitan aspiration is that humanity will overcome national differences and conflicts in a global civil society.

Kant's pious position was adjudged extremely dangerous by Carl Schmitt, for whom its initiator was a judge of heresy and a theologian rather than a lawyer. According to Schmitt, Kant's cosmopolitan teachings anticipated the (feeble) attempts in the twentieth century (and one could add the much more

35 Recent research has given the lie to the other cliché that democracies do not commit atrocities. Michael Mann, *The Dark Side of Democracy: Explaining Ethnic Cleansing* (Cambridge, Cambridge University Press, 2005) argues persuasively that ethnic cleansing and genocide happen when the *demos* and the *ethnos* coincide or when the nation legitimises its claim to power through democratic means.

successful in the twenty-first) to impose morality on international relations.[36] But for many important commentators and social theorists, we are now well on the way to a new type of cosmopolitanism. For Jürgen Habermas, our choice is between a Kantian pacific cosmopolitanism and a regressive and aggressive loyalty to one's tribe.[37] Similarly for Anthony Giddens, globalisation is defined as the clash between a cosmopolitan outlook and fundamentalism. The battle-ground of the twenty-first century will pit fundamentalism against cosmopolitan tolerance. Indeed, for David Held[38] and Mary Kaldor,[39] the emergence of a cosmopolitan order is a historical inevitability.

Are we moving to such an order? I think the answer is yes and this is what brings modernity to its end. But its nature is very different from the Kantian ideal. Let us have a quick look at the most influential and compelling versions of the cosmopolitan project, those of Hans Kelsen and Jürgen Habermas. Hans Kelsen, the great Austrian jurist, borrowed and developed Kant's cosmopolitan ideals of perpetual peace, federalism and world citizenship. The world state of the future, Kelsen believed, will unite all states under a federal constitution. As a philosophical positivist and a lawyer, Kelsen placed greater emphasis than his inspirer on the legal components of the world state. He had already developed in the 1920s a unified concept of law, according to which the legal system constitutes a single normative hierarchy with international law at its apex and domestic law beneath it, the whole arranged in a pyramidal shape.[40] In this grand scheme, the validity of norms is a logical or transcendental phenomenon. Rules are derived coherently and seamlessly from those above them in the edifice. Every legal decision is a logical and determinate judgment in which low generality norms are subsumed to those above them all the way to the last point of ascription or basic norm, that of international law. In such a system national laws cannot be in conflict with international norms and still be valid. In a direct reference to Kantian metaphysics, Kelsen argued that the unity of the legal system mirrors the moral concord of humanity and gives international law its highest component, moral nature. The legal unity of humanity was akin to the *civitas maxima* of the Roman Empire.

---

36 Carl Schmitt, *The Concept of the Political* (G. Schwab, trans.) (Chicago, IL, University of Chicago Press, 1996), Chapter III.
37 Jürgen Habermas, 'Kant's Idea of Perpetual Peace, with the Benefit of Two Hundred Years' Hindsight', in James Bohamn and Matthias Lutz-Bachmann, eds, *Perpetual Peace: Essays on Kant's Cosmopolitan Ideal* (Cambridge, MA, MIT Press, 1997), 130.
38 David Held, *Democracy and the Global Order* (Cambridge, Polity, 1995).
39 Mary Kaldor, *New and Old Wars: Organised Violence in a Global Era* (Cambridge, Polity, 1999).
40 Hans Kelsen, *The Pure Theory of Law* (Berkeley, CA, University of California Press, 1934).

Starting from these premises, Kelsen argued that a concept of right, emanating exclusively from the pyramid of domestic laws and judicial decisions, is inadequate and insufficient. To be complete, national law should be placed within an international legal order creating an integrated whole. Such a universal legal system would bring together legality and morality and put an end to conflict among states. Legal right would coincide with 'the organisation of humanity and would therefore be one with the supreme ethical idea'.[41] Observing the newly created United Nations, Kelsen thought that it was a step towards Kant's project of a cosmopolitan world government. In this new world order, all states would be formally equal. Its law would be both superior to that of individual states and encompass them all ensuring internal security and international stability. Based on this rather outlandish conception of the international legal order, Kelsen promoted the idea of 'legal pacifism', of a peace founded and promoted through respect for the international rule of law. For this to be achieved, however, the constitutional arrangements of the world order should be improved. Both the League of Nations and the United Nations had placed inordinate emphasis on their respective councils with their political composition and predominantly executive role. This was a design error; greater importance should be placed on a new world court. The court should become the highest legal authority and have the power to decide whether a state is in breach of international law and order reprisals or even war against it. Peace through law would be guaranteed only through the creation of such an international legal authority, which should stand above state disputes and have at its disposal a police force with sufficient powers of enforcement.

Kelsen went on to argue that on the way to the future cosmopolitan order and despite the lack of an authoritative legal authority, war could be used as a 'legal sanction' against states violating international law under an implicit legal authorisation.[42] In a paradoxical extension of his position, the formalist and pacifist Kelsen saw a rejuvenated theory of just war as the beginning of the future perpetual peace. Repeating Kant's accusations, Kelsen denounced realist international lawyers for abandoning the normative terrain for pragmatic calculations and the consolations of realpolitic. His belief that law had replaced religion and morality as the ultimate criterion of going to war made him see 'the ethical doctrine of "just war" as the condition for the legal legitimacy of

---

41 Hans Kelsen, *Das Problem des Souveranität in die Theorie des Volkerrechts* (Tübingen, Mohr, 1920) 205 quoted in Hardt and Negri, op. cit., 5.
42 Hans Kelsen, *Principles of International Law* (3rd edn) (New York, Holt, Rinehart, Wilson, 1967), 29–33.

the international system'.[43] But as Danilo Zolo put it, the political core of the primacy of international law and of legal pacifism in international politics is the 'inverted image of imperialism'.[44]

Postmodern cosmopolitanism

Kants' idealism is not convincing in our post-metaphysical world and Kelsen's vision has remained just that, an unrealistic and unrealised vision. Recently, however, Jürgen Habermas has undertaken the task of rescuing and updating the Kantian vision. Habermas starts by distinguishing Kantian cosmopolitanism from conventional international law, which is unable to deliver the cosmopolitan order. Public international law, based on the principle of national sovereignty, allows states to renounce violence and even join a league of nations through multilateral agreements while retaining their independence. As a result, their voluntary coalition can be dissolved at will, if they decide that it acts against their interests. Only a self-imposed moral duty would keep them in the league since there would be no binding legal obligation. For Habermas, this is unsatisfactory. Cosmopolitanism should bring this Hobbesian 'state of nature' to an end. Its law should be based on binding and strict constitutional arrangements, unlike the loose and flexible agreements of alliances and federations.

Kant had been understandably suspicious of constitutionally organised alliances of nations, because such groupings had acted as the main tool of power politics in his age. In Kant's philosophy of history, the 'great artist nature' would make political interest and moral duty coincide. Habermas does not need such an exalted insurance policy. He believes that the cosmopolitan idea had started taking concrete roots after the Second World War. Nuremberg was the turning point. The introduction of the concepts of crimes against peace, created under the Briand–Kellog pact of 1928 but first prosecuted in Nuremberg, and crimes against humanity was epoch-making. These two innovations removed the immunity of states and seriously undermined the presumption of innocence of political and military leaders. But the Kantian scheme needs to be radicalised further. Combining Kant's philosophy and Kelsen's jurisprudence, Habermas envisages a world political system in which a single world government would replace the nation-states. Cosmopolitan law

---

43 Danilo Zolo, *Invoking Humanity* (Federico and Gordon Poole, trans.) (London, Continuum, 2002), 88.

44 Danilo Zolo, 'Hans Kelsen: International Peace through International Law' 9/2 *European Journal of International Law* 306 (1998), 323.

must be institutionalised and bind governments while the use of sanctions will ensure that states act lawfully. Second, world citizenship rights, similar to the human rights enjoyed currently by Western citizens, should be given to everyone. The world citizens of cosmopolitanism will have a direct and unmediated relationship with a single sovereign centre as free and equal persons. Cosmopolitan law 'goes over the heads of the collective subjects of international law to give legal status to the individual subjects and justifies their unmediated membership in the association of free and equal world citizens'.[45] Finally, the world government should have full executive powers and adequate mechanisms of enforcement to punish those who violate cosmopolitan law and human rights. This universally valid code of law would bring together the Kantian principle of normative universalisation and the globalised world of economic transactions and instant communications in what could be called a universalistic globalisation and a cosmopolitan citizenship.

But the German tradition represented by Habermas includes dissenting voices. For Friedrich Nietzsche, morality is the eternalisation of temporary relations and universalism the moralisation and absolutisation of the balance of power. Warming to this theme, Carl Schmitt attacked the moralisation of politics. Cosmopolitanism would lead to the world hegemony of a single power, which, based on some version of absolute morality, would attack its enemies as 'evil', impose its will under a cloak of implementing human rights and destroy politics and the pluralism that characterised the pre-Second World War international scene. How can Habermas answer these telling criticisms? How can he jettison the noblest part of the German *Rechtsstaat* tradition, namely the separation between law and morality? This was the greatest achievement of legal modernity; it removed religion and morality from politics and subjected power to legal rules. Habermas accepts partly the legitimacy of Schmitt's critique which, like those of Hegel and Horkheimer, is 'directed against the false and transfiguring abstraction of a Platonic general concept with which we often only cover up the dark side of the civilisation of the victors'.[46] He is also aware of the political objection that recent wars and sanctions can be seen as part of a renewed imperial project, which uses a strong moral language as a tool against political enemies. To answer them, Habermas introduces a crucial distinction between human rights and morality. Human rights are the creations of law not morality. They are juridical concepts, the origins of which lie in the tradition of individual civil liberties. Modern morality, on the other hand, derives from the Kantian 'philosophical revolution'. But while their

---

45   Habermas, op. cit., 128.
46   Ibid. 145.

histories differ, human rights and morality share the same foundation and can be justified in the same manner.

Following standard liberal theory, Habermas argues that human rights do not impose or promote a particular version of the good life or a partial moral viewpoint. They are the progeny of two parallel universalist traditions, one moral the other legal. As legal entitlements, legislated in Bills of Rights and international treaties, human rights carry the legitimacy of democratically enacted legislation; as moral claims, they carry the normative validity of universal rationality bestowed on them by the values they promote. This means that human rights and moral norms share form and function. While their validity derives from their legal history and legislative enactment, it points beyond any particular legal order. As legal rights, they stand higher than the ordinary rights given by states to their citizens. They are given to people not on account of their membership in some group, such as nation, state, class or profession, but simply because of their common humanity. This gives them their moral appeal. At the same time, human rights and morality share what Habermas calls their 'structure of validity', their justification: they have a common foundation, the 'fundamental discourse principle', which precedes the historical separation between law and morality. This is an elaboration of the Kantian categorical imperative with a Rawlsian inflection: 'just those action-norms are valid to which all possible affected persons could agree as participants in a rational discourse.'[47] Furthermore, the universalism of law and morality are similar. 'Basic rights are equipped with such universal validity claims precisely because they can be justified *exclusively* from the moral point of view.'[48] But their common justification does not turn human into moral rights. The differences remain: unlike morality, human rights retain their status as actionable legal claims; their enforcement is entrusted in legal remedies and courts of law; they are tools for acting out individual desires; finally, they enjoy preference over duties, with the latter arising only as legal restrictions on individual liberties. Cosmopolitan law extends the juridical logic beyond the frontiers of the state. In the cosmopolitan order, human rights violations are not moral wrongs but criminal actions similar to war crimes and crimes against humanity. Interventions to stop them are not just wars but police action against criminals.

This is the most sophisticated argumentation for postmodern cosmopolitanism. Following this analysis, Habermas argued that the Kosovo war was an attempt to push international law towards its cosmopolitan phase, by creating

---

47 Jürgen Habermas, *Between Facts and Norms: Contributions to a Discourse Theory of Law and Democracy* (W. Rehg, trans.) (Cambridge, MA, MIT Press, 1996), 107.
48 Ibid. 138.

and upholding rights to universal citizenship. In a highly controversial article,[49] Habermas wrote that until the full cosmopolitan order has been introduced and international institutions have been reformed in accordance with his blueprint, the border between law and morals will be blurred. In Kosovo, the dual legitimacy of law was split. NATO appealed to the moral validity of human rights and to norms of peacekeeping and rescue, which are clearly part of the evolving cosmopolitan dispensation although not actually applied or upheld by the international community. In an unacknowledged revival of Kelsen's position, Habermas argued that NATO's action was legitimate despite the lack of Security Council authorisation, because it anticipated the future cosmopolitan order while at the same time promoting its advent. The cosmopolitan project of peace through law will put an end to murderous ethnic nationalisms and will transcend international law in the direction of Kant and Kelsen.

Are these claims about an emerging cosmopolitanism credible? Is cosmopolitanism an alternative or a supplement of empire? Habermas's discussion and elaboration of the Weberian link between legality and legitimacy has been one of his most celebrated contributions to social theory. By promoting their radical separation, Habermas is realising one of the worst nightmares of Max Weber. Even the uber-cosmopolitan Ulrich Beck has difficulties with the principle that 'human rights trump international law'. We cannot tell, Beck admits, what is more dangerous, the old system of sovereign states, the 'murky complex' of international institutions in hock to powerful states or the 'self-authorisation of a hegemonic power which "defends" human rights in foreign territories'.[50] Carl Schmitt has a clear answer to Beck's question. Cosmopolitanism inevitably leads to world hegemony, the subjection of politics to morality and the destruction of the pluralism of the international stage. Habermas, who seems to be ceaselessly fighting with Schmitt's ghost, accepts that his opponent's dread about the moralisation of politics is partly justified. This fear will be realised, however, only if the sphere of legal protection breaks down and politics becomes directly subjected to morality without the mediation of law. The 'legal presupposition of an authority that judges impartially and fulfils the conditions of neutral criminal punishment' saves the day.[51]

This is a rather meek defence of the principle of separation between law and morality. It is an example of the adverse effects John Rawls's *Theory of Justice* has had on political theory. It is also a symptom of the recent attraction

---

49   Jürgen Habermas, 'Bestialität und Humanität', *Die Zeit*, 29 April 1999.
50   Beck, op. cit., 121.
51   Habermas, op. cit., fn. 37, 147.

law holds for those who know little about the long critical legal tradition, to which the early Frankfurt School was such an important contributor. Rawls's revisionist definition of justice in terms of rights had the effect of turning political philosophy into a branch of jurisprudence. His followers have presented political, social and economic conflict as a matter of rights and have replaced the understanding of antagonism with a discussion of legitimacy. Habermas's recent writings have moved in the same direction. He combines Rawls's American liberalism with German constitutionalism in directions that are alien to both. His over-hasty adoption of claims about the neutrality of law and judges, after two centuries of legal demystification from Marxist, realist and critical legal perspectives, is not convincing. Abstract legality and impartial lawyers are hardly sufficient, if law is to act as the judge and arbiter of the new cosmopolitanism. The emphasis on the judiciary follows the proliferation of criminal trials, which accompanies the defeat of the new order's enemies. Whatever their merits, however, criminal trials are backward-looking and cannot give much guidance about the legality of a future war or the direction of foreign policy.[52] International lawyers turned to morality to justify the Kosovo and Iraq wars precisely because the law ran out and was of little help.[53] Their admission that the law would face great difficulties in the Herculean task Habermas assigns to it is far more realistic and cannot be answered by the latter's grand claims about the shared foundations of law and morality.

By neglecting the insights of 200 years of legal critique in favour of an unrepresentative view of law, Habermas has paved the way for an assortment of social theorists to use the law as the answer to the problems facing political and social theory. One has argued that the legal moralism of human rights should be extended towards an 'ethical judicialism' (*sic*) that would expand the legalisation of culture.[54] Another insists that having cosmopolitan trials expresses

52   Milocevic was indicted while still the President of Yugoslavia; Saddam Hussein was repeatedly threatened with criminal prosecution before the attack on Iraq. In this sense, judicial proceedings have become tools for putting pressure on leaders and states. But this is not a case of expanding the judicial regulation and oversight of foreign policy in a cosmopolitan direction. It is a pre-emptive use of criminal law to accompany the pre-emptive use of military force.

53   See Chapter 9.

54   Tom Osborne, 'What is Neo-Enlightenment', 2/4 *Journal of Human Rights* 523 (2003). Osborne starts from the standard appropriation of juridical practices but distances his position from that of Habermas. His neo-humanism is based not on Kantian moral principles but on 'ethical' norms and practices. A human rights culture, Osborne claims, comes about through ethical performances, dialogical practices, truth commissions, reconciliation, etc. Neither universal nor local, it leads to immanent and performative problem-solving through the use of e.g., shaming practices rather than through overarching moralities. According to Osborne,

a 'wordliness as the practical wisdom of those who by hook or crook know how to construct a touch of humanity in the most forbidding circumstances'.[55] Finally, a third believes that it is possible to adopt a legalistic cosmopolitan approach to politics 'without elevating that universal principle to an essential absolute which finds everything that resists it expendable'.[56] The law has become the *deus ex machina* of cosmopolitanism. It is brought in when the concepts of social theory or the resources of politics run out. As a proponent puts it, 'cosmopolitan social theory may be viewed as a multi-disciplinary attempt to reconstruct the core concepts of the human sciences – society, political community, democracy, culture, sovereignty etc'.[57] Ulrich Beck responded to the call by launching 'cosmopolitan social science' and the 'new grammar' of the social and the political and by conducting 'the epistemological turn, the empirical-analytical cosmopolitanism'.[58] Cosmopolitanism may not launch a thousand ships or even a thousand campaigners or protesters, but it will certainly launch a thousand academic books and learned articles.

Many of these theorists are opposed to the imperialist direction of the new world order. What they cannot explain, however, is how a court of law and judges with armies at their disposal could avoid becoming either an Imperial Court themselves or a tool in the plans of the Great Power. As Bill Rasch sardonically commented, 'with this fine differentiation between moral fundamentalism and legal constitutionalism, the police actions undertaken by a world government . . . can be positively contrasted with repressive moral or cultural crusades'.[59] The response by Robert Kagan, an avowed American imperialist, is even more telling. Commenting on European double standards over Kosovo (morality trumps legality) and Iraq (legality trumps American national interest), Kagan ironically retorts:

> Any 'rules-based' international order must apply the same sets of rules to different situations. Otherwise we return to a world where nations individually or in groups decide for themselves when a war is and is not

human rights ethical culture may be leading us to a 'contextualism of the universal', a rather interesting paradox that would have profited from a discussion of the Hegelian 'concrete universal'. In normative terms, neo-humanism is identical with the standard version and is an exalted title for pragmatism.

55 Bob Fine, *Political Investigations: Hegel, Marx, Arendt* (London, Routledge, 2001), 162.
56 David Hirsch, *Law Against Genocide: Cosmopolitan Trials* (London, Glasshouse, 2003), 154.
57 Bob Fine, 'Cosmopolitanism and Social Theory' quoted in Hirsch, ibid. xii.
58 Beck, op. cit., 33.
59 William Rasch, *Sovereignty and its Discontents* (London, Birkbeck Law Press, 2005), 61.

justified, guided by their own morality and sense of justice and order. In fact that is the world we live in, and the only world we have ever lived in. It is a world where those with power, believing they have right on their side, impose their sense of justice on others.[60]

Let us move to the claim that Kosovo was the first step towards a cosmopolitan order with a binding constitution and rights of world citizenship. There is little evidence to indicate that a world constitution is emerging in the way that such instruments are initiated. Domestically, this could happen through revolution or a constitutional convention. A global constitution on the other hand could emerge either through agreement among a majority of states and possibly, as in the European case, popular referenda around the world; or, through occupation and imposition of the law by the victors on the vanquished. The most important formal move in the direction of rewriting international law recently was the unilateral and unlawful declaration of war in Kosovo, Afghanistan and Iraq and the successful conduct of these campaigns. Habermas had to admit as much after the Iraq war. In an article published in 2003, he accused the United States of violating international law with their attack. Focusing his criticism on the Bush doctrine of spreading liberal states and free markets through violence, Habermas claims that while the United States was the 'pacemaker of progress on the cosmopolitan plan', Iraq meant that it has 'given up its role as guarantor of international rights . . . its normative authority lies in ruins'.[61] Habermas distinguished Kosovo from Iraq arguing that in the former, war was justified because it aimed at preventing ethnic cleansing, it followed 'the provision of international law for emergency aid' and, finally, it was carried out by democratic and rule of law states. The Americans can claim, of course, that all three criteria were similarly met in the case of Iraq. The war aimed, among other issues, to stop extensive human rights abuses, it had a higher degree of international law legitimacy than Kosovo and, it was carried out by the two oldest democracies in the world.

Habermas concludes his extraordinary confession, which comprehensively undermines the cosmopolitan position, by arguing that there is little difference between classical imperialism and American hegemonism. Imperial campaigns spread 'the universal values of their own liberal order, with military force if necessary, throughout the entire world. This arrogance doesn't become any more tolerable when it transfers from nation-state to a single hegemonic

---

60   Robert Kagan, *Paradise and Power* (London, Atlantic Books, 2004), 130–1.
61   Jürgen Habermas, 'Interpreting the Fall of a Monument', 4 *German Law Journal* 7 (1 July 2003). The essay originally appeared in the *Frankfurt Allgemeine Zeitung* on 17 April 2003.

state'.[62] This is the closest Habermas comes to a genuine *mea culpa* and an admission that despite the brutal attacks, Carl Schmitt may have carried the day. As Chapters 9 and 10 argue, the suspension of international law and the state of exception these attacks introduced can be interpreted as the beginning of a new legal order. This order and the space it applies on are the result of the action of the hegemon who, by violating and suspending the law, becomes the sovereign of an empire in the making. Instead of moving to a cosmopolitan order, this brutal assertion of sovereignty is an attempt to move the world towards a global principle of sovereignty in search of empire.

We will examine the role of human rights in the new world order in the next chapter. Here, I would like to address briefly two related cosmopolitan claims. First, the proposition that a cosmopolitan citizenship is the necessary building block of a world republic and, second, the accompanying assertion that human rights are given to people on account of their humanity rather than membership of narrower groups. The citizen is the Roman translation of the Greek *polites*, the man of the city who participates in political deliberation and decision-making about common affairs. Citizenship has always been situated; it is political belonging to a city, a nation or a state, it is citizenship of Athens or Rome, England or France. Today, citizenship is still closely linked with state sovereignty, which acts as both its effect and putative cause. It is the law of a particular state that recognises someone as its citizen with the associated rights and duties. The separation between human and citizen is the main characteristic of modern law (Chapter 4). The modern subject reaches his humanity by acquiring political rights of citizenship by being admitted to the 'nationality' of a nation-state. In a world in which every part of the world comes under the direct or indirect rule of the 'condensed' sovereign to be without the legal protection of state citizenship, rather than opening to a world citizenship, is equivalent to civic death. If human rights were given to people simply because they are members of the human species, as Habermas claims, one would expect that those who do not enjoy citizen rights, such as refugees, should have the greatest possible protection of their human equivalent. Refugees have left the protection of their state of origin but have not as yet received the protection of a receiving state. Their only characteristic is their humanity, as it is for those confined to legal black-holes, such as Guantánamo Bay or Abu Ghraib. And yet, they have none. All the evidence shows, that those abandoned by state law and citizenship rights do not enjoy some higher human or cosmopolitan protections but they become just 'bare life', people who can be tortured, abused or sacrificed with total impunity, the *homines sacri*[63] of the new world order.

---

62   Ibid.
63   Agamben, op. cit.

Despite the hopes of Habermas and his continuous references to the German philosophical and legal tradition, a commitment to humanity or his 'constitutional patriotism' cannot replace (German or American) nationalism. The language of humanity has often been the tool of imperial expansion. According to Reinhart Koselleck,

> the dualistic criteria of distribution between Greek and Barbarian, and between Christian and Heathen, were always related, whether implicitly or explicitly, to humanity as a totality ... the *genus humanum*, was a presupposition of all dualities that organised humanity physically, spiritually theologically or temporally.[64]

For the Greeks, who introduced a distinction between us and the others, the barbarians were simply foreigners, people who spoke gibberish (bar-bar), an incomprehensible language. The Christian ecumenical mission of salvation changed that. Every person has a soul and can be saved and, as a result, the conquest of the heathens' lands and their brutal proselytisation or extermination is justified in order to bring them to Christ's ecumenical truth. The civilising mission of the Christians has now been transferred to the humanitarians.

Carl Schmitt's prescience in predicting the shape of recent events is quite unnerving. 'When a state fights its political enemy in the name of humanity, it is not a war for the sake of humanity, but a war wherein a particular state seeks to usurp a universal concept against its military opponents', Schmitt wrote in 1934.[65] Humanity cannot wage war because it has no enemy, at least not on this planet. Logically, 'humanity' excludes the concept of the enemy, because an earthly enemy does not cease to be a human being. When a state fights its political enemy in the name of humanity, it is not a war for the sake of humanity, but a war where a particular state seeks to usurp the universal concept against its military opponents. As Proudhon put it, 'whoever invokes humanity wants to cheat'.[66] When humanity becomes the ground concept, its enemies are in a worse position than the barbarian for the Greeks or the infidel for the Christians. This is because the term 'human' may be commonly seen as a factual distinction or classification, but its action is evaluative and normative. For the Christians, both believers and infidels belong to the same species. Humanity was the wider category, which enabled the distinction. But according to Carl Schmitt, 'only

---

64   Reinhart Kosseleck, *Futures Past: On the Semantics of Historical Time* (Cambridge, MA, MIT Press, 1985), 186.
65   Schmitt, op. cit., 54.
66   Ibid.

when man appeared to be the embodiment of absolute humanity did the other side of this concept appear in the form of a new enemy: the *inhuman*'.[67] As William Rasch puts it, in his great defence of sovereignty and politics, humanity is not part of the distinction but its horizon. But once 'the term used to describe the horizon of a distinction also becomes also that distinction's positive pole, it needs its negative opposite . . . something that lies beyond the horizon . . . completely antithetical to horizon and positive pole alike . . . the inhuman'.[68]

Furthermore, cosmopolitical space turns all relations into domestic affairs. The cosmopolis leaves no barbarians outside the gates because the frontiers are gradually removed. As there is no outside every threat appears close, interconnected and frightening. The barbarians are now in our midst in the ghettoes and *banlieus* of the metropolitan lands and the more remote badlands of Kosovo, Afghanistan, Iraq, Lebanon, Iran, Sudan. John Rawls, *The Law of the Peoples*, is a good example. Reasonable liberal and 'decent hierarchical' peoples possess superior institutions, culture and moral character. They are entitled to attack outlaw states when they violate human rights. Liberal aggression is justified because liberalism provides the universal standard of decency, while the indecent character of the rogues makes wars against them just.[69] Anthony Anghie concludes his examination of international law at the time of the conquest of the Americas, stating that the Indians were 'included in the system only to be disciplined'.[70] Some four hundred years later, we can generalise: 'To be truly human, one needs to be corrected.'[71]

Second, civil and political rights and, later, economic and social rights were fought for and won by people who exercised them as an aspect of democratic citizenship and an expression of popular sovereignty and participation in the legislative activity of the state. Morality and the natural entitlements of humanity do not endow people with rights, only with moral claims that may or may not be granted by the sovereign, who is still the only power recognising and enforcing rights. Are we moving towards a cosmopolitan citizenship?

---

67 Carl Schmitt, *Nomos of the Earth in the International Law of the Jus Publicum Europaeum* (New York, Telos, 2003), 104.
68 Rasch, op. cit., 143.
69 John Rawls, *The Law of the Peoples* (Cambridge MA, Harvard University Press, 2001). Tony Judt has called the (left) liberals who have rallied to our recent wars and provide them with intellectual legitimacy, 'the useful idiots of the War on Terror', 'Bush's Useful Idiots', *London Review of Books*, 21 September 2006, 3.
70 Antony Anghie, 'Fransicso de Vitoria and the Colonial Origins of International Law', 5 *Social and Legal Studies* 321 (1996), 331.
71 Rasch, op. cit., 145.

In the Stoic definition, the *cosmopolis*, the city of gods and men, combines the *demos* with law, justice and sophistication. None of these elements exists today or is likely to develop soon. There is no *demos* in the cosmos, no people of the world exist, brought together in community through what Chapter 11 calls bare sovereignty and cosmopolitan jurisdiction. The only common law we have is the disintegrating public international law; the only common justice, that of neo-liberal economics; the only sophistication, that of jet-setting cosmopolitans. If we are on the way to a world state with a sovereign capable of creating and enforcing citizens' rights this would be imperial rather than cosmopolitan. Massimo La Torre, a supporter of cosmopolitanism, reaches the obvious conclusion others avoid: the only way of creating a world citizenship would be if the United States take the 'Ancient Romans great example and give American nationality to all members of the globalised world community'.[72] A dominant centre of power is still the inescapable precondition of global citizenship but such an admission would fatally undermine the cosmopolitan project.

Cosmopolitanism in its different versions starts as a philosophical and moral universalism but it degenerates each time into imperial globalism. The ancient conflict between *cosmos*, the ideal order of the world, and *polis*, empirical social existence, is one of the great metaphysical divides. *Cosmopolis*, the name of its transcendence, one of the greatest early utopias. Diogenes, Zeno and Clemes found in the universal reason, virtue and eros of the *cosmos* the refutation of the artifice, greed and injustice of the *polis*. The *cosmopolis* must be first a place of the mind and soul before it becomes a place in the map, if it ever does. The cosmopolitanism of the Cynics and the Stoics was utopian. But is there any other? Let us have in conclusion a brief look at the sociological, philosophical and political positions of its contemporary proponents.

Ulrich Beck, the sociologist, claims that the human condition itself has become cosmopolitan. Cosmopolitanism has 'left the realm of philosophical castles in the air and has entered reality . . . it has become the defining fixture of the era of reflexive modernity'.[73] But if this is the case, cosmopolitanism in its final and complete incarnation has lost its radical energy. Reason, the universal critical perspective of the Stoics, in its reflexive stage, acts as a buffer-zone by turning critical dissent into its opposite. According to Beck's rather exaggerated assertion, cosmopolitanism has been so effective in co-opting

---

72 Massimo La Torre, 'Global Citizenship? Political Rights under Imperial Conditions', 18/2 *Ratio Juris* 236 (2005), 255.
73 Beck, op. cit., 2.

dissent to its goals and effects that it managed to turn 'the anti-globalisation movement into the motor of cosmopolitanisation'.[74] Diogenes has left the barrel, has become a world citizen and meets Alexander in cocktail parties.

For the analytical philosopher Kwame Appiah, cosmopolitanism reminds us of the powerful ties that connect people across religions, cultures and nations, while also valuing differences. Its two strands are the 'we have obligations towards others . . . beyond those to whom we are related by the ties of kith and kind' and that 'we take seriously the value of particular human lives [and] learn from our differences'.[75] Cosmopolitanism is about valuing sameness, difference and values themselves. As a prospectus, this covers the totality of liberal political philosophy but adds little to our understanding or normative commitments. Martha Nussbaum is a little more specific.[76] Humanism and cosmopolitanism involve cultivating a critical examination of our way of life, the capacity to identify with others in different groups, cultures or nations, and a 'narrative imagination' that helps us understand and empathise with others. The underlying principle is that common needs and aims are differently realised in different circumstances. This principle could become an important normative source leading to greater reflexive self-understanding, in the context of a world of many diverse cultures and perspectives. Discussing Marcus Aurelius's cosmopolitanism, Nussbaum praises the way in which humanism can weaken anger and hatred, the damaging effects of politics. Even when we disagree with political opponents, we can see still see them as part of humanity rather than as 'inhuman others'. But, as argued above, it is precisely the absolutisation of local moralities and their equation with humanity that creates the inhuman others. Furthermore, anger and hatred are justified reactions by the oppressed. It is fine for emperors, generals and philosophers to preach to the dominated *ataraxia* and moderation towards their rulers, justifying their subjugation. A political ideology that hails from Diogenes and Zeno on the other hand is critical towards unjust power and institutions and angry towards their apologists.

Finally, the political scientist David Held argues that

> there is the significant entrenchment of cosmopolitan values concerning the equal dignity and worth of all human beings; the reconnection between international law and morality; the establishment of regional and

---

74 Ibid. 118.

75 Kwame Anthony Appiah, *Cosmopolitanism. Ethics in a World of Strangers* (London, Allen Lane, 2006), xv.

76 Martha Nussbaum, *Cultivating Humanity: A Classical Defence of Reform in Liberal Education* (Cambridge, MA, Harvard University Press, 1997).

global systems of governance; and growing recognition that the public good . . . requires coordinated multilateral action.[77]

Every single one of these propositions is contestable at the empirical level and highly problematic normatively. At least, however, this type of cosmopolitical approach retains a certain distance from reality and to that extent we could call it 'utopia lite'. None of its rather blunt premises exists or is about to come to life soon. But bluntness is its main problem: institutionalised cosmopolitanism risks becoming the normative gloss of globalised capitalism at its imperial stage. Once more, the hope of the cosmos will have been subjected to the will and power of the polis.

---

77 David Held, 'Violence, Law and Justice in a Global Age' in Daniele Archibugi, ed., *Debating Cosmopolitics* (London, Verso, 2003), 191.

Chapter 8

Human rights

Values in a valueless world?

The new world order emerging after the collapse of communism is, we are told, 'not only anchored by liberal democracy but ... is a genuinely liberal democratic order'.[1] It is founded on 'judicial equality, the constitutional protection of individual rights, representative government and market economics based on private property rights'.[2] The victory of the West means that the ideological controversies of the past have given way to general agreement about the universality of Western values and have placed human rights at the core of international law. Human rights have become the driving force of international relations, a way of conducting politics according to ethical norms. The geopolitical framework of the new millennium is liberal cosmopolitanism. Its signs are everywhere.

In humanitarian wars, military force has been placed in the service of humanity. Economic sanctions have been repeatedly imposed unilaterally and multilaterally allegedly to protect nations and people from their evil governments. Politics are legalised through the increased use of criminal procedures against political leaders in domestic and international courts. Finally, human rights and good governance clauses are routinely imposed by the West on developing countries as a precondition for trade and aid agreements. Human rights appear to have triumphed in the world.[3] They unite left and right, the

---

1 Anne-Marie Slaughter, 'Government Networks: The Heart of the Liberal Democratic Order', in Gregory Fox and Brad Roth, eds, *Democratic Governance and International Law,* (Cambridge, University of Cambridge Press, 2000), 235.
2 Anne-Marie Slaughter, 'Law Among Liberal States: Liberal Internationalism and the Act of State Doctrine', 92 *Columbia Law Review* 1909 (1992).
3 *The End of Human Rights* opened with the statement 'human rights have triumphed in the world'. Reviewers and commentators have challenged this view from opposing perspectives. Hilary Charlesworth (at the 'End of Human Rights?' symposium, which took place at the Australian National University, Canberra, 11 April 2006) and Bill Bowring (12 *King's College Law Journal*, 2001) have disagreed because they believe human rights should become

pulpit and the state, the minister and the rebel, the North and the South. Human rights are the fate of our societies, the ideology after 'the end of ideologies', the only values left in a valueless world after 'the end of history'. Kosovo, Afghanistan and Iraq were the first wars of the new world order formally conducted in the name of human rights, the postmodern *justa causa*. If these wars established the parameters of a new type of limited independence for those outside the circle of friends and satellites of the global hegemon, they also sketched out the evolving map of a world order no longer based on the nation-state or traditional sovereignty. And yet, many doubts persist. Lebanon is relentlessly bombed as I write these lines and not one day passes without newspaper reports about the latest atrocity somewhere in the world. Triumph and disaster are never far apart.

Postmodern cosmopolitans as well as the British and American governments argue that traditional notions of sovereignty and non-intervention in the internal affairs of states cannot stand in the way of rescuing people from their evil governments. Sovereignty and human rights are presented as a zero sum game. In the new world order, sovereignty bends the knee before morality. This image of human rights resisting and piercing sovereign claims is historically inaccurate, however. The close internal link between human rights (the moral perspective on politics) domestic policy consideration and national sovereignty, evident from the beginning of the human rights movement, was discussed in Part 1 of this book. Morality and power or human rights and sovereignty, the two allegedly opposing principles about to be reconciled in postmodern cosmopolitanism, are two sides of the same coin. They have combined in varying ways during state and empire-building. Every polity, state or empire promotes a version of morality and of people's entitlements that accords with its priorities and interests. Natural rights accompanied the establishment of the modern nation-state in the eighteenth century.[4] Human rights were the (contested) moral foundation of the post-Second World War international order.

the accepted norm of international relations but are still a long way from achieving this. Stewart Motha and Thanos Zartaloudis have argued, on the contrary, that human rights should be resisted and not allowed to become the accepted norm. Statements like mine concede too much to the promoters of human rights (Stewart Motha and Thanos Zartaloudis, 'Law, Ethics and the Utopian End of Human Rights', 12 *Social Legal Studies*, 243–268, 2003). I partly agree and disagree with both positions, hoping this way to avoid the centre. Human rights are the dominant ideology of our age, I believe, although not its fully accepted legal norm. When human rights become policy tools for governments and international institutions or the public expressions of insatiable individual desire they lose their way. The main end of human rights is to resist public and private domination and oppression. When they lose this end their function comes to an end.

4   Costas Douzinas, *The End of Human Rights* (Oxford, Hart, 2000), Chapter 5.

After the collapse of communism, human rights and humanitarianism have become the morality and ideology of the new world order.

The endless process of international and humanitarian law-making put into operation in the last fifty years aims at protecting people from their governments, the putative representatives of popular sovereignty. Why has so much energy been placed on this attempt to decide what are the entitlements of the human being? The standard explanation is that 'it is quite conceivable', as Hannah Arendt put it, 'that one fine day a highly organized and mechanized humanity will conclude quite democratically – namely, by majority decision – that for humanity as a whole it would be better to liquidate certain parts thereof'.[5] The 'market' of human dignity and equality did not conceal a 'hidden hand', and people voted and still vote for regimes and parties determined to violate all human rights, as the examples of Hitler's Germany and Milosevic's Yugoslavia show. To paraphrase Nietzsche, if God, the source of natural law, is dead, he has been replaced by international law.

Yet, the key principle of international law, from the United Nations Charter to all major treaties, has been that of national sovereignty and non-intervention in the domestic affairs of states. After the Second World War, the victorious powers fought tooth and nail over the definitions and priorities of human rights (civil against economic, individual against collective). They unanimously agreed, however, that these rights could not be used to pierce the shield of national sovereignty. Human rights were a major tool for legitimising nationally and internationally the post-war order, at a point at which all principles of state and international organisation had emerged seriously weakened from the war. The supposed contradictory principles of human rights and national sovereignty, schizophrenically both paramount in post-war international law, served two separate agendas of the great powers: the need to legitimise the new order through its commitment to rights, without exposing the victorious states to scrutiny and criticism about their own flagrant violations. As Norman Lewis put it,

> the debate about human rights and the upholding of human dignity, was in reality a process of re-legitimation of the principles of sovereignty and non-intervention in the domestic affairs of sovereign states. The most powerful states, through the human rights discourse, made their priorities the universal concern of others.[6]

Human rights became an instrument for underpinning the power of states.

5 Hannah Arendt, *The Origins of Totalitarianism* ((San Diego, CA, Harvest Books, 1979), 299.
6 Norman Lewis, 'Human Rights, Law and Democracy in an Unfree World' in Tony Evans, *Human Rights Fifty Years On* (Manchester, Manchester University Press, 1988), 89.

The huge enterprise of human rights legislation and codification, which started with the 1948 Universal Declaration of Human Rights, has become the safest haven of a *sui generis* nationalism. Codification, from Justinian to the *Code Napoléon*, has always been the ultimate exercise of legislative sovereignty, the supreme expression of state power. In the same way that the early declarations of rights helped to bring about the absolute, indivisible and illimitable power of the sovereign, so too the post-Second World War expansion of international human rights turned the principle of non-intervention in the domestic affairs of states into the cornerstone of the law and founded the power of the new international institutions. Law-making in the human rights business has been taken over by government representatives, diplomats, policy advisers, international civil servants and human rights experts. As Chapter 1 argues, the agenda for the codification of human rights was set by the great powers and in particular the United States. But priests, princes and prime ministers are the enemy against whom nature, natural rights and human rights were conceived as a defence. The business of government is to govern, not to follow moral principles. Governmental actions in the international arena are dictated by national interest and political considerations, and morality enters the stage always late, when the principle invoked happens to condemn the actions of a political adversary. Government-operated international human rights law is the best illustration of the poacher turned gamekeeper.

The same applies to international institutions. The way in which both right and left insisted, in the days leading to the Iraq war, that if the war was authorised by the Security Council their objections would disappear, was baffling.[7] This is the Council of which three members, China, Russia and the United States, consistently and flagrantly violate the rights of their own citizens. No liberal cosmopolitan would be seen dead in supporting the treatment of Tibetans or Chechens, the death penalty so generously meted in China and the US or the treatment of minorities in all three countries. Yet they are happy to accept this triumvirate of rogues as the final arbiters of international and domestic morality and indeed to accept any government as the judge of what human rights, the practice of resistance to government and dissent from the clichés of public opinion, are.

Planetary policy was always created by the great powers, the subjects of the world system. Smaller states are its objects following the rules introduced by the powerful. The alleged cosmopolitan character of contemporary politics does not derive from their global subjection to universal rules. The reverse is

---

7 Matthew Craven, Susan Marks, Gerry Simpson and Ralph Wilde, 'We are all Teachers of International Law', 17 *Leiden Journal of International Law*, (2004) 363–74.

true: universal rules are created as ideal accompaniments of global phenomena by those who can exercise world policy. Domestic considerations have always played an important role in the calculation of the great powers and determine the ways in which foreign relations are exercised. This leads to a crucial distinction between globalisation and universalisation, which has been almost totally elided in the debate on human rights. Universalisation is the methodology of Kantian moral philosophy. It accepts a particular answer to a moral dilemma, if it is applicable to every similar case without contradiction or exception and elevates a principle of action into a moral rule if it can become a universal maxim. The variable universalism of classical natural law or of normative universalisation acted as regulative principles: they gave a perspective from which each particular action could be judged, in theory at least, in the name of the universal.[8] The empirical globalisation of human rights, on the other hand, is not a normative principle. It refers to the factual matter of counting how many states have adopted how many and which treaties, or how many have introduced which reservations or derogations from treaty obligations. When normative universality becomes a calculable globalisation, it turns from a lofty, albeit impossible, ideal into the lowest common denominator of state interests and rivalries. Every state and power comes under the mantle of the international law of human rights, every government becomes civilised as the 'law of the princes' has finally turned into the 'universal' law of human dignity. But this is an empirical universality, based on the competitive solidarity of sovereign governments and on the pragmatic concerns and calculations of international politics. Oona Hathaway, in an exhaustive quantitative study of state accession to human rights treaties, has concluded that the ratification of such treaties by major Western countries and increased advocacy by human rights NGOs not only did not improve conditions in target countries but on the contrary increased violations.[9] The community of human rights is universal but imaginary: universal humanity does not exist empirically and cannot act as a transcendental principle philosophically.

The underlying tendencies of international law and politics have been accelerated after the collapse of communism. The global arrangements under construction follow moral principles of universal applicability. International human rights have become the universal morality and ideology of the age. They aim to impose moral principles on the exercise of (domestic and international) power – to moralise politics. The moralisation of international

---

8   Douzinas, op. cit., Chapters 2, 3 and 4.
9   Oona Hathaway, 'Do Human Rights Treaties Make a Difference?', 111 *Yale Law Journal* 1935 (2002).

relations is evident at a number of levels. Let me mention briefly some of the favourites of academics promoting the new order. First, a new type of international community is emerging, in which peace, liberal democracy and human rights are the preconditions of 'complex interdependence'. The international community is 'regulated by law and considerations of justice'.[10] Second, the way a government treats its people has become a concern of international law, institutions and governments. 'Democracy, freedom and the promotion of "civil society" is the contemporary zeitgeist. They are supposed to place constraints on the way a sovereign power is organised and exercised internally'.[11] Finally, the process of standard-setting of human rights norms is being rapidly replaced by measures to improve the enforcement machinery and guarantee compliance. Law, courts, tribunals and lawyers are central to these developments. As Ruti Teitel, one of the most authoritative international law scholars put it, 'a new international legalism – or "humanity's law" – [has developed which] assists in framing and legitimating the form of policymaking choices in present global politics'.[12]

According to Teitel, 'humanity's law' is the result of a merger between the old law of war (traditionally called 'humanitarian' law) and human rights law. The law of war limited state action in periods of conflict, human rights during peacetime. The new global rule of law has expanded both temporally and spatially. Temporally, no distinction can be drawn between war and peace. International criminal justice, in particular, used to be invoked after the end of hostilities against the vanquished enemy. Now it is invoked before or during the war and becomes part of the conflict and its solution. Future criminal proceedings against Milosevic became part of the pressure put on Serbia before and during the Kosovo war. Spatially, emphasis has shifted from the protection of national borders to the upholding of certain (legal) concepts and values. Support from states and international institutions is no longer mobilised as a response to threats to territorial sovereignty. Rather, humanitarian wars are triggered by attacks on human rights or the stability of populations through ethnic cleansing, atrocities, etc. As Teitel puts it, 'the emerging legal regime

---

10 Cornelia Navari, *Internationalism and State in the Twentieth Century* (London, Routledge, 2000), 270; see Ann-Marie Slaughter, 'Government Networks' in G.H. Fox and B.R. Roth, eds, *Democratic Governance and International Law* (Cambridge, Cambridge University Press, 2002).

11 Louis Henkin, 'The Future of International Law' in C. Ku and P.F. Diehl, eds, *International Law: Classic and Contemporary Readings* (Boulder, CO, Lynne Rienner Publishers, 1998), 552.

12 Ruti Teitel, '"Humanity" Law: Rule of Law for the New Global Politics', 35 *Cornell International Law Journal*, 355 (2002), 357.

plays a role in shaping current political policymaking, chiefly by reframing and restructuring the discourse in international affairs in a legalist direction'.[13] The most important and violent effect, however, is the use of military force for 'humanitarian interventions' by the United States or American-led coalitions with or without United Nations authorisation. The justification for the violation of sovereignty in the first stage of the new order was that flagrant violations of human rights should override the cardinal principle of international law. For Teitel, 'the new legalism offers an ongoing justificatory apparatus for unilateral and multilateral international intervention'.[14] David Kennedy agrees: the new disposition could lead to a situation where 'governments would be recognised and states admitted to the international community when they complied with the norms of international human rights'.[15] Humanity's law reconstitutes the structure, subjects and core values of the international system. It is arguably well on the way to becoming the constitution of the new world order.

Teitel's 'humanity law' has striking similarities with Michael Hardt and Antonio Negri's claim that empire appears as a 'juridical formation' with its own distinct supranational constitution and a new form of sovereignty. Its constitutional structure unites the various components 'under a single logic of rule' and creates a new notion of supranational right, 'a new design for the production of norms and legal instruments of coercion'.[16] Old imperialism created 'an extension of the sovereignty of the European nation-states beyond their boundaries' and a hierarchy between centre and periphery. In empire, nation-states have declined as sources of normativity; sovereignty consists of a series of national and supranational 'organisms' united under a single logic of rule. This new source of juridical production is effective on a global scale and has assumed the sovereign juridical role. New sovereignty can no longer be restricted as empire becomes spatially boundless and normatively limitless.[17]

Spatial boundlessness, temporal extension and the withering away of sovereignty bring together the lawyers' 'humanity's law' and Hardt and Negri's 'supranational right' despite the political differences of their promoters. Their similarity is further indicated by the claim that concepts rather than territories demarcate the contours of the new order. As Ulrich Beck, an ardent

---

13 Ibid. 365.
14 Ibid. 381.
15 David Kennedy, *The Dark Side of Virtue* (Princeton, NJ, Princeton University Press, 2004), 169–70.
16 Michael Hardt and Antonio Negri, *Empire* (Cambridge, MA., Harvard University Press, 2000), xii, 9.
17 Ibid. xii.

cosmopolitan puts it, 'the problem is not boundarylessness, but that boundaries are no longer being drawn along national lines'.[18] During the British Empire, maps marked states in different colours and painted large tracks of the world in the blue of empire. 'Concepts', in other words ideology, have obvious attractions as cartographic devices. They allow their initiators and promoters to determine the 'concept' and to provide its authoritative interpretation. They offer simple and easily understood blueprints for deciding who counts as citizen, denizen and barbarian. They give an indication only of what is allowed and what not, leaving the penitent unsure about their exact meaning and import. Finally, they simplify the colour of the world map. There is no doubt that 'concepts' are an easy and flexible way for arranging the world, much easier than frontiers, rivers and mountains. But what is the concept or norm of humanity's law?

In August 2006, Tony Blair argued that our recent wars were not about regime change but about 'values change'. 'We could have chosen [national] security as the battleground. But we didn't. We chose values.'[19] For Teitel and most lawyers, human rights are the key value rearranging the world. It has many attractions. It is moral, it claims universality and it is, to a certain extent, legally binding. It formed the main rhetorical and ideological weapon of the early humanitarian wars under Clinton, it has wide international legitimacy and it can call upon a well-organised international, state and non-governmental institutional structure. 'Humanity' is semantically flexible and can be put to the service of all kind of causes, as Chapter 3 argued. One of the responses to the prioritisation of security after 9/11 is characteristic. 'National security' has been the privileged term giving the state discretion to override policies and human rights when it feels threatened by real or imaginary enemies. But Western states have now replaced national with 'human' security as the basis for engagement in world politics, 'a conception more attentive to the concerns and insecurities of persons and people'.[20] The substitution of human insecurity for national security hugely expands the scope of state action both domestically and internationally. In the climate of fear of terrorists, criminals and other rogues assiduously cultivated by Western governments, personal insecurity is an ever-present existential condition offering open-ended authorisation for all kinds of preventive and protective action. It extends from British internment to American torture to Israel's bombing and killing of hundreds of Palestinians and Lebanese in order to achieve the release of four soldiers.

18   Ulrich Beck, *Cosmopolitan Vision* (Cambridge, Polity, 2006), 110.
19   Peter Wilby, 'Tony Blair and His Values', *The Guardian*, 4 August 2006.
20   Richard Falk, *The Declining World Order* (New York, Routledge, 2004), 11, 16.

The other candidate for the position of cardinal value is freedom. Interestingly, for Hardt and Negri, freedom is the main value of empire and the greatest legacy of the United States constitution. In the period between the presidencies of Thomas Jefferson and Andrew Jackson, 'a new principle of sovereignty is affirmed, different from the European one: liberty is made sovereign and sovereignty is defined as radically democratic within and continuous process of expansion. The frontier is the frontier of liberty'.[21] It is true that the heart of American ideology is to be found in the 'concept' or value of freedom. But freedom is a notoriously ambiguous and contested term. Its open-endedness can support opposed actions and regimes, as the proverbial 'terrorist and freedom fighter' quip shows. Tom Farer, in a recent review of the link between human rights and American domestic and foreign policy, has argued that four features characterise American ideology. Religiosity, the failure of socialism and Christian democracy, a constitutional culture that promotes the rights of the individual and suspects government except when it acts in the name of national security and, finally, laissez-faire capitalism.[22] The core meaning of freedom is economic. It is unfettered freedom to buy and sell goods, capital, land and labour. As Peter Fitzpatrick put it, the liberty of the frontier referred to an acquisitive world, in which 'voracity [is] a virtue'.[23] Based on this premise, trade has always been seen as a means of liberation. Its imposition on others (even by force) does not undermine their freedom. President Bush Jr expressed the idea in his usual simple terms: 'Open trade is not an economic opportunity, it is a moral imperative.' [24] Trade liberates people, makes them more prosperous and spreads American values in the bargain too. These values are 'supposed to be universal, valid for everyone: expressed in the rhetoric of "liberty" and "freedom" that Americans employed ubiquitously, without, in most cases, any sense of the intrinsically problematical aspects of these ideals'.[25]

21 Hardt and Negri, op. cit., 169. We should add here that while freedom may be the core concept of American ideology it is not its 'principle of sovereignty'. The politico-theological sovereignty of modernity does not have 'principles'. Its distinguishing characteristic is the unfettered power of decision.

22 Tom Farer, 'The Interplay of Domestic Politics, Human Rights and US Foreign Policy' (forthcoming, on file with author).

23 Peter Fitzpatrick, 'The Immanence of Empire' in Jodi Dean and Paul Passavant, eds, *Empire's New Clothes* (New York, Routledge, 2004), 49.

24 Quoted in Roger Burbach and Jim Tarbell, *Imperial Overstretch* (London, Zed Books, 2004), 129.

25 Bernard Porter, *Empire and Superempire* (New Haven, CT, Yale University Press, 2006), 70.

Capitalism has always moralised the economy and applied a gloss of righteousness to profit-making precisely because it is so hard to believe it. From Adam Smith's 'hidden hand', to the religious nature of the development discourse,[26] to the assertion that untrammelled egotism promotes the common good or that beneficial effects 'trickle down' if the rich get even bigger tax exemptions, capitalism has consistently tried to claim the moral high ground. The predominantly negative meaning of freedom as absence of external constraints – a euphemism for keeping state regulation of the economy at a minimum – has recently taken a more sinister bend, however. President Bush Jr used the word freedom thirty-seven times, in his 2005 Inaugural Address. 'Freedom is the Almighty's gift to every man and woman in this world and as the greatest power on earth we have an obligation to spread freedom', he intoned. America's history is 'freedom for everyone', its mission, 'to liberate the oppressed of the world'.[27] But Bush menacingly qualified his message: 'the survival of liberty in our land increasingly depends on the success of liberty in other lands'.[28] America is threatened unless the causes of anti-American resentment and hatred are eliminated. 'To make her own peoples safe, America has to revolutionise the world.'[29]

In Iraq, the meaning and values of this revolution is quite clear. Paul Bremer, the first post-war viceroy, imposed what the *Economist* called a 'capitalist dream regime'. It included 'the full privatisation of public enterprises, full ownership rights by foreign firms of Iraqi businesses, full repatriation of foreign profits . . . the opening of Iraq's banks to foreign control . . . the elimination of nearly all trade barriers', the imposition of a regressive flat tax, the outlawing of strikes and the restriction of trade union rights.[30] What is patently missing is any concern for human rights in general and for minimum economic and social rights in particular. The great advantage of making 'concepts' or values the foundation of the world order is their flexibility; the more general and vague, the greater their flexibility. Values can be widened or narrowed according to current priorities; potentially problematic rights can be discarded through the invocation of opposed rights. In the occupied lands, the 'freedom' of property and trade trumps economic and social rights. In a strange historical twist, human rights became the dominant ideology and started receding at precisely the same time.

26   Jennifer Beard, *The Art of Development* (London, Cavendish-Routledge, 2006).
27   President's Inaugural Address to the Nation delivered on 20 January 2005.
28   Quoted in Porter, op. cit., 108.
29   Ibid.
30   Quoted in David Harvey, *The New Imperialism* (Oxford, Oxford University Press, 2005), 214–15.

Most legal academics welcoming the turn to values do not spend much time discussing its historical provenance, philosophical premises and ideological parameters. They offer a strained apology based on outlandish discussions of international law and recent political events. The disciplines of international law and international relations are somewhat problematic intellectual fields. International law is in a state of permanent crisis, as Chapter 9 discusses, while scholarship in international relations takes often the form of (more or less) sophisticated journalism. The crash empiricism, outlandish pragmatism and uncritical acceptance of the pronouncement of Western governments make many of these texts painful to read. The unreality of their claims is matched by their ideological convictions. The claim that the protection of human rights was the intended effect or a main concern of recent wars, for example, is ridiculed by the uncounted deaths, up to 100,000 according to some reports, and the misery of Iraqi civilians since the invasion. Indeed 'humanity's law' conflation of human rights law with the law of war forgets that 'humanitarian law contemplates a starting point of death, violence and destruction that is repugnant to the essence of human rights law'.[31] The intellectual distortions of attempts to reconcile the two bodies of law are quite amazing. They are exemplified by a recent article, which discovers a 'human rights-based law of war' around the principle that 'individuals may be killed intentionally if their expected death is compensated [*sic*] by more than an equivalent expected increase in enjoyment of human rights'.[32] In this humanitarian calculus, enjoyment trumps death; the death drive and *jouissance* of the cosmopolitan saviours overrides the pleasure and survival principle of those to be rescued through their death. But the naive frankness of this 'modest proposal' indicates the problem of the wider and unavoidable difficulties when the law is entrusted with the job of preventing and punishing atrocities. Hannah Arendt accurately identified them, first, during the Eichmann trial.[33] The translation of genocide, atrocities or torture into professional legal language is hugely problematic. Like all law, terrible evil must be presented according to strict procedures, expressed in legal doctrines replete with their principles and counter-principles, their rules always accompanied by exceptions. It must confront interpretative tricks and respond to technical defences. These open-ended and formalistic techniques not only cannot accommodate the enormity of evil; they often banalise it and can even help absolve it. Martti Koskenniemi succinctly identifies the harm:

---

31 Audrey Benison, 'War Crimes: A Human Rights Approach to a Humanitarian Law Problem at the International Criminal Court', 88 *Georgia Law Journal*, 141 (1999), 152.

32 David Koller, 'The Moral Imperative: Towards a Human Rights-based Law of War', 46/1 *Harvard International Law Journal* 231 (2005), 251.

33 Hannah Arendt, *Eichmann in Jerusalem* (London, Penguin, 1992).

[It] lies in the suggestion that law may condemn evil, however massive, only if legal technique allowed this when this technique always contains a justifying principle as well: perhaps genocide by nuclear weapons resulted from self-defence, was an unintended consequence of action or was necessary to prevent some greater evil. Perhaps the acts did not fall under some definition of war crime or torture, the claimant lacked *locus standi*, or the lawyer was devoid of jurisdiction.[34]

The assertion that the protection of rights is the basis of new enforcement mechanisms cannot explain why all attempts to bring the NATO leaders to court after Kosovo and Iraq failed, despite claims about the centrality of law and human rights. The War Crimes Tribunal for Former Yugoslavia decided not to investigate the claims that NATO had engaged in violations of international humanitarian law. The growing acceptance of humanitarian war concludes the process in which the humanitarian impulse that 'started out as an expression of empathy with common humanity [has transformed] into a lever for strategic aims drawn up and acted upon by external agencies'.[35] Finally, these arguments ignore a basic jurisprudential insight. Human rights provisions more than other pieces of law and litigation are profoundly ambiguous and must be interpreted in complex political and legal situations. Human rights are the one area in which the realist and critical legal claims have been almost universally confirmed.[36] In brief summary, the critics argue that human rights provisions are indeterminate; that they are always subjected to wide and similarly indeterminate restrictions;[37] that rights are inescapably involved in conflicts with other rights (freedom against security, expression against privacy)

---

34 Martti Koskenniemi, 'Letter to the Editors of the Symposium', 93/2 *American Journal of International Law* 351 (1999), 358.

35 David Campbell, 'The Road to Military Humanitarianism: How the Human Rights NGOs Shaped New Humanitarian Agenda' 23 *Human Rights Quarterly* 678 (2001), 700.

36 Duncan Kennedy, *A Critique of Adjudication* (Cambridge, MA, Harvard University Press, 1977) 304–9; Martti Koskenniemi, 'The Effects of Rights on Political Culture' in Philip Alston *et al.* (eds) *The European Union and Human Rights* (Oxford, Oxford University Press, 1999) 99–116; David Kennedy, 'The International Human Rights Movement. Part of the Problem?', 3 *European Human Rights Law Review* 245–67 (2001).

37 The right to freedom of expression in Article 10 ECHR is subjected to such 'formalities, conditions, restrictions or penalties as are prescribed by law and are necessary in a democratic society in the interests of national security, territorial integrity or public safety, for the prevention of disorder or crime, for the protection of health or morals, for the protection of the reputation of the rights of others, for preventing the disclosure of information received in confidence, or for maintaining the impartiality of the judiciary'. A cynical soul might observe that every possible restriction on speech can be justified under this litany of exceptions.

or with the same rights of others; that their open-ended language means that they acquire meaning and effects in acts of interpretation and application, in which all kinds of non-principled considerations are involved; finally, that the context of application is much more important than the text of the provisions.

The claim, for example, in Article 2 of the European Convention on Human Rights that 'everyone has a right to life' gives no answer whatsoever to questions about the legitimacy of abortion, euthanasia or the use of lethal force by the military against civilians and the security services against presumed terrorist threats.[38] Human rights provisions do not wear their meaning on the sleeve of the relevant treaty clause. Whether, for example, events in Rwanda amounted to genocide (according to the Security Council they did not) or, whether the persecution of Albanians in Kosovo to a 'humanitarian catastrophe' (no according to the Security Council, yes according to NATO) is not answered by treaties and conventions but by the politicians and diplomats interpreting them in the context of state interests. An ardent supporter of the new order admits 'any substantive issue could be labelled as a human rights violation'.[39] If one combines this recognition with law's intrinsic indeterminacy, which means that 'the legal argument inexorably and quite predictably, allows the defence of whatever position',[40] it becomes clear that the trust put on lawyers' ability to resolve conflict through the tool of human rights is seriously misplaced.

These responses to the unthinking paeans to the new world order do not answer the question how and why did this new international norm emerge? What forces brought it about and what are the stakes behind its adoption? Human rights and their dissemination are not simply the result of the liberal or charitable disposition of the West. Cosmopolitanism, universal morality and human rights, express and promote the quasi-imperial configuration of the new times. Its signs are everywhere. The ideological battles of the cold war were

---

38 In a number of cases the European Court has stated that states retain a 'margin of appreciation' (in other words discretion) in deciding their obligations under the Convention (*Handyside* v. *UK*, Series A, ECHR, No 24, Judgment of 7 December 1976); that 'even if one assumes that Article 2 protects the unborn life, the rights and interests involved have been weighed against each other in a reasonable way' (*Open Door Counselling Ltd* v. *Ireland*, ECHR, Series A, No 246, Judgment of 29 October 1992); that 'the value of life to be protected can and must be weighed against other rights of the person in question' (*McCann and others* v. *UK*, ECHR, Series A, No 324, Judgment of 27 September 1995).

39 Katarina Tomasevski, *Responding to Human Rights Violations: 1946–1999* (The Hague, Martinus Nijhoff, 2000), 405.

40 Martti Koskenniemi, 'Letter to the Editors of the Symposium', 93/2 *American Journal of International Law* 351 (1999), 354.

fought over human rights. The West promoted civil and political rights and castigated the Soviets for their violations. The communists retorted that economic and social provision was more important than formal liberties. The collapse of communism signalled the victory of the principles of market capitalism and human rights. In the same way that the victory of the Christian Emperor Constantine over his pagan enemies led to the spread of Christianity around the known world, the American triumph over the 'evil empire' has led to the global dissemination of the principles of universal human rights. Small and weak states were given a clear signal about what matters in the world today. Indeed, the continuous reference to moral values, human rights and freedom in American and British pronouncements creates the (false) impression that an enforceable public international law is in the making, which will override the sovereignty of non-compliant states.

Global moral and civic rules are the necessary companion of the globalisation of economic production and consumption, of the completion of world capitalism that follows the dogmas of neo-liberalism. Over the last thirty years, we have witnessed, without much comment, the creation of global legal rules regulating the world capitalist economy, including rules on investment, trade, aid and intellectual property. Robert Cooper has called it the voluntary imperialism of the global economy:

> It is operated by an international consortium of financial Institutions such as the IMF and the World Bank . . . These institutions . . . make demands, which increasingly emphasise good governance. If states wish to benefit, they must open themselves up to the interference of international organisations and foreign states.

Cooper concludes that 'what is needed then is a new kind of imperialism, one acceptable to a world of human rights and cosmopolitan values'.[41] Michael Hardt and Antonio Negri, agree with Cooper's diagnosis but they do not find it as reason for celebration: 'Although the practice of Empire is continually bathed in blood, the concept of Empire is always dedicated to peace – a perpetual and universal peace outside of history.'[42]

Cooper refers to the extensive imposition of market liberalisation and deregulation policies on developing and former socialist countries by the World Bank, the IMF and the WTO. We examined in Part I the way in which domestic politics has been subjected to economic and moral considerations. The same

---

41 Robert Cooper, 'The New Liberal Imperialism', *The Observer,* 1 April 2002, 3.
42 Hardt and Negri, op. cit., xv.

is happening at the international stage leading to a convergence of the domestic and the global. Morality in the guise of human rights replaces politics in international affairs and neo-liberal economics is imposed by international institutions on governments everywhere. Anne Orford, in an exhaustive review of the activities of these institutions, concludes that the conditions imposed on developing states in loan and aid agreements 'constrain the ability of peoples or their representatives to make decisions about wage levels for workers, education policy, health policy, social security provision, provision of services, constitutional reform, levels of unemployment, and federal/state relations within federations'.[43] These conditions determine 'economic restructuring', a euphemism for the imposition of neo-liberal policies on debtor states in purely technocratic terms. Third World parliaments and even prime ministers are regularly excluded from the decision-making process and quite often do not even have access to the necessary information. The major powers and international institutions take it for granted that 'in the South, democracy is subordinate to their own economic and strategic interests, and they try to shape democracy in such a way that it becomes a mere form of free-market management'.[44] Similar policies are followed by the WTO. According to Orford, TRIPS and GATS restrict democracy in three main ways. Their investment liberalisation agenda puts transnational corporations in a dominant position, promoting private interests and denying local people the information necessary to make decisions about economic policy. Second, these agreements impose the privatisation of public services and utilities. Third, patenting provisions privilege research generated knowledge in agrochemicals and pharmaceuticals making it expensive to obtain while leaving unprotected traditional and community-based knowledge. Orford develops these ideas by arguing that the trumpeted 'linkage' between trade and human rights, which would allegedly 'humanise' global capitalism, is impossible. Trade agreements follow a Christian model of sacrifice in which the 'market' has replaced God. Human rights and democracy claim to break away from the sacrificial economy circulating between father (God, Abraham, the market) and son (Christ, Isaac, economic man). Anne Orford's delightful parallel reading of trade agreements and human rights cases indicates that the subject of rights and the economic man of trade coincide and are both constituted through the sacrificial logic of the market. The history of international law shows that the formal benefits of the culture of human rights, democracy, etc. are always

---

43 Anne Orford, 'Locating the Internationals: Military and Monetary Interventions after the Cold War', 38/2 *Harvard International Law Journal* 465 (1997).

44 Jochen Hipples, quoted in Orford, 468, 469.

predicated on people 'being produced as civilised subjects of that culture else-where', in the strictures of colonial law, the mandate and trusteeship systems or, today, in the demands of neo-liberal capitalism formalised in international economic law.[45]

The often violent imposition of neo-liberal economic policies upon the rest of the world has been a consistent policy of recent American administrations. It was President Clinton, first, who argued that globalisation is the historical stage of American dominance and adopted policies promoting the penetration of American capital around the world: 'Open and competitive commerce will enrich us as a nation.' As a result, it had become 'time for us to make trade a priority element of American security'.[46] The rhetoric used for this combination of trade and security is of 'enlargement and "openness"': 'we want "enlargement" of both our values and our Pizza Huts. We want the world to follow our lead and become democratic and capitalistic, with a Web site in every pot, a Pepsi on every lip, Microsoft Windows on every computer and with everyone, everywhere pumping their own gas.'[47] Openness on the other hand, is

> the removal of barriers to the movement of goods, capital, people, ideas, thereby fostering an international order conducive to American interests, governed by American norms, regulated by American power, and, above all, satisfying the expectation of the American people for ever-greater abundance.[48]

The proclaimed spread of freedom and democracy must be placed within the much longer and consistent policy of opening doors to capitalist markets. This is carried out at two levels: American foreign policy promotes and helps financially, militarily and through technology transfers capitalist client states irrespective of their political systems or human rights records. International institutions, on the other hand, set the rules and supervise 'openness' under guidance from the dominant powers. Politics has become economics, democratic decision-making technocratic expertise and capitalism the end point of history.

---

45 Anne Orford, 'Beyond Harmonisation: Trade, Human Rights and the Economy of Sacrifice' *Leiden Journal of International Law* 179–213 (2005).
46 Quoted in Andrew Bachevich, *American Empire* (Cambridge, MA, Harvard University Press, 2002), 96.
47 Thomas Friedman, 'A Manifesto for the Fast World', *New York Times Magazine*, 28 March 1999, 43.
48 Bachevich, 88.

For a brief moment around 1990, globalisation and the collapse of communism seduced people into believing that conflict had become pointless and obsolete. In that climate of euphoria, economic rules, free markets and capitalist institutions started being gradually supplemented by moral and civic regulations and directives. The combination of the two would prepare the individual of the new order, a world citizen, highly moralised, highly regulated but also highly differentiated materially, despite the common human rights that everyone enjoys, from Helsinki to Hanoi and from London to Lahore. We can find parallels with the emergence of early capitalism. The legal system first developed the rules necessary for the regulation of capitalist production, including rules for the protection of property and contract and the development of legal and corporate personality. Only later did civic rules emerge, mainly with the creation of civil and political rights, which led to the creation of the modern subject and citizen. These rules gave the man of the classical declarations the legal tools and public recognition necessary to cut his traditional ties, abandon any residual ideas of virtue and duty and organise his activities and life-plan according to a calculation of interest borne by the institution of rights. Similarly today, the globalisation of the *sui generis* morality of human rights follows the gradual unification of world markets. As economic practices, legal rules and governance are standardised, a unified ethics, semiotics and law becomes the international lingua franca. This common language promises perpetual peace but forgets its own founding violence. According to the 2000 UN Development report 30,000 children die every day of malnutrition and the life expectancy in sub-Saharan Africa is thirty-six years. The extreme injustice of global distribution is invisible to cosmopolitan law and is reduced to the sphere of the private; natural inevitable and humanitarian intervention will not confront the regime of intellectual property that condemns millions of people to death by disease. Poverty, disease, lack of food and clean water, violence against minorities and women, HIV/Aids are the main causes of misery and death in the world. But they are not seen as worthy of 'humanitarian' intervention. They are demoted to the private and domestic, they become an invisible and normalised part of the contingencies of life for which not much can be done. They are left to the magnanimity of philanthropists and the goodwill of pop stars. Despite the rhetoric of universal international law only a tiny part of the world comes under its purview and only a few problems of interest to the West are defined as crises.[49]

---

49 Hilary Charlesworth, 'International Law: a Discipline in Crisis', 65 *Modern Law Review* 377 (2004).

The universalism of rights was invented by the West, but will be used now by the South and East to make claims on the distribution of the world product. The recent converts to universal values are led to believe that improvement of domestic human rights will strengthen their claim against world resources. Milosevic was extradited to the Hague for a few hundred million dollars in aid to Serbia, while the Afghan regime is given aid if it polices successfully the borders of empire. Aid agreements routinely impose privatisation, market economics and human rights as the new gospel of liberation. Neo-liberal economic policies and human rights appear to promise an inexorable process of equalisation between East, South and West. Poor states are treated like the Western workers of old, as dangerous and valueless partners at worst (rogue states) or, as suffering and deserving recipients who must get the chances and philanthropy proletarians were offered in earlier times. Aid and human rights are the contemporary version of alms and Sunday school, of poor law and skills training.

As we know from Western histories, formal liberties cannot be contained in their formalism for too long. Soon, the workers with the vote and freedom of speech will demand the income and resources needed to make their new-found freedoms real: they will ask for the material preconditions of equality. Lecturers in China and farmers in India will demand to earn as much as those in Helsinki or southern France, something that can only be done through a substantial reduction in the Western standard of living. The (implicit) promise that market-led home-based economic growth will inexorably lead the South to Western economic standards is fraudulent. The Western ability to turn the protection of formal rights into a limited guarantee of material, economic and social rights was based on huge transfers from the colonies to the metropolis. While universal morality and rights now militate in favour of reverse flows, Western policies on development, aid, trade and Third World debt, and American policies on oil pricing, gas emissions and defence spending, indicate that this is not politically feasible. Indeed, unsustainable living standards at the core depend on flows of wealth from the periphery. As Immanuel Wallerstein put it, 'if all humans have equal rights, and all the peoples have equal rights, then we cannot maintain the kind of inegalitarian system that the capitalist world-economy has always been and always will be'.[50] When the unbridgeability of the gap between the missionary statements on equality and dignity and the bleak reality of obscene inequality becomes apparent, human rights rather than eliminating war will lead to new and uncontrollable

---

50   Immanuel Wallerstein, 'The Insurmountable Contradictions of Liberalism', 94 *Southern Atlantic Quarterly* (1995), 176–7.

types of tension and conflict. While human rights appear to be universal and uninterested in the particularities of each situation, their triumph means that they have now become prime weapons in political conflict, something that undermines their claim to universality. The reference to their common values will not stop their polemical use, by those who have been at the receiving end of our humanitarian wars. Spanish soldiers taken prisoners met the advancing Napoleonic armies who were spreading modernity and liberty, with banners inscribed 'Down with freedom!' It is not difficult to imagine people meeting the 'peacekeepers' and humanitarians of the new times with cries of 'Down with human rights!' The devastating bombings against the Baghdad Red Cross headquarters and United Nations compound in 2003 were the beginning of a counter-attack by the Iraqi insurgency. When the insignia of universal morality are embossed on the flags of occupiers, the local insurgents interpret them like the cross on the crusaders' banners: they become symbols of oppression and humiliation and the most particular expressions of self-interest.[51]

Universalist morality claims to muster agreement about the content of its prescriptions. But universal human rights cannot work in the abstract. As they become the lingua franca of the new times but are unable to eliminate conflict, the formal struggle over human rights will revolve predominantly around their interpretation and application. They can only operate as an instrument of the leading powers of the new times or by the citizens claiming not just formal but material equality. As always, the universal is placed at the service of the particular: it is the prerogative of a particular to announce the universal. The enunciating particular can place itself towards the universal in two positions: either it can attach an opt-out clause and exclude itself from the applicability of the universal or it can arrogate itself the exclusive power and right to offer the correct interpretation of the universal. France was the enunciator of the universal in early modernity, the United States in the new times, and they have adopted both practices.

The imperial opt-out clause is most apparent when the Americans adopt what can be called their 'universalist exceptionalism' and denounce the jurisdiction of the new International Criminal Court declaring that under no circumstances will they allow American personnel to be tried by it. But they also claim the power of the sole authoritative interpreter of the law. During the Afghan campaign, President Bush declared that, despite the unanimous view of international lawyers to the contrary, his interpretation of the Geneva

---

51 K. Anderson, 'Humanitarian Inviolability in Crisis: the Meaning of Impartiality and Neutrality for UN and NGO Agencies Following the 2003–4 Afghanistan and Iraq conflicts', 17 *Harvard Human Rights Journal* 41–74 (2004).

Conventions was the only valid one and accordingly, the prisoners held in the Guantánamo Bay camp would be designated not as prisoners of war, but would instead fall into the novel category of 'unlawful combatants'.[52] Similarly, the interpretation of the meaning of torture by American legal officers, practised in Abu Ghraib, Guantánamo Bay and the various destinations of the process of 'exceptional rendition', wildly diverges from the accepted legal position.

It is a little ironic that, while the insurgents approach the universal as the most aggressive version of the particular and colonial, the same approach in reverse can be observed in the other major objective of American foreign and military policy, the spread of democracy. Susan Marks in an extraordinary review of the cosmopolitan claim that a 'democratic norm' has developed in international law, under which the law requires and imposes democratic forms of government, concludes that the democratic norm thesis works 'to stabilise existing power relations by identifying democracy with low intensity democracy' and 'global democracy with pan-national democracy'.[53] But even the 'low intensity' democracy of elections and basic rights was unacceptable to the White House when the election results in the Palestinian territories, Iran, Venezuela and Bolivia did not go the way the Americans wanted despite the large aid given to the opposition. In the case of Palestine, relations were broken with the freely elected government of Hamas, while the democratically elected presidents of Venezuela, Iran and Bolivia have been repeatedly denounced. On the other hand, the Pakistani dictatorship and the absolute monarchies of Saudi Arabia and the various Emirates are beyond reproach if they align themselves to American foreign policy. The principles of human rights and democracy are universal, only if they promote the interests of the most particular.

Social and political systems become hegemonic by turning their ideological priorities into universal principles and values. The rulers must adjust their ideas to those of the ruled to have them accepted and adopted; in reverse, the ruled accept the (adjusted) ideology of the rulers as their own. In the new world order, human rights are the perfect candidate for this role. Their core principles, interpreted negatively and economically, promote neo-liberal capitalist penetration. Under a different construction, their abstract provisions could subject the inequalities and indignities of late capitalism to withering attack. But this cannot happen as long as they are used by the dominant powers

---

52   'Bush Says No to POW Status for Detainees' (2002) CNN.com <http://www.cnn.com/2002/US/01/28/ret.wh.detainees/> at 23 July 2002.

53   Susan Marks, *The Riddle of All Constitutions* (Oxford, Oxford University Press, 2000), 100.

to spread the 'values' of a nihilistic ideology. This is why Jacques Derrida denounced the

> discourse on human rights and democracy [which] remains little more than an obscene alibi so long as it tolerates the terrible plight of so many millions of human beings suffering from malnutrition, disease, and humiliation, grossly deprived not only of bread and water but of equality or freedom.[54]

The critique of injustice cannot be formulated in the terms of a discourse that supports the arrangements producing injustice. The short-circuit between human rights as ideology and human rights as critique is complete. In a historical first, the end of human rights coincides with their rise.

54 Jacques Derrida, *Rogues* (Pascale-Anne Brault and Michael Naas, trans.) (Stanford, CA, Stanford University Press, 2005), 86.

Chapter 9

The brief glory and the long crisis of international law

At around March 2003, international law came briefly out of its closet of well-oiled diplomatic lunches and obscure academic seminars and gloried in a few months of fame. The stakes were high, indeed the highest a government and a nation can face: going to war. The law has played a secondary walk-on role in the drama of this ultimate decision of life and death in the last fifty years. What distinguished the discussions in the House of Commons in early 2003 and for a few months afterwards was the impression that international law had moved to the front of the stage and become the protagonist in deliberations and decision-making. Newspapers were full of articles and letters by international lawyers, people discussed the finer points of the UN Charter and various Security Council resolutions, the chattering classes dissected the small print of hitherto obscure treaty clauses and legal concepts. Academics often complain that the world does not listen to them and, as a result, important decisions are taken without a full understanding of the issues. In the debate leading to the Iraq war, this changed radically.

International law has suffered something of a bad press among lawyers and academics. The charges are well known. It is a kind of soft law without bite, highly dependent for compliance on the good will of states rather than the usual sanctions of domestic law. The lack of a world government and a global law-maker is accompanied by the absence of a proper court to interpret the law and a serious police force to enforce it. Academically, international law is seen as a peripheral exercise, closer to the doubtful pursuits of international relations rather than to a fully formed legal discipline.[1] International lawyers

---

1 Martti Koskenniemi, 'International Law in Europe', 16 *European Journal of International Law* 113 (2005); Hilary Charlesworth, 'International Law: a Discipline in Crisis', 65 *Modern Law Review* 377 (2004); Matthew Craven *et al.*, 'We are the Teachers of International Law', 17 *Leiden Journal of International Law* 362 (2004); David Kennedy, 'When Renewal Repeats: Thinking against the Box', 32 *International Law and Politics* 335 (2000).

are often treated as apologists who add a veneer of unworthy respectability to base motives and low campaigns.[2] As a renowned international lawyer puts it, it is quite usual 'for legal academics from other fields to think the internationalist jurisprudentially naive and politically suspect. Either a utopian socialist or free-market cosmopolitan'.[3] In short, it is a commonly held view that international law is an intellectually indifferent discipline pursued in the main by smooth-talkers more interested in world travel than in the hard graft of the library and the seminar room.

All that changed in a short eighteen months in 2002 and 2003. The media and a large part of the public discussed extensively the legality or otherwise of the pending war. International law was considered crucial for the initial decision to go to war, for its legitimate conduct, for the conduct of the ensuing occupation of Iraq and for the potential criminal liability of political and military leaders. International law and lawyers experienced suddenly a huge increase in their market value. A number of conferences and new organisations were set up and capitalised on the newly found respectability of the discipline. Legal theorists took an increasing interest in a discipline that until recently was not discussed much.[4] It was an exciting period for international lawyers and academics more generally. An international lawyer friend told me that he hated going to parties in the spring of 2003 because he was interminably interrogated about the importance of Security Council resolutions and the veto powers of the permanent members of the Council. I suspected that he loved it. Doctors complain that they are regularly accosted at cocktail parties for a quick diagnosis and advice for some mild symptom. International lawyers were the last group, one would expect, to be inflicted with this particular occupational hazard. International law had arrived on the world stage or, at least, on the television screen.

But it was not here to stay. The moment was short-lived. The short period of international law glory has now come to an end and a number of recent books by prominent international lawyers have conducted the post-mortem or, better, offered a eulogy for the brief period of prominence or at least attention that the subject enjoyed in the hectic months of 2002 and 2003.[5] Our interest

2 Martti Koskenniemi, *From Apology and Utopia. The Structure of International Legal Argument* (Helsinki, Finnish Lawyers Publishing Company, 1989).

3 David Kennedy, 'A New World Order', 4 *Transnational Law and Contemporary Problems* 329 (1994), 339.

4 A new European Conference of International Law was launched in Florence in 2005, while Harvard Law School held a major international conference on the changing world order in 2004.

5 David Kennedy, *The Dark Side of Virtue* (Princeton, NJ, Princeton University Press, 2004); Philippe Sands, *Lawless World* (London, Allen Lane, 2005); Jack Goldsmith and Eric Posner, *The Limits of International Law* (Oxford, Oxford University Press, 2005); Michael Byers, *War Law* (New York, Atlantic, 2005).

in returning to these glory days is more general. In an expression overused in international law scholarship, the period from 1989 to the Iraq war has been described as a 'Grotian' moment.[6] The aim is to examine the legal and institutional framework of the new times. Have we witnessed a profound change in the normative foundations of the world order? What is the character of new international law? How does it relate to the imperial and/or cosmopolitan proclamations of the dominant powers? We will start with a brief review of recent international law theory.

Intellectual histories of international law, particularly of its post-Second World War period, argue that its foundation and function has moved on a spectrum between realistic pragmatism and legalistic formalism. At one end, the role of international law is to facilitate the achievement of the aims of foreign policy. According to this view, international lawyers should become inter-disciplinary, adopt a realist 'law in context' approach and examine causes and potential effects of actions rather than their quaint description in law books and international treaties. This way, lawyers would be able to help statesmen and states to pursue their aims and improve their professional profile.[7] This instrumentalisation and politicisation of international law was promoted by the American scions of the new discipline of international relations such as Hans Morgenthau, Myres McDougall and Harold Lasswell.[8] The most extreme proponents of this tendency have merged their discipline with international relations, creating what can be called a 'functional' or 'pragmatic' jurisprudence that pays lip-service only to legal rules and judicial reasoning.

   At the other end, optimistic followers of Hans Kelsen stand by the traditional normative function of law. They argue that, despite difficulties and setbacks, an international rule of law has gradually developed in the post-Second World War world. Like domestic law, this international body of rules is distinct from (indeed, above) politics and places constraints on power and the powerful. Its rules have (or ought to have) internal consistency and coherence in exactly the same way as domestic legal systems. The palpable disregard for the 'international rule of law' 'periodically displayed by the Great Powers' was not the result of weaknesses in the law but of contingent political factors militating against its full adoption. During the cold war, it is explained, domestic

6   Ibarahim Grassama, 'International Law at a Grotian Moment', 18 *Emory International Law Review* 1–52 (2004). Grassama writes that while international law 'was at odds with itself' over the legality of the Iraq war, this placed it at the centre of a passionate debate and was 'a boon for the discipline', at 3. Unfortunately the boon did not last for long.
7   Martti Koskenniemi, *The Gentle Civilizer of Nations* (Cambridge, Cambridge University Press, 2002).
8   Ibid. Chapter 6.

politics were predominantly normal and rational and allowed legal regulation. The international scene, on the other hand, was dominated by the exception, the struggle for national survival and the ultimate experience of life and death. The predominance of the national interest and of the so-called 'Hobbesian' view of international relations was reflected in the veto power given to the five permanent members of the Security Council and used extensively to prevent the imposition of sanctions against states violating the principles of the Charter. As a result, conflicts between the superpowers and their satellites were largely excluded from the purview of the post-Second World War legal regime and the sanctity of sovereignty became the guiding principle of international law. States and their lawyers were happy to get around the veto difficulty by bypassing the Security Council. Authorisation for sanctions and military action came from the General Assembly (the case of the Korean War) or the General Secretary, whose power to send peacekeepers into various parts of the world became one of the main ways through which the United Nations became involved in regional struggles with a cold war temperature about them.

According to this narrative, international politics followed the prerogatives of state interest and global ideological confrontation and sidelined the law. Lawyers had to adjust to this reality and, as a result, 'largely gave up any attempt to conceive the balance of powers in terms of legal rules and principles'.[9] The end of the cold war brought this sorry situation to an end and emancipated international law. After the collapse of communism, the cosmopolitan project of fashioning international politics according to the Western rule of law could start in earnest. In the aftermath of these momentous events, triumphalist commentators and lawyers hailed the 'end of history' and the dawn of a new age. As professor of international law David Kennedy put it, 'the end of the Cold War and the simultaneous completion and expansion of the Western market seemed to signal the triumph of humanitarianism as the new language for international affairs. The vocabulary of human rights was central to both efforts'.[10] Legal rules should now be able to give answers to all difficult legal questions, including the thorniest of all: when is it lawful (or moral or just) to start a war. A group of international lawyers acting like revellers after a long and hard period of fasting abandoned their previous abstinence and, through a creative reinterpretation of the UN Charter and the mushrooming body of international treaties and practices, returned to the 'just war' doctrine (Chapter 10). Ancient quasi-religious opinions about moral justifications for warfare were turned into legal arguments about 'humanitarian interventions', pre-emptive wars and lawful first strikes. Through a merger of old ideas and new

9   Ibid. 441.
10 Kennedy, op. cit., 169.

practices, the novel language of 'international humanitarian virtue' or 'humanity's law' came into being, most apparent in the renewed and expanded 'law of force'.

The humanitarians are on the march. The term 'cosmopolitan' has acquired legal and political meanings beyond those of a glossy magazine and busy jetsetters. But conflicting ideological and professional approaches survived and were evident in the debates about the legality of the Kosovo and Iraq wars. These debates are the best laboratory for examining the contemporary status of public international law. The next two sections examine them briefly, in an attempt to understand the role of law in the new times.

Kosovo and the morality of law

Suppose that three eminent criminal lawyers debate a particularly gruesome homicide. All three agree that the act was clearly a murder under the law. But as the murderer was a powerful man and claimed good motives for his act (the victim apparently was abusing his wife, although some witnesses testified that the motives were more complex; the murderer had tried desperately to buy a plot of land from the victim with no success), the crime was turned into a legitimate act. Indeed, our experts agree with some nuanced differences that accepting this act as criminal but legitimate ought and will eventually lead to the development of a necessary exception to the law of murder, which would allow the powerful to kill the weak with impunity, if they claim to act morally.

This is an absurd position in English or any other domestic law. Yet it was the conclusion emerging from a debate about the legality of the Kosovo war between Professors Antonio Cassesse, Bruno Simma and Michael Glennon, three of the most eminent international lawyers.[11] In articles written immediately after the war, all three agreed that the use of force against Yugoslavia was illegal under international law and contrary to the United Nations Charter. For Cassesse, the illegality perpetrated by NATO was grave; indeed unlike the Iraq war, NATO did not even attempt to put forward a justification for its attack on Yugoslavia based on the UN Charter. Simma agreed. The

---

11   Antonio Cassesse, '*Ex Injuria Jus Oritur*: Are We Moving Towards International Legitimation of Forcible Humanitarian Countermeasures in the World Community?', 10 *European Journal of International Law* 23 (1999); Bruno Simma, 'NATO, the UN and the Use of Force: Legal Aspects', 10 *European Journal of International Law* 1 (1999). See also the editorial comments on 'Kosovo and the Law of "Humanitarian Intervention" in 93 *American Journal of International Law* 824–62 (1999). With the exception of Christine Chinkin, an equally eminent group of international lawyers invited to comment by the AJIL accepted the 'illegal but legitimate' position.

overwhelming majority of contemporary legal opinion agrees that no right of 'humanitarian intervention' exists. One would expect that such strong statements would be the end of the matter. But they are not. Cassesse argues that respect for the international rule of law should be sacrificed at the altar of human compassion. Resort to armed force was justified from 'an ethical viewpoint'. In Cassesse's view, this illegal but moral action was a clear breach of international law but has started a process that will eventually modify the legal position. Illegality will gradually lead towards the creation of a general customary rule of law authorising the use of force for the purpose of putting an end to atrocities. Such a rule 'would constitute an exception to the UN Charter of collective enforcement based on the authorisation of Security Council'.[12]

For Bruno Simma, on the other hand, the Kosovo war was unique. NATO decided to act out of overwhelming humanitarian necessity justified by special circumstances. No precedent or general rule should be drawn from that. Indeed, the overwhelming morality of the motives made the Kosovo exception almost legal (only a thin red line separated, according to Simma, NATO's action in Kosovo from extant international legality). But hard cases make bad law; the exception should not be turned into a general policy, Simma concludes. Their American counterpart, Michael Glennon, goes further. As he puts it rather grandiosely, 'the higher, grander goal that has eluded humanity for centuries – the ideal of justice backed by power – should not be abandoned. If power is used to do justice, law will follow'.[13] The war was 'illegal but legitimate',[14] a conclusion also reached by the Independent Commission on Kosovo, chaired by Judge Richard Goldstone.[15]

The three eminent lawyers agreed that the war was illegal. Their differences were relatively minor: will or should Kosovo lead to the creation of a new type of customary international law with a moral inflection or should it be treated as a one-off exception from the general rule respecting sovereignty? The moral viewpoint, the demands of justice and compassion, replaced hard-nosed technical definitions based on the UN Charter and international treaties, the beloved activity of lawyers. These generic references to morality give the impression that a common and universal ethical position or moral code has developed and can be invoked over the language of law or the strife of politics.

12 Ibid. 26.
13 M.J. Glennon, 'The New Interventionism: the search for a just international law', 78/3 *Foreign Affairs* 7 (1999).
14 Ann-Marie Slaughter, 'Good Reasons for Going Around the UN', *New York Times*, 18 March 2003, A33.
15 *The Kosovo Report: Conflict, International Response, Lessons Learned* (New York, Oxford University Press, 2000).

Yet, lawyers are not normally given to grand moral statements. The proud and self-proclaimed achievement of legal modernity was precisely the exclusion of ethics from the realm of law. Morality was excluded from the legal domain because of the modern experience of relativism and pluralism and the fear of nihilism. For a positivist lawyer, law is the answer to the irreconcilability of values, the most perfect embodiment of human reason. Its operation should not be contaminated by extrinsic, non-legal considerations, such as morals, ideology or politics. Law's empire is full of statements about its non-moral, neutral character that stands above politics. Let us list some. Private law turns social conflict into technical disputes, the resolution of which is entrusted to public experts and technicians of rules and procedures. Public law imposes constitutional limits and normative restrictions upon the organisation and exercise of state power. Rules depersonalise power and structure the exercise of discretion by excluding subjective values in the interpretation of the law by judges and its application by administrators. This insulation of law from ethico-political considerations allegedly removes any bias from the exercise of power and guarantees the equal subjection of citizens and state officials to the dispassionate requirements of the 'rule of rules' as opposed to the 'rule of men'. Indeed, the rule of law is presented as the law of rules, which, like facts, have singular and incontrovertible meanings turning the law into a guide to universal right and the route to objective truth. On the reverse side of the separation between morality and legality, ethics is presented as personal, subjective, an unreliable guide for public action. Lawyers profess a lack of interest in morality, a trait extensively ridiculed in world literature from Shakespeare to Dickens. As a 'disillusioned radical' barrister put it 'as a lawyer you don't have moral choice because the law makes the moral choices for you. I have no morality'.[16] And a former Chairman of the Bar went further: 'It's easy for the lawyer: there are rules. There are lighthouses all along the route for me and I haven't got to make moral judgements as I go. I am not a social worker. The rules fix my morality for me.'[17]

Displaced on the world stage, the same characteristics are encountered in international law. Both the domestic and international rule of law ideas have been based on the clear demarcation between legal and extra-legal considerations. International law came to existence by rejecting and abandoning the theological attempts to define the justice of war. By the end of the nineteenth century, natural law-type arguments were comprehensively discarded. Indeed, the key concepts and strategies of international law are incompatible with a

16 'Clean Hands Murky Deeds', *The Guardian*, 6 February 1991, 21.
17 Ibid.

moral view of the world. They include the pre-eminence of sovereignty, the contractual treaty-based character of the law and the *realpolitik* nature of international relations, law's object of regulation. International law and its terrain of operation (initially the 'society of princes', today the 'international community') share their birthday with modernity. Its predominantly contractual nature makes it the modern law par excellence and the perfect example of modernity's emphasis on individual freedom. In domestic law, contracts can exceptionally modify the law; in the international domain, contracts (treaties) make the law.

But the separation of law from politics and morals, which founded modern international law, has been increasingly coming under pressure. As David Bederman put it, while the split has been 'historically the demarcation of international law's domain', it is the 'ultimate heart of darkness' of international law and must be abandoned![18] In abandoning the cardinal principles of modernity, new international law becomes the first self-proclaimed postmodern law. The admission by eminent international lawyers that the project of insulating law from morals, in other words the attempt to build a self-contained and professionally operated legal system, has failed is a pretty devastating indictment of the discipline. Nevertheless, the reference to moral values is not particularly convincing. Lawyers freely admit that they are not professionally trained or knowledgeable in the tradition of ethics.

This is evident in the writings on Kosovo. The eminent professors assume that only one school of morality and a single universally accepted conception of justice exists whose demands are self-evident. For the professors of law, virtue ethics, the ethics of care or the ethics of otherness are not even considered as potential ways of addressing the moral problems of the Balkans.[19] But the problem is greater. Wars are not conducted according to the other-worldly Kantian morality; they follow utilitarianism, its greatest opponent. The absolute Kantian duty implied in the 'moral point of view' is continuously trumped by the fact that political and military planners and soldiers have little time for absolute principles. They are involved in utilitarian calculations, continuous cost-benefit analyses and balancing between conflicting policies, intended effects and unintended consequences. If the declaration of war was piously Kantian, as the lawyers claimed, its conduct was aggressively Benthamite. Joining the party of morality in the matter of war leads inevitably to double standards. First, to the hypocrisy of responding to some humanitarian crises

18 David Bedrman, *The Spirit of International Law* (Athens, University of Georgia Press, 2002), 140, 154.

19 Costas Douzinas and Ronnie Warrington, *Justice Miscarried* (Edinburgh, Edinburgh University Press, 1994), Chapter 4.

only and not to even worse others; second, the equally significant 'internal' duplicity: the means of conducting 'moral' wars are profoundly non moral. It is a typical instance of a 'performative contradiction': you must act immorally in order to be moral.

An example will explain the point. Military planners were under huge political pressure to prevent American casualties. This was achieved through the increase of 'collateral damage' among civilians in Serbia and Kosovo. A few weeks after the start of the war, General Michael Short of the US Air Force told journalists that hitting civilian morale was necessary for success. His tactic was going to be 'no power to your refrigerator. No gas to your stove, you can't get to work because the bridge is down – the bridge on which you held your rock concerts and all stood with targets on your heads. That needs to disappear'.[20] Civil targets were easier to identify and bomb. Some fifty bridges were destroyed as well as a number of TV and radio stations, hospitals, schools and nurseries, cultural, economic and industrial sites, computer networks and electricity generating plants.[21] Indeed, the bombing of Belgrade, a major capital city, carried out allegedly in order to protect Albanians hundreds of miles away in Kosovo, defied both logic and morality. The Americans do not keep count of enemy civilian casualties; it has been estimated however that 500 civilians were killed on the ground in Yugoslavia, up to 4,000 in Afghanistan and many tens of thousands in Iraq. The targeting of the civilian infrastructure and the repeated mistakes led Mary Robinson to state, after the first four weeks of bombing, that the campaign had 'lost its moral purpose'.[22]

None of this created much reaction among the humanitarian international lawyers. This moral laxity was supported by repeated statements about the atrocities of the Serbs, the great suffering of the Kosovars, the 'new genocide taking place not in some remote African republic but right here in Europe'. There is no doubt that the Serbs acted appallingly towards the Albanians, their resident 'barbarians'. On the other hand, even Michael Ignatieff, an ardent supporter of the war, admitted what was obvious to everyone except for the eminent international lawyers:

20 *The Observer*, 16 May 1999, 15.
21 Professor Ian Brownlie, the eminent human rights expert, in evidence to the International Court of Justice said, on 10 May 1999: 'There is no general humanitarian purpose to the [bombings] . . . the pattern of targets indicates political purposes unrelated to humanitarian reasons', *The Guardian*, 11 May 1999, 8. The Court declined the Serbian government's application to declare the bombing illegal, although it expressed concerns about its effects on civilians.
22 'Shift in Bombing a Warning to Serbs', *The Guardian*, 29 May 1999, 4.

Humanitarian intervention in Kosovo was never exactly what it appeared.
It was never just an attempt to prevent Milosevic from getting away with
human rights abuses in Europe's backyard. It was also a use of imperial
power to support a self-determination claim by a national minority . . .
that used violence in order to secure international notice and attention.[23]

The lawyers' monotonously repeated claims, based on what turned out to be
hugely exaggerated evidence of atrocities, would have been more convincing
had they been accompanied by equally vigorous condemnations of Serb victimisation. In their one-sided form, they remain ideological claims masquerading
as moral arguments. They also indicate a wider moral deficit. New international
law as a field in the making, needs, more than other areas, the legitimacy of
professors and intellectuals. International customs acquire legal validity after
long usage by a large number of states accompanied by the actors' belief that
they follow a legally binding rule. The applicability of this principle to recent
humanitarian wars has been a central aspect of the eminent professors' debate.
But whatever their conclusion about the *opinio juris* and the ability of the
Kosovo war to create a new international custom, the *opinio jurisconsulti* has
helped justify the actions of the dominant powers. It was a case of academics
and lawyers as apologists for empire.

We need to turn to Jürgen Habermas, a non-lawyer, to find a considered
examination of the law–morality nexus and a powerful moral argument for
the legality of the Kosovo war. We examined in Chapter 7, Habermas's presentation of the Kosovo war as a 'step on the path from the classical international
law of nations towards the cosmopolitan law of a world civil society'.[24] But
if we compare the position of the international lawyers with that of Habermas,
bed-fellows on the Kosovo issue, a strange conclusion emerges. For the
lawyers, moral considerations must be introduced in the argument because
amoral international law runs out. They may be a little hazy about the mode
or organisation of moral arguments or about the different schools of ethics.
But they are certain that the law on its own is inadequate to the task of saving
humanity. Habermas, on the other hand, is weary of turning politics and war
into moralistic arguments, a prospect that raises the dreaded spectre of Carl
Schmitt. Schmitt's 'kernel of truth is that an *unmediated* moralisation of law
and politics does in fact break through those protective zones that we want to
have secured for legal persons for good, indeed, moral reasons', Habermas
reluctantly admits.[25] Because morality must not be allowed to resolve on its

23   *Empire Lite*, op. cit., 70–1.
24   Jürgen Habermas, 'Bestialität und Humanität', *Die Zeit*, 29 April 1999.
25   Jürgen Habermas, *The Inclusion of the Other* (Cambridge, Polity, 1998), 198–9 (italics in
     original).

own difficult political conflicts, the law is called in to play the role of the *mediator*, of a universal but disinterested arbiter. But since the law has been shown to be inadequate, human rights are bifurcated, as we saw, into a juridical component and its moral foundation and justification. Despite their differences, morality and legality share the same foundation and a similar kind of universal validity.[26]

Habermas poses the problem and its answer in precisely the reverse terms from those addressed by the lawyers. For the latter, morality saves politics from (inadequate) law, for Habermas, law saves politics from (potentially problematic) moralisation. The sleight of hand is evident: morality and human rights are identified in their form and content but separated in their action. The legal facet of human rights saves the day. Universalism establishes its principles and values by testing them according to criteria of universal applicability following the protocols and procedures of reason. But, as communitarians have convincingly argued, morality is only in small part guided by formal procedures, logical protocols and tests of universality. Universalism has been historically associated with the promotion of the interests of its proponents. This

> counter-intuitive nature of universalism can lead its proponent to extreme individualism: only myself as the real moral agent or as the ethical alliance or as the representative of the universal can understand what morality demands. Moral egotism easily leads into arrogance and universalism onto imperialism: if there is one moral truth but many errors, it is incumbent upon its agents to impose it on others.[27]

And this is indeed the prospectus of our recent military humanism.[28] For Habermas, the barbarian Serbs were rightly bombed by NATO. Ann-Marie Slaughter argues that liberal international relations theory mandates a distinction between liberal and non-liberal states and international law cannot accommodate both.[29] Similarly for John Rawls, sanctions and even war are justified against 'non well-ordered states', which should be made to follow the global rules.[30] Michael Ignatieff is more honest. The function of humanitarian

---

26 See Chapter 8.
27 Costas Douzinas, *The End of Human Rights* (Oxford, Hart, 2000), 137.
28 Costas Douzinas, 'Humanity, Military Humanism and the New World Order', 32/2 *Economy and Society* 159 (2003); 'Postmodern Just Wars and the New World Order', 5/3 *Journal of Human Rights* 355 (2006).
29 Ann-Marie Slaughter, 'International Law in a World of Liberal States', 6 *European Journal of International Law* 504 (1995).
30 John Rawls, *The Law of the Peoples* (Cambridge, MA, Harvard University Press, 2001).

wars is to repel the barbarians and impose order on the frontiers of empire. But as David Rieff, a non lawyer, stated about Kosovo 'such interventions, no matter how disinterested, or wrapped up in the mandate to the UN or new international law, are colonising enterprises'.[31] Behind the high-minded words about ethical foreign policies and rogue states on the one side and results, accountability, calculation of consequences on the other, one can hear bombers leaving the aircraft carriers or guns blazing and tanks rolling into a sandy Iraqi town.

If the *eminences grises* of international law believe that the war in Kosovo was unlawful but moral, just or simply legitimate, the very existence and status of law becomes highly problematic. One is tempted to say that there is something seriously flawed with this branch of law. Its morality is not good enough for the lawyers, but its legality saves us from excessive and imperialist moralism, for the philosophers. Its palindromic nature makes it more elastic than a rubber band. Let us turn to the Iraq war, in an attempt to delve further into the nature of the problem.

Iraq and the 'lawless world'

The Kosovo war was hailed by many as the dawn of a new and invigorated moral state of the world, in which sovereignty and state borders cannot stop the writ of the international rule of law. The next step in the unravelling of international law was taken in the shifting sands of the war on Iraq. During the run-up to the war a number of legal arguments were put forward. Britain, in particular, placed huge emphasis on the legality of the campaign. The advice of the Attorney-General to the government became a major issue of political contention. Philippe Sands, a British international lawyer, recently disclosed the machinations of the British government aimed at overriding and then changing the advice of its law officers about the legality of the war.[32] Sands claims that as early as March 2002, Tony Blair committed Britain to Bush's campaign against Iraq. Following that, the issue of the war's legality became a major bone of contention in the British Cabinet and the media, giving international law its few months of glory. In reverse order of credibility and validity, three legal justifications were canvassed before the war: liberation of the Iraqi people; pre-emptive self-defence against future terrorist attacks; and, finally, the existence of weapons of mass destruction, in violation of Iraq's legal obligations.

31   David Rieff, *A Bed for the Night* (London, Vintage, 2002), 117.
32   Philippe Sands, *Lawless World* (London, Allen Lane, 2005).

The most extravagant claim was that the war should be seen as a humanitarian intervention for 'regime change' – in other words, a just war to liberate the Iraqis from Saddam Hussein. This argument linked Iraq with the debates on Kosovo. It would take the cosmopolitan project initiated in the Balkans to the Middle East. Indeed, the obvious illegality of the Kosovo war was used as an argument for the legality of the pending attack. After the end of the Kosovo campaign, the UN Security Council had indirectly legitimised the war and the occupation, it was claimed, by placing the province under an international mandate. The initial illegality had been mitigated, the argument went, and the world was moving the Habermas and Cassesse way, by narrowing the distance between moral legitimacy and formal legality. Legal scholars were working full-time to establish new legal principles and customs, which would justify future humanitarian wars. But unlike the (rather exaggerated) claims about Kosovo, Iraq could not be presented as a current and pressing humanitarian disaster. Saddam Hussein had been ruling Iraq for some thirty years and had been consistently doing business with the West without many complaints about his human rights record. The greatest catastrophe to have visited the Iraqis in recent years was the imposition of American-led UN sanctions, which, according to some estimates, had cost the lives of up to 500,000 people.

The second argument was that the war would amount to a pre-emptive strike in self-defence, because of a possible link between Iraq and Islamic terrorists. But, as even Lord Goldsmith, the Attorney-General, had to admit both arguments were legally unsound. Regime change cannot be used as a legal basis for war. Similarly pre-emptive self-defence is unknown to international law. The only avenue for a lawful declaration of war was through the authorisation of the Security Council. It soon became clear, however, that such authorisation was not forthcoming, because of potential vetoes by the French and the Russians. For the Americans, this was a further sign of European (and particularly French) perfidy. While the Europeans were willing to run roughshod over international law in Kosovo, a few years later they rediscovered their great admiration and belief in its values. As an exasperated American commentator put it,

> European leaders, knowing well that [humanitarian principles] could be stretched to fit many circumstances, wanted to close all loopholes. They scuttled away from the moralistic principles they had used to justify Kosovo and began demanding a much more rigid adherence to the UN Charter.[33]

---

33 Robert Kagan, *Paradise and Power* (London, Atlantic Books, 2004), 129.

In the face of European intransigence, a way out was found in Iraq's disarmament obligations under Security Council resolutions, issued in 1991 and 2002. Resolutions 678 and 687 of 1991, which followed the Gulf War and ordered Iraq to destroy its chemical, biological and nuclear weapons, were interpreted as authorising the use of force, if Iraq was in 'material breach' of its disarmament obligations. Resolution 1441 of 2002 gave Iraq a final opportunity to disarm and sent inspectors to check its compliance. But who could judge the existence of a 'material breach' of Iraq's obligations after the inspectors report appeared to indicate that Iraq was abiding by them? The United States and Britain asserted the power to do so. They claimed that the assorted old resolutions created a sufficient basis for war and that in any case they were entitled to attack in self-defence without explicit authorisation. The legal basis of these arguments was rejected by the overwhelming majority of international lawyers, by the Security Council and the Secretary-General of the United Nations, who denounced America's 'lawless use of force'.[34] After the end of the war, when it became clear that the regime did not possess any prohibited weapons, the priorities changed. Like a moveable feast, the aim of the war now became the liberation of the Iraqi people and the importation of democracy and freedom to their ancient land.

According to Philippe Sands's influential narrative, the Iraq war was illegal from the start. It was the culmination of the persistent undermining of the 'international rule of law' by President Bush and Tony Blair. Sands deplores this Bush–Blair 'anti-law' campaign, evident in Bush's dismissive statement that 'I don't care what the international lawyers say' and Blair's campaign to rewrite international law through new global humanitarian rules 'as though the achievements of the past sixty years count for nought'.[35] President Bush had decided to revamp international law well before 9/11. The delightfully entitled *Project for the New American Century*, a right-wing think-tank close to the president, had repeatedly attacked rules of international law for constraining the United States, undermining its sovereignty and threatening its national security. The wrath of the neo-conservatives had many targets, among them the laws used to detain former Chilean President Pinochet in Surrey, the International Criminal Court and assorted international conventions, such as various arms control treaties and the Kyoto climate control agreement.[36] As Philippe Sands put it, the United States opted for an 'a la carte

---

34 'At UN, Bush is Criticised over Iraq', *The Washington Post*, 24 September 2003, A1.
35 Sands, op. cit., 225, 234.
36 Harold Koh, 'On American Exceptionalism', 55 *Stanford Law Review* 1549–1527 (2003).

multilateralism': 'pick and choose the bits of international law you like and drop the rest'.[37]

Rationalising this approach, John Bolton, President Bush's adviser and American Ambassador to the United Nations, argued that international treaties are politically, not legally binding and could be dropped if political expediency dictated it. The president adopted the advice; the United States withdrew from Kyoto, 'unsigned' the ICC treaty while the protocol on biological weapons was abandoned. The eminent international lawyer Michael Glennon agreed in the context of the 'war on terror': the UN Charter provisions on the use of force 'cannot guide responsible US policy-makers in the US war against terrorism or elsewhere'.[38] On the other hand, however, international economic law and treaties promoting globalisation and liberalisation of markets are forcefully promoted. As a result, international law is split: its parts that promote 'the opening of overseas markets and protecting America's international investments' are good, while those that pose 'unacceptable constraints on the American way of life' are bad and disposable.[39]

The 'war on terror' extended this approach to the law of war, to criminal law and to the treatment of prisoners. Parts of these bodies of law were selectively abandoned and new legal regimes developed. The most symbolic departure from accepted legality was Guantánamo Bay, which, placed formally – although not in substance – outside American jurisdiction, allowed the administration to create a legal 'limbo' or 'black hole' and to treat detainees without regard for rules of domestic or international law. Two aspects of the treatment of prisoners stand out. First, and against the advice of the overwhelming majority of international lawyers, the detainees were designated not as prisoners of war but as unlawful combatants, a novel legal category. As a result, the constraints and limitations of the Geneva Conventions on the treatment of POWs were declared not to apply. The brutal effects of this disapplication became famously clear in the many tales of torure of Guantánamo prisoners. Second, Jay Bybee, the Assistant Deputy Attorney-General, advising on standards of conduct on torture argued that the prohibition of torture covers the most extreme acts and the infliction of pain so severe that it could not be endured by the victim. Physical pain amounts to torture if it is akin in intensity to what accompanies serious physical injury such as death or organ failure. Anything less is not torture. Mental pain requires lasting psychological harm such as seen in mental disorders or in post-traumatic stress disorder. The torture

37 Sands, 229.
38 M.J. Glennon, 'The Fog of Law: Self-defence, Inherence and Incoherence in Article 51 of the United Nations Charter', 25 *Harvard Journal of Law and Public Policy* 539, 541 (2001).
39 Sands, 225–6.

practices carried out under this interpretation of the law have now become known around the world through the publication of the infamous Abu Ghraib pictures.[40]

Philippe Sands's *Lawless World* is a devastating attack on American attitudes to international law under Bush Jr. It represents the prevalent attitude of liberal Europeans towards the Bush presidency and 'neo-conservatism'. The United States under Bush have been acting outside the law, indeed in violent breach of their legal obligations. The indictment finds sufficient confirmation in various, shocking to European ears, statements from conservative American commentators. 'America is the dominant power in the world,' wrote Charles Krauthammer in 2001, 'more dominant than any since Rome. Accordingly America is in a position to escape norms, alter expectations and create new realities. How? By unapologetic and implacable demonstrations of will.'[41] Anticipating the imperial turn, Bolton had also argued that 'we should be unashamed, unapologetic, uncompromising American constitutional hegemonists'.[42] Sands concludes that the political and moral responsibility of governments and academics is to return to the pre-Bush state of rule-governed international relations. Despite the drawbacks of Iraq, the question whether a war is legal under international law remains of great importance to many people, even though 'it is not the only relevant question'.

This is a last-ditch defence of a slightly old-fashioned but honourable legal orthodoxy without the cosmopolitan heavy-breathing. It belongs to the legalist tradition of Kelsen but has abandoned, in typical English fashion, its Germanic formalism. Law is placed above partisan considerations and policies and has the last word in deciding the great issues of the day. In the felicitous and totally unrealistic words of Ronald Dworkin, legal rights 'trump' policies and, in the international lawyer's reformulation, legal rules 'trump' governmental interests. Both premises of this argument are factually wrong, however. The Iraq war was not a legal anomaly; Iraq was the third war by the United States considered illegal by the majority of international lawyers in the space of four years.[43]

---

40   See further Chapter 5.

41   Charles Krauthammer, *Time Magazine*, 5 March 2001.

42   John Bolton, 'Is There Really "Law" in International Affairs?', 10 *Transnationaal Law and Contemporary Problems* 1 at 48 (2000).

43   In the case of *Nicaragua* v. *USA*, 184 *International Court of Justice Reports* (1986), the Court accepted that a resolution of the United Nations General Assembly banning aggression is binding in international law and reaffirmed that so-called 'humanitarian interventions' are unlawful (at 14). The case arose out of the violent US campaign against Nicaragua under the Sandinista government, which included mining its ports and supporting the anti-government terrorist activities of the Contras. The American argument was that the violent intervention was in self-defence because Nicaragua was harbouring rebels attacking

Second, rather than being opposed to policy, law itself is used instrumentally as one policy consideration among many.

The wars in Kosovo and Afghanistan did not have stronger claims to legality than that in Iraq. Indeed, the NATO powers involved in the Kosovo war failed to show a single compelling legal reason for going to war. Kosovo was at least as blatant a violation of international law as was Iraq, but it did not attract the ire of liberal lawyers. In a book entitled *Lawless World*, not a single page is devoted to Kosovo or Afghanistan, except for the oblique comment that 'the intervention in Kosovo provided the only real hint that the rules of international law might need to be revisited, but this would be in order to promote respect for human rights'.[44] The attack on Kosovo had the support of many Western European governments. Under international law its illegality was greater than that of the Iraq war, where an arguable although risible case of UN authorisation and self-defence could be made. It should be added that, if the Iraq war was not lawful, it was a war of aggression. According to the Nuremberg tribunal, a war of aggression is 'the supreme international crime, contain[ing] within itself the accumulated evil of the whole'. The European contradiction, if not hypocrisy, in an area riddled with double standards, has understandably angered American commentators:

> These days most Europeans argue, that by invading Iraq without Security approval, the United States 'has torn the facric of the international order'. But if there ever was an international order of the kind they describe, then Europe undermined it in 1999, too. In fact the fabric of this hoped-for international order has yet to be knit.[45]

El Salvador and, second, that it was carried out in order to protect the human rights of Nicaraguans. The American government withdrew from the Court's jurisdiction before the case, but this was not accepted because of a previous American statement that a six-month notice would be given before withdrawal. Following this, the Americans refused to participate in the case and withdrew their consent to the Court's jurisdiction in relation to future cases. The Court ruled that the United States were not acting in 'self-defence', since they could eliminate the danger to the Salvadorian government without attacking Nicaragua. On the second point, the Court was even more categorical: 'The protection of human rights, a strictly humanitarian objective, cannot be compatible with the mining of ports, the destruction of oil installations, or again with the training, arming and equipping of the Contras' (133–4). The ICJ asked the US 'to cease and to refrain' from activities against customary international law and not to use force. But as the 'Iran-Contra scandal' showed this did not happen. American foreign and military policy has not been particularly worried about such illegalities despite Philippe Sands's claim that 'America is a nation of rules and lawyers' (op. cit., 228).

44   Sands, 231.
45   Kagan, op. cit., 131.

No valid legal argument for war existed in Kosovo, a case of a postmodern just war based on controversial evidence. It was the blatant illegality of that war that made the discussion of international lawyers about Kosovo such an interesting case study about the status of this brand of law.

It did not take long for the debate on the Iraq war to imitate that of Kosovo: is it legal, is it moral, is it both or neither? For Sands, the war was illegal and therefore immoral. At the other end, the *Sunday Telegraph* called the question of the war's legality a 'giant irrelevance', while an *Observer* commentator stated that the question was not whether the 'Iraq invasion was "legal" but whether it was "good"'.[46] The rather confused position emanating from the Anglo-American allies was that the morality of liberating the Iraqis from Saddam supplemented the meagre legal case. For Sands, legality rules; for the warriors, morality trumps legality. By the standards of legal formalism, the war was clearly illegal. But Kosovo and Iraq indicated beyond reasonable doubt that international law is only peripherally the domain of the textualist and the legalist. The United States and Britain had decided to go to war and whether it was called legal or illegal, moral or immoral, the trumpets of war would sound.

Sands concludes that 'tough guys are not enough in international relations. In the twenty-first century you need rules, and proper lawyers too'.[47] And in a recent talk, he appeared even more optimistic. 'Despite attacks international law is alive and kicking and the world is not as lawless as many may wish. And although it is not the only question to ask, the question is it legal under international law is of great importance to many people.' One gets a sense of relief that good international lawyers, clever advisers and people at large have started taking notice of the great problems of a lawless world and are returning to the virtues of the international rule of law. Sands himself admits that the recent 'great advances' of international law amount to a 'silent global revolution' and 'most people are blissfully unaware quite how much international law there is'.[48] It is true that international law has expanded into areas hitherto belonging to domestic regulations, such as trade, the environment, migration, etc. But the normative characteristics of these areas have been set internally; international law replicates them globally. The normative specificity of international law lies with the regulation of sovereign conduct, of which war is the ultimate instance. Reading the misadventures of the Iraq war saga, one concludes that people are not wrong to remain in their blissful ignorance and indifference towards this branch of law. What Sands shows with great clarity

---

46 Leader, *The Sunday Telegraph*, 29 February 2004, 24; David Aaronovitch, 'A War of Words', *The Observer*, 6 March 2005, 25.

47 Sands op. cit., 239.

48 Philippe Sands, 'Lawless World: International Law after 9/11 and Iraq' University of Melbourne Law School Alumni Lecture, 15 June 2005 (on file with author).

is that his beloved ideal of an 'overarching commitment to the international rule of law' and of a new 'rule based system' of international relations has remained something of an ineffectual secret shared almost exclusively by the cognoscenti (international lawyers and diplomats) and its beneficiaries (the various international civil servants and NGO operatives).

The evidence of the last thirty years does not indicate that the Bush administration is against international law but that American policy has been consistently and independently of recent neo-conservative excesses violating, obeying or re-fashioning the law according to its perceived strategic interests. International law is one more weapon in the pragmatic political calculations of the great powers of the new times. Like foreign policy, economic argument and military strategy, law is one more consideration governments take into account before deciding how to act. It can be wheeled out when it supports their interests and it is easily discarded if it creates a real or imaginary constraint on them. The idea that a little more or a little better law or that its more robust enforcement would release us from strife, war and atrocities is one of the great chimeras of our time, the noble lie of international relations. Blair with his disregard and manipulation of the legal advice did his best to expose this lie *malgré lui,* while Sands, who exposed Blair's lies, buries his head in the sand by trying to perpetuate it. *Inter armes silent leges* states the classical maxim. It expresses a basic and still valid realistic observation: law as a technical means of resolving or neutering conflict works until and unless one of the parties decides that no peaceful resolution is possible. When *raison d'état* or *raison d'empire* speaks, the law is silent; if it keeps speaking, it gets shut up or seriously cut down to size.

Pragmatism as the ideology of empire

Philippe Sands thankfully does not subscribe to the grandiose cosmopolitan designs of Habermas and his followers. His defence of international law is more modest. But his brave attempt to rescue and rehabilitate the law ultimately misfires. The legalist project despite its good intentions seriously misrepresents the nature and function of law. The hope that international law can constrain the plans of the great powers is not supported by the evidence. While international lawyers keep arguing about the state of their discipline, Baghdad is burning.

It is precisely this impotence of traditional notions of law that motivates the dominant American approach to international law. The conservative commentator Robert Kagan claimed recently that a state's support for international law is in direct relation to its strength in the global system.[49] The Kelsenian

49   Kagan, *Paradise and Power, passim.*

normative universe is a smokescreen dreamt up by outdated formalists, while the cosmopolitan idea, a last resort by old Europeans anxious to retain their waning influence. When the United States were weak, they relied on rules to protect their interests; now they are powerful they have turned unilateralist and abandoned international law. European states, on the other hand, having lost their world dominance, promote an idealised vision of the world in which nations share common values and follow international law. The Sophist Callicles in classical Athens and Friedrich Nietzsche in modernity have argued that morality is a cunning trick by the inferior and the weak to constrain the strong. The project to create a Kantian cosmopolitanism of perpetual peace, 'the new European civilising mission', is the latest example of such hypocrisy. In reality, it is an attempt to build a *cordon sanitaire* around American power. It is born out of the weakness of the Europeans and their inability to look after their own security. But rules neither restrain power nor provide security. European cosmopolitanism can 'flourish only under the umbrella of American power exercised according to the rules of the old Hobbesian order'. In its role as the 'international sheriff', the United States is 'enforc[ing] some peace and justice in what Americans see as a lawless world where outlaws need to be deterred or destroyed, often through the muzzle of a gun'.[50] To do so, concludes Kagan, America 'must refuse to abide by certain international conventions that may constrain its ability to fight effectively in [the] jungle. It must support arms control, but not always for itself. It must live by a double standard.'[51]

According to Harvard lawyer David Kennedy, international law and its more forward-looking practitioners are already embracing this 'double standard' approach. The new world order can be both effective and benign, if international lawyers forget their unreal legalistic inhibitions and help its consolidation by offering whatever useful tools they have at their disposal. Kennedy develops this argument in his book *The Dark Side of Virtue*, published at around the same time as Sands's *Lawless World*.[52] Kennedy provides a troubling picture of the normative universe after the end of the cold war. His main argument is that something called 'humanitarian pragmatism' has become the official ideology of the New Times bringing together politicians, journalists, human rights activists and the military. This ideology provides 'an integrated way of thinking about warfare' and a 'modern constitutional scheme for global governance'.[53] It has the characteristics of the constitution of the new world order but is the exact opposite of the dreams of Kelsen and Habermas.

---

50 Ibid. 73, 36.
51 Ibid. 99.
52 David Kennedy, *The Dark Side of Virtue* (Princeton, NJ, Princeton University Press, 2004).
53 Ibid. 237.

On almost every issue, Kennedy offers a mirror image of Sands.[54] The legalist position is wrong descriptively and prescriptively. International law has become intensely anti-formalistic; indeed, it has lost many of the attributes a traditional lawyer would ascribe to law. According to Sands, the legal order offers clear rules and standards to judge disputes, supreme among them the legality of going to war. For Kennedy, on the other hand, the law is not a set of external rules embodied in a 'sacred text'. It is a 'professional vocabulary' used by similarly minded people to conduct arguments. As Richard Falk put it, if lawyers stick to the textual analysis of the relevant legal norms and to old-fashioned legalism, the 'self-marginalisation of international law and international lawyers is assured in contemporary situations involving claims to use force, consigning their vocational fate to the demeaning roles of "apologist" or "utopian"'.[55]

There are no right answers in law; when a lawyer voices a professional opinion about the legality of war, he does so as a rebuttable argument and not as the truth of the matter. Legal standards are 'too malleable to provide definite guidance for statesmen or scholars'.[56] Rather than offering neutral standards for judgement and decision, the law provides a vocabulary for conducting disputes and a job for commentators. Questions such as whether the war on Iraq amounted to a pre-emptive strike in self-defence or, whether the actions of Saddam were a gross violation of Iraqis' human rights do not have one right answer. No war is ever simply aggressive and no violence is ever wanton, except that carried out by rogue states and 'not well-ordered societies', the contemporary descendants of the uncivilised barbarians. All recent wars can be justified by persuasive legal claims conducted within the frame of the UN Charter. Opposing arguments about the legality of action can be easily translated into the humanitarian vocabulary of necessity, proportionality, etc., and present equally compelling cases.[57] The formalist attachment to the text of law and Sands's 'international rule of law' are akin to the irrational beliefs of theologians, attempts to exorcise social evils by the indefatigable repetition of magic formulae.[58] If this is the case, lawyers advising governments or the military should open up to psychological and sociological evidence and theories, examine the consequences of their action and balance the expected positive results against the likely harms.

---

54 There is one exception. Kennedy is as concerned as Sands to defend the professional status of international lawyers.
55 Richard Falk, 'Kosovo, World Order and the Future of International Law', 93 *American Journal International Law* 847 (1999), 853.
56 Kennedy, op. cit., 266.
57 Ibid. 260–265.
58 Koskenniemi, op. cit., 459.

This tirade follows a well-known position developed by realist legal critics at the turn of the twentieth century and continued, in a slightly confused fashion, by the American Critical Legal Studies movement in the 1970s and 1980s.[59] In its broad outline, law cannot be distinguished from politics and cannot act as the neutral arbiter of conflict. Politics and power are as much part of legal operations and ideology as of any town-hall meeting. Legal texts are full of contradictory concepts, such as principles and policies, laws and facts, form and substance, freedom and determination, which allow competent lawyers to reach opposing decisions with equally compelling argumentation.[60] Human rights law, for example, both generalises too much by promoting similarities among people and downgrading differences; and particularises too much by concentrating on individuals and their rights and neglecting groups and classes.[61]

Anti-formalism was a reaction and a necessary antidote to the exalted claims of legal orthodoxy. For legal traditionalists, the spirit of the law develops its own internal logic and has answers to all types of social, political and economic conflict. Indeed, the role of law is to translate social strife into technical disputes about the meaning and interpretation of rules and pass them to rule-technicians, lawyers and judges, to find solutions and pacify conflict. Critical legal studies rebelled against this inaccurate and complacent view of law. Legal formalism misrepresents legal practice by exaggerating the rational rule-bound character of the legal and, in particular, the judicial enterprise and by underplaying the creative and therefore political, ideological, moral or aesthetic input of judges.

For the pragmatist, Habermas and Kagan commit a similar error although at the opposite ends of the political spectrum. They take claims about the certainty and effectiveness of international law at face value. For Habermas, international law can be used to promote world security and citizenship rights; for Kagan, it is the main tool the waning Europeans mobilise to defend their interests against the Americans. David Kennedy insists, on the contrary, that the law was never able to do either of these things. As a result, the European hope is plainly silly. The Europeans are as much committed to regime change in their

---

59 Costas Douzinas and Adam Gearey, *Critical Jurisprudence* (Oxford, Hart, 2005), Chapter 9.
60 Martti Koskenniemi, another major critical scholar in international law, puts it like this: 'As I learned from David Kennedy, the legal argument inexorably, and quite predictably, allowed the defence of whatever position while simultaneously being constrained by a rigorously formal language.' 'Letter to the Editors of the Symposium', 93/2 *American Journal of International Law* 351 (1999) at 354.
61 Kennedy, op. cit., Chapter 1.

own backyard as the Americans. They carried it out by incorporating Eastern Europe into the European Union and imposing brutal market and political reforms that caused untold misery. The Americans did it by occupying Iraq. The aim was the same, only the means differed; international law had very little to say about the justice of either course of action. International lawyers should therefore stop looking at treaties for rules and norms and focus on context and results. They should cultivate

> rule scepticism – a well-developed and ubiquitous practice of criticising rules in the name of anti-formalism – and a blurring of the boundary between law and . . . policy, a mix of expert argument about how disputes should be resolved and institutions developed that opens legal analysis in the United States to all sorts of interdisciplinary input and social considerations which might elsewhere seem more like 'politics'.[62]

Nowadays, no legal scholar can neglect the devastating attack on formalism by the school of critical legal studies. David Kennedy has been at the forefront of anti-formalist international law and is a key member of the American Critical Legal Studies movement.[63] It is against this background of political activism and critical thinking that his approach appears so problematic. His crucial argument is that the international system does not depend on the tergiversations of international lawyers and plenipotentiaries. On the contrary, it evolves in low-level policy work in international institutions, government departments and political associations. Abandoning legal text and high diplomacy, Kennedy calls for a turning of political praxis into technique, legal formulae into sociological and psychological analyses and lawyers into political and military advisers and policy-makers. But to what end? Why should lawyers abandon their traditional terrain of textual interpretation, argumentation and practical reasoning for the reason of state? It is highly paradoxical for an international lawyer to claim that there is no international law worthy of the name in a number of lengthy articles in international law journals. This may

---

62 David Kennedy, 'The Disciplines of International Law and Policy', 12 *Leiden Journal of International Law* 9 (1999), 26.

63 David Kennedy has been exemplary as scholar, teacher and sponsor of younger academics. He has educated and supervised the research of generations of international lawyers at Harvard and his disciples are eminent legal academics around the world. The David Kennedy 'stable' has changed the face of international law scholarship and has rejuvenated the discipline theoretically and politically. It is against this background of political activism and critical thinking that David's book is so problematic.

be further expression of the existential angst international lawyers experience about their professional identity.[64] Nevertheless, the epistemological and political problems associated with this type of pragmatism are much deeper and have wider repercussions.

Max Weber showed, at the turn of the last century, how Leibniz's critique of reason's inability to ground its own rational activity extended to all spheres of society, including law. In a disenchanted world, natural law and its author, the preferred moral foundation of early modernity, cannot ground the legal system and give it metaphysical dignity.[65] This was the beginning of European normative positivism, for which norms derive endlessly from higher and more abstract norms and no original stopping point, no Mount Sinai moment, can be found. As a result, law cannot ground its own legality; challenges to its legitimacy or justice are law's inescapable condition. At the foundation of states, empires and legal systems stands an original violence, not a founding norm.[66] The narratives, according to which law began in some idyllic past, the myths of foundation and the tales of hallowed longevity are attempts to bestow authority on current values and priorities and undermine resistance to the actually existing. It cannot be otherwise. In a society of conflict, domination and exploitation, no common value system can represent the whole, let alone the 'international community', the beloved trope of both formalist and pragmatic lawyers. This community is the descendant of the 'comity of civilised nations', its law the heir to the 'law of European princes' with all the violence these traditions carry. As Sundhya Pahuja puts it,

> the international community is imagined as being composed of the aggregate of particular nations, but is also posited at the same time as the source of 'universal values' on which international institutions draw to justify their characterisation of these particular values as universal.[67]

Indeed, one should say with David Rieff that there is no such thing as an international community. 'There are international treaties and international institutions

64 Matthew Craven, Susan Marks, Gerry Simpson and Ralph Wilde, 'We are all Teachers of International Law', 17 *Leiden Journal of International Law* 363–74 (2004).

65 Peter Fitzpatrick, *Modernism and the Grounds of Law* (Cambridge, Cambridge University Press, 2003).

66 Jacques Derrida, 'Force of Law: "The Mystical Foundations" of Authority', 11 *Cardozo Law Review* 919–1046 (1990). See Chapter 10.

67 Sundhya Pahuja, 'The Postcoloniality of International Law', 46/2 *Harvard International Law Journal* 459 (2005), 465.

. . . but an international community presupposes a common understanding of how the world should be ordered and manifestly that does not exist'.[68]

The ultimate attitudes to life are irreconcilable and the need for decisive choices, particularly in cases of life and death or war and peace, cannot be avoided. This is the reason why the abandonment of the normative potential of law and morality in favour of a technical policy-driven agenda is not a neutral choice of means to achieve results. It is a highly political choice against politics. The ultimate ends of the new order have been set by its hegemonic power and are not open to questioning or disagreement. In this context, the political and moral duty of critical intellectuals has always been and still remains not to match ends to means but to question and challenge the ends themselves.

Pragmatism dislikes political action outside expert knowledge and the machinations of policy-makers. An example of this lack of interest in politics took place on the eve of the Iraq war. David Kennedy reprimanded a number of British and Australian legal academics, who wrote to the *Guardian* newspaper expressing the view that the planned military action was illegal. Kennedy argued that the critics had seriously undermined the critique of formalism to which many were committed by using international law, as if it could give right answers or stop the war.[69] That international law could not stop the war was evident to all. Kennedy was right. But Tony Blair had raised the war's legality into a main plank of his government's attempt to legitimise it. The formalistic arguments of the international lawyers were put to purely pragmatic use. In a debate carried out in terms of legal expertise, they had used their position as legal experts to give arguments that could be mobilised by the anti-war lobby. Academic opinion and technical expertise rarely acquires immediate political significance. This was one of those rare occasions. Legal opinion became a tool for both formal and protest politics, reversing the pragmatist priorities. Lenin said that he would use the rope capitalists sold to him to hang capitalism. But when policy replaces politics, we end up not with good law but with bad politics.

Pragmatism stands opposite cosmopolitanism. It rightly rejects and abandons the platitudes about international community, global citizenship and human rights for a hard-nosed look at the realities of the situation and the pursuit of concrete and measurable results. And yet this necessary debunking of legal fetishism could provide the most advanced normative support for a new imperial dispensation. Kennedy accepts that spreading capitalism and a

---

68 David Rieff, 'On the Wishful Thinking of Eminent Persons: the Independent Commission's Kosovo Report', 1/1 *Journal of Human Rights* 115 (2002).

69 This example is based on conversations with David Kennedy in London and Melbourne in 2004.

modicum of 'low-intensity' democracy, the declared aims of our just wars, are beyond challenge.[70] His enthusiasm for disseminating the American way of life to the rest of the world indicates the ideology of American nationalism at its imperial stage.[71] There is no acknowledgement of the fact that the value system of the American (and British) elites might not be the best recipe for everyone else.

Pragmatism and messianism are the twin brothers of American ideology. In the early 1990s, President Clinton set the tone for post-cold war unilateral military action as a supreme realist. His administration defined American interests as 'ensuring uninhibited access to key markets, energy supplies, and strategic resources' and anything that could be considered a vital interest by a 'domestic jurisdiction'.[72] Secretary of State Colin Powell, on the other hand, was given to more Christian rhetoric. America is the 'first universal nation', he stated, and 'the motive force for freedom and democracy in the world'.[73] James Der Derian, examining the 2002 *National Security Strategy* with its repeated evocations of virtue and freedom, concludes that it reads more like late-nineteenth-century poetry: 'the rhetoric intends to mobilise the moral clarity, nostalgic sentimentality, and uncontested dominance reminiscent of the last great empires against the ambiguities, complexities and messiness of the present world disorder.'[74] This is a fake version of 'Kant's view of Europe as the pinnacle of progress . . . As we are civilised, we are also in advance of history while the lives of others are only provisional'.[75]

The combination of messianic eschatology and pragmatic instrumentalism is the poor man's Hegelianism: the motive for the Iraq war was the 'grand vision of remaking societies of the Middle East as stable, open, middle-class countries . . . to link these nations more closely to the West, and even simply to stand up for what seemed "right"'.[76] The world is inexorably moving towards

---

70 This is the term used by Susan Marks in her devastating critique of the claim that international law has developed a democratic norm under which it does and ought to spread democracy around the world. Susan Marks, *The Riddle of all Constitutions* (Oxford, Oxford University Press, 2000).

71 Americans apparently believe that American nationalism does not exist. Instead they have patriotism and civic republicanism. Anatol Lieven, *America Right or Wrong: An Anatomy of American Nationalism* (London, HarperCollins, 2004). See also Chapter 6 in this volume.

72 Noam Chomsky, *Rogue States* (London, Pluto Press, 2002), 4.

73 Quoted in Andrew Bachevich, *American Empire* (Cambridge, MA, Harvard University Press, 2002), 219, 216.

74 James Der Derian, 'Decoding the *National Security Strategy* of the USA', 30/3 *Boundary 2* 19 (2003).

75 Martti Koskenniemi, 'International Law in Europe: Between Tradition and Renewal', 16 *European Journal of International Law* 113 (2005), 120.

76 Kennedy, *Dark Side*, 300.

a pale version of the American suburbs and our duty is to accelerate the process and turn everyone into a little American in order for the Americans to live safely and happily. This vision is evident in Kennedy's description of a visit to the aircraft carrier USS *Independence* patrolling the Gulf in March 1998. We are treated to an almost lyrical celebration of the regulated life, strict discipline, fancy uniforms, submissiveness and sheer *joie de vivre* of sailors and pilots as they prepare to strike Iraqi targets. 'Modern humanitarian law does seem particularly suited to the highly technical and professional operations of the American navy, and to the broader culture of submission to rule and pragmatic means–ends calculation one finds in such environments', Kennedy enthuses.[77] Consistent with anti-formalism, however, these metabolised 'standards of self-defence, proportionality and necessity are so broad that they are often routinely invoked [by the pilots] to refer to the zone of *discretion* rather than limitation'.[78] The juxtaposition of humanitarian law and massive air strikes is unnerving.

Kennedy's advice to international lawyers may be useful, if the purpose of the balancing act is to impose a morally sounding imperial will on the rest of the world. Instrumental reason can provide tools for carrying out specific tasks once the aims of the enterprise have been set. This is the logic of the cliché 'the end justifies the means'. The correspondence and fitness of means to ends is a matter of a technical not political judgement. The political and moral duty has always been to discuss and justify the ends themselves, as something that transcends the narrow interests of the person, class or nation that adopts them. If the ends have not been set, if they are not clear or if they are wrong, pragmatic calculation and technical efficiency offers nothing more than the self-aggrandisement of its practitioners. The logic of the argument that hopes to salvage the law by making it an instrument for the values or decisions of the powerful is 'if it works let it be law'.[79] This way, however, 'without the ability to articulate political visions and critiques, international law becomes pragmatism all the way down, an all encompassing internalisation, symbol and reaffirmation of power'.[80] One can go further; for the pragmatist with a conscience, a 'successful' outcome is taken as evidence of the justice of the cause. But can we reduce the worth of a cause to its apparent success? Are the defeated wrong just because they were defeated? Can you criticise power by using exclusively the arguments and priorities of power?

The abandonment of the admittedly threadbare claims of legal orthodoxy can turn pragmatism into a virulent ideology of the American empire. According

77   Ibid. 293–4.
78   Ibid. 290.
79   Koskenniemi, *Gentle Civilizer*, 484.
80   Ibid. 516.

to Christine Chinkin, the derisory way in which the United States has treated the claims of international law shows

> the new world order as a Western hegemon . . . The West continues to script international law, even when it ignores the constitutional safeguards of the international legal order . . . the alleged doctrine seems to exemplify international law-making by the West for is own application, in the name of its 'civilising' mission. Internal disorder and human rights violations are explained in terms of local nationalisms and power struggles without reference to other causes of violence such as economic intervention. The West assumes that its wealth, power and assurance bestow a normative authority that discounts alternative views.[81]

Or, as David Bowie puts it more succinctly, 'If God is an American, then God forbid if you're an immigrant (Iraqi, Iranian or Cuban) in search of the American dream.'

The cosmopolitan depoliticises politics by turning them into a local application of universalist ethics; the pragmatist, by turning them into a technically delivered accountancy for the powerful. As Anne Orford puts it, international law becomes the

> new imperial law operating through the administration of daily life and the harmonisation of systems of control and coercion to create a new global subject . . . Hardt and Negri present a genealogy of juridical forms that led to, and now leads beyond the supranational role of the UN and its varied affiliated institutions . . . Moral interventions prepares the stage for military intervention and vice versa.[82]

The industrial–military complex has been replaced by the humanitarian–military project.[83]

---

81 Christine Chinkin, 'Kosovo: A "Good" or "Bad" War?', 93 *American Journal of International Law* 841, 846–7 (1999).

82 Anne Orford, 'The Gift of Formalism', 15 *European Journal of International Law* 179 (2004). It is intriguing to note that Australian women international lawyers have consistently provided the most interesting writings on international law and have attacked the rather shaky foundations of their macho American and European counterparts. This group includes Australian academics working overseas and non-Australians who have worked in Australia for long periods.

83 See Chapters 7, 8 and 10.

The constitution of empire

Ubi societas (respublica) ibi constitutio. This is the motto of modern juridical thinking. The constitution is the outward sign and institutional design of an emerging order, including a world one. The desire to build a constitution and the ideology of constitutionalism unites international lawyers and their political opponents, the radical thinkers Michael Hardt and Antonio Negri. Negri has been a legal thinker throughout his career, a typical example of European *nomophilia*.[84] Their *Empire* states categorically that a fully functioning global constitution is emerging. It includes a new concept of supranational right, a new design for the production of norms and new instruments of coercion. This imperial constitution supersedes national and international law and creates the legal framework for regulating global social, economic and political processes. Its norm-generating institutions include the United Nations and economic and financial bodies such as the World Bank, the IMF and the WTO. A similar desire to constitutionalise the global order is evident in the writing of international lawyers. The standard American international law textbook states that 'the idea of human rights has become a universal political ideology and a central aspect of the ideology of constitutionalism'.[85] Jürgen Habermas agrees: 'Cosmopolitan law is a logical consequence of the idea of the constitutive role of law. It establishes for the first time a symmetry between the juridification of social and political relations both within and beyond the state's borders.'[86] The rather onerous task of spiriting into existence a world constitution out of the parsimonious provisions of the UN Charter and the Delphic (and often non-binding) pronouncements of the World Court, has been undertaken in the main by American and German legal academics.

Despite major ideological and political differences, both legalists and pragmatists share the belief (and hope) that a world constitution is under construction. This is particularly pronounced in recent writings on the UN Charter. The formalists claim that the Charter is a 'constitution for the world community';[87] that it 'constitutes a self-contained system which claims

---

84   Antonio Negri, 'Postmodern Global Governance and the Critical Legal Project', 16/1 *Law and Critique* 27 (2005).

85   Lari Darmosch *et al.*, *International Law: Cases and Materials* (St Paul, West Group, 2001), 586.

86   Habermas, *Inclusion of the Other*, 199.

87   Bruno Simma, ed., *The Charter of the United Nations: a Commentary* (2nd edn, Oxford, Oxford University Press, 2002), 16. Anne Orford's review of this prohibiting tome ('The Gift of Formalism', 15 *European Journal of International Law* 179 (2004)) was extremely useful in understanding the constitutional aspirations of international lawyers.

priority over other agreements';[88] that the General Assembly is 'the world's most important political discussion forum';[89] that the Security Council is 'the executive of the international community' and its resolutions can be seen as law on a global level.[90] David Kennedy agrees with the diagnosis. The emerging world constitution is 'realistic, ethical, humanist, legally valid and politically practical' and promotes democracy and freedom.[91] It includes 'a universal ethic, a political institution linked to the great powers, powers articulated through constitutional standards and limited by legal rules'.[92] The constitution privileges a results-orientated policy, which prioritises tasks, efficiency and success. For the constitutionalists, on the other hand, the United Nations can be seen as the repository of an inchoate police power, which may be used to authorise intervention, if consistent with Charter principles and the new humanitarian dispensation.[93] This putative world constitution started with the creation of the United Nations but is now coming to completion as the grand scheme of the new world order. The humanitarian turn was crucial in the process: humanitarianism spread 'from the narrow group of . . . Red Cross experts to politicians, media commentators, human rights activists and military strategists thinking more broadly about the use of force'.[94] But the individual components have now been transcended and the law of war is now turning into the law *tout court*, the constitution for the world community.[95] To defy it would be to defy the world and civilisation.

The different priorities and demands of the new legal order have brought together legalists and pragmatists in a complementary relationship. As *legal*, the new order must continuously refer back to constitutional texts; as *order*, it is more concerned with efficiency and results rather than principle and value. Constitutionalism and the rule of law are the rallying cries of cosmopolitans and legalists. Jürgen Habermas and Richard Falk advocate the decentralisation of power through the transfer of sovereignty to supranational bodies, the

88 Ibid. 495.
89 Ibid. 248.
90 Ibid. 702, 508.
91 Kennedy, op. cit., 262
92 Ibid. 263
93 Ibid. 260–3 and at 262. It is not clear whether David Kennedy agrees with this process of legalisation – in which case it would be seen as part of the pragmatic agenda - or disagrees because of the continuing strong link with humanitarianism. The overall drift of the argument, however, indicates that military humanitarianism is the most positive aspect of the new humanitarian dispensation.
94 Ibid. 236–7
95 Orford, *Humanitarian Intervention*, 158–85.

strengthening of global civil society and the construction of transnational democratic institutions. Philip Sands wants a return to the principles of the rule of law and a strengthening of international courts, tribunals and legal processes. Joining forces with the cosmopolitans, in terms of ends if not means, David Kennedy agrees that sanctions must be legally justified and force linked to the promotion of human rights and the export of freedom and democracy. This new type of humanitarian and humane war has become the most advanced instrument of the legal order. Its ideology combines some of the hopes of the legalists and cosmopolitans with a large dose of pragmatic utilitarianism and, to that extent, it transcends the old debates between constitutional fetishists and political realists. Developments in Kosovo and Iraq have made it possible to use force legally in order to export modernity and free markets to parts of the world Western values have not yet reached. For the first time since the abandonment of the attempt to define just war, we have acquired a vocabulary through which the Western civilised nations can discuss, judge and justify violence. Its completion and realisation depends on its full internalisation by politicians, bureaucrats and the military. The cosmopolitans were right to support the Kosovo war but did not fully understand its implications. The war was not an old style just war nor was it mainly motivated by a love for suffering humanity. It was the first war of the new order, in which hard-nosed humanitarians wear khaki, fly in bombers and apply the World Constitution. Like early international law, which emerged out of the religious doctrine of just war and the laws of war, humanity's law is evolving into the constitutional ideology of global governance.

Hardt and Negri seem to agree with these descriptions but they denounce their normative implications. The new order is closer to a strange empire rather than to Kelsenian cosmopolitanism. Its ideological underpinnings are traced back to the centrality of freedom in the American constitution, which allegedly distinguished it from its European sovereignty-obsessed counterparts and, second, to its tendency to disregard state frontiers and expand outwards. The next step towards the imperial constitution was taken by the creation of the United Nations, which owes more to the European constitutional tradition and the writings of Kant and Kelsen. For Hardt and Negri, Kelsen's hope that the UN Charter would become the foundation of a complete legal system and take priority over domestic law is coming true in the new world order. In the current phase, however, the practice of the imperial constitution is 'bathed in blood' while its concept is dedicated to perpetual peace. Despite their attacks on Hegelian dialectics, their constitutional blueprint brings together and sublates cosmopolitan aspirations and a darker, Schmittian conception of conflict. In the planetary terrain of Empire, Ignatieff's 'barbarians' are no longer menacing the frontiers. Deterritorialisation turns all enemies into 'enemies within' and makes the war against them temporally and spatially limitless. The old 'amity line', which separated the Europe of civilised princes from the newly 'discovered' lands where atrocities, genocide and plunder were allowed, is being redrawn, along a line that goes from Russia through the Balkans and the Arab world. Neutrality has withered and the distinction between belligerents and neutrals has stopped making sense now that force has become the instrument of the international community. A more appropriate distinction is that between the international community and 'rogue states', who opt for wanton violence and aggressive wars. Or, as Bush would put it, 'whoever is not with us is against us'.

Are we, then, on the way to developing a global constitution and a novel type of universal non-national sovereignty as Hardt and Negri suggest? Is 'humanity's law', or perhaps 'freedom's law', the organising principle, the norm of the world order? Is international law being superseded by a new supranational norm? Will domestic law follow national sovereignty and wither away replaced by the laws and regulations of supranational public and economic institutions? By examining the normative evidence and the actions of the new world order so far, we can start the process of understanding – which is the first step towards resisting it.

Sovereignty is the first principle and begetter of new constitutions and polities. There is no doubt that sovereignty is going through a period of radical transformation. Does this mean, as often claimed, that the principle has been weakened or is about to pass away? Are Hardt and Negri right to argue that imperial sovereignty is 'not American and the United States is not its centre' although it has a 'special place' in it? [96] Sovereignty as the foundation of law and supporter of the unity of a people belongs to the symbolic order, as Chapter 11 discusses. When a part of national sovereignty is removed or surrendered, it does not leave the symbolic order. It gets transferred and condensed in another pole, augmenting its aura and power. A concept of European law can help us understand the evolution of sovereignty. Under the principles of direct effect and direct applicability, a large number of European legal provisions can be invoked by citizens of the Union in their domestic courts and any conflicting provisions of national law cannot be applied and evetually must be amended or repealed. The European Court of Justice rationalised this huge incursion on legal sovereignty by arguing that member-states, by entering the Union and recognising the jurisdiction of European law in its areas of competency, restricted their sovereignty accordingly. This 'surrendered' national sovereignty was then transferred to the Brussels institutions creating

96   Hardt and Negri, op. cit., xx, 384.

a gap in national law. In applying European law even when in conflict with domestic legislation, judges apply the only valid law, since domestic law has vacated the relevant areas.

One could argue, by analogy, that while most states have 'lost' the full attributes of traditional sovereignty through developments in humanitarian and economic law, lost sovereignty has not disappeared but has been condensed in the hegemonic power which directs the initiatives that gnaw at it. The sovereignty transfer and deficit of some states concentrates the lost part in a *super-sovereign*. This sovereignty transfer lies behind the debates among international lawyers about the appropriate response to humanitarian crises. Should the response be carried out at international, regional or national level? The answer is that both the response and its form depend almost exclusively on the decision of the United States. The fluidity of the range of responses, however, indicates that frontiers no longer protect the weakened states nor do they restrict condensed sovereignty. In more prosaic terms, our recent wars teach states to align themselves with the US, in which case they can freely violate the human rights of their citizens. 'Humanity's law' is a powerful tool for undermining national sovereignty and territorial integrity. Humanitarian wars are asymmetrical however. They allow the super-sovereign to intervene in the affairs of the weak but under no circumstances could the reverse take place.

While sovereignty is being weakened at the periphery and condensed at the centre, the nation-state remains the organising principle of the world. Whether inter-national, supra-national or trans-national, Hardt and Negri's 'imperial right' or Teitel's 'humanity's law' is still a relationship among nations and a formal and material extension of domestic legal principles. The nation has always stood as the representative of the universal. This has not changed at the present imperial or cosmopolitan stage. As Ruth Buchanan and Sundhya Pahuja put it, 'empire assumes the very nation-state it would ostensibly transcend. Nation is the pivot between domestic and international law'.[97] The mutual dependence of the national and the more-than-national (international, imperial or cosmopolitan) is evident at many levels.

The nation-state and domestic law remain an inescapable component of the political economy of globalisation. Both public and economic international organisations are managed by state delegations and national emissaries according to various criteria of regional representation. The Americans dislike the UN and its agencies partly because of the formal equality of its 190-odd

97 Ruth Buchanan and Sundhya Pahuja, 'Legal Imperialism' in Dean and Passavant, op. cit., 85.

members, which could – but rarely do – override American interests. It must be more than simple coincidence that the attack on sovereignty started after the process of decolonisation had raised a large number of former colonies, dependencies and other 'uncivilised' places to the status of full statehood, sovereignty and formal equality with their erstwhile colonial masters. In the area of international trade, multilateral agreements, the most important driver of globalisation, are on the retreat. The Doha round of trade negotiations failed and was abandoned in 2006, a development which, if confirmed, could lead to the sidelining of the WTO, the most powerful globalising institution. Bilateral treaties, a characteristic expression of the national principle and of the contractualism of modern law, have replaced multilateral negotiations. Their attraction to the powerful is evident. They emphasise both the formal equality of sovereignty and the material imbalance of the partners. The United States has already negotiated a number of bilateral deals, using its hegemonic position to impose unfavourable trade terms on its negotiating partners. Singapore and Chile were forced to renounce the use of capital controls, deployed by Malaysia during the Asian financial crisis, while Australia had to accept extended periods of validity for patents augmenting the privileges enjoyed by American companies. Finally, human rights were invented as protection against state power and became a paradoxical addition to national laws and constitutions. Their respect or violation is still a matter of national policies under the supervision and threat of sanctions by the imperial centre. Human rights can meaningfully survive only within the context of the nation-state.

The continuing centrality of the nation-state despite attacks from right and left can be easily explained. The capitalist mode of production separated a sphere of economic activity from the political realm, where the territorial and legal sovereignty of the state developed. Capitalist accumulation and the commodification of social relations need the state to help with the twin tasks of coercion and ideological legitimacy. David Harvey has convincingly argued that, while in imperialism the logic of capital and of the state often diverge and even come into conflict, they are united in their overall aim of securing the reproduction of capitalism. Capitalist appropriation at the age of globalisation still needs the protection of coercive laws and policies; the state is the only institution able to provide them. The logic of capital exploits 'the uneven geographical conditions under which capital accumulation occurs and . . . takes advantage of the "asymmetries" that inevitably arise out of spatial exchange relations', while the logic of state is 'to try to preserve that pattern of asymmetries in exchange over space'.[98] The fact that globalisation has

98 Harvey, op. cit., 32.

extended capital's economic powers beyond the range of any single nation-state means that 'global capital requires *many* nation-states to perform the administrative and coercive functions'.[99]

The international lawyers' diagnosis of an emergent 'humanity's law' eating away at the sovereign structure of weak states is correct. Geographical and political boundaries are being replaced by open-ended concepts, such as humanity and freedom. But against their complacent enthusiasm, the emerging public law does not express the triumph of sympathy and solidarity for human suffering but the structural asymmetries of the world order and the dominant role of the hegemonic power. Its condensed sovereignty turns the United States into the strongest political and military imperial power the world has ever seen, an emperor in search of empire. Michael Hardt and Antonio Negri are right to emphasise that the new order's rule penetrates all levels of social life integrating economic, social, cultural and political domination. But their emphasis on the biopolitical organisation of social life and on sovereignty's non-national character cannot explain the recent endless wars. They argue that empire is committed to eternal peace but involved in permanent war. To support this conclusion, they adopt Carl Schmitt's concept of the state of exception, which determines the normal operation of the law. But the eclectic addition of a Schmittian sovereign on Foucaultian biopolitics undermines their conception of empire. According to Schmitt, the supreme characteristic of the sovereign is the power to declare a state of exception in order to save the law. But if this is the case, the sovereign, both logically and historically, must be a single person, natural or metaphorical. *Empire*'s sovereign, on the other hand, consists of a combination of international institutions, norm-generating jurisdictions and biopolitical functions. To paraphrase Henry Kissinger's quip about the European Union, how many fighter-bombers and tanks does such a sovereign have? Their reluctance to name the United States as the sovereign centre of empire makes their weird edifice unconvincing.

We can conclude that neither a constitution nor a supranational norm has emerged at the world stage. It could not be different. The constitution is the base, the plinth upon which a community stands, the expression of its members coming together. This coming together singularly and plurally is evident in the etymology of *constitution*, the primal law-founding jurisdiction.[100] The Indo-European root **sta* is one of the most potent markers of the philosophical tradition. It appears in the Greek stasis (standing, stopping, rebellion) and its

99 Ellen Meiksins Wood, 'A Manifesto for Global Capital?' in Gopal Balakrishnan, ed., *Debating Empire* (London, Verso, 2003), 68.

100 Chapter 11, below.

derivatives (*hypostasis*, *anastasis*), in the Latin-derived stance, substance, constance, *vorstellung*, etc. Constitution is the place, ground or stand upon where people come to presence together (*cum-stance*). It expresses the co-appearance and standing together of a people in their common space and time. But no community or *demos* exists on the world stage and no principle or ground brings people across the globe together. We may not have a constitution or community but we already have a uniquely powerful hegemonic power and are well on the way towards the creation of empire.

Excursus: the existential problem of the international lawyer

International law is both more and less law-like than its national counterpart making its practitioners feel both superior and inferior compared with their domestic brethren. On the one hand, international lawyers enjoy what one could call a certain 'interpretative pre-eminence'. The absence of a global legislator and of a real court interpreting the law authoritatively turns the texts of international law into an ultimate but indeterminate reference point. Its practitioners, lawyers and diplomats, have much greater power in deciding the meaning and import of the law than domestic lawyers who must always defer to higher authority. International law practice is closer to the Protestant tradition under which individuals interpret the holy texts freely rather than to the Catholic authoritative renditions by the Church. Even pragmatist international lawyers, despite their interdisciplinary interests (or because of their interest in achieving results) are necessarily immersed in the legal text deeper and are unavoidably more legalistic than their domestic cousins. The international lawyer is the lawyers' lawyer, someone who spends a lifetime pouring over the text of treaties, their *traveaux préparatoires* and the few 'soft' decisions of international tribunals. But if she accepts the extreme version of pragmatism and becomes fully multidisciplinary, she turns from a respected knower of the law into a second-class sociologist or psychologist.

On the other hand, the more certain the law, the least its power (when a strong state disagrees with it) and the greater and more embarrassing its demise, as Kosovo and Iraq showed. Uncertain, indeterminate law is better-suited to its function as a tool of the great powers. The international lawyer's professional identity is in direct conflict with her practical effectiveness. As a result, international lawyers live in a permanent existential crisis. Their *hazar professionel* is that they are the ultimate exponents of a law whose power is in reverse proportion to its certainty. This combination of ideological significance and political irrelevance shadows the debates of international lawyers like Hamlet's ghost. Their endless musings about the status of their discipline is quite unique in the legal academy. Anxiety about the nature of international law and the identity of its personnel is evident throughout the academic literature. Conferences often seem to become exercises in group therapy. For one critical commentator, international law has all the characteristics of kitsch.[101] For another, the law is in a permanent state of crisis and is burdened with the anxiety of influence.[102] As a confused essay written by academics who objected to the war on legal grounds characteristically states:

> But what would [our legal objections to the war] ultimately mean? Could we seize the legal ground without being simultaneously imprisoned within it? How were we to understand what was going on? Was this a case of critical sensibilities dulled by political thrill-seeking? A temporary and strategic embrace of the doctrinal? Or legalism's united front threatening to dissolve in self-doubt?[103]

This sounds like a cry for help brought about by international law's brief glory.

Academic debates commonly turn from a defence of the law into an apology for its practitioners. For Sands, the American government's preference for the advice of ignorant political appointees rather than that of competent lawyers was a main reason for the rush to war. The legal opinion written by Assistant Attorney-General Jay Bybee legitimising the use of torture by American interrogators should become 'compulsory reading for every student of international law. It makes for a mildly entertaining read'.[104] In the lead to the war, according to Sands, no constituency tried to defend international law and academic lawyers remained silent. David Kennedy, on the contrary, attacks those who tried to use international law to stop the Iraq war. They confused the UN Charter with humanitarianism, evaluated military action in moral terms and silenced those 'favouring the war [who] were simply not permitted to say why they did so'![105]

The combination of the belief that right answers exist in law (shown up for its naive optimism in Kosovo and Iraq) with despair about the general indifference or disrepute accompanying their discovery, marks the dilemma of the legalist. The pragmatist's problem is the opposite: the law cannot provide

---

101 Martti Koskenniemi, 'International Law in Europe: Between Tradition and Renewal', 16 *European Journal of International Law* 113 (2005), 119.

102 Susan Marks, *The Riddle of all Constitutions* (Oxford, Oxford University Press, 2000).

103 Matthew Craven, Susan Marks, Gerry Simpson and Ralph Wilde, 'We are Teachers of International Law', 17 *Leiden Journal of International Law* 362 (2004) at 366.

104 Sands, op. cit., 229.

105 Kennedy, fn. 52, 302.

right answers, but as a result there is no resting place in the quest for solutions. The law must be seen in its context; but as the context is infinite and therefore mute, the answers are given by the powerful. The problem with international law is not that it is under attack by detractors and must be defended by people who believe in international legality. The main difficulty is that it is highly malleable:

> Customary international law changes under this definition when state practice changes which led former Attorney-General Bill Barr to opine: 'Well as I understand it, what you're saying is the only way to change international law is to break it'. This telling remark shows the incoherence of treating 'customary international law' as law.[106]

This is the general characteristic of the law beyond its customary part. Its obvious admixture of principle, pragmatism and generalised national interest allows states to use it when it suits them and to discard it when it does not.

We can conclude that international law can offer justification for the application of sanctions and constraints against 'rogue' states or small powers when they assert their independence vis-à-vis the great, but it is no constraint or limitation against the great powers themselves. In the Kosovo war, the great Western powers were all on the same side and the breach of the law was overlooked and excused. In Iraq, the great split into two and the weaker Europeans were sidelined despite their credible legal arguments. Hardt and Negri are exaggerating when they claim that international law has been replaced by a new supranational right and the constitution of empire. A form of international law will survive as long as the world order (including an imperial one) will continue using the nation-state as its main constituent. But as the new or 'postmodern' international law adjusts to the demands of the world order, liberal cosmopolitans and the hard-nosed pragmatic practitioners of *realpolitik* are coming together. International law with all its contradictions and paradoxes is leading us into empire.

106 Bolton, op. cit., 6

Chapter 10

War, violence, law

A short history of just war

Throughout history, people have gone to wars and sacrificed themselves at the altar of religion, empire, nation or class. Religious and secular leaders know well the importance of adding a veneer of high principle to low ends and murderous campaigns. This is equally evident in Homer's *Iliad*, in Thucidides' chilling description of the Athenian atrocities at Melos and Mytilene, in the chronicles of the Crusades and in the films about the Gulf Wars and Somalia. The ability of kings and generals to present their side's war as morally justified and their opponents' as evil, combined with the lack of a moral arbiter who could sift through conflicting rationalisations has made just war doctrine one of the hardest moral mazes. For the warring parties, there is nothing more certain than the morality of their respective causes. For observers, there is nothing more uncertain than the rightness of the combatants' conflicting moral claims. As Wyndam Lewis put it 'but what war that was ever fought, was an unjust war, except of course that waged by the enemy'. The wars, tortures, forced migrations and other calculated brutalities that make up so much of history have, for the most part, been carried out by men who earnestly believed that their actions were justified, indeed, demanded by divine will or human righteousness.

It is against this background of moral undecidability that we must examine the history of the morally justified or 'just' war. In premodern societies, the power to go to war was a natural and undisputed part of their political organisation, an anthropological given. The conduct of war was regulated by the warriors' customs, which flexibly determined the rituals necessary for starting the war, the treatment of opponents and hostages and the respect owed to the dead of both sides. The *Iliad*, the *Trojan Women* and *Antigone* offer ample evidence of the customs that guided combatants. Plato, for example, stated in the *Republic* that it is an abominable outrage for either party in civil war to ravage the lands or burn the houses of the enemy, a practice acceptable and often used in war against foreigners. It is not true therefore that unregulated warfare is unlimited warfare. Every community develops its own internal rules and customs for organising this ultimate test of life. These customs have often led to reciprocal recognition and minimum respect between enemies.

The concept of the *bellum justum* appeared first in Rome. Following Greek precedent, it meant that war was initiated and conducted according to certain customs and rituals. Before the beginning of hostilities, the *fetials*, a college of priests, determined whether the conditions for going to war existed. Legal formalities such as the issuing of the *jus fetiale*, a demand for just satisfaction which, if unmet, led to formal declaration of war, complemented religious practices, like the taking of the auguries before battle. Cicero, a general, lawyer and politician writes that 'in a republic the laws of war are to be maintained in the highest degree . . . wars must be undertaken for this cause: that life may go on in peace without injustice'.[1] Cicero adds that republican laws and customs limit the conduct of war. Soldiers should be formally enlisted before they fight, faith and the law of oaths should be kept with enemies and vanquished enemies should be spared if they lay down arms and seek the protection of the victors.[2] These procedures were based on the belief that the outcome of battles and wars was decided by the gods. Observance of the rituals guaranteed that the war would be blessed by divinity and good fortune. A combination of sacral functions, religious rituals and legal regulation formed the ancient structure of war. It is still with us today.

It was the early Church, after the conversion of Emperor Constantine to Christianity, that first developed a consistent theory of just war in an attempt to serve Caesar without abandoning fully its pledges to God. From the earliest theologico-political attempts at determining the morality of war, emphasis was placed on its just ends. For Augustine, one of the early Church Fathers, a just war is designed to restore the violated moral order. Just are wars '*quae ulciscuntur injurias*', which redress a wrong suffered. Strict conditions should be met. War should be undertaken as the last resort and should be declared by legitimate authority. But the element that allowed a war to be fully blessed was its *justa causa*. Typically, wars were considered just if conducted in self-defence against aggression or for restitution and retribution after unjust acts or conquests. Additionally, the war should have a reasonable prospect of success. Once the just demands had been met all further violence was prohibited. The aim of war was not victory but the establishment of '*tranquillitas ordinis*'

1   Cicero, *On Duties*, 1.34–35.
2   Ibid. 1.33–37 *passim*.

an ordered or just peace.[3] It was fought justly, if its conduct followed religious, customary or positive rules of engagement restraining its excesses. Introduced into law, this distinction took the form of the *jus ad bellum* (the lawful initiation of war) and the *jus in bello* (the lawful conduct of war).

Just war theory became a crucial part of medieval political theology. After the disintegration of the *Respublica Christiana* and the rise of many small principalities and communities at permanent war, the mediating role of the emperor was gradually transferred to public law. Secular ideas followed canon law and recognised the exclusive power of princes and knights to declare war. The great glossator Bartolus and his contemporary Johannes de Legnano argued that war was originally a divine institution, a remedy or medication for the elimination of disease and the return to a just peace. Only the Pope, however, could wage this type of divine war in defence of the faith. For the warring princes, on the other hand, war was part of general law and was connected with the dominant idea of reprisals for wrongs suffered. As no superior judge existed to decide the justice of the cause, each prince could decide whether a legitimate cause for war or reprisals existed, according to the dictates of Christian doctrine.[4] This combination of theology, ethics and the law of the Justinian code created a highly convenient theory for the warring sides. It blessed military campaigns, strengthened the authority of princes and buttressed their willingness to protect the Church. Not unlike contemporary humanitarianism, just war theory was a marriage of convenience between prudence and morality consecrated by the establishment of the day. As a result of the religious–moral influence, medieval political theology became preoccupied with the justice of the cause, which was sought in the Bible and the disputations on natural law. A just war should be conducted in line with its declared aims. Little attention was paid to the means used. The divine duty to punish infidel and evil-doer made the prosecution of some wars limitless. It justified the unremitting violence of the Crusades, the genocidal attacks on the Indians and indigenous people of the newly discovered lands and, later, the atrocities of the religious wars, which, conducted on both sides in the name of the true faith, knew no limit in their attempt to annihilate the morally degraded enemies.

With the collapse of the medieval order, the Reformation and Counter-Reformation replaced the common religious ethics with various conflicting moral standpoints. The Christian empire broke up into a number of warring

---

3 Augustine, *De Civitate Dei* (M. Dods, J.J. Smith and G. Wilson, trans.) (New York, Hapfner, 1948), XIX, 13.

4 Joachim von Elbe, 'The Evolution of the Concept of Just War in International Law', 33/4 *American Journal of International Law* 669–73 (1939).

empires and states, all armoured with powerful militaries and a supreme sense of rightness. Lawyers abandoned God-sanctioned natural law for the conventional law of nations and gave up the search for universal standard of justice. That justice does not belong to the concept of war has been generally recognized since Grotius's *De Jure Belli ac Pacis*, the foundational text of international law. Grotius echoed the theological debates of the previous age; he emphasised the punitive aspect of war for crimes committed against a state but did not include justice in the definition of war.[5] As Christian Wolff put it, the question of the justice of wars falls outside the pale of international law.[6]

The emergence of the *Jus Publicum Europaeum* in the seventeenth and eighteenth centuries secularised the idea of the just cause and made the initiation and conduct of war part of international law.[7] The medieval debates had assumed that only one of the warring parties could be just, as it would be contradictory for both parties to pursue a just cause at the same time. The theologians determined the justice of the cause from god's all-seeing perspective. When lawyers inherited this task, they could not claim god's omniscience, even though they have always fancied themselves as a priesthood and as messengers of a higher truth. Francisco de Vitoria, the Spanish lawyer who combined classical just war theory with an understanding of the changed international scene, introduced the idea that while a war could not be just on both sides, '"invincible ignorance" on the part of those who wage objectively unjust wars in good faith is a "complete excuse"'. Gentilis took it further: 'a war may be just on one side, but on the other is still more just.' The warring parties resembled two litigants before an impartial judge, none of whom could be called unjust.[8]

Under the new 'subjective' conception of justice, both warring parties could validly believe in the morality of their cause. The early modern theory of the just war is the clearest sign of the emergence of a system of international relations based on sovereign states demarcated by clear and recognised territorial boundaries. The modern nation-state could freely determine its causes for going to war. The law of war, one of the earliest components of international law, disassociated the idea of just war from its *justa causa* and related it to a just enemy, defined as an external sovereign, a foe who shares the formal attributes of statehood. After the Treaty of Westphalia, a war between European sovereigns was just because the combatants were formally equal actors (*hostes*

5 Grotius, *De Juri Belli et Pacis*, vol.1, Book 1, Chapter 1, para. 2, 49.

6 Wolff quoted in von Elbe, op. cit., 682.

7 Carl Schmitt, *Der Nomos der Erde in Volkerrecht des Jus Publicum Europaeum* (Berlin: Ducker & Humblot, 1997 (1950)).

8 von Elbe, 675, 676.

aequalitur justi). The sovereign decided the justness of the cause and moral justifications became redundant. Indeed, the principle that war must be accounted just on both sides is absolutely necessary, if any type of restraint is to be introduced into its conduct. Emphasis was now placed on the development of a detailed *jus in bello*, legal rules regulating the conduct of war without overburdening the parties with excessive concern for the collateral damage of their action. These customs, practices, rules and procedures, some introduced in international treaties others developed more gradually, have been grouped under the principles of discrimination and proportionality and form the bulk of humanitarian law. Discrimination distinguishes between military staff and civilian populations and targets and prohibits attacking, targeting or otherwise harming non-combatants except when absolutely necessary. The principle of proportionality, on the other hand, attempts to adjust the means and scope of military action with its legitimate objectives. Taken together the two principles present war today as an intrinsically limited activity, which must be directed only at legitimate, predominantly military, targets.

When the regulation of military conduct was first introduced, it presupposed that the warring parties were formally equal. A sense of minimum faith, of trust in the enemy, was necessary if restraints were to be successful. Warfare considered illegal on one side would create chaotic conditions and the resulting peace would always be challenged as unjustly achieved, argued Vattel.[9] Indeed, the term just war became a pleonasm, as all wars among sovereigns were considered formally just. As a result, international lawyers abandoned the attempt to classify and abolish war in order to minimise its impact and for this reason Kant accused them, in the person of Grotius, as 'miserable comforters'.[10] For Kant, who revived the idea of a just peace, reason condemns war. A sovereign not prepared to abandon the warring state of nature of international relations in favour of the promised peaceful cosmopolitan order is an unjust enemy.[11] For Kant, force can be used ethically in very few instances. The use of force and war as a tool of foreign policy should be banned by law. The aim of cosmopolitan society, first evangelised by Kant, was defined negatively: it is the abolition of war. We examine the cosmopolitan project in some detail in Chapter 7.

---

9   Ibid. 683.
10 Immanuel Kant, 'Towards Perpetual Peace: A Philosophical Sketch' in H. Reiss, ed. *Kant: Political Writings* (Cambridge, Cambridge University Press, 1986), 103.
11 Kant, 'Idea for a Universal History from a Cosmopolitan Point of View' and 'Perpetual Peace' in H. Reiss, ed. *Kant: Political Writings*, (Cambridge, Cambridge University Press, 1986), 164–74.

While the war between homogeneous Christian sovereigns became regulated and limited, this 'normalisation' was grounded on an exception. A crucial difference separated the war between Europeans and that between Europeans and non-Europeans or among Europeans outside continental Europe. In the war against 'savages', the *jus in bello*, premised on a society of homogeneous Christian sovereigns, did not apply. The so-called European 'amity line' allowed a degree of civilisation of war in the metropolitan lands, while the New World became the terrain of a dual barbarity: the presumed barbarity of the indigenous people but also the space for the release of European brutality. Francis Bacon, for example, justified genocide because certain people, such as the Indian nations, are subhuman and are proscribed by nature itself, because they eat human flesh. Anthony Anghie has shown how the colonial experience was central to the formation of international law. Francisco de Vitoria, one of the forefathers of international law, argued that although Indians had a form of government, this was inadequate because they did not have proper laws or judges and were not even capable of controlling their family affairs. Spanish occupation and rule was in their own interests because it provided them with proper government.[12]

In a related development, the concept of the 'enemies within' emerged. They are political and social forces that challenge the internal *ordre publique*. They do not deserve any respect and they cannot invoke the constraints of international law in their treatment by the King's police and army because they have no sovereign status. They are reduced to the condition of bandits, terrorists, rebels, infidels to the claims of sovereign statehood. This faultline led to the distinction between war, civil strife and police action. These different types of violence can be distinguished by observing the state's response and not the identity of the combatants. Modernity with its religious and ideological fervour reversed Plato. It placed certain restrictions on the conduct of war but left civil strife unregulated. War is partly regulated, while civil war has no limits and is considered as the most brutal and cruel of warfare. Rebels are treated as absolute enemies, ripe for elimination or, as targets of boundless police action and criminal sanctions that conceal their political status. The distinction between war and police action indicates the way in which the sovereign posits itself towards the law.

The early modern undermining of the theological conceptions of the good or the just meant that the absolute power of sovereignty and *raison d'état*

---

12 Antony Anghie, *Imperialism, Sovereignty and the Making of International Law* (Cambridge, Cambridge University Press, 2005); Nathaniel Berman, 'In the Wake of Empire', 14 *American University International Law Review* 1521 (1999).

replaced the morality of war. In modernity, the ends of war belong exclusively to the sovereign; war is the ultimate expression of the sovereign nature. By declaring and waging war, the sovereign accomplishes his nature in absolute opposition to another, he acts against his alter ego *ad mortem*. This change in the character of war was acknowledged by the gradual decline of the *jus ad bellum*. The decision to go to war is the sovereign decision par excellence, the exception and suspension of law and, as such, the confirmation of the sovereign in his majesty. As Karl von Clausewitz, the paramount theorist of modern warfare put it, 'war is an act of force which theoretically can have no limits'.[13] In this sense, there is no act of violence, cruelty or brutality that falls outside the conduct of war 'for the logic of war simply is a moral thrust toward moral extremity'.[14] If war is the ultimate expression of the sovereign power to decide to suspend the law and act in excess, the *jus in bello,* the lawful conduct of law, is a concession by the sovereign and an implicit contract between the warring parties. *Inter armes silent leges* stated the classical maxim; its essence was confirmed in the limited and voluntary acceptance of restraints by the European powers. The suspension of law in the declaration of war as much as its acceptance in the form of the law of war was a confirmation of the paramount brilliance of sovereignty.

Modern war, beyond its immediate aims, has always had the further end of accomplishing the sovereign's proper essence. The two new types of war created by modernity, the war of independence and the war of liberation, fully upheld sovereign right. The first, modelled on the American War of Independence, confirms the sovereign order by aiming to create a new sovereign. The second, modelled on the French Revolution, claimed to uphold and spread the natural rights of humanity but ended in the Napoleonic campaigns and the creation of the French Empire. Revolutions and wars of liberation were supposed to create a new type of logic that transcended the sovereign order. But the 'people's war' was born and entered its museum phase at the same time. War has remained the highest expression of sovereignty and has formed the foundation of most state sovereigns and their legal systems. Despite attempts to conceal the link, war is the father of law.

The law understands its debt to war, it knows that its foundation is drowned in violence and that the laws of war exist by virtue of a sovereign concession. Police action, on the contrary, appears to give law back its normality. Policing appears as war according to law, a war that takes place when the sovereign

---

13 Carl von Clausewitz, *On War* (M. Howard and P. Paret, eds) (Princeton, NJ, Princeton University Press, 1976), 76.
14 Michael Walzer, *Just and Unjust Wars* (New York, Basic Books, 1977), 23.

voice is silent. But sovereign action and policing cannot be easily distinguished. The treatment of the internal 'enemies of the state' by regimes of all kinds has been more brutal than that of external foes. The links between war and policing have been extensively discussed by Walter Benjamin[15] and Carl Schmitt. As Giorgio Agamben commenting on their work put it,

> whereas the sovereign is the one who, in proclaiming a state of emergency and suspending the validity of the law, marks the point of indistinction between violence and law, the police operate in what amounts to a permanent 'state of emergency'. The principles of 'public order' and 'security', which the police are under obligation to decide on a case-by-case basis, represent a zone of indistinction between violence and law perfectly symmetrical to that of sovereignty.[16]

War and police action are both at the limit of law. A modernist convention calls the internal use of force policing while the external war. The first projects sovereign power in its momentary splendour while the latter carries within it the permanent potential of sovereign exception. Their difference lies elsewhere. War exemplifies the sovereign decision while police action, the war of law, operates within limits set elsewhere, between the first principle of law's violent foundation and the final ends always decided in sovereign decisions. Indeed, the idea of law becoming sovereign, of war in the name of humanity so that lawful peace would replace war, would have to wait until our recent just wars.

The twentieth century changed somewhat the main elements of this picture. The Second World War was seen as the ultimate failure of the League of Nations system. But the determination to continue and complete the League's task of banning war became stronger. The first court in the Nuremberg indictment was for Nazi crimes against peace. Indeed, Justice Jackson started his address to the tribunal by stating that he had the 'privilege of opening the first trial in history for crimes against the peace of the world'. Waging a war of aggression was 'the supreme international crime, contain[ing] within itself the accumulated evil of the whole'. The devastation of the war led to a desire not just to control but to prevent and outlaw war. Nuremberg introduced the principle that planning and waging a war of aggression constituted a crime in international law and this led to a return of a substantive *jus ad bellum*. Building

---

15 Walter Benjamin, 'Critique of Violence' in *Reflections* (E. Jephcott, trans.) (New York, Schocken Books, 1978).

16 Giorgio Agamben, 'The Sovereign Police' in Brian Massumi, ed., *The Politics of Everyday Fear* (Minneapolis, MN, University of Minnesota Press, 1993), 62.

on this beginning, the UN Charter established a distinction between aggressive and defensive or unjust and justified wars upon which the Security Council's right to impose sanctions rests. A main purpose of the post-Second World War order was to maintain peace and the law was used, in part, as a tool to achieve this objective. States and their sovereigns were no longer free, in law at least, to go to war except in a relatively well defined and strict set of circumstances. Broadly speaking, states could go to war in self-defence or on the authorisation of the Security Council acting on its obligation to prevent and stop violations of peace. In this sense, just war theory returned, creating a new juridical *jus ad bellum*.

A distinction between aggressive (read unjust) and defensive (just) wars was introduced. But this was not a return to religious just war theory. The new and terrifying total war, the development of mass destruction technologies, the ideological fervour of the age and the erosion of the military/civilian distinction combined to transfer morality from the pulpit to the legal chambers. The legal banning and the regulation of warfare became characteristic of late-twentieth-century international law and moved the just war arguments from moralists to diplomats and from catholic seminaries to statesmen's conferences. A type of morality was incorporated into the law; but it was a forced marriage, a cohabitation of limited convenience.

The new law of war was of an exceptionally 'soft' character. While denouncing aggressive war and proclaiming its faith in human rights, the post-Second World War order reinforced the inviolability of sovereignty. The principle of non-intervention in the internal affairs of states schizophrenically accompanied the claims to universal justice implicit in the definition of just war and in the international treaties of human rights that characterised the post-war order. The attempt by international lawyers to codify the idea of crimes against peace was unsuccessful and has been abandoned. But the apparent failure of lawyers and diplomats to create a detailed legal definition of (un)just war, a double-edged sword for the major powers, has been compensated by the emergence of the much more extensive moral order of human rights and humanitarianism, an order from which the West can easily exempt itself.

The changes in the last twenty years have been quite dramatic. The modernist divide between international politics guided by state interest and domestic politics that respect the rule of law and civil liberties has started to collapse. After the fall of communism, human rights and humanitarianism became the dominant ideology of the new times, as we discuss throughout this book. At the same time, the previously impossible prospect of a limited war by powerful against weak states, which would not risk a major conflagration between nuclear powers, became available. This combination led to the novel idea of wars for humanitarian purposes, of military invasions to save people. Bosnia and Kosovo were the first examples of the new military humanitarianism. The cosmopolitans became the postmodern policy-makers at the turn of the twenty-first century. Politics bends the knee before right, we are told. In a strange historical reversal, neo-Kantians have turned the master on his head. While Kant wanted to outlaw war, his putative followers argue that morality demands the use of sanctions and humanitarian wars.[17] Michael Walzer, someone who championed just war even when it was not fashionable, claims that just war theory has now triumphed.[18] Similarly, Fernando Teson, a self-proclaimed follower of Kant, has denounced the principle of non-intervention in the internal affairs of sovereign states, the contemporary expression of the ban on war, as the outcome of the removal of morality from law.[19] For Teson, a passionate advocate of humanitarian intervention, this ban was the result of amoral positivism and of the 'fetishisation' of the state by the followers of Hegel (!) who see it as a morally free entity. The idea that international lawyers and statesmen follow Hegel is rather bizarre. It follows a rather unconvincing attempt to claim that a right to humanitarian intervention was endorsed by Grotius and Vattel. If this was the case (it was not), it must have been undermined by someone and the 'Hegelian' international lawyers are as good a candidate as the Freemasons or the Knights of the Temple.[20]

The *justa causa* for war was a major topic of conversation among the theologians who kept discussing and developing it throughout the Middle Ages. Despite its frequent use it does not get similar attention today. The closest we came to a contemporary just war doctrine was in a speech by Tony Blair during the Kosovo war. 'This is a just war', Blair claimed, 'based not on any territorial ambitions but on values.' Occupying the high moral and political ground, Blair claimed that an 'international community' has come into existence and spoke on its behalf:

> We are all internationalists now, whether we like it or not. We cannot re-fuse to participate in global markets if we want to prosper. We cannot

---

17 It has been argued, however, that since Kant's cosmopolitan project would involve some states imposing their views on justice on others in order to reform them and establish a just peace it could end up with a 'perpetual war for perpetual peace' (K. Waltz, *Man, the State and War* (New York, Columbia University Press, 1959), 113. This is not the position of modern humanitarians although it may be its effect.

18 Michael Walzer, *Arguing about War* (New Haven, CT, Yale University Press, 2004), 3–22.

19 Fernando Teson, *Humanitarian Intervention: An Inquiry into Law and Morality* (2nd edn, Dobbs Ferry, NY, Transnational Publishers, 1997).

20 Simon Chesterman, *Just War or Just Peace? Humanitarian Intervention and International Law* (Oxford, Oxford University Press, 2002), 20–22.

ignore new political ideas in other countries if we want to innovate. We cannot turn our back on conflicts and violations of human rights within other countries if we want still to be secure. . . . We need new rules for international cooperation and new rules of organising our international institutions.[21]

The economic foundations of globalisation were clearly spelt out. They would not sound out of place in a neo-conservative conference or in the offices of the World Bank: 'We all understand the need to ensure flexible labour markets, to remove regulatory burdens and to untie the hands of business if we are going to succeed.' Based on these premises, Blair went on to formulate a postmodern doctrine of just war, posing five questions or criteria for deciding when and how to intervene militarily to rescue a population: Are we sure of our case? Have we exhausted all diplomatic options? Are there military operations we can sensibly and prudently undertake? Are we prepared for the long term? Do we have national interests involved?

The most interesting omission in this restatement of just war doctrine is international law; the most striking innovation, the insertion of national interest. Simon Chesterman's exhaustive and careful examination of the history of international law has shown beyond reasonable doubt that there is 'no "right" of humanitarian intervention either in the UN Charter or in customary international law'.[22] Blair's doctrine needed to neglect, if not dismiss, international law pending its radical rewriting. International law's strictures would come back and torment him when the legality of the Iraq war became a political issue. The addition of national interest is more revealing. Wars based on national interest, the traditional way of war, are limited. They are judged according to utilitarian criteria and follow the cold calculation of costs and benefits. A war of values, on the other hand, follows a strict moral calculus, which imposes considerations of consistency and coherence. As David Rieff puts it, wars of values have no limits and each 'conflict, rather like a judicial decision that establishes a legal precedent, is viewed by its proponents as a basis for future conflicts'.[23] If Kosovo introduced the logic of a war for human rights, greater humanitarian crises in Rwanda, Sudan or Chechnya should equally create duties to invade and rescue. And yet, this did not happen. Humanitarian wars are crusading ventures; their only limits are prudential.

---

21 *Doctrine of the International Community*, remarks by Tony Blair to the Economic Club of Chicago, 22 April 1999.
22 Chesterman, op. cit., 226.
23 David Rieff, 'Kosovo: The End of an Era', in Fabrice Weissman, ed., *In the Shadow of 'Just Wars'* (London, Hurst & Co, 2004), 293.

The introduction of the national interest criterion, a palpable contradiction if not refutation of moral principles, reveals the postmodern just war logic. It allows cases to be distinguished from pressing precedents while insisting that the moral motives for (in)action are fully adhered to. Human rights and humanitarianism offer the gloss of moral universalism without the discipline of moral consistency. This combination of moral stringency and utilitarian laxity makes the millenarian ambitions of humanitarianism the perfect cover for empire and, national interest, the perfect imperial opt-out clause. As an ardent supporter of humanitarian imperialism put it, 'empires that are successful learn to ration their service to moral principle to the few strategic zones where the defence of principle is simultaneously the defence of a vital interest, and where the risks do not outweigh the benefits'.[24]

National interest was the only Blair criterion the Iraq war could possibly meet. Post-war events, however, revealed a serious miscalculation. America's international strategy, on the other hand, is much more open and unashamed about its combination of morality and interest. It places freedom, democracy and human dignity at its centre but subordinates them to the quest for security from real or imagined threats and for the opening of markets and economic privileges for American business. Thomas Friedman, the ideologue of globalisation, is quite explicit:

> The hidden hand of the market will never work without a hidden fist. McDonald's cannot flourish without McDonnell Douglas, the designer of The US air force F-15. And the hidden fist that keeps the world safe for Silicon Valley's technologies to flourish is called the US Army, Air Force, Navy and Marine Corps.[25]

The recent wars were called 'Operation Enduring Freedom' and 'Operation Iraqi Freedom'. The double pillars of the international community of globalisation, neo-liberal economic policies and humanitarianism, were both present. War, violence and their permanent threat are an integral part of economic globalisation.

Let us conclude this short history. War and just war have been important strategies through which sovereignty has come to existence and has been put to work. War is a central element of the Western symbolic, of the way in which the West has conceived its existence, territory and importance. War brings

---

24 Michael Ignatieff, *Empire Lite* (London, Vintage, 2003), 111.
25 Thomas Friedman, *The Lexus and the Olive Tree* (New York, Farrar, Strauss & Giroux, 1999).

states to life, literally as most states have been the outcome of war or revolution, metaphorically by energising nations and metaphysically by raising them to the universal. Moreover, war has always acted as the litmus test for man and nation. For Hegel, the greatest philosopher of history, war and the fear of death have great metaphysical value:

> In order not to let [people] become rooted and set in this isolation, thereby breaking up the whole and letting the community spirit evaporate ... government has from time to time to shake them to their core by war. By this means the government upsets their established order, and violates their right to independence, while the individuals who, absorbed in their way of life, break loose from the whole and strive after the inviolable independence and security of the person, are made to feel by government in the task laid on them their lord and master, death.[26]

By confronting the combatants with the negativity that encircles life, war helps them rise from their daily mundane experiences towards the universal, a necessary step towards the acquisition of full consciousness. Jacques Derrida comments that, according to Hegel,

> war would prevent people from rotting; war preserves 'the ethical health of peoples', as the wind agitating the seas purifies them, keeps them from decomposing, from the corruption, from the putrefaction with which a 'continual calm' and a 'perpetual peace' would infect health.[27]

At a more mundane, although more pervasive level, the importance of war has been a constant motif of modernity, one of its responses to its nihilism, individualism and anomie. 'War is to men as maternity to women' Mussolini, an 'expert' on the travails of masculinity is supposed to have said while, for Yitzhak Shamir, 'war is inescapable because without this, the life of the individual has no purpose'.[28] Indeed over the last twenty years many commentators in the West mourned the passing of war and attributed many of our social ills from hooliganism and drug abuse to the crisis of the family and masculinity to the rotting effect of semi-perpetual peace.[29]

---

26 Georg Hegel, *The Phenomenology of Spirit* (A.V. Miller, trans.) (Oxford: Oxford University Press, 1977), 272–3.
27 Jacques Derrida, *Glas* (Lincoln, NB, University of Nebraska Press, 1986), 101 and 131–49.
28 Quoted in Corey Robin, 'Protocols of Machismo', *London Review of Books*, 19 May 2005, 12.
29 See among others, Jeremy Paxman, *The English* (London, Penguin, 1999).

The health of the nation, paralleling the life of the individual, has been largely attributed to the benefits of war. War memorials, national holidays and festivals celebrate the great victories or disasters of the past turning them into the foundation stone of the nation. These celebrations become widespread and even absurd in their grandiosity at times of moral and political uncertainty. The first few years of the twenty-first century were marked in the United Kingdom by continuous celebrations of the victory in the Second World War. They were not unrelated to the wide popular dissatisfaction with the Iraq war. The World War did not allow moral doubt or prevarication. It was a 'good' war necessitated by an extreme emergency posed by evil enemies and threatening the very survival of the nation. The persistent references to that earlier victorious and righteous war reminded the nation of the glory and morality of war and tried to transfer some of its symbolic capital to the unpopular current conflict.

The problem was that proper war, a war that pits sovereigns against each other and in so doing underpins the structure of sovereignty, nation and self has been retreating from the Western stage for some fifty years. It was first suspended in a cold war and now in the war against terrorism, wars that do not follow the traditional ways of war. Globalisation has drained the nation-state, we are told, networks have replaced the sovereign, the rule of law and international institutions prioritise elements of sovereign action exempt from violence and force. '[I]t is no longer the power of one state, or a plurality of states, but rather law that determines what constitutes peace. Ultimately, belligerent global politics would be replaced by global law', claims Ulrich Beck.[30] Everything from economics to law, politics and even love has turned into a communication system, which reproduces itself autopoetically with scant regard for other systems and their environment. Power has allegedly dissolved in legal rules, sublimated in administrative procedures. The state has accepted voluntarily a degree of self-control, and has adopted the barely sovereign role of regulative, juridical and social administrator.

But war has now returned triumphantly to our symbolic space in the Gulf, in Kosovo, in Afghanistan, in Iraq and Lebanon. It has returned, in a mixture of warlike fantasies, of police action and law. The lack of epic achievements by heroic warriors is filled with technological marvels, which have turned the war into spectacle. We all felt a little cheated when the Afghan and Iraq wars finished quickly. The West had been prepared by the media and the military for a long and hard campaign, the outcome of which was conveniently predetermined but whose conduct would bring together the symbolic of war and victory with the imaginary of spectacle. It was presented as a celebration

---

30   Ulrich Beck, *Cosmopolitan Vision* (Cambridge, Polity, 2006), 141.

of the bravery of fighting and the brilliance of technology – in other words, of sovereign action, something the West had been lacking for a long time. It is not surprising, therefore, that war on behalf of human rights appears to have relegitimised a certain image of sovereignty. But is the return of war a sign of the sovereignty of old, or has the Aristotelian good and Kantian cosmopolitanism replaced the principle of sovereignty? We will discuss the nature of the sovereign in some detail in Chapter 11. One should insist, however, that still today and forever, the decision to go to war is in form and force a sovereign decision. When a state speaks on behalf of the rights of man and uses them to start war, this is still a sovereign decision and leads to an increase in its sovereignty.

Whether recent events mark a return to old imperialism or the appearance of a new hybrid form, the world moral order joins the premodern attack on the uncivilised infidel with modern police action in the powerful image of the postmodern just wars. Humanitarian wars return us to sovereignty and to the ancient link between the sacred and the legal. The *jus ad bellum*, the power to declare war and carry it out as policing, is the reassertion of sovereign brilliance against the complacency of accountants and lawyers. It may be that this is a new type of imperial sovereignty or just the ghost of old sovereignty, which needs the spectacle of war to convince us that it has not passed away in networks of economic, cultural and political governance. The *jus in bello* has been replaced by the efficiency and sophistication of technology. Finally, the *justa causa*, humanity and its rights, becomes the new sacred order in a disenchanted world. It raises the national interest to the status of moral duty. As Michael Ignatieff, a promoter of these wars puts it, 'this is why modern imperial ethics can only be hypocritical'.[31]

The normative force of violence

The proponents of humanitarianism claim that our recent wars obeyed the demands of the law and followed the dictates of morality. Cosmopolitans, on the other hand, place their hopes for a just and peaceful world order on the belief that international law can tame violence and regulate war before its eventual abolition. Kant's dream of perpetual peace will be the end state in a long process of legalisation of international relations and pacification of conflict. In this sense, law and violence are involved in a zero-sum game. Civilisation leads to the progressive subjection of violence to the law, as legal rules replace physical conflict with technical argument. This is the premise of

---

31 Michael Ignatieff, *Empire Lite* (London, Vintage, 2003), 111.

all positivism: the state enjoys moral and political legitimacy and has the monopoly of violence. The state's use of violence is therefore legitimate while all other violence is unlawful or criminal. More generally, reason, law, morality are the antitheses of violence; they either tame it or use it as means for their ends. Hegel's moral state (*sittlichkeit*) or positivism's benign sovereign power bring together reason and violence in a dialectical synthesis.

But this argument is historically wrong and morally dubious. Normativity relates to violence as its cause and effect; violence carries out or generates normative commands. The link between law, morality or normativity and violence is complex and permanent. Its exploration belongs to the phenomenology of power. Violence founds and institutes law. War is the father of states and violence the midwife of law. War is fought in excess of law and creates a new distribution of sovereigns. But law, too, is intimately connected with force. Most modern constitutions and legal systems were introduced in violation of the protocols of constitutional legality at the time of their adoption, as a result of war, revolution, occupation or liberation. Revolutionary violence suspends laws and constitutions and justifies itself by claiming to be founding a new state, a better constitution and a more just law to replace the corrupt or immoral system it rebelled against. Violence will be condemned as illegal, brutal and evil at the point of its occurrence. But when it succeeds, revolutionary violence will be retrospectively legitimised as the necessary means to the end of social and legal transformation. Furthermore, there is no law if it cannot be potentially enforced, if there is no police, army and prisons to punish and deter possible violations. In this sense, force and enforcement are part of the very essence of legality. Modern law coming out of the endless feuds of princes and local chiefs claimed a monopoly of violence in the territory of its jurisdiction and used it to protect the ends and functions it declared legal, but also to protect the empire of the law itself. The violence following the law routinely and forming its background has been called by Walter Benjamin 'law-preserving'.[32] It guarantees law's permanence and enforceability. Its regular exercises both display the awesome power in the hands of the state and conceal or gloss it over in the language of its superior legitimate, legal ends. Violence acts in material and symbolic ways: it coerces its targets, stifles challenges and, at the same time, bestows legitimacy upon itself.

The French Revolution was retrospectively legitimised by its *Déclaration des droits de l'homme*, the American by the Declaration of Independence and the Bill of Rights. These foundational documents carry in themselves the violence of their birth. Their 'founding' violence is re-enacted in the great

32 Benjamin, *Critique of Violence.*

pageants that celebrate nation and state-building and is repressed and forgotten in acts of interpretation of the Constitution and enforcement of the new law. The American Bill of Rights is an obvious example. The violence of the militias, so important in the War of Independence, is perpetuated in the constitutionally protected right to bear arms, which, some two centuries after the Revolution, still keeps the United States in a state of war. Similarly, capital punishment reproduces the founding violence of war in every execution, which accompanies the legal operation as the dark and empowering side of legal normality. These re-enactments of the traumatic genesis of the new law are interpreted, however, as demands of legality; the original violence is thus both continuously revealed, repeated and repelled, consigned to oblivion. The creation of a dominant approach to constitutional interpretation is one of the most important strategies in this politics of forgetting. Once victorious, revolutions or conquests produce 'interpretative models to read in return, to give sense, necessity and above all legitimacy to the violence that has produced, among others, the interpretative model in question, that is, the discourse of its self-legitimation'.[33] But the repressed always returns. The founding and preserving types of violence cannot be separated. Law-founding violence is encrypted within the legal system and regularly emerges whenever the empire of law is challenged, while law-preserving violence carries out its daily tasks in the name of its violent origin. Law is not just the opposite of violence or its antidote. Law and violence are intertwined and contaminate each other, as acts of legal enforcement repeat the original law-making violence that established the law. As a result, the efforts to impose a universal morality on politics and to present law as a neutral protector of peace consolidates and freezes the established system of domination and balance of powers and makes resistance immoral, criminal, illegitimate.

The same applies to international law. War is a means for creating new law through the use of force, the counterpart to revolution. The key moments of international law and institutions were a result or reaction to war. Its foundational text, Grotius's *De Jure Belli ac Pacis* (Of War and Peace), is an extensive treatise on war and an attempt to regulate its conduct. The function of war, writes a famous Italian international lawyer, in 1914, is 'to bring positive law in conformity with fact'.[34] The League of Nations and the United Nations and their agencies were responses to the two World Wars. Colonialism and imperialism have had a major influence in its development.[35] Governments

---

33 Jacques Derrida, 'Force of Law: "The Mystical Foundations" of Authority', 11 *Cardozo Law Review* 919–1046 (1990), 993.
34 Quoted by von Elbe, op. cit., 686.
35 Anghie, op. cit.

and cosmopolitans have painted a picture in which international institutions are 'the opposite of the social breakdown of war'.[36] But history shows that every new type of international order was 'created by war'.[37] As Anne Orford puts it, in her extraordinary *Reading Humanitarian Intervention*,

> at the heart of the establishment of international law was, and is, the legitimacy of the violence exercised as sacrifice or punishment against those constituted as law's savage, barbaric, others. In this sense, the international community shares something with those national or 'tribal' communities against which it constitutes itself – the wounding and killing of its others as an organic and necessary part of its foundation.[38]

What about the wars of the new world order?

Antonio Cassesse, a judge of the War Crimes Tribunal for Yugoslavia and a supporter of the Kosovo war, entitled an essay on that war *Ex Injuria Jus Oritur* (the law is born out of crime).[39] Kosovo, Afghanistan and Iraq were clear reminders of the continuing, indeed increasing, implication of war and violence with law, although this was not the sense in which Cassesse used the Latin maxim. Cassesse, Habermas and Sands believe that the international rule of law can and should subject war to legal regulation. Our recent wars, however, indicate the opposite dynamic. Their most important normative effect was the wholesale undermining and destruction of existing law. This is the case in the conquered countries, the constitutions of which have been radically reformed in time-honoured fashion, according to the dictates of the conquerors as the only way of incorporating these prodigal sons back into the international community. The same applies to international law and the United Nations, its most important institution, both of which are in the process of being drastically reorganised. In the summer of 2005, an extraordinary UN summit solemnly adopted the report of the Secretary General's high-level panel entitled 'a more secure world: our shared responsibility' and declared the 'responsibility to protect civilians' during conflict, calling it one of the most urgent global priorities.[40] This initiative was part of the reform of international law in the

---

36 David Kennedy, 'The Move to Institutions', 8 *Cardozo Law Review* 841 (1987), 846.

37 Michael Howard, *The Invention of Peace* (New Haven, CT, Yale University Press, 2001), 47.

38 Anne Orford, *Reading Humanitarian Intervention* (Cambridge, Cambridge University Press, 2003), 196–7.

39 Antonio Cassesse, '*Ex Injuria Jus Oritur*', 10 *European Journal of International Law* 23 (1999).

40 UN Doc. A/59/2005, 21 March 2005.

wake of the difficulties the United States and Britain faced during Kosovo and Iraq. In the absence of a fully legalised right of humanitarian intervention, the declaration loosened the protective shield of sovereignty and state frontiers, following the advice of liberal cosmopolitans and pragmatic globalisers. Yet, as I write these lines in August 2006, the Israeli bombardment of Lebanon continues with hundreds of dead Arab civilians. Kofi Annan, the UN General Secretary, called for a ceasefire and an end to the Israeli 'excessive use of force', ten days after the bombing of Lebanon started but the US and Britain fully backed the aggression and blocked attempts to advise caution on the Israelis. Terje Roed-Larsen, the UN envoy in the Middle East, agreed with Israel that conditions were not ripe for a ceasefire. The new 'responsibility to protect' was promptly shown for what it is: an easily discarded method for adding a moral veneer to the strategic priorities of the hegemonic power and its satellites. Violence begets law, illegality legality; the punishment for the crime is to be turned into the new law.

A number of commentators have argued that Kosovo was fought in order to destroy and reorganise the post-war international legal order, marginalise and reconfigure the United Nations.[41] According to Andrew Bachevich, a conservative former soldier, 'assertions that the United States and its allies acted in response to massive Serb repression of Kosovar Albanians simply cannot survive close scrutiny. [The Kosovo war] was neither planned nor conducted to alleviate the plight of the Kosovars'.[42] As in all complex political events, there can be no single cause for that or any war. President Clinton stated before the start of the bombing that 'if we're going to have a strong economic relationship that includes our ability to sell around the world, Europe has got to be a key . . . That's what this Kosovo thing is all about'.[43] Richard Holbrooke, the American diplomat and negotiator, elaborated that the American action in the Balkans marked 'a watershed in the use on American power not just in the region but in the world . . . It showed the tired European and the dispirited UN . . . what America can accomplish when it uses ruthless means . . . to achieve peace'.[44] Keeping to the legal parameters, it is arguable that a main effect of the action was the transformation of the international legal order. The limited multilateralism of the late twentieth century is being replaced by

---

41 Peter Gowan, 'Making Sense of NATO's war on Yugoslavia' in L. Panitch and C. Leys, eds, *Socialist Register 2000: Necessary and Unnecessary Utopias* (London, Merlin Press, 1999), 272–7.

42 Andrew Bachevich, *American Empire* (Cambridge, MA, Harvard University Press, 2002), 104.

43 Quoted ibid. 105.

44 Quoted in Michael Ignatieff, *Virtual War* (London, Vintage, 2001), 17

the unipolar world of global capitalism led by the US, which is rewriting the rule-book to its own recipe. It is curious, commented a 'baffled' Michael Ignatieff, a vocal supporter of humanitarian wars, 'how little place' American strategy 'accords the United Nations'[45] and gives the answer himself: 'America's entire war on terror is an exercise in imperialism.'[46] The opposite would have been curious. As Richard Perle, a key adviser to the Bush administration, boasted during the Iraq war, the death of the United Nations dates from Kosovo.[47]

Speculation about the geopolitical motives of American administrations is not part of this book. But the legal objectives and certainly the legal outcome of the Kosovo and Iraq wars were to free the US from the legal framework of the United Nations and international law, to make right out of wrong. Antonio Cassesse hopes that the Kosovo exception would soon become (customary) law. The argument was that very few states argued that NATO's war violated the UN Charter.[48] However, the elusive element necessary for the creation of a new international customary norm (long and consistent usage of the norm under question accompanied by a 'psychological element', that is belief that in acting according to the norm states follow the law) was missing. Some 133 states denounced the right of humanitarian intervention and two independent commissions admitted lack of consensus about the creation of a wide-ranging precedent. Michael Glennon, someone who shares Cassesse's political viewpoint, despaired: 'Although the UN's rules purport to represent a single global view – indeed universal law – on when and whether force can be justified [the Kosovo war showed that] the UN's members (not to mention their populations) are clearly not in agreement.'[49]

Giorgio Agamben, following Carl Schmitt, has discussed extensively the power to impose a state of exception in times of emergency.[50] According to liberal jurisprudence, the rule of law and its international version offer a consistent hierarchy of norms, which should be able to answer all legal questions. But the decision to impose the state of exception is not legal; it cannot be reached according to the protocols of legal judgment and does not use the resources of the legal system. When a state or regime is threatened in

45 Ibid. 31.
46 Ignatieff, *Empire Lite,* op. cit., 79.
47 Richard Perle, 'Thank God for the Death of UN', *The Guardian*, 21 March 2003.
48 Antonio Cassesse, 'A Follow-Up. Forcible Humanitarian Countermeasures and *Opinio Necessitatis*', 10 *European Journal of International Law* 791 (1999).
49 Michael Glennon, 'Why the Security Council Failed', 82/3 *Foreign Affairs* (May/June 2003), 16.
50 Agamben, *Homo Sacer.*

its very existence, someone or some institution has the power to impose a state of emergency and suspend normal legal operations for its duration. In normal times, a legal judgment applies law to the facts. The exception indicates that standard legality has failed. The ultimate decision to suspend the law in order to save it belongs to law's field of operation; at the same time, it is outside the legal system. Both outside and inside the law, the state of exception guarantees normal legality. 'The exception is that which cannot be subsumed; it defies general codification, but it simultaneously reveals a specifically juristic element – the decision in absolute purity'.[51] This is why liberal theory approaches the exception as an anomaly that must be hidden in order to maintain the fiction of law's unity and purity. As William Rasch puts it, 'the exception presents itself as the ineluctable necessity of choice precisely at the moment when none of the normal criteria is available to guide selection'.[52] The name of the person or institution who has the power to impose the exception is the sovereign. According to Carl Schmitt, 'it is precisely the exception that makes relevant the matter of sovereignty'.[53] The sovereign, the indivisible and omnipotent font of the legal order, introduces the exception to save the law from lethal threats. Sovereignty is the cause and effect of both normal law and its suspension; the sovereign, he who decides exceptionally and performatively about the exception, he who has or takes the power to suspend the law. The sovereign creates *ex nihilo* as God's representative, disciple and heir. Sovereignty as a political and legal concept is the perfect secular displacement of the theological heritage. This is why liberalism has always suspected the sovereign and is now campaigning for its abolition.

The Kosovo and Iraq wars were illegal under international law, but victory led to the smashing of old sovereignty and reaffirmation of the principle that war and violence found the law. The debate among international lawyers and Cassesse's claim that law is born out of injustice indicate that the decision to go to war was, when taken, an exception to the current state of international law and, for many, of domestic and constitutional law too. The Anglo-American decision amounted to a massive violation of international law and led inexorably to a suspension of many of its provisions. This violation and suspension of the law acted in a performative manner. For Schmitt and Agamben, the power to impose the state of exception indicates who is the sovereign. In our recent wars, the aim of law's suspension was not the *salutus populi*. The claim that Iraq was attacked in (pre-emptive) self-defence referred back

---

51 Carl Schmitt, *Political Theology: Four Chapters on the Concept of Sovereignty* (Cambridge, MA, MIT Press, 1985), 13.
52 William Rasch, *Sovereignty and its Discontents* (London, Birkbeck Law Press, 2005), 27.
53 Schmitt, op. cit., 12.

and acknowledged that tradition, but it was palpably untrue. The wars pursued hegemonic interests and allowed the United States to assert the position of the sovereign in the new world order. The action was a modification of Schmitt's law: by deciding on the exception, the United States places itself in the position of the sovereign. There is more. The exception does not just create the rule; it also constitutes the imaginary global space over which it will rule and creates the terrain of its application. In this act, empire's sovereign, its law and its putative space are created. In a historical reversal, an emperor is emerging but the empire is still under construction.

War as/and policing

The apparent divergence between the declared moral purpose and the atrocious results on the ground indicates the character of new humanitarianism as a combination of morality and might, of values and effectiveness. Inequality of means promotes the idea of inequality of status and ends. The powerful considers his superiority as an indication of moral righteousness, of a just cause that allows him to turn the enemy into a common criminal. The impotent enemy becomes an internal rebel, the war against him takes the character of police action.

Recent wars have been presented as policing operations against criminals and bandits. This became undeniably clear when huge pressure was put on the Belgrade regime to surrender Milosevic to the Hague tribunal, in violation of the Serbian Constitution, in return for large sums in aid, a practice reminiscent of the rewards and bounties offered for the arrest 'dead or alive' of great criminals. Wars have been characterised by a 'posse' mentality, the declared aim of which was to arrest some evil person who violates the universal moral codes for selfish, cruel or mad ends. Noriega in Panama, Mohammed Aideed in Somalia, Sadam Hussein in Iraq, Milosevic in Yugoslavia, Osama Bin Laden are the master criminals, personifications of evil, a tactic that can often backfire. A painful lesson from recent terrorist atrocities is that enemies of the new moral order, themselves the keepers of another truth and the enforcers of a different morality, have gladly adopted the role of great criminals. When politics becomes policing and policies moral action, some political opponents willingly take on the rogue roles assigned to them and bring to atrocious completion the caricatures of their motives and evil.

The terrorist attacks on American targets have all the characteristics of an evil reversal of the new order. The terrorists used hijacked passenger airliners as a combination of fighter aircraft and missile, as manned and guided missiles. By doing this, they adopted and reversed the globalising principle that the most symbolic strike and most effective punishment of enemies/infidels is delivered from the air. The immediate reaction to the atrocities illustrated the conceptual difficulties created by the emergence of the new order while the ideas, arrangements and principles of the old are still alive. When President Bush announced the war on terror and those who harbour terrorists, a clamour of voices from the least hawkish commentators responded 'yes, but who is the enemy?'. The question keeps coming back: how can we speak of war if we do not have an enemy state, government or president against whom we can declare war? The imagery of sovereign states and of recognisable enemies still dominates the Western imaginary. At the same time, the American, and even more, the British governments consider their response as both war and policing. As Wesley Clark, a former allied commander in Europe put it, we should use 'decisive force' and involve 'information, law enforcement and military force'.[54] The police/war continuum of the war on terror creates major conceptual difficulties in the absence of an enemy state.

The role of law enforcement in the war against terror is further evidence of the normative impasse of the emerging world order. Liberal commentators argued that the 'most effective response may not be the instant vengeance of a cruise missile but concerted international police work that leads to arrest, extradition, trials and imprisonment of perpetrators'.[55] Geoffrey Robertson went furthest in this respect arguing that the terrorist attacks should be described as 'crimes against humanity' and treated according to the remedies and sanctions available in international law. Others less aware of the fine distinctions of international law called the attacks 'war crimes' arguing that they were acts of war and crimes at the same time, indicating again the conceptual difficulties created by this new type of unconventional hostilities and the acceptable response to them. To be sure, current international law still wedded to the remnants of state sovereignty does not recognise non-state-sponsored terrorism as a crime against humanity. Robertson has argued consistently that terrorism of all kinds should be subjected to the laws of war irrespective of its links with a state or states. Its perpetrators should be delivered to the International Criminal Court, while international law provisions and restraints should be applied to the military action against the culprits. But the main character of the new moral order is precisely that it does not make clear distinctions between moral and legal arguments or between enemies and criminals. Policing operations follow a different logic from that of wars, which are supposed to comply with the niceties of international law. As a more realistic professor of international law put it 'terrorists benefit from no privilege as soldiers under the laws of war ... They are therefore, legally speaking, "unprivileged combatants" – to be

---

54   Wesley Clarke, 'Decisive Force', *The Guardian*, 15 September 2001.
55   Michael Ignatieff, *Financial Times*, 13 September 2001.

fought on military terms with respect to non-combatants in their midst but if captured treated as criminals'.[56] War and police operations have been merged in the same way that morality and force have become largely interdependent.

The arguments from international law have some limited value. But from a wider perspective, they miss the point: in a just war against criminals, international law can be seen as part of the process of moralisation of politics with all the problems presented above. Moral argument and force support each other harmoniously so that the old distinction between just ends and just means of violence, meticulously analysed by Walter Benjamin in his *Critique of Violence*, is no longer relevant. Moral ends justify the overwhelming means and overwhelming force generates morality. While in modernity, morality and might were related externally as ends and means and were often in conflict, they have now become fully integrated into a morality/force amalgam. The wide acceptance of the morality of action increases its effectiveness and the success of an action augments its moral force and persuasiveness. To that extent, the success of an operation cannot be judged morally in isolation from its military conduct and, similarly, the morality of an action cannot be separated from its military outcome. Morality exists if it is effective and military action is moral if it succeeds. On those grounds, Kosovo was the first postmodern just war; Iraq the extension of cosmopolitanism towards fully fledged empire.

'Shock and awe' or the imaginary empire

Moral righteousness is supported by overwhelming force. A structural asymmetry, a huge economic, military and technological inequality characterised the relations between the United States and the rest of the world. Recent American administrations have pursued absolute superiority in most areas. They have achieved, in particular, the military and technological superiority necessary to overcome any conceivable combination of enemies. National Security Adviser Samuel Berger claimed in 1999 that 'military expenditures are larger than those of all other countries combined'.[57] While this was exaggerated boasting, it is not far from the truth. A permanent garrison is maintained in Europe despite the end of the cold war, while some 100,000 troops are stationed in the Asian Pacific region, mainly in Korea and Japan. Smaller mobile units and military bases are scattered all over the world with one

---

56 Kenneth Anderson, 'Language, Law and Terror', *Times Literary Supplement*, 21 September 2001.

57 Samuel Berger, 'American Power: Hegemony, Isolationism or Engagement'. Lecture to the Council on Foreign Relations, New York, 21 October 1999. A more accurate estimate compares US fire-power favourably with the aggregate power of the next twenty states.

commentator estimating that US troops are stationed in 150 foreign countries.[58] According to Eliot Cohen, President Clinton's Secretary of Defence,
a major reason for such extensive deployment of forces is 'to shape people's
opinions about us in ways that are favorable to us. When people see us, they
see our power, they see our professionalism, they see our patriotism, and
they say that's a country that we want to be with'.[59]

Overwhelming force and huge technological superiority characterised the
Kosovo, Afghanistan and Iraq campaigns. Michael Ignatieff concluded that
the Kosovo war was fought

> by no more than 1,500 NATO airmen . . . in VTC conference rooms, using
> targets flashed up on a screen, and all that a commander like Clark ever
> saw of the rush of battle was the gun camera footage e-mailed every night
> on secure internet systems to his headquarters in Belgium.[60]

This differentiation has a number of important normative effects. The most
striking is the strict hierarchisation of the value of life, the putative foundation
of all lists of human rights. In Kosovo, the bombers flew at extremely high
altitudes, which put them beyond the reach of anti-aircraft fire and used smart
bombs and stealth technology. The tactic was successful and NATO forces
concluded their campaign without a single casualty. But there were serious
side-effects. Total air domination did not stop Serb atrocities. Ethnic cleansing
intensified and the worst massacres of Albanians occurred after the start of
the bombing campaign. If the declared war aim was to 'avert a humanitarian
catastrophe', it failed badly. Second, the high flight altitudes of the bombers
increased significantly civilian 'collateral damage'. Civilians were killed in
trains and buses, in TV stations and hospitals, in the Chinese Embassy and
other residential areas. The most grotesque incident was the killing of some
seventy-five Albanian refugees whose ragtag convoy was hit repeatedly
because, according to NATO, tractors and trailers cannot be easily distinguished
from tanks and armoured personnel carriers at an altitude of 15,000 feet.
Civilian deaths can never be justified. When it is clearly foreseeable that
hostilities will unavoidably cause civilian deaths, despite the smartness of the
bombs and the 'humane' nature of warfare, and are still pursued, the killings
become murder; if they are numerous they amount to war crimes. But as

58 Chalmers Johnson, *The Sorrows of Empire: Militarism, Secrecy and the End of the Republic*
    (New York, Metropolitan Books, 2004), 154.
59 Quoted in Bachevich, op. cit. 129.
60 *Virtual War*, 111.

Jean-Hervé Bradol has aptly said, 'the production of order at the international level – just as at national and local levels – demands its quota of sacrificial victims . . . the construction of a "better world" inevitably comes at a price – the lives of others'.[61]

The largely undefended bombardments of Yugoslavia, Afghanistan and Iraq were ultimate signs of the military superiority. Bombardment has become 'the instrument of choice of America's foreign policy' enthused an American general.[62] If the wars between Spain and England represented two opposing world views, an old land-based one and a new global principle based on control of the seas and communications, the principle of the new order is planetary. As the US Space Command enthused in 2001, it is the 'synergy of space superiority, which missile defence will bring, with land, air and sea superiority' that will protect Western interests from the increasing gap between haves and have-nots. The extensive and often exclusive use of the air weapon is also symbolic of a new type of boundless power not constrained by geographical boundaries and state frontiers. Territory and place, the dominant characteristics of modern statehood, wedded to geographical landmarks, historical divisions and political demarcations, are being replaced by a boundless global space, which, unlike the mountains, seas, rivers and frontiers of twentieth-century international relations, rather than hindering operations, they have become an infinite resource of the new order.

It is no coincidence that the first wars of the new order were air campaigns, as was the attack on Manhattan and the Pentagon, which, according to President Bush, was the 'first war' of the twenty-first century. While modern sovereignty was bound to place, the new order is both modelled on the openness of space and uses the air as its most appropriate conduit. It is organised horizontally alongside planes of activity, which bear no relation to the constraints earth places on human activity. Space with its all-seeing, all-listening satellites, its all-conquering rockets, its vastness syncopated by the non-communicating billions of stars, creates a mirror for the earth of the new millennium. Technology and communications provide the means of global presence and 'humanity's law', the foundational values of its action. Space and time have become the terrain of operation of the new moral order. Limits placed hitherto by state sovereignty simply call for the local adjustment of action; public opinion reservations, for an intensification of the moral message that qualifies the action. The only limits to military campaigns are those of logistics

---

61 Jean-Hervé Bradol, 'The Sacrificial International Order and Humanitarian Action' in Weissman, op. cit., 4–5.

62 Quoted in Bachevich, 155.

and utilitarian calculations: Rwanda did not have much strategic, political or economic interest for the new order, as was the case with Afghanistan after the Soviet defeat. But when events showed that 'remote' places like Afghanistan are possible sources of disturbance, American policy included them in its list of candidates for correction. Nation-building in Bosnia, Kosovo and Afghanistan, Ignatieff concludes, 'is imperial because its essential purpose is to create order in border zones essential to the security of great powers – and because armed force, an instrument only great powers can use with impunity, is critical to the task'.[63] No area of the globe can be abandoned, since the new integrated order can be disturbed by activities in its most remote reaches and no time limit exists in the 'long war' on terror.

From Homer to this century, war introduced an element of uncertainty: the possibility that the mighty might lose or suffer casualties. But in Kosovo and Afghanistan, the role of the military was not to fight but to deliver ordnance. As an American pilot put it, the task was 'to club 'em like baby seals . . . and then come home'.[64] In this sense, these were not wars but a type of hunting: one side was totally protected while the other had no chance of effectively defending itself or counter-attacking. A war without casualties for your side, an electronic game type of war or Reagan's unbeatable 'star wars' may be the dream of every military establishment. But a war in which a soldier's life is more valuable than that of many civilians cannot be moral or humanitarian. In valuing an allied life at hundreds of Serbian, Afghan or Iraqi lives, the declaration that all are equal in dignity and enjoy an equal right to life was comprehensively discredited.

The extensive use of technology aimed at reducing friendly casualties has been hailed as a sign of the humanisation of warfare. Technology is presented as the bloodless substitute for the absence of heroism that characterised the Western warrior.[65] This technological utopianism is based on

an illusion that a ludic substitute for war has already been discovered, and that technology has ushered in a new Enlightenment in which a set of rational and logical strategies designed to disarm the enemy . . . can be implemented with weapons that greatly minimize, if not totally eliminate, human killing.[66]

63 Ignatieff, *Empire Lite*, 109.
64 Quoted in Bachevich, 236.
65 Christopher Coker, *Humane Warfare* (London, Routledge, 2001).
66 Ibid. 231.

But certain crucial distinctions should be made. The everyday technology of the Internet and the advanced technology of 'smart bombs', 'humane' warfare, stealth aircraft and satellite surveillance should not disguise the fact that war is the technology of the sovereign and its technologisation is part of the wider turning of the world into technology. According to Jean-Luc Nancy

> there is no 'question of technology' in general, that is, a question put to technology or its subject and involving criteria that do not belong to it. War-with-missiles is neither better or worse that war-with-catapults; it is still a question of war.[67]

Indeed, the emphasis placed on the 'marvels' of military technology displaces the key questions of war's ends and of war-as-manifestation of sovereign power and replaces them with a discussion of war's means. In doing so, we abandon the most crucial consideration in every war and implicitly accept its legitimacy and justice.

Our zero-death imperial wars have brought to an end the warrior's heroic sacrifice at the altar of great symbolic values. Democracy and human rights or oil and strategic influence cannot replace the great belief systems of religion, nation or ideology. The loss is crippling. We unleash death of others but have banned death for our own, defied its sovereignty over the battlefield, turned war into a game that produces no body bags. Death in action has become both meaningless and terrifying, as it cannot be redeemed by the blandishments of sacrificial logic. War has become a spectacle, a series of images that do not threaten the Western public. But the outward defiance of death has made our lives death-bound. We die many 'deaths' a day, small deaths created from our innumerable fears of death, persecuted by an infinite number of risks, by criminals terrorists, ecological disasters, mutant genes and viruses.

The sense that our military victories in the name of human rights are bloodless, with no adverse repercussions, is reproduced through the partial nature of the accountability mechanisms after the war. War crimes trials establish respect for authorised violence, while condemning and punishing outlawed forms.[68] The technologies of the powerful, such as aerial bombardment, are not outlawed by the laws of war and the victorious powers are never subjected to post-war trials. A case brought to the European Court of Human Rights, by the victims of the NATO bombing of a television station in Belgrade,

---

67 Jean-Luc Nancy, *Being Singular Plural* (Stanford, CA, Stanford University Press, 2000), 116.
68 Simon Chesterman, 'Never Again . . . and Again: Law, Order, and the Gender of War Crimes in Bosnia and Beyond', 22 *Yale Journal of International Law* 299 (1997).

was rejected because the bombings did not take place within the territorial jurisdiction of the NATO states.[69] The Court distinguished this case from situations where a respondent state had invaded and occupied a territory, had effective control over its inhabitants and exercised all or some of the public powers normally exercised by the government.[70] It held that the Convention operates only 'in the legal space of the Contracting States. The FRY clearly does not fall within this legal space'.[71] The historian of bombing Sven Lindqvist has shown that bombing allowed European powers to exercise 'control without occupation' and to pacify 'restless natives', most notably in Iraq in 1920.[72] The Human Rights Court legalised this strategy by accepting that aerial bombardment does not need to meet the legal restrictions applying once a state has gained control over a territory. As space becomes the privileged terrain of operations of the new world order, aerial bombardment is its physical and symbolic expression. But this is also a lawless space, like the lands discovered by the conquistadores, the 'terra nullius' the common law declared Australia to be and the old and new concentration camps.

The obvious failures in the aftermath of our recent wars, the extensive ethnic cleansing and murder of Serbs, the large number of civilian casualties in Afghanistan and Iraq, the alleged increased appeal of terrorist activities among disaffected youth in the West can be seen as the not totally undesirable side-effects of the new order. Both President Bush and Tony Blair have repeatedly stated that we have never lived in greater danger. This is quite remarkable, coming after a period when a nuclear Armageddon was an ever-present possibility (or so we were told).[73] When morality replaces politics and military action policies, ubiquitous dangers, powerful fears and a sense of permanent crisis with recurring emergencies descends on the world.

These remarks lead us to a number of wider considerations about the use of violence. Recent wars have been carried out in the form of brief and violent raids. They aim at maximum short-term destruction and at creating a sense of shock and awe both among their targets and among the wider viewing public around the world. 'In Afghanistan, awe is maintained not by the size of the

69 *Bankovic and others* v. *Belgium and others.* Admissibility Decision, 12 December, 2001, available at http://hudoc.echr.coe.int/hudoc/ViewRoot.asp?Item=0&Action=Html&X= 806064118&Notice=0&Noticemode=&RelatedMode=0.

70 Ibid. para. 71.

71 Ibid. para. 80.

72 Sven Lindqvist, *A History of Bombing* (London, Granta, 2001), 100–2.

73 On the uses and abuse of fear, see Joanna Bourke, *Fear: A Cultural History* (London, Virago, 2005).

American presence but by the timeliness and destructiveness of American air power.'[74] Similarly, the images of massive bombardment, extensive destruction and 'clinical' strikes emerging from Iraq promoted an aesthetic of wonder and bewilderment around the world. 'Shock and awe' is the politician's and soldier's language for the sublime feeling. 'The sublime is not strictly speaking something which is proven or demonstrated', writes Boileau, 'but a marvel, which seizes one, strikes one, and makes one feel.'[75] For Kant, the sublime feeling is created as a reaction to the presentation of the non-representable. The imagination casts aside the barriers of the sensible world and, in this presentation of the infinite, it ascends to a feeling of being unbounded by the senses. In his discussion of the *Analytic of the Sublime,* Kant presents 'aesthetic ideas' as representations of the imagination, which 'strain out beyond the confines of experience . . . and no concept can be wholly adequate to them'.[76] They are 'sensible forms', the 'attributes of an object, the concept of which, as an idea of reason, cannot be adequately presented'.[77] The sublime role is now projected onto the use and image of violence.

'Shock and awe' aims at projecting an image of American power as incomparably large and vindictive, hugely disproportionate and boundless. Power *incomparably* large: the level of military superiority and strike power makes all challenge futile. A Pentagon document, leaked in 1992, argued that America should not allow military powers to emerge in any region of the world that could challenge in the future American dominance within that region.[78] Dick Cheney and Paul Wolfowitz were reputedly among the drafters of this document. This approach has dominated American diplomatic and military strategy, for which the greatest threat are not incidents of disobedience by hostile powers, but their acquisition of potent weapons or other strategic advantages that could deter future interventions in a particular region. The obsession with Iraq's non-existent weapons of mass destruction, with Iran's and North Korea's nuclear capacity and with challenges to Israel's predominance in the Middle East are part of this principle of incomparable superiority. The strategic thinking behind 'pre-emptive' wars is that no potential threat, however insignificant or unlikely, should be allowed to mature. The American

---

74 Michael Ignatieff, *Empire Lite* (London, Vintage, 2003) 89.
75 Jean-François Lyotard, 'The Sublime and the Avant-garde', in A. Benjamin, ed., *The Lyotard Reader* (Oxford: Blackwell, 1989), 202
76 Immanuel Kant, *Critique of Judgment* (J.C. Meredith trans.) (Oxford, Clarendon, 1985), 176.
77 Ibid. 177
78 David Armstrong, 'Dick Cheney's Song of America: Drafting a Plan for Global Dominance' *Harper's Magazine*, October 2002, 76–83.

plan, according to a close observer, calls 'for dominion over friends and enemies alike. It says not that the United States must be powerful, or most powerful, but that it must be absolutely powerful'.[79] The military option is therefore used when its outcome is safely predetermined. Any evidence of weakness, the slightest doubt about the nature of power and its invincibility would undermine its pretensions. Victory is what matters in the presentation of war.[80] Its symbolic principle: the gap between imperial centre and others cannot be closed, the hegemon cannot be defeated, resistance is futile.

Power incomparably *large*: it is power gone both mad and routine, unimaginable in its reality and fully domesticated through its continuous display in front rooms around the world. Violence and its spectacle have become the normative sources of the new order both at the symbolic and imaginary levels. The American strategies of bombing and torturing represent the metaphysics of infinity. They try to control the life of states and people by turning terror into a reality show. At the symbolic level, neither constitutional nor international law can restrain this violence because they operate in the space violence opens for them. It is the space between zero-death wars and thousands of sacrificial victims, where the inhuman and the non-human are brought together to create our postmodern humanity. The (fake) infinite, violence unbound constitutes the metaphysics of American power.[81] God-like power, creating *ex nihilo* and returning life to *nihil.*

The unleashing of disproportionate and destructive violence against weak states in wars with no great stakes indicates that the empire under construction complements its violent reality with a strategy of *imaginary* identification. The global coercion against recalcitrant enemies cannot be carried out always by the imperial power and its allies or their local representatives. The imperial centre must be therefore imagined as incomparably more powerful than potential rivals, as invincible without a shred of a doubt. The strategy of imaginary identification uses both visual images and works on people's imagination. The structural asymmetry which characterises the relationship between the centre and the rest of the world must be seen, omnipotence and invincibility must be displayed. This visual aspect is carried out by the regular displays of the deadly power of military technology, by the images of the 'shock and awe' attacks on Baghdad and elsewhere, by the photographs and videos of the atrocious torture techniques. Displays of military force indicate that

---

79　Ibid. 79.

80　Jean-Luc Nancy, 'War, Right, Sovereignty – Techne' in *Being Singular Plural* (Stanford, CA, Stanford University Press, 2000), 101–44.

81　See Alain Badiou, *Circonstances 2* (Paris, Lignes et Manifestes, 2004).

if it cannot be everywhere all the time, it can go anywhere, any time, and cause massive damage. The result has been a pattern of military interventions in which means are disconnected from any particular ends, a pattern of wars without objectives, exit strategies or geographical boundaries.[82]

The imperial omnipotence is staged, confirmed and repeated in an almost theatrical mode.[83] In the tale of the emperor's new clothes, the emperor had no clothes on, he was naked. But his subjects, except for one cunning boy, could not bring themselves to believe their eyes. In our case, the tale is reversed. By displaying lavishly ornamented jewellery, absurdly gilded robes and synthetic diamond-encrusted slippers, the aspiring emperor aims to persuade the world that he is not an impostor, that he is the real thing.

There is a second aspect to the imaginary empire. It is presented as a world community that we, its members, (ought to) desire, identify with and bring into existence. Humanitarianism has a key function here. Omnipotence has a moral purpose, the displays of destruction are carried out for our benefit. We want or should want to live the American way. When commentators condemn the Americans for not having a post-war strategy in Iraq, they are missing the point. The United States does not follow the traditional imperialist strategy of direct rule over colonies nor its postmodern version of 'nation-building', the preferred modus operandi of 'old Europe'. The 'gunboats and ghurkas' strategy of the British Empire has been adopted and exported from the military to political level. Once the missiles have stopped falling and victory has been secured, the local allies, the KLA in Kosovo, the Northern Alliance in Afghanistan, the various Kurdish and Shiite groups in Iraq, are supposed to take over and stabilise the post-war country. What matters is the fast victorious conclusion to the war and the staging of invincible, incomparable force, even if disconnected from major interests (Kosovo), even if the enemy is insignificant (Afghanistan). War as the *mise-en-scène* of terrible force, war as the theatrics of violence.

Violence sustains the new world order. As the Real of this order, it organises the relationship between the hegemonic power and the rest. As its imaginary principle, it asks of us, the citizens and metics of empire to identify with its policies, priorities and values. The people of Baghdad and Beirut may have conflicting or no views about the morality or the aims of the American and Israeli bombers. What they have experienced and the rest of the world seen, however, is the invincible reach of a highly visible power that strikes from above at will on behalf of humanity.

82 Ellen Meiksins Wood, 'A Manifesto for Global Capital?' in Gopal Balakrishnan, ed., *Debating Empire* (London, Verso, 2003), 71.
83 Olivier Todd, *Après l'empire* (Paris Gallimard, 2002), 157.

Seven theses on the relationship between violence and normativity

1   The conflict between violence and law is more apparent than real. It should be replaced with an examination of the amalgam violence/law, in which violence is placed at the service of law and creates law while law both uses and begets violence.

2   State violence protects dominant interests and the established balance of power, but it is always exercised in the name of ideal ends (even if highly abstract and general such as God, Nation, Law, Peace or Humanity). The violence sustaining the structure of domination is that of means towards high ends. This is the ideological process *par excellence*.

3   All force leads to counter-force, all violence to counter-violence, all systems of domination create resistances.

4   The job of ideology is to turn the violence of the dominant powers into an exercise of legitimate force and to present all resisting counter-force as violence, criminality, brutality. In the dialectic between violence and counter-violence, state action reverses the causal and chronological sequence and presents itself as countering or pre-empting an original (social, political) violence. Social or political violence is evil, it pre-dates and leads to the creation of state counter-violence in response.

5   The principle of state violence is pre-emptive action against evil violence in the service of higher normative ends.

6   Systems of domination are supported by an organisation of violence, which coerces, criminalises and disposes of those who resist it or are surplus to its requirements. State or 'objective' violence normatively justified triggers extreme forms of 'subjective' violence, which idealises hatred and attempts to cleanse self and society from all evidence of otherness. The extreme brutality of the Iraqi insurgents is closely linked to the normative and 'humanitarian' justifications of the violence of the occupiers.[84]

7   The invocation of morality serves the perpetuation of systems of domination. As long as there is domination, as long as violence is used to defend it, there will be resistance and counter-violence. Moralising, criminalising or outlawing counter-violence freezes the current balance of power and awards perpetual (moral as well as material) supremacy to the dominant forces.

---

84   This position is developed in response to Etienne Balibar's excellent argument in 'Violence: Ideality and Brutality' in *Truth and Politics* (Athens, Nissos, 2005), 97–122.

Chapter 11

Bare, theological and cosmopolitan sovereignty

What remains of sovereignty today? Over the last few years, sovereignty has become an endangered concept. Each of the themes examined so far is eating away at the sovereign edifice. Humanity's law, cosmopolitanism, international law, universal jurisdiction, humanitarian wars and imperial violence are all involved in a concerted attack on sovereignty. The apparent conflict between sovereignty and rights is being resolved in favour of morality. Sovereignty has degraded, it is passing away and is replaced by humanity.

But this picture of beastly sovereignty deserving its inevitable decay has not gone unchallenged. William Rasch, in an extremely interesting book, offers a spirited defence of sovereignty and shows how many of its detractors have misunderstood its function.[1] Jacques Derrida addressed repeatedly the problems of sovereignty in the last years of his life. He emphasised how sovereignty is founded on theological ideas both in absolutist and democratic regimes. 'We did not have to wait for Schmitt', he states, 'to know that the politico-juridical concept [of sovereignty], like all the others, secularises the theological heritage.'[2] Undoubtedly, this theological foundation is intimately connected with sovereignty's claims to absolute and indivisible power, its ability to suspend the law and introduce a state of exception, finally its link with war. For Derrida, sovereignty must be questioned philosophically and practically and the latter is happening

> in the name of the universality of human rights, or at least their perfectibility . . . that the indivisible sovereignty of the nation-state is being more and more called into question, along with the immunity of sovereigns,

---

1 William Rasch, *Sovereignty and its Discontents* (London, Birkbeck Law Press, 2005).
2 Jacques Derrida, *Rogues* (Pascale-Anne Brault and Michael Naas, trans.) (Stanford, CA, Stanford University Press, 2005), 154.

be they heads of state or military leaders, and even the institution of the death penalty, the last defining attribute of state sovereignty.[3]

Derrida seems reluctant, at the same time, to join the ranks of the rabid cosmopolitans, who demand the immediate and comprehensive abandonment of sovereignty. The classical principles of freedom and self-determination are part of the tradition of sovereignty, he believes, and an all out attack on sovereignty would jeopardise these great achievements of the Enlightenment. Human rights emerged and acquired purchase and protective power within the nation-state. Rights were paradoxically both the creation of the sovereign and a main defensive weapon against its cannibalistic power. There is no easy way out from the recognition that there would be no rights and protections for citizens without the sovereign power and those state institutions, which are, at the same time, their greatest foe and antagonist. Derrida goes further:

> Nation-state sovereignty can even itself, in certain conditions, become an indispensable bulwark against certain international powers, certain ideological, religious, or capitalist, indeed linguistic hegemonies that under the cover of liberalism or universalism, would still represent, in a world that would be little more than a marketplace, a rationalization in the service of particular interests.[4]

We should add that the humanitarian interventions of the cosmopolitans address a limited agenda of interest only to the great powers and totally neglect, indeed actively promote, forms of globalisation that commit grave and irreversible violence against the excluded of the South and the poor and unrepresented of the North.

Derrida's approach to sovereignty is highly nuanced.[5] Against the triumphalism of the liberals and the knee-jerk reaction of cosmopolitans, he consistently emphasised the aporetic nature of sovereignty. He reminded us of its auto-immune condition, of the proximity of its absoluteness with the unconditionality of the ethical act at its purest,[6] finally, of the similarity between the indivisibility of sovereignty and that of the individual. Both the victim of sovereignty and the beneficiary of human rights, the modern individual was

---

3   Ibid. 157–8.

4   Ibid.

5   One of Derrida's last and still unpublished seminars was entitled 'The Sovereignty and the Beast' and discussed at length Robinson Crusoe. See J. Hillis Miller, 'The Late Derrida' in Costas Douzinas, ed., *Adieu Derrida* (London, Palgrave, 2006), 134–52.

6   Jacques Derrida, 'The University Without Condition' in *Without Alibi* (Peggy Kamuf, trans. and ed.) (Stanford, CA, University of Stanford Press, 2002), 202–37.

born as a mirror image of the sovereign.[7] Derrida's negotiation of the aporia, in his calls for 'a democracy to come' or a New International, takes a well-known deconstructive form. We must both analyse and deconstruct the 'geopolitical axioms and the assumptions of international law, and everything that rules its interpretation, back to its European, Abrahamist and predominantly Christian filiation (with the effects of hegemony that this inherently involves)' and at the same time, never give up the 'universal, universalizing exigency . . . that tends irresistibly to uproot, to de-territorialise, to dehistoricise this filiation, to contest its limits and the effects of its hegemony (all the way to theologico-political concept of sovereignty)'.[8] What are the reasons, philosophical and practical, that have made sovereignty a prime example of the paradox? Is the Schmittian analysis of sovereignty coming to an end in the new cosmopolitan dispensation of Kosovo and Iraq? We need to go back, before its beginning, in an exploration of the metaphysics of sovereignty that will help understand its contemporary predicament.

Bare sovereignty

> The metaphysical image that a definite epoch forges of the world has the same structure that the world immediately understands to be appropriate as a form of its political organization . . . metaphysics is the most intensive and the clearest expression of an epoch.[9]

For Carl Schmitt, the metaphysics of a society and epoch is best displayed in its politics. Modernity's political organisation was characterised by the centrality of sovereignty. But sovereignty has started withdrawing and its loss of power is closely related to the image of the world our age has developed. But the trumpeted retreat of sovereignty is relative only. Lost sovereignty has not disappeared. It has been absorbed and condensed into a super-sovereign centre.[10] If the clearest expression of an epoch's (self-)understanding is its metaphysics, the metaphysical urge of our age is to deconstruct essences. It is arguable, therefore, that the retreat does not mean that sovereignty has lost its power but its ability to make sense according to modernist protocols. To trace these mutations, we will follow sovereignty from its first emergence

7 Costas Douzinas, *The End of Human Rights* (Oxford, Hart, 2000), Chapters 7 and 8.
8 Jacques Derrida, 'Globalisation, Peace, and Cosmopolitanism' in *Negotiations* (Elizabeth Rottenberg, trans. and ed.) (Stanford, CA, Stanford University Press, 2002), 373.
9 Carl Schmitt, *Political Theology: Four Chapters on the Concept of Sovereignty* (Cambridge, MA, MIT Press, 1985), 46.
10 Chapter 10.

in a simple community to the God-like sovereign of Carl Schmitt to the somewhat unclear, confusing sovereign of the new world order. The move from bare to cosmopolitan sovereignty and from a simple community to the new world order follows a Hegelian dialectical methodology. Each step is conceptually presupposed in the more advanced form but it also represents a stage in the historical trajectory of the concept. In this sense, bare sovereignty is both an inescapable condition of every sovereign structure but it also represents a historical period before the rise of the theological sovereignty in modernity. As sovereignty allegedly withdraws in humanitarian wars and cosmopolitan designs and is replaced by humanity, it becomes the best testing ground for an examination of the sense of our globalised world and its cosmopolitan community.

A space, terrain or collection of people becomes community when these people gather themselves in common. By gathering in common, the terrain becomes territory, the collection collectivity or community and the space of relationships society. As Jean-Luc Nancy writes, 'before even the tie of Law, there is the network of the world. Before the symbolic, there is this spacing out without which no symbol could symbolise: there is being-in-common, the world'.[11] A community comes forth as polis, empire or state by circumscribing itself in its interiority, demarcating its proper interior from an outside, legislating (and therefore changing) this being-in-common. Community's outside may be seen as open space (the New World to old Europe), as uncircumscribed relations (the barbarians beyond the borders) or as another foreign community (Sparta to Athens or France to England). This coming together is expressed through certain figures, which project the common in its singularity. They include a spatial demarcation, a proper name (Athens, Rome or England) and an institutional organisation (the constitution of Athens or France), which open the political as a space of being together. The polis launches itself when it sets the *arché* (beginning) and the ends of its common existence, when a community gives itself to itself formally in self-expression and self-constitution.

A community becomes political, a *polis,* when the relationships among its members are circumscribed, regulated. The maxim *ubi societas ibi jus* expresses the recognition that a collection of people becomes a people in common, when this or that law is declared as common law, transforming relations from open and unregulated to ordered, closed, encircled. Law is the way in which a people addresses itself and in so doing constitutes itself as the people and as a coming together of singularities. This setting of the common law as the expression and organisation of community may take place through

---

11 Jean-Luc Nancy, *The Sense of the World* (Jeffrey Librett, trans.) (Minneapolis, MN, University of Minnesota Press, 1997), 48.

a long process of acknowledging and sanctifying a certain 'natural' order of things, the *dike* of the world, or through the enunciation of a new law and constitution in an act of taking hold of the space and the people.[12] In all instances, the setting and acceptance of a common law both brings forward and expresses the will of a people to be together.

To take classical Athens as an example, Jacques Rancière has argued that democracy came to existence when everyone and anyone became *polites*: both addressors of law and policy and its addressees on issues of public concern, irrespective of their class, knowledge or qualifications, indeed because they had no qualification to rule. The law of community represents the community becoming law through a mutual address of all people to each other.[13] The mutual address, the reciprocal stating of the law, institutes the *demos*, the people, as ultimate bearers of power, and its members, as equal within it. Law-making is the expression of being in common, of maintaining communication, both as a plurality of individuals and in their being together, in common. In this sense, law in its essence expresses an ontology in which Being is not a thing or predicate but the intertwining acts of a plurality of beings.

Since Rome at least, the name for this self-constitution has been jurisdiction. Solon introduces law to Athens, Lycurgus to Sparta, the Constitutional Assembly to the nascent United States and a new community comes forth. In this minimal and structural sense, jurisdiction is the name of the appearance of a community, the decision and determination to be in common. A community gathers itself as common in jurisdiction, in *juris dicere*, the speaking of law and the outward appearance of a community in its uniqueness. The act of setting the law as the common law is the presupposition of political life. It initiates and expresses community in its uniqueness but it also constructs the political as such.

There is no community without jurisdiction, since a community comes together in the speaking of the law. With a certain anachronism, we can call this minimal expression of community, the degree zero of sovereignty or bare sovereignty. It expresses the coming together, the *cum* or together, the *com* of community or the *con* of the constitution. There can be no community without bare sovereignty, which means without common law and an instance that enunciates it. Bare sovereignty is the setting of the origin and the ends of a community, the act or acts by means of which a community gives itself to

12 Douzinas, op. cit., Chapter 2; Costas Douzinas and Adam Gearey, *Critical Jurisprudence* (Oxford Hart, 2005), Chapter 4.
13 Jacques Rancière, *On the Shores of Politics* (Liz Heron, trans.) (London, Verso, 1995); *Disagreement: Politics and Philosophy* (Julie Rose, trans.) (Minneapolis, MN, University of Minnesota Press, 1999).

itself. If community is a coming together, it must gather itself by asserting its bare sovereignty, as the outward expression and inner arrangement of its very facticity. This assertion often presupposes the positing of a mythical or heroic past or of a promised glorious future. But it is the expression of the being together itself, the recognition of the community's singularity and difference from other similar communities, that brings it into existence. Bare sovereignty is the coming together of jurisdiction, law and politics in community.

Jurisdiction (the expression of the emergence of a communal space and common identity), politics (the determination to be together) and law (the regulation of the interiority/exteriority of space and continuity in time) emerge at the same time, they are the synchronic expressions of commonality. *Polis* is the name, politics the content, law the form of community. The provenance and nature of jurisdiction has been neglected by legal and political philosophy. This chapter argues that an understanding of its structure may help explain some of the conundrums of sovereignty.

The metaphysics of jurisdiction

Let us start with the etymology of the term. Jurisdiction speaks the law: it is *juris diction*, the diction of law, law's speech and word. Law's speech, as a double genitive, has two aspects inescapably implicated. It refers both to the diction that speaks the law, law's enunciation through words and, law's speech, what the inaugurated law says. The Romans believed that the law speaks. For the Greeks, the word for jurisdiction is *dikaiodosia, diken didonai*, the giving of *dike*, of order and, later, of the law. Jurisdiction is the gift of law (but who gives this gift?) and law's gift (but what does the law donate?) If we accept Ulpian's opinion in the Digest that the word for *jus* (law) derives from *justitia* (justice), jurisdiction is the diction of justice, justice's talk.

The law speaks and the law gives and this law-talk is associated with justice. In jurisdiction, a speech or utterance, the most particular and singular, offers law, the most general and abstract. The universal as *ratio*, concept or law conjoins the most fleeting, the saying of a word or the happening of an event. Which speech establishes its power to legislate in its act of speaking? What utterance brings about this formidable result through the mere uttering of words? How does jurisdiction arise in its original form? The speech that gives law is a command, legislation or judgment. The nature of law-giving is most apparent in constitution-making, the inaugural act of the power to legislate. In all legislation but particularly in constitution-making, the political in its form as decision, act or judgment attaches itself to law as the precondition of law's coming into being. But for the law to come to existence, it must declare itself to be the law of a specific community and attach to a particular polity. The juridical, too, links itself to the political, to the *polis* as its constituting provision. We have a double linking of a judgment that singularly institutes the law, of a unique act that pronounces legitimacy in general; a particular judgment about the generality of law and a general judgment about the particularity of a polity and its sovereignty. Jurisdiction contains the motif of a declaration that gives now and prospectively reproduces the power of law as always linked with a polity and a politics.

In jurisdiction, legal speech both constitutes and states the law, it introduces the constitution (an act of utter singularity, indeed the very definition of the unique and unrepeatable event) and presents its principles and norms (a return to the universality of law and the uniformity of its application). Two axes are rolled into one: the universal and the particular as well as the performative and the constative. To unpick the structure of jurisdiction, we must separate the four poles. According to a crucial semiotic distinction, the subject of enunciation and the subject of statement are two separate speaking positions. In literature, for example, the subject of enunciation is the author of a novel; the novel's fictional narrator, on the other hand, is the subject of the statement, (s)he who tells the story. The lack of distinction between the two positions, the confusion of the distinct subjects of the diction, permeates jurisdiction and is at its most apparent in constitution-making. The French Declaration of the Rights of Man and Citizen starts by claiming to derive from God and to speak on behalf of all humanity and its eternal and inalienable rights. 'All men are born free and equal' it states but then proceeds to give the newly inaugurated rights to the only people it can legislate for, French citizens. The South African Constitution starts 'We the people of South Africa recognise the injustices of our past, honour those who suffered and adopt this constitution.' The subject of enunciation is the Constitutional Assembly, the body creating the new institutions, structures and rights. Its statement is attributed, however, to a totally different subject, God, humanity, the people. The subject of enunciation, the constitutional legislator or the new sovereign, is utterly unique. It is the agent and outcome of revolution, the historical expression of triumphant political will, a singularity. The revolution and its agent represent the essence of the history-making event in its utter unpredictability and uniqueness. Yet, this representative of the event speaks the law, by referring it back to another speaker, a putative higher authority. The particular and the universal are rolled together as are the different subjects of enunciation and statement. One obvious explanation is that referral backwards or upwards to the universal acts as an ideological trope, aiming to justify or legitimise the utter uniqueness of the action and diction. And yet, like many obvious explanations, it is not sufficient.

The confusion, the rolling together through the rhetorical figure of *metalepsis* (the part stands in for the whole) is implicit in the nature of all jurisdiction and not only in post-revolutionary constitution-making. Enunciation is the general precondition for the existence of all discourse, since without its communication to at least one other person, discourse would remain a private matter. Similarly, since Rome at least, the diction of *jus*, its public pronouncement, is its necessary prerequisite and constraint. Discourse requires a speaking subject. Jurisdiction, following this constraint, demands

> the existential positing of a *judex*, of an unique individual who says the right, and who is unique not because he takes this power to himself . . . nor because people have decided to give it to him [but because] only a single individual can speak.[14]

If the law must speak in order to exist, the law needs a mouth and voice. We, the law's addressees, must hear law's word and accept law's gift. But if the law needs a mouth, the mouth attaches to a face and a body. The law to speak must be one, only a unique individual can utter it. Because the law must be spoken, the great legislators, Moses, Solo, Lycurgus, Plato, Zarathustra enter the stage. Eventually, the great representatives of sovereignty, God, King, the People, will emerge.

Theological sovereignty

The legislator or judex, the sovereign himself, is a function of law's speech, of the speaking requirement of law. Indeed, the great legislators are divine figures and God's representatives. God's law-giving address personifies the unitary principle of jurisdiction in monotheism and brings God into life through his address. The people addressed by the lawgiver, on the other hand, become community by receiving the law and by recognising in the law the ground of their commonality and, in God, the unity of their emerging identity. The voice that speaks the law comes to personify the community in its sovereignty. This logical presupposition and historical expression of community, of any community, modifies bare sovereignty into its theological version. The theological element, so much emphasised by Carl Schmitt, refers primarily not to God's presence (or, today, absence) but to the unitary source of the speaking, law-giving voice. This transforms sovereignty from an

---

14 Jean-Luc Nancy, 'The Jurisdiction of the Hegelian Monarch' in *The Birth to Presence* (Mary Ann and Peter Caws, trans.) (Stanford, CA, Stanford University Press, 1993), 132.

expression of plural beings together into that of a singular body politic, the One-All or Hobbes' Leviathan, who mirrors the singularity of the law-giver in the multitude composing his body.

Hegel offers the most advanced defence of the principle of unitary sovereignty and of the monarch (the *monos archon* or single ruler).[15] Hegel argues that the content and aim of the state is the union of all. Politics and the state transcend and dialectically sublate the collective life of social relations and, similarly, the citizen transcends the private individual of civil society. Sovereignty exists in the form of a subjectivity without foundation, a personality that enjoys complete self-determination. The monarch personifies and incarnates this transcendence empirically and metaphysically. He is 'the summit and base of everything'[16] in the state, the truth of its truth, the truth of 'union as such'.[17] The oneness and uniqueness of the monarch, the monistic *arche*, both presents the truth of the union of all in the state and is its empirical instantiation. The monarch is the supreme individual but also the whole of the state, someone whose personal unity accomplishes the union of the state as individuality. This individuality encloses both the utterly unique biological person of the ruler and the whole of the relations of the state. The monarch as a real person is the truth of the union, its very existence. In Hegelian dialectics, the unity of the state is personal, the sovereign, a unitary person. Indeed, the state has legal personality and is real 'only if it is a single person'.[18] The monarch incarnates the principle of sovereignty and affirms the essence of union by converting it into the unity of a real person.

What creates the need for such a unique and universal person, what gives the monarch his two bodies and turns him into the secular *imitatio Christi*? It is the demand that the right be posited. '*Right is by its essence an actual positing* . . . The actuality of right is its *sensible declaration* to the intelligence, and the exercise of its legitimate power.'[19] Hegel derives the need and nature of the singular, individual personification of sovereignty precisely from the requirement that law speaks. Jurisdiction is the positing of the law. The right of the people, which is the expression of the Spirit in the ethical state, must be spoken and acquire empirical existence. 'The juris-*diction* of the monarch, on this account, is only the naming of right, of union as right.'[20] Right is the

---

15 Georg Hegel, *The Philosophy of Right* (T.M. Knox, trans.) (Oxford, Oxford University Press, 1967).
16 § 278.
17 § 279.
18 § 278.
19 Nancy, op. cit., 119 (italics in original).
20 Ibid. 131 (italics in original).

presupposition of the union of the people, but it must be pronounced to become real. The monarch, the unique and sole ruler, comes into existence in order to voice this right. The long and tortuous metaphysical argument ends up with the same conclusion. The monarch is a function of jurisdiction, the historical mouthpiece the Spirit spirits into existence in order to announce the right of the people. The sovereign is born because Spirit as right must be actualised in the world. The

> signature, the name, and the mouth of the monarch who says 'I will' (§ 279) constitute and are the decision that, even if it adds nothing to the content of the people's right, transforms the saying of the law and of the councils into the doing of subjectivity.[21]

Hegel believes that the right(s) of people and the law a polity introduces through its sovereign are identical.[22] 'Concrete right is the absolute necessity of spirit.'[23] Law enacts right as result of historical necessity, more accurately, law becomes law because it enacts what reason demands about people's right. The experience of the last two centuries, however, undermines this optimistic philosophy of history. Rights are the effect and not the metaphysical begetter of law. The figures of sovereign and right or of legislator and people take a different inflection. It is the particular who speaks, the constitutional assembly, the legislator or the judge but their utterance is figured in the name of a silent partner for whom they speak, God, King, the People or law. The saying of law, *juris-diction*, is what brings together the universal and the particular and articulates their relation.

Here, we reach the original and basic structure of what one could call the theologico-political form of sovereignty. The sovereign repeats the gesture of Moses in Sinai. Moses speaks and gives the law as a mouthpiece or a ventriloquist's dummy; in reality, it is God who speaks and dictates to Moses his words. According to Carl Schmitt, the sovereign is he who declares the exception and metes out excess and incalculability.[24] The function of juris-diction is to bring the sovereign to life and give him voice and then, by confusing the person who speaks and the subject who states, to gloss over sovereignty by confounding its creative, performative aspect with the rule of

---

21 Ibid.
22 Costas Douzinas, 'Identity, Recognition, Rights: What Can Hegel Teach us About Human Rights', 29 *Journal of Law and Society*, 379–405 (2002).
23 Hegel, op. cit., § 28.
24 Political Theology, op. cit.

law and by concealing the sovereign's power of exemption.[25] Even more importantly, the configuration of individual and universal creates a body politic, which mirrors the individuality of the *juris-dictator* (he who speaks the law). This unified body, while plural and therefore silent, wills the law singularly and speaks through its foil and representative, the sovereign, legislator or judge.

Bare sovereignty is the name of community opening to itself, in its self-institution or constitution. Bare sovereignty expresses, in other words, the autonomy of the social and political world. But all self-institution, all processes in which the 'self is made to self itself' are infinite.[26] In classical Hegelian terms, self or community are constituted by going out into the world and coming back to themselves after this sortie. In the Odyssey of the spirit, Odysseus does not acquire identity before his return to Ithaca. Self is not given before its alienation, before consciousness's negation by the objective world and by others and its return to itself from the exteriority of the world. Similarly, bare sovereignty as the self-constitution of community is an infinite process, in which inward-looking autonomy is negated by the external world and other communities. This negation by the foreign introduces the stranger at the heart of community and brings it to self-recognition through the recognition of the other. The autonomy of a community is nothing more than its never-ending self-constitution, the infinity of its becoming through its negation by others.

But the infinite returns to finitude, the boundless becomes demarcated and assumes a recognisable figure in history. The dialectical self-constitution of outward movement, negation and return is temporarily interrupted every time (which is all the time) a figure comes to personify the infinite and close it down. Whenever self-constitution is precipitated into something, every time a figure, person or concept (God, King, the people) comes to occupy the place of self-constitution as the creator, law-giver, etc., autonomy disappears in the heteronomy of a law given from outside rather than emerging in the midst of community. Finitude takes the form of someone or something, a person or concept substitutes for the temporal continuum of becoming-community. In this sense, theological sovereignty is nothing else but the precipitation of bare sovereignty into the definite figure of the sovereign. The infinite process of self-constitution is displaced and projected onto the mortal existence of the personifier. The finite source of law assumes the transcendent, grandiose epiphany of the sovereign, a fake God incarnate, the king's second mystical body. This is the reason why the sovereign appears not as superiorly great or

---

25 For the difficulties of lawyers and political philosophers with the state of exception, see Giorgio Agamben, *Etat d'Exception* (Paris, Seuil, 2003).

26 Jean-Luc Nancy in conversation with author at the *Adieu Derrida* seminar and lecture series at Birkbeck College, on 5 May 2005 (tape with author).

supremely high but as absolutely great. 'The sovereign One is a One that can no longer be counted; it is *more than one* [*plus d'un*] in the sense of being *more than a one* [*plus qu'un*], beyond the more than one of calculable multiplicities.'[27] The infinite openness to the world masquerades in the fraudulent sacredness of its substitutes, who must appear as beyond comparison, incalculable. When this process of endless self-constitution is interrupted, a community ceases being autonomous.

At this point, the modern sovereign, according to Carl Schmitt's influential theory, makes its entry. The sovereign is, famously, he who decides on the exception. The emphasis on the exception has both logical and historical reasons. Law's origins and its limits are non-legal, they depend on decisions that cannot be fully accounted within law. No rule is applicable to total disorder and chaos, to a total lack of relationships. Before legal order is introduced, a rudimentary order must be established upon which the law will come to apply its logic of normality, predictability and security. Before law there must be order, before normality there must be relations, before security there must be a space upon which what is to be secured dwells. This is what we called bare sovereignty, the decision of a community to be together expressed in its speaking of law.

Schmitt insists that legality is based on a decision that cannot take the form of law.[28] The original jurisdiction, which established law's power and set the ends of community returns in states of emergency, when normality is abandoned and the original non-legal power to set the law suspends legality in order to save it. But the state of emergency or the declaration of war is only one instance of the original power. Normal rules, commands or regulations operate because a border has been set between law's inside and outside, between what is properly and purely legal and what is not. The decision that determines the normativity of norms or the rule-like character of rules cannot be made from within the legal system and cannot take the form of a norm or a rule. This is the reason why for a legal system to exist a decision that exceeds the law and gives it its legality must be made both setting the law into circulation and setting its limits and ends.

The sovereign, on the other hand, decides on its own limits and is therefore illimitable, the 'ungrounded ground of the law', according to a felicitous phrase.[29] Although the sovereign 'stands outside the normally valid legal system, he nevertheless belongs to it, for it is he who decides when the

---

27   Derrida, fn. 2, 168.

28   Schmitt, op. cit., 46.

29   Andrew Norris, 'The Exemplary Exception', 119 *Radical Philosophy*, 9 (2003).

constitution needs to be suspended in its entirety'.[30] Sovereignty is a borderline, paradoxical concept because, as Agamben argues, it is both inside and outside the law, since the law acknowledges its power to impose an exception to legality, to proclaim a state of emergency and suspend its own validity.[31] To explain this paradoxical position, which gives rise to justified objections, we should return to the metaphysics of sovereignty. A community constitutes itself in an infinite process in which it comes back to itself. The sovereign interrupts this process by assuming a finite figure and imposing it on the infinite self-constitution. The decision to impose the exception and suspend the law is similarly an interruption of the process of community's self-constitution. Schmitt's metaphysics and his emphasis on the sovereign and the state of emergency can now be understood. Self-constitution is always interrupted as self and community comes back to itself from its exit to the world and confrontation with negation; interruption is its necessary prerequisite. The sovereign represents precisely the crystallisations self-constitution periodically assumes, the finite disruptions of an infinite process, which simulate the infinite in their finite figures. The sovereign is not therefore the 'ungrounded ground of law'; on the contrary, it is the temporary pause of the process of self-constitution through jurisdiction, the effect rather than cause of law. Similarly, the state of exception is the precondition of law's normality because self-constitution through law's speech must be interrupted so that the law can acquire its positivity.

If the sovereign is the illimitable power to impose the exception, it is also the very definition and expression of the nature of the exception, of the exceptionality of the exception. The normal situation applies because it is tolerated by the power of exception. Normality exists on sufferance, it is the exception or suspension of the exception. Indeed, in this sense every norm, rule or judgment can be seen as a special case of the exceptional decision. If exceptions exist beyond the normative and regulative power of law then all law, including the normal law of determinate judgments and applied rules, is exceptional, because 'all law is situational law'. As Vico reviving Aristotle put it, the jurist is not the master of positive law, but someone with sharp judgment, who knows how to judge cases and decide which require the application of equity and which demand the exception.[32] Following this line of argument, Agamben argues that 'the exception does not subtract itself from the rule; rather, the rule, suspending itself, gives rise to the exception and,

---

30 Schmitt, 7.

31 Giorgio Agamben, *Homo Sacer* (Stanford, CA, Stanford University Press, 1998), 15–29.

32 Schmitt, 13. As Schmitt put it 'the decision becomes instantly independent of argumentative substantiation and receives an autonomous value', ibid. 31.

maintaining itself in relation to the exception, first constitutes itself as rule'.[33] The exception is included through the suspension of order's validity, as the order withdraws and abandons it. This seemingly paradoxical situation is the basis of the modern system of the rule of law, both domestic and international.

The all-powerful sovereign is modernity's modification of bare sovereignty, of the process of self-constitution of community. But the finite figure of each sovereign is itself interrupted by the ongoing infinite process of self-constitution. Democratic theory argues that sovereignty comes from and addresses the people, that the people constitute themselves in a process of self-interpellation. In Claude Lefort's felicitous phrase, the place of power becomes empty in modern democracies. Popular sovereignty, the people's jurisdiction, could potentially become its own continuous interruption. But this initial secularization of power and desubstantialisation of the sovereign does not guarantee openness. The 'people' or the democratic leader can wear the garments of the infinite-become-transcendent as easily as gods and kings. As Derrida has noted, the democratic majorities expressing popular sovereignty are always concerned with their size. But if the majority is numerical and calculable, it falls short of the 'general will of the sovereign or the monarch [which] cannot be divided. The One (of God, of the monarch, of the sovereign) . . . is absolutely great and thus above measurable greatness'.[34] Indeed, modern totalitarianism, by presenting the personification of infinity as the servant and representative of the people, incorporates the body politic into the mortal flesh of the 'dear leader' more radically than any king ever did. This is the dreadful strength of totalitarian regimes that explicitly adopt the shiny garments of fake mystical sovereignty and a major problem for their pale imitations by democracies. 'The people' of liberal democracy do not signify a continuous process of self-becoming or an empty place where the community addresses itself. They are one further link in the chain of substitutions of the metaphysical principle of the One.

We can see this sleight of hand in English constitutional theory. Its classic statement in A.V. Dicey and Walter Bagehot distinguished between political and legal sovereignty. The former belongs to the electorate and has only ideological significance. Legal sovereignty by contrast is perpetual, indivisible and illimitable. It resides in the 'Queen in Parliament'. The paradox of an 'indivisible and illimitable' sovereignty, which is divided, however, into two parts has been repeatedly commented upon.[35] This bifurcation has long

---

33 Agamben, op. cit., 18, 19.
34 Derrida, op. cit., fn. 2, 168.
35 Martin Loughlin, *Public Law and the Constitution* (Oxford, Oxford University Press, 1992), Chapter 7.

historical provenance and a prospective function. The division between the two spheres retains the distinction and bond between the divine and secular, which permeates the modern theory of sovereignty. The anaemic 'political' sovereignty of the 'electorate', on the other hand, hides the fear of democracy and the looming entry of the masses into politics. For Maine, 'the gradual establishment of the masses in power is the blackest omen for all legislation founded on scientific opinion';[36] for Bagehot, 'the common ordinary mind is quite unfit to fix for itself what political questions it shall attend to';[37] while Dicey dreaded 'the passing of laws, and still more the administration of the law, in accordance . . . with the immediate wishes of a class, namely the class of wage earners'.[38] The dangerous electorate is accorded a higher but ethereal 'sovereignty', while the real principle of power is concentrated into the combination of monarch and parliament (for which today read the executive). The real attributes and powers of *Deus* (the power to create *ex nihilo*, for example) have been passed to the political institution (parliament can make and unmake any law whatsoever); its nature as *absonditus* has been transferred to the people, declared supreme in their submission. The idea of popular sovereignty, so popular (and unrealistic) elsewhere, never took roots in England. We cannot detect, however, many adverse effects of its absence, when comparing Britain with states proclaiming the 'people' sovereign.

Let us summarise the argument so far. Jurisdiction, the enunciation of law as the common law, creates community. This is the zero degree of sovereignty or bare sovereignty. Bare sovereignty is the expression of coming together of a community. There can be no community without bare sovereignty, the mode in which community comes together and acts on the world or, without the jurisdiction of common law. Jurisdiction as enunciation means, first, that there is an instance that speaks and, second, that this instance in order to speak must have a singular voice. This singularity enunciates the law and its speech act is the performative par excellence: by speaking the law it brings together and creates the community out of an open space of uncircumscribed relations. But the requirement that the law is spoken and the people addressed for community to emerge leads to the figure of the unique, all-powerful modern sovereign. As successor to God, the sovereign projects his unity on the body politic and turns the autonomy of self-constitution into the heteronomy of the subjects receiving the law.

36 Henry Maine, *Popular Government* (London, John Murray, 1885), 98.
37 Walter Bagehot, *The English Constitution* (London, Kegan Paul, 1965), 274.
38 Quoted in Loughlin, op. cit., 143.

For Carl Schmitt (and Walter Benjamin), the pre-legal decision that opens the field of legality is violent. But bare sovereignty indicates that the only precondition the original decision to come together in community must meet is to set the common law. Its violent or peaceful character is a contingent matter depending on empirical circumstances. Being with the other, being together, is the way is which being is revealed. But inescapable togetherness, being with others, does not necessarily mean being together in friendship and peace. While togetherness is the primordial ontological condition, being with the other in amity (Levinas) or enmity (Schmitt) is an ontic not ontological category. The Jew and the Palestinian are inescapably together (and they would remain with each other even if one or the other was to be removed from the disputed lands). But the normative contours and political ramifications of their co-existence can change radically. This is because bare sovereignty carries within it both the decision to be together expressed in the setting of common law and the negation of that decision, symbolised by the masks the theological sovereign assumes as he suspends the process of self-constitution.

Sovereignty and justice

What type of common and in-common does law's enunciation bring forth? We argued above that law as the expression of community circumscribes social relations, turns them from open and undetermined into closed and self-sufficient. From Aristotle to Kant and Rawls, law defines the social as the terrain of external relationships, of agreements, contracts and restitution. The exteriority of legality becomes particularly pronounced in modernity, when it designates and supports autonomy as the metaphysical principle, subjectivity as the expression of freedom. This is also the period in which sovereignty proper appears and bare sovereignty becomes subsumed and even foreclosed under the sovereign's extravagant gestures. The counterpart of the all-powerful sovereign is the legal subject envisaged in the discourse of rights. Legal rights construct the social as a set of relationships among autonomous legal persons, who are devoid, or indifferent to value or follow antagonistic values. If sovereignty is the logical and historical presupposition of community, the speaking sovereign is also the presupposition of subjectivity as legal personality. The legal person comes into existence as a sub-ditus, as she who hears or takes the word of law, called by the sovereign voice; she is the *subjectum* or sub-jected, the proper target and creation of sovereign domination.[39] This subjection

---

39   Etienne Balibar, 'Subjection and Subjectivation' in Joan Copjec, ed., *Supposing the Subject* (London, Verso, 1994).

is the precondition of autonomy guaranteed by law and realised in legal rights. The legal person is this or that person, any person within a sovereign community. It is a person to the extent that her relations with others are arranged as external, material and relative either through legal rights, typically of a contractual nature or as relations of obedience towards the sovereign voice. The law is the place of calculation, circulation and exchange. It is also the institutional terrain in which the metaphysics of subjectivity find their most prominent expression.

Rights are the best expression of the value of law as the relativisation of value. We see this in Hegel's argument that rights support a conception of the subject as this or that person, a universal person, with dignity, respect and self-respect but without interiority or content.[40] We find it in Kant, who inaugurates the *nomophilia* of modernity by insisting that law and right take precedence over any conception of the good or virtue and conceives law as a positive morality. We revisit it in Rawls, for whom liberalism supports subjectivity by being strictly indifferent to any substantive conception of the good or substance.[41] Recently, we encounter it in various theories of legal formalism and proceduralism, according to which the value of law is precisely its valuelessness, its commitment to rules and procedures, to 'exchange value', and its turning away from 'use value'. Legal rights express and support individual desire, an absolute desire for which everything in the world except itself is relative. They are the sign of the relativisation of value, another name for the absence of value or nihilism. When a human rights lawyer recently stated that human rights are the values in a valueless age, she conceded *malgré elle* that human rights are the perfect expression of modern nihilism.[42] The value promoted by legal rights and autonomy is the value of desire or desire as ultimate value. The modern community of rights is indispensably nihilistic, both in the sense that it is based on the lack, the negativity of desire and in the sense that its end is its endless reproduction and expansion.

The community of bare sovereignty is not yet complete, it has the contours of a circumscribed space of relations. To acquire full identity, it needs to go out in the world and acquaint itself with its foreignness. Similarly, the legal person, recognised in his desire but not in his substance, is still an 'empty vessel', as Hegel put it, 'a negativity blocked in on itself and deprived of dialectical fecundity'.[43] Negativity and alienation must be filled, the community

40   Douzinas, *The End*, Chapter 10.
41   John Rawls, *Political Liberalism* (Chicago, IL, University of Chicago Press, 2005).
42   Francesca Krug, *Values for a Godless Age: The History of the Human Rights Act and its Political and Legal Consequences* (London, Penguin, 2000).
43   Nancy, op. cit., 162.

and the legal person must return to themselves from their foreign travels, absorb the negativity that surrounds them and add value to the sovereign speaking voice and formal rights. Self as concrete human being has identity and recognition beyond those given by legal rights. The valuelessness of rights, in other words, must be accompanied by positive value and supplemented by meaning.

According to Jean-Luc Nancy, the mythical, the belief in the plenitude of value and fullness of meaning, has always shadowed and opposed Western nihilism. In Nancy's terminology, myth designates absolute value and value as absolute, as ultimate ground of community or indispensable *telos* of its politics and law. In modernity, this mythical task belongs to justice. After the withdrawal of the pre-modern figures, classical *dike* as the order of the world and God as source of absolute transcendence, justice has filled the space of withdrawal of value. From Plato's *Republic* to Augustine's *City of God* and Marx's *Communist Manifesto*, justice signals the origin of a fallen world or the *eschaton* of a utopian or antinomian future. Justice is fullness of meaning in its absence, the presence of a lacking world. As origin or destination, as nostalgia or prophesy, the presence of justice has been absent, an edenic past or a future arcadia that is always still to come. This absent meaningfulness, this lacking value is the essence of modern mythology, justice is the mythical par excellence. No wonder why when we speak of justice we always go back to an Antigone or a Prometheus. No wonder also that nostalgia and utopia, are the only revolutionary fantasies of modernity. Without utopia, we are only left with simple nihilism. If rights express the absence of value except for the value of rights, justice is the fulfilment of value as origin or destination but never as a presence in law.

Modern law inaugurates the common as a space of external relationships, justice gives the common the interiority upon which identification and recognition will be projected. Justice as absolute and absent value opens the symbolic space, in which the figures of belonging such as nation, people, culture or, recently, multi-culturalism and humanity appear. This way, the community of bare sovereignty becomes this or that community, England or France, this culture or subculture, this life-style or that political commitment. Nietzsche said that morality is the absolutisation and eternalisation of temporary relations of power. Similarly the diction of law and its constraint, to be spoken by an individual, present the social as in-dividual or undivided, the mirror image of law's speaker. The distance between he who performs (the legislator) and he who states (the people or law) is where the One and All are rolled together. The singular speaking voice, dressed in the colourful garments of value as absent justice and its substitutes, projects on community the figure of One, of a *pater communitatis*, of *communitas* in *imago dei*, in unity and homogeneity, as nationalism, populism, tribalism, fundamentalism. The unity of community mirrors the sovereign. Together, law and (absent) justice open the space of modern politics in two forms: belonging and exclusion or domination and resistance.

We encounter a similar operation when we turn to the constitution of subjectivity. If the law guarantees the desire of the subject, if rights are what make us autonomous, it is only within a sovereign organisation of community that individuals become legally endowed. The law as common law brings us to freedom as the instantiation of valueless desire. The substitutes of absent justice, on the other hand, allow the subject to fill the garments of legal rights with the flesh and blood of belonging to nation, people, class or group, the predicates of identity. If the subject relates to others as external to self, as hostile, indifferent or objects of calculation; if he relates to the common as the superficial and artificial arrangement of legal rights or the expression of domination; belonging to the substitutes of (absent) justice allows the subject to acquire interiority, spirituality, substance and to move from legal person to full being.

The confounding of particular and universal and of bare and theological sovereignty can be unravelled, however. Because the claim of the sovereign can fail, because the gap between particular and universal can be seen as two separate moments not necessarily or automatically connected, violence and critique launch themselves in law. Violence is the closing down or forgetting of the gap, critique the care for the distance, the cultivation of its memory and possibility. The closing down is violence *stricto sensu*. It appears in its sharpest form when a new sovereign and its law are established through the overthrow and destruction of the old. But violence operates in a more mundane form when the *I* is forced to become part of the *We*, of a community or a communion where we find our essence through the identification with the spirit, the tradition or the history of that community. All such violent identification is mythological: it asserts a common being in which the law speaks to its subjects as One and All or as All in One.

Forgetting the gap is the more common form in our liberal and democratic societies. Judicial interpretation and judgment are precisely organised in a way that conceals the original performance of the law in favour of its reasoned and coherent statement. And yet this forgetting is at its most fragile when the jurisdiction of a court or judge is challenged. Jurisdiction always involves a clash of jurisdictions and is therefore open to contestation. Both the Nuremberg and the Yugoslav war crimes tribunals resorted to the sheer fact of their establishment by the victorious powers to get around the challenge to their jurisdiction. When jurisdiction is itself called into question then the original difference between creating and stating the law returns like the repressed. This exceptional challenge to jurisdiction, which had to take shelter in the political and violent act of its inauguration, is the background of all adjudication. Every trial explicitly or implicitly addresses the power of the court to judge. It is in this sense that we should understand Benjamin's statement that there is something rotten in law. What is rotten in every legal act and in every judgment is the violence at law's inception, the original performative *dictio*, which established the law and which, in the modern nation-state, takes predominantly the form of exclusion of other people, nations and races. This originary force is entombed in every legal act as a residue or excess, as the force which created law by cutting off an outside and then mirrored itself as the proper or inside, a force that shadows and guarantees the juridical. If jurisdiction tries to conceal its creation of law and figuring of community, it always returns and, when challenged, reveals the contingency of origins and the fragility of communal construction.

Sovereignty and community are the institutional expressions of modern metaphysics. Bare sovereignty constructs community as common, while theological sovereignty gives it identity. Legality recognises and valorises individual desire only in accordance to a domination or subjection to the sovereign, who expresses both the commonality of a community of external relations and the oppression of its immanence. But, similarly, bare sovereignty leads to the sovereignty of absent completeness and plenitude as its inevitable supplement, which circles back again to a sovereignty of lack simple. In the same way that bare sovereignty and the law of external relations mobilise justice in order to become community and subjectivity, justice, too, can become nihilistic, when it abandons the remembrance or promise of absent value for absence simple. At this point, humanity emerges as the organising concept of our symbolic space. Where does sovereignty withdraw and what are the ends of humanity?

Cosmopolitan sovereignty

The withdrawal is precipitated and advertised by our recent wars, the war on terrorism and the postmodern just wars. In modernity, the setting of ends, including the ends of law, was the prerogative of the sovereign. War is the ultimate expression of the sovereign end. The return of war indicates that sovereignty is not retreating but losing its ability to make sense. The decision to go to war is the sovereign decision par excellence and beyond its immediate aims, war's end is to accomplish the sovereign's essence. The nature of the enemy in the 'war on terror' may help us understand this changing essence. The enemy is both banalised as a mere criminal and absolutised as radical evil-doer and our wars take the form of police action, of a war of law. As a criminal, the terrorist testifies to the emergence of a common law and, as evil-doer of a universal lingua franca of ethics and semiotics governing the entire world. The terrorist as criminal violates the one legal order and as evil-doer repudiates our common ethics. The creation of this symbolic space is infinitely more important than toppling Saddam Hussein or catching a few Al Qaeda members. This is the symbolic space of a global community organised according to the effectiveness of planetary technology, world capitalism and a legal system given to the endless circulation of causes and effects without end. But as we saw, no common law or ethics, no world constitution or supranational right has or can emerge. War is called police action and economic competition, violence has taken a lawful, humane, civilised form, nesting everywhere and nowhere, linked to any number of ends but not to a supreme end. Community without commonality, law without justice, terrifying sovereign action that has made the exception permanent; these are the normative contours of the new world order. Finally, law's action veers between a sovereignty that has given up on determining its end and a humanity that cannot determine ends. In this sense, war may be the return to sovereignty, but of a bastard sovereignty without community, which acts without end, except the end of endless aggrandisement.

One can argue, therefore, that the withdrawal of sovereignty, its alleged subjection to legal and moral rules, and its replacement by humanity refers to the withdrawal of bare sovereignty, the sovereignty of autonomous self-constitution. Theological sovereignty on the other hand, withdraws from the weak states and gets condensed in its quasi-imperial centre. It is a sovereignty of absent value, a nihilistic theology that retains all the trappings of absolute power including absolute military, technological and economic superiority, which has as its end the endless circulation of exchange value. As bare sovereignty is the logical and historical presupposition of all community including a world one, what withdraws is the space that came between bare and theological sovereignty or between citizen and subject, in other words politics. If sovereignty infused with value was predominantly that of blood and soil, the sovereignty of the absence of value is the postmodern sovereignty of globalisation and empire. The deconstruction of sovereignty, the destruction of the sense of the world leaves us with a super-sovereignty for which violence has replaced value.

The metaphysics of humanity, of the human added to legal rights in the form of human rights cannot provide a postmodern principle of justice because humanity like rights carries no intrinsic value. Absent justice, the mythological principle of modernity, becomes infinitely relativised, it abandons the remembrance or promise of absent value for absence simple. Its justice is what we find when law and justice are collapsed into each other, justice becomes bare and nihilistic, the productivity or efficiency of law regulating external, material, relative relations. At this point, the symbolic space of a new world order opens. Cosmopolitan sovereignty, the only type of global sovereignty on offer, claims the garments of value (freedom, dignity, emancipation) but is realised in the ubiquitous violence of economic competition, war as police action and empty but ever-present legality. Law as validity without significance is the main form of the social bond. There can be no community at the global level. The jurisdiction of the global hegemon, rather than expressing of autonomy and self-constitution of community marks its heteronomy and decline. Because nihilism and value, solely as exchange value, cannot finish community and subjectivity, the simulacra of value (atrocious nationalism, nihilistic terrorism, religious fundamentalism) appear, no longer as the opposite and supplement of nihilism but as its mirror and bastard progeny.

Humanity cannot act as the a priori nihilistic or mythological source of legal and moral rules. Let me repeat: humanity's function lies not in a philosophical essence but in its non-essence, in the endless process of redefinition and the necessary but impossible attempt to escape external determination. Humanity has no foundation and no ends, it is the definition of groundlessness. But if humanity has no ends, it can never become a sovereign value and war fought in its name will always be fake. If rights express the endless trajectory of a nihilistic and insatiable desire, humanity's only sacred aspect is its ability to endless sacrifice in order to resacralise the principle of sovereignty as terrible and awe-inspiring or as its slightly ridiculous simulacrum. At this point, the new sovereign will have achieved its end and could even gradually wither away as humanity will have come to its final definition. But this would also be the withering away of humanity. The principle of just war will have finally won, in the proclamation of a perpetual peace drowned in endless violence.

Chapter 12

Epilogue
The cosmopolitanism to come

Positive law does not have an independent internal morality contrary to the claims of the cosmopolitans. The pragmatists are right to remind us of this fact. But the pragmatist denunciation of all external ethical positions leaves us devoid of value in a world where meaning and value has been drained. Law is linked with justice in a paradoxical way. When law violates its established procedures; when it does not recognise or uphold rights already given; when it violates basic principles of equality and dignity – the law acts unjustly according to its own internal criteria. We can call this first type of injustice, legal injustice; it is negative, internal to the law and operates when the law does not match its own standards and principles. But throughout history, another type of transcendent justice has appeared, to which the law as a whole is accountable. The law of the polis has been judged from the position of the cosmos, with its universal but absent principles and found wanting. Let us call it 'cosmopolitan' justice. What are its principles today?

The philosophical tradition has persuasively argued that the metaphysics of our age is 'the metaphysics of the deconstruction of the essence and of existence as sense'.[1] Theory has deconstructed well, a little too well, meaning and value. But in the wake of this final stage in secularisation, it is the dominant political and cultural powers that announced the end of history and turned nihilism into the ultimate value. As Jean-Luc Nancy puts it, there is no longer any value or spirit, 'nor is there any history before whose tribunal one could stand. In other words, there is no longer any sense of the world'.[2] Jürgen Habermas agrees from a different perspective: 'Lacking a universe of intersubjectively shared meanings, [individuals] merely observe one another and behave towards one

---

1 Jean-Luc Nancy, *The Sense of the World* (Jeffrey Librett, trans.) (Minneapolis, MN, University of Minnesota Press, 1997), 92.
2 Ibid. 4.

another in accordance with imperatives of self-preservation.'[3] This absence of meaning leads to an absence of world. The world is not just the context or background of sense; world is precisely sense, a unique arrangement of meaning and value.

What world do we have in the era of globalisation, of global communications, of *mondialisation* (worlding) and cosmopolitanism?

- Our *polis*: the nation, the state, the nation-state.
- Our *cosmos*: the inter-national, the interval or in-between nations and states, with its international institutions, faking equality and democracy, mimicking our thin equality and emaciated democracy.
- Our *international institutions*: in awe of sovereignty, aping it and aspiring to acquire their own.
- Our *personas* (masks): the *human*, the soul man of the theological tradition, the cipher of indeterminate humanity or the vessel of the spirit of community and tradition.
- The *polites*, the citizen of the state, mirror image and foil of the sovereign.
- The *subject*, subjected to endless regulation and external determination.
- The *legal person* of the limited recognition and identity the symbolic order offers.
- Our *sense*: the nihilism of insatiable desire and endless exchange and the (fake) value of sacrificial traditions, nationalisms and religions.

This denudement of sense and value marks the withdrawal of the world. In this period of greatest mobility and wealth, we suffer from a poverty of world. The trumpeted globalisation

> is more inegalitarian and violent than ever . . . less global or worldwide than ever, where the world, therefore, is not even there, and where we, we who are worldless, *weltlos, form* a world only against the backdrop of a nonworld where there is neither world nor ever that poorness-in-world that Heidegger attributes to animals.[4]

Slavoj Zizek attributes this worldlessness to capitalism, which 'although it is global, encompassing all worlds, it sustains a *stricto sensu* worldless ideological constellation depriving the great majority of the population of any meaningful

---

3 Jürgen Habermas, *The Inclusion of the Other* (Cambridge, Polity, 1998), 125.
4 Jacques Derrida, *Rogues* (Pascale-Anne Brault and Michael Naas, trans.) (Stanford, CA, Stanford University Press, 2005), 155.
5 Slavoz Zizek, *The Parallax View* (Cambridge, MA, MIT Press, 2006), 318.

"cognitive mapping"'.[5] Global capitalism has denuded the world of meaning and humanitarian violence has drained the moral universe of value. Human rights and cosmopolitanism contribute to this loss. They are supposed to be the defences of the weak and poor, to add meaning to our world as the values of a 'valueless age'. But the withdrawal of sense has made human rights infinitely reversible, both tools of resistance and struggle and the pretext for imperial campaigns, which help integrate and subordinate the oppressed and dominated.

Jacques Derrida has denounced the

> discourse on human rights that will remain inadequate, sometimes hypocritical, and in any case formalistic and inconsistent with itself as long as the law of the market, the 'foreign debt', the inequality of techno-scientific, military, and economic development maintain an effective inequality as monstrous as that which prevails today, to a greater extent then ever in the history of humanity.[6]

Against imperial arrogance and cosmopolitan naivety, we must insist that global neo-liberal capitalism and human-rights-for-export are part of the same project. The two must be uncoupled; human rights can contribute little to the struggle against capitalist exploitation and political domination. Their promotion by Western states and humanitarians turns them into a palliative: it is useful for a limited protection of individuals but it can blunt political resistance. The cosmopolitanism of legalists and pragmatists expands the imperial writ further, turning us into citizens of a world under a global sovereign in a state of well-defined and terminal humanity. This is globalisation of the lack of world, the imperialist and positivist end state to which cosmopolitanism has always descended. Human rights can reclaim their redemptive role in the hands and imagination of those who return them to the tradition of resistance and struggle against the advice of the preachers of moralism, suffering humanity and humanitarian philanthropy.

In our thoroughly secular era, cosmopolitan justice must be discovered in history, the *cosmopolis* immanent to the *polis*. This is the promise of Derrida's *New International*[7] or, what we could call, the *cosmopolitanism to come*.[8] Phenomenology explains that I cannot know the other as other, I can never comprehend fully her intentions or actions. I can have no immediate access to

---

6 Jacques Derrida, *Spectres for Marx: The State of the Debt, the Work of Mourning and the New International* (Peggy Kamuf, trans.) (New York, Routledge, 1994), 85.
7 Ibid. 77–94.
8 See Chapter 7 in this volume.

the consciousness of the other, no perception of otherness; the other is never fully present to me. I can approach her only by analogy of the perceptions, intentions and actions available to me. But I am always with the other, my being is a being together, exposed to the singularity of the other and to otherness. In cosmopolitan ontology, each singular being is a cosmos, the point of intertwining and condensation of past events and stories, people and encounters, fantasies, desires and dreams, a universe of unique meanings and values. Each cosmos is a point of *ekstasis*, of opening up and moving away, of being outside ourselves in our exposure to and sharing with others, immortals in our mortality, symbolically finite but imaginatively infinite; existence, our only essence. The other as a singular, unique finite being puts me in touch with infinite otherness. In this ontology, community is not the common belonging of communitarianism, a common essence given by history, tradition, the spirit of the nation. Cosmos is being together with one another, ourselves as others, being selves through otherness. It means '*being-to* or *being-toward* [*être-à*]; it means rapport, relation, address, sending, donation, presentation . . . of entities or existents *to* each other'.[9] The *cosmopolis* is the coming together of multiple and singular worlds, each exposed to each other in the sharing of the cosmos.

The other comes first. I exist through my relating to the 'existence of others, to other existences, and to the otherness of existence'.[10] To be just to the other we need criteria but those available misfire. Turning justice into an abstract theory (as some Marxists did) or a series of normative statement (as extant cosmopolitanism does) is unjust. Their application would turn the uniqueness of the other into an instance of the concept or a case of the norm and violate their singularity. The axiom of cosmopolitan justice: respect the singularity of the other. We should not give up, however, the universalising impetus of the imaginary 'polis in the sky' of Diogenes and Zeno, of a cosmos that uproots every city, disturbs every filiation, contests all sovereignty and hegemony. We must invent or discover in the European genealogy of cosmopolitanism whatever goes beyond and against its institutionalisation, the principle of its excess. The cosmopolitanism to come extends beyond nations and states, beyond the nation-state. It must limit the logic of sovereignty, of nation and state, it must tame its illimitability, indivisibility and theological metaphysics. The questioning of sovereignty is philosophically necessary and has already started. Human rights attack the omnipotence of the sovereign, humanitarianism

---

9 Nancy, op. cit., 8.
10 Jean-Luc Nancy, *The Birth to Presence* (Brian Holmes, trans.) (Stanford, CA, Stanford University Press, 1993),155.

the brutality and excess of its unlimited power. But we should be careful: this attack on sovereignty does not take place in the name of non-sovereignty but in that of another sovereign, the individual. This is not a campaign against sovereignty but the civil war of Sovereign versus sovereign. 'Human rights pose and presuppose the human being (who is equal, free, self-determined) as the sovereign. The Declaration of Human Rights declares another sovereignty; it thus reveals the autoimmunity of sovereignty in general'.[11] The principle of sovereignty remains intact even though some sovereigns have been weakened and some frontiers breached.

What must be attacked is the theological mask of sovereignty, represented today by the hegemonic power rather than its pale homonymic imitations. This is necessary for two reasons. The absolute, monstrous, all-powerful sovereign of modernity was born in order to protect the political balance of powers and reproduce the social order. While the trajectory of sovereignty has often diverged and even opposed dominant socio-economic forces, the state and its heights still remain intimately linked with and dependent upon the priorities of capital. Attacking the sovereign without putting its actions in their socio-economic and international setting falls into the depoliticising trap of human rights (Chapters 4 and 8). But we must be aware that we cannot fight sovereignty and the nation-state in general without risking giving up the principles of equality and self-determination to the emerging super-sovereign. These principles were inaugurated by, with and against national sovereignty. They are today an indispensable barrier against ideological, religious, ethnic or capitalist hegemonies which, masquerading as universalism or cosmopolitanism, claim the dignity of a cosmos that is nothing more than a marketplace or the moral rationalisation of particular interests. When a hegemon attacks the weakened sovereigns around the world, resistance may demand supporting the local against the global.

Dissatisfaction with nation, state, the international comes from a bond between singularities. What binds me to an Iraqi or a Palestinian is not membership of humanity, citizenship of the world or of a community but a protest against citizenship, against nationality and thick community. This bond cannot be contained in traditional concepts of community and cosmos or of polis and state. What binds my world to that of others is our absolute singularity and total responsibility beyond citizen and human, beyond national and international. The cosmos to come is the world of each unique one, of whoever or anyone; the polis, the infinite number of encounters of singularities. The cosmopolitanism to come is neither the achievement of humanity nor a

11   Derrida, *Rogues*, 88.

federation of nations; neither a constitutional arrangement nor an alliance of classes, although it draws from the treasure of solidarity. It is the reassertion of bare sovereignty as the will to be together. Bare sovereignty without the gilded robes of theological oneness will be 'a vulnerable nonsovereignty, one that suffers and is divisible, one that is mortal even, capable of contradicting itself or of repenting'.[12] The principle of the cosmopolitanism to come: the other as singular, unique finite being putting me in touch with infinite otherness, the other in me and myself in the other.

Derrida's 'democracy to come' is closely linked with the utopian tradition.[13] Utopia is the name of the power of imagination, which finds the future latent in the present even in the ideologies and artifacts it criticises. Utopia unsettles the linearity of empty historical time: the present foreshadows and prefigures a future not yet and, one should add, not ever.[14] The future projection of an order in which man is no longer 'degraded, enslaved or despised being' links the best traditions of the past with a powerful 'reminiscence of the future' and disturbs the linear conception of time. This non-place has been the vocation and aim of great philosophers, religious figures and lawyers, who have built a remarkable edifice of radical political inspiration. Similarly, the 'democracy to come' is

> not something that is certain to happen tomorrow, not the democracy (national, international, state or trans-state) of the future, but a democracy that must have the structure of a promise – and thus the memory of that which carries the future, the to-come, here and now.[15]

The co-presence of present and future in the structure of the promise again unsettles, disjoins linear time.

This memory of the future must be complemented by the image of the past. For those whose lives has been tarnished by the catastrophes of history, for

---

12   Ibid. 157.

13   Derrida calls his 'to come' a 'messianism without a messiah' inseparable from an 'affirmation of otherness and justice' and wants to distinguish it from the Greek utopian tradition with its expectation of a perfect collective future (Jacques Derrida, 'Marx & Sons' in *Ghostly Demarcations*, Michael Sprinkler, ed. (London, Verso 1999), 249. But the messianic is another name for utopianism. The 'cosmopolitanism to come' brings together the ontology of plural singularities or worlds and the social aspect of a polis which incarnates the universality of cosmos.

14   Costas Douzinas, 'Theses on Law, History and Time', 7/1 *Melbourne Journal of International Law* 13 (2006).

15   Jacques Derrida, *The Other Heading* (Pascale-Anne Brault and Michael Naas, trans.) (Bloomington, IN, Indiana University Press, 1992), 78.

those who resist the degradation, oppression and domination perpetrated in the name of humanity, modernity, morality, the past is the most important normative source for the promise of the future. For Derrida, the past returns in spectral form, as a ghost that cannot be laid to rest. Walter Benjamin's philosophy of history takes a more material form.[16] History is not a timeline but a porous surface whose holes provide windows into discarded memories. Memories live not in a historically rigid sequence but in a simultaneity in which we may choose from many possibilities to create the present. It is not the past that casts its light on the present nor the present on the past: historical truth is like an image, a photograph in which the Then and the Now come together into a constellation, like a flash of lighting.[17] The relationship of the present to the past is temporal, the relationship of then to the now is dialectical, imagistic not temporal. The image, dialectics at a standstill.[18] It emerges in the now time through its recognition. Memory as image doesn't belong to a certain time, but becomes legible at a certain time. The image belongs radically to the present because it is only in the present that it can be understood. But the image is also radically historical, and the past can only be realised now. Every present is determined by those images that are synchronic with it: every now is the now of specific recognisability, loaded to the bursting point with time.[19] The past can be seized only as an image that flashes up at the instant; if it is not recognised by the present as one of its own concerns, it disappears. To understand the past means to seize hold of a memory as it flashes at a moment of danger.[20] If not, it disappears alongside the trace it carried. The address of the past will not have been received if it is not read by the present that it enables. That is how the past is saved, but this is a past that never was. Historical knowledge is to read what was never written. The structure of historical event follows that of the photograph. Justice is the legibility of the past, what lies underneath and transmits every Then offering it in the Now as the image that calls for redemption.

Zeno's *Republic* was attacked in antiquity and more recently as an unrealistic utopia, its virtuous and wise lovers, figments of a feverish imagination. And yet, Zeno criticised Plato precisely because he placed his *Republic* in an edenic past or a remote future. For Zeno, the 'polis in the sky' can and must be achieved here and now, indeed it is already part of extant experience.

16   Walter Benjamin, *Illuminations* (Harry Zohn, trans., 1968 edn) (London, Pimlico, 1999); *The Arcades Project* (Cambridge, MA, Harvard University Press, 1999).

17   *Arcades*, 462.

18   Ibid. 462–3.

19   Ibid.

20   Walter Benjamin, 'Theses on the Philosophy of History' in *Illuminations*, op. cit., 247.

His message took the form of an injunction: 'make your own city, with your own friends, now, wherever you happen to live'.[21] The democracy to come combines two paradoxical injunctions, a position well-known in negative theology: the desire that it is understood by anyone and everyone and includes all (as democracy must) with the injunction

> to keep or entrust the secret within the very strict limits of those who hear/understand it *right*, as secret, and are then capable or worthy of keeping it. The secret, no more than democracy or the secret of democracy, must not, besides, cannot, be entrusted to the inheritance of no matter who.[22]

If cosmopolitanism was an early utopia, the opposition between cosmos and polis has now become the struggle between law and desire, in their widest meaning. Law, the principle of the polis, prescribes what constitutes a reasonable order by accepting and validating some parts of collective life, while banning, excluding others, making them invisible. Law (and rights) links language with things or beings; it nominates what exists and condemns the rest to invisibility and marginal existence. As the formal and dominant decision about existence, law carries huge ontological power. Radical desire, on the other hand, like the cosmos of old, is the longing for what does not exist according to law; for what confronts past catastrophes and incorporates the promise of the future. Following Diogenes, Zeno and the utopian tradition, the 'cosmopolitanism to come', this being together of singularities, is constructed here and now with friends, in acts of hospitality, in cities of resistance. This cosmopolis brings together here and now the just *polis* and the principles of resistance of the *cosmos* already incarnate in our present cities.

21 Malcolm Schofield, *The Stoic Idea of the City* (Cambridge, Cambridge University Press, 1999), 149.
22 Jacques Derrida, *On the Name* (Thomas Dutoit, trans.), (Sandford, CA, Stanford University Press, 1995) 83–4.

Bibliography

A and others v. *Secretary of State for the Home Department* UKHL 56 [16 December 2004] .

Aaronovitch, David, 'A War of Words', *The Obserser*, 6 March 2005, 25.

Ackerman, Bruce, *Before the Next Attack* (New Haven, CT, Yale University Press, 2006).

Agamben, Giorgio, *Homo Sacer. Sovereign Power and Bare Life* (Daniel Heller-Roazen, trans.) (Stanford, CA, Stanford University Press, 1998).

Agamben, Giorgio, *Means Without Ends* (Vincenzo Binetti and Cesare Casarino, trans.) (Minneapolis, MN, University of Minnesota Press, 2000).

Agamben, Giorgio, 'Bodies Without Words: Against the Biopolitical Tatoo', 5/2 *German Law Journal* (2004).

Agamben, Giorgio, *Etat d'Exception* (Paris, Seuil, 2003); *State of Exception* (Kevin Attell, trans.) (Chicago, University of Chicago Press, 2005).

Alcock, S.A. *et al.*, eds, *Empires. Perspectives from Archaeology and History* (Cambridge, Cambridge University Press, 1999).

Alston, Philip, *et al.*, eds, *The European Union and Human Rights* (Oxford, Oxford University Press, 1999).

Althusser, Louis, *For Marx* (Ben Brewster, trans., ed.) (London, Verso, 1969).

Anderson, Fred and Cayton, Andrew, *The Dominion of War: Empire and Conflict in America, 1500–2000* (London, Atlantic, 2005).

Anderson, Kenneth, 'Language, Law and Terror', *Times Literary Supplement*, 21 September 2001.

Anderson, Kenneth, 'Humanitarian Inviolability in Crisis: the Meaning of Impartiality and Neutrality for UN and NGO Agencies Following the 2003–4 Afghanistan and Iraq Conflicts', 17 *Harvard Human Rights Journal* 41–74 (2004).

Anghie, Antony, 'Francisco de Vitoria and the Colonial Origins of International Law', 5 *Social and Legal Studies* 321 (1996).

Anghie, Antony, *Imperialism, Sovereignty and the Making of International Law* (Cambridge, Cambridge University Press, 2005).

Appiah, Kwame Anthony, *Cosmopolitanism. Ethics in a World of Strangers* (London, Allen Lane, 2006).

Archibugi, Daniele, ed., *Debating Cosmopolitics* (London, Verso, 2003).

Archibugi, Daniele and Held, Daniel, eds, *Cosmopolitan Democracy* (Cambridge, Polity, 1995).

Arendt, Hannah, *The Origins of Totalitarianism* (San Diego, CA, Harvest Books, 1979).

Arendt, Hannah, *Eichmann in Jerusalem* (London, Penguin, 1992).

Armstrong, David, 'Dick Cheney's Song of America: Drafting a Plan for Global Dominance', *Harper's Magazine*, October 2002, 76–83.

Augustine, *De Civitate Dei* (M. Dods, J.J. Smith and G. Wilson, trans.) (New York, Hapfner, 1948).

Aurelius Antoninus, Marcus, *Meditations* (C.R. Haines, trans.) (London, Heinemann, 1959).

Bachevich, Andrew, *American Empire* (Cambridge, MA, Harvard University Press, 2002).

Badiou, Alain, *Ethics* (Peter Halward, trans.) (London, Verso, 2001).

Badiou, Alain, *Saint Paul: the Foundation of Universalism* (Ray Brassier, trans.) (Stanford, CA, Stanford University Press, 2003).

Badiou, Alain, *Circonstances 2* (Paris, Lignes et Manifestes, 2004).

Badiou, Alain, *Being and Event* (Oliver Feltham, trans.) (New York, Continuum, 2005).

Bagehot, Walter, *The English Constitution* (London, Kegan Paul, 1965).

Balakrishnan, Gopal, ed., *Debating Empire* (London, Verso, 2003).

Balibar, Etienne, *Masses, Classes, Ideas: Studies on Politics and Philosophy Before and After Marx* (London, Routledge, 1994).

Balibar, Etienne, *Politics and Truth* (Athens, Nissos, 2005).

Bankovic and others v. *Belgium and others*. Admissibility Decision, 12 December 2001, available at http://hudoc.echr.coe.int

Bankowski, Zenon, *Living Lawfully: Love in Law and Law in Love* (London, Kluwer Academic, 2001).

Barret-Kriegel, Blandine, *Les droits de l'homme et le droit naturel* (Paris, PUF, 1989).

Bauman, Zygmunt, *Postmodern Ethics* (Oxford, Blackwell, 1993).

Baxi, Upendra, *The Future of Human Rights* (New Delhi, Oxford University Press, 2000).

Beard, Jennifer, *The Art of Development* (London, Cavendish Routledge, 2006).

Beauvoir, Simone De, *La Force des Choses*, Tome 2 (Paris, Gallimard, 1963).

Beck, Ulrick, *Cosmopolitan Vision* (Cambridge, Polity, 2006).

Bedrman, David, *The Spirit of International Law* (Athens, University of Georgia Press, 2002).

Benison, Audrey, 'War Crimes: A Human Rights Approach to a Humanitarian Law Problem at the International Criminal Court', 88 *Georgia Law Journal* 141 (1999).

Benjamin, Andrew, ed., *The Lyotard Reader* (Oxford, Blackwell, 1989).

Benjamin, Walter, *Reflections* (E. Jephcott, trans.) (New York, Schocken Books, 1978).

Benjamin, Walter, *Illuminations* (Harry Zohn, trans., 1968 edn) (London, Pimlico, 1999).

Benjamin, Walter, *The Arcades Project* (Cambridge, MA, Harvard University Press, 1999).

Berger, Samuel, 'American Power: Hegemony, Isolationism or Engagement', Lecture to the Council on Foreign Relations, New York, 21 October 1999.

Berman, Nathaniel, 'In the Wake of Empire', 14 *American University International Law Review* 1521 (1999).

Bloch, Ernst, *Natural Law and Human Dignity* (Dennis Schmidt trans.) (Cambridge, MA, MIT Press, 1988).

Bohamn, James and Lutz-Bachmann, Matthias, eds, *Perpetual Peace: Essays on Kant's Cosmopolitan Ideal* (Cambridge, MA, MIT Press, 1997).

Bolton, John, 'Is There Really "Law" in International Affairs?', 10 *Transnational Law and Contemporary Problems* 1 (2000).

Bourke, Joanna, *Fear: A Cultural History* (London, Virago, 2005).

Bourke, Joanna, 'The Theshold of the Human. Sexual Violence in the War on Terror', Oxford Amnesty lecture, 7 February 2006 (forthcoming).

Brennan, Rony, 'Contradictions of Humanitarianism', 7 *Alphabet City* 140 (2000).

Brown, Wendy, *States of Injury* (Princeton, NJ, Princeton University Press, 1995).

Brown, Wendy, 'Human Rights and the Politics of Fatalism', 103 2/3 *South Atlantic Quarterly* 453 (2004).

Brownlie, Ian, *The Guardian,* 11 May 1999, 8.

Burbach, Roger, *The Pinochet Affair* (London, Zed Books, 2003).

Burbach, Roger and Tarbell, Jim, *Imperial Overstretch* (London, Zed Books, 2004).

Burke, Edmund, *A Philosophical Enquiry into the Origin of Our Ideas of the Sublime and Beautiful* (J.T. Boulton, ed.) (London, Routledge & Kegan Paul, 1958).

Byers, Michael, *War Law* (New York, Atlantic, 2005).

Cadava, Eduardo, Connor, Peter and Nancy, Jean-Luc, eds, *Who Comes After the Subject?* (New York, Routledge, 1991).

Cain, Kenneth, Postlewait, Heidi and Thomson, Andrew, *Emergency Sex* (London, Ebury Press, 2004).

Campbell, David, 'The Road to Military Humanitarianism: How the Human Rights NGOs Shaped the New Humanitarian Agenda', 23 *Human Rights Quarterly* 678 (2001).

Cassesse, Antonio, '*Ex Injuria Jus Oritur:* Are We Moving Towards International Legitimation of Forcible Humanitarian Countermeasures in the World Community?', 10 *European Journal of International Law* 23 (1999).

Cassesse, Antonio, 'A Follow-Up. Forcible Humanitarian Countermeasures and *Opinio Necessitatis*', 10 *European Journal of International Law* 791 (1999).

Chandler, David, *From Kosovo to Kabul* (London, Pluto Press, 2002).

Charlesworth, Hilary, 'Author, Author!: a Response to David Kennedy', 15 *Harvard Human Rights Journal* 127 (2002).

Charlesworth, Hilary, 'International Law: a Discipline in Crisis', 65 *Modern Law Review* 377 (2004).

Chesterman, Simon, 'Never Again . . . and Again: Law, Order, and the Gender of War Crimes in Bosnia and Beyond', 22 *Yale Journal of International Law* 299 (1997).

Chesterman, Simon, *Just War or Just Peace? Humanitarian Intervention and International Law* (Oxford, Oxford University Press, 2002).

Chinkin, Christine, 'Kosovo: A "Good" or "Bad" War?', 93 *American Journal of International Law* 841 (1999).

Chomsky, Noam, *Military Humanism* (London, Pluto, 1999).

Chomsky, Noam, *Rogue States* (London, Pluto, 2002).

Chow, Rey, *The Protestant Ethnic and the Spirit of Capitalism* (New York, Columbia University Press, 2002).

Cicero, *De inventione* (H.M. Hubbell, trans.) (London, Heinemann, 1949).

Cicero, *On Duties* (M.T. Griffin and E.M. Atkins, eds) (Cambridge: Cambridge University Press, 1991).

Cicero, *Republic* (N. Rudd, trans.) (Oxford, Oxford University Press, 1998).

Clark, Grenville and Sohn, Louis, *World Peace Through Law* (Cambridge, MA, Harvard University Press, 3d edn, 1966).

Clarke, Wesley, 'Decisive Force', *The Guardian,* 15 September 2001.

Clarke, Wesley, *Waging Modern War* (Oxford, Public Affairs, 2002).

Clausewitz, Carl von, *On War* (M. Howard and P. Paret, eds) (Princeton, NJ, Princeton University Press, 1976).

Clement of Alexandria, *Opera* (4 vols, W. Dindorf ed.) (Oxford, 1869).

Cmiel, Kenneth, 'The Emergence of Human Rights Politics in the United States', 86/3 *Journal of American History* (1999).

Coker, Christopher, *Humane Warfare* (London, Routledge, 2001).

Colas, Alex, *Empire* (Cambridge, Polity, 2006).

Copjec, Joan, ed., *Supposing the Subject* (London, Verso, 1994).

Cooper, Robert, 'The New Liberal Imperialism', *The Observer*, 1 April 2002, 3.

Craven, Matthew, Marks, Susan, Simpson, Gerry and Wilde, Ralph, 'We are all Teachers of International Law', 17 *Leiden Journal of International Law* 363–74 (2004).

Danner, Mark, *Torture and Truth. America, Abu Ghraib and the War on Terror* (London, Granta Books, 2005).

Darmosch, Lari, *et al.*, *International Law: Cases and Materials* (St Paul, West Group, 2001).

Dean, Jodi and Passavant, Paul, *Empire's New Clothes* (New York, Routledge, 2004).

Derian, James Der, 'Decoding the *National Security Strategy* of the USA', 30/3 *Boundary 2* (2003).

Derrida, Jacques, *Glas* (Lincoln, NB, University of Nebraska Press, 1986).

Derrida, Jacques, 'Force of Law: "The Mystical Foundations" of Authority', 11 *Cardozo Law Review* 919–1046 (1990).

Derrida, Jacques, *The Other Heading* (Pascale-Anne Brault and Michael Naas, trans.) (Bloomington, IN, Indiana University Press, 1992).

Derrida, Jacques, *Spectres for Marx: the State of the Debt, the Work of Mourning and the New International* (Peggy Kamuf, trans.) (New York, Routledge, 1994).

Derrida, Jacques, *On the Name* (Thomas Dutoit, trans.) (Stanford, CA, Stanford University Press, 1995).

Derrida, Jacques, "Globalisation, Peace, and Cosmopolitanism' in *Negotiations* (Elizabeth Rottenberg, trans. and ed.) (Stanford, CA, Stanford University Press, 2002), 373.

Derrida, Jacques, *Without Alibi* (Kamuf, Peggy, trans. and ed.), (Stamford, CA, University of Stamford Press, 2002).

Derrida, Jacques, *Rogues* (Pascale-Anne Brault and Michael Naas, trans.) (Stanford, CA, Stanford University Press, 2005).

Dershowitz, Alan, *Why Terrorism Works* (New Haven, CT, Yale University Press, 2002).

Douzinas, Costas, 'Antigone Death and Law's Birth: on Ontological and Psychoanalytical Ethics', 16 *Cardozo Law Review* 1325 (1995).

Douzinas, Costas, *The End of Human Rights* (Oxford, Hart, 2000).

Douzinas, Costas, 'Identity, Recognition, Rights: What Can Hegel Teach us About Human Rights', 29 *Journal of Law and Society* 379–405 (2002).

Douzinas, Costas, 'The End(s) of Human Rights, 26/2 *University of Melbourne Law Review* 445 (2002).

Douzinas, Costas, 'Humanity, Military Humanism and the New World Order', 32/2 *Economy and Society* 159 (2003).

Douzinas, Costas, 'Postmodern Just Wars and the New World Order', 5/3 *Journal of Human Rights* 355 (2006).

Douzinas, Costas, 'Theses on Law, History and Time', 7/1 *Melbourne Journal of International Law* 13 (2006).

Douzinas, Costas, ed., *Adieu Derrida* (London, Palgrave Macmillan, 2006).

Douzinas, Costas and Gearey, Adam, *Critical Jurisprudence. The Political Philosophy of Justice* (Oxford, Hart, 2005).

Douzinas, Costas and Nead, Lynda, eds, *Law and the Image: the Authority of Art and the Aesthetics of Law* (University of Chicago Press, IL, 1999).

Douzinas, Costas and Warrington, Ronnie, *Justice Miscarried: Ethics and Aesthetics in Law* (Edinburgh, Edinburgh University Press, 1994).

Downes v. *Bidwell* (1901) 182 US 244.

Eaves, Elizabeth, 'Defining Deviancy Down', *Harper's*, September 2004, 6.

Elbe, Joachim von, 'The Evolution of the Concept of Just War in International Law', 33/4 *American Journal of International Law* (1939) 669–673.

Evans, Tony, *Human Rights Fifty Years On* (Manchester, Manchester University Press, 1988).

Falk, Richard, 'Kosovo, World Order and the Future of International Law', 93 *American Journal International Law* 847 (1999).

Falk, Richard, *The Declining World Order* (New York, Routledge, 2004).

Farer, Tom, 'The Interplay of Domestic Politics, Human Rights and US Foreign Policy' (forthcoming, on file with author).

Ferguson, Euan, *The Observer*, 3 July 2005, 2.

Ferguson, Niall, 'Welcome the New Imperialism', *The Guardian,* 31 October 2001, 13.

Ferguson, Niall, *Colossus* (London, Penguin, 2004).

Ferry, Luc and Renault, Alain, *From the Rights of Man to the Republican Idea* (Franklin Philip, trans.) (Chicago, University of Chicago Press, 1990).

Fine, Bob, *Political Investigations: Hegel, Marx, Arendt* (London, Routledge, 2001).

Finkielkraut, Alain, *In the Name of Humanity* (New York, Columbia University Press, 2000).

Finley, Moses I., *The Use and Abuse of History* (London, Chatto & Windus, 1975).

Fitzpatrick, Peter, *Modernism and the Grounds of Law* (Cambridge, Cambridge University Press, 2003).

Foley, Conor, 'Caught in the Crossfire', *The Guardian*, 7 May 2004, 23.

Foucault, Michel, *Power/Knowledge* (Brighton, Harvester, 1980).

Foucault, Michel, *The History of Sexuality* (Harmondsworth, Penguin, 1981).

Foucault, Michel, *The Uses of Pleasure: The History of Sexuality, Vol. 2* (London, Penguin, 1989).

Foucault, Michel, *Society Must Be Defended* (David Macey, trans.) (London, Allen Lane, 2003).

Fox, Gregory H. and Roth, Brad R., eds, *Democratic Governance and International Law* (Cambridge, Cambridge University Press, 2000).

Freud, Sigmund, 'A Child is Being Beaten' in James Strachey, ed., *Collected Papers*, vol. 2 (London, Hogarth Press, 1934), 173.

Friedman, Thomas, *The Lexus and the Olive Tree* (New York, Farrar, Strauss & Giroux, 1999).

Friedman, Thomas, 'A Manifesto for the Fast World', *New York Times Magazine*, 28 March 1999, 43.

Fukuyama, Francis, *Our Postmodern Future* (London, Profile, 2002).

Gearey, Adam, *Globalisation and Law* (Lanham, MD, Rowman & Littlefield, 2005).

Gearty, Connor, 'With a Little Help From our Friends', 34/1 *Index on Censorship* 47 (2005).

Gewirth, Alan, *Self-Fulfilment* (Princeton, NJ, Princeton University Press, 1998).

Glennon, Michael J. 'The New Interventionism: the Search for a Just International Law', 78/3 *Foreign Affairs* 7 (1999).

Glennon, Michael J., 'The Fog of Law: Self-defence, Inherence and Incoherence in Article 51 of the United Nations Charter', 25 *Harvard Journal of Law and Public Policy* 539 (2001).

Glennon, Michael, 'Why the Security Council Failed', 82/3 *Foreign Affairs* 16 (May/June 2003).

Goldsmith, Jack and Posner, Eric, *The Limits of International Law* (Oxford, Oxford University Press, 2005).

Goldstein, Richard, 'Bitch Bites Man!', in *Village Voice*, 10 May 2004.

Grassama, Ibarahim, 'International Law at a Grotian Moment', 18 *Emory International Law Review* 1 (2004).

Green, Peter, *Alexander of Macedon* (Oxford, University of California Press, 1991).

Griffith, Guy. T., ed., *Alexander the Great: the Main Problems* (Cambridge, Heffer, 1966).

Grotius, *De Jure Belli ac Pacis*.

Guehenno, Jean-Marie, *The End of the Nation-state* (Victoria Elliott, trans.) (Minneapolis, MN, University of Minnesota Press, 1995).

Habermas, Jürgen, *Between Facts and Norms: Contributions to a Discourse Theory of Law and Democracy* (W. Rehg, trans.) (Cambridge, MA, MIT Press, 1996).

Habermas, Jürgen, *The Inclusion of the Other* (Cambridge, Polity, 1998).

Habermas, Jürgen, 'Bestialität und Humanität', *Die Zeit*, 29 April 1999.

Habermas, Jürgen, 'Interpreting the Fall of a Monument', 4 *German Law Journal* 7 (1 July 2003).

Habermas, Jürgen, *The Future of Human Nature* (Cambridge, Polity, 2003).

Hadas, Moses, 'From Nationalism to Cosmopolitanism in the Greco-Roman World', 4/1 *Journal of the History of Ideas* 105 (1943).

Halttunen, Karen, 'Humanitarianism and the Pornography of Pain in Anglo-American Culture', 100/2 *American Historical Review* 303 (1995).

Halward, Peter, *Badiou: A Subject to Truth* (Minneapolis, MN, University of Minnesota Press, 2003).

Handyside v. *UK*, Series A, ECHR, No 24, Judgment of 7 December 1976.

Hardt, Michael and Negri, Antonio, *Empire* (Cambridge, MA, Harvard University Press, 2000).

Harvey, David, *The New Imperialism* (Oxford, Oxford University Press, 2005).

Hathaway, Oona, 'Do Human Rights Treaties Make a Difference?', 111 *Yale Law Journal* 1935 (2002).

Heater, Derek, *World Citizenship and Government* (London, Palgrave, 1996).

Hegel, Georg, *Philosophy of Right* (T.M. Knox, trans.) (Oxford, Oxford University Press, 1967).

Hegel, Georg, *The Phenomenology of Spirit* (A.V. Miller, trans.) (Oxford, Oxford University Press, 1977).

Hegel, Georg, *Vorlesung über die Philosophe des Rechts* (Frankfurt, Suhrkamp, 1983).

Held, David, *Democracy and the Global Order* (Cambridge, Polity, 1995).

Hirsch, David, *Law Against Genocide: Cosmopolitan Trials* (London, Glasshouse, 2003).

Hobbes, Thomas, *Leviathan* (Richard Tuck, ed.) (Cambridge, Cambridge University Press, 1996).

Hobsbawm, Eric, 'After the Winning of the War', *Le Monde Diplomatique*, June 2003, 6.

Hoffman, Natalie, *Human Rights Treaties and the Senate: a History of Opposition* (Chapel Hill, NC, University of North Carolina Press, 1990).

Howerd, Michael, *The Invention of Peace* (New Haven, CT, Yale University Press, 2001).

Howerd, Michael, 'Smoke on the Horizon', *Financial Times* 7 September 2002, Weekend section, 1.

Ignatieff, Michael, *Virtual War* (London, Vintage, 2001).

Ignatieff, Michael *Human Rights as Politics and Idolatry* (Princeton, NJ, Princeton University Press, 2001).

Ignatieff, Michael, 'Is the Human Rights Era Ending?' *The New York Times*, 5 February 2002.

Ignatieff, Michael, *Empire Lite* (London, Vintage, 2003).

Ignatieff, Michael, 'The Burden', *New York Times Magazine*, 5 January 2003, 24.

Ignatieff, Michael, *Empire Lite* (London, Vintage, 2003).

Ignatieff, Michael, *The Lesser Evil* (Edinburgh, Edinburgh University Press, 2004).

Ignatieff, Michael, 'Lesser Evils', *New York Times Magazine*, 2 May 2004, 3.

Independent International Commission on Kosovo, *The Kosovo Report: Conflict, International Response, Lessons Learned* (New York, Oxford University Press, 2000).

Johnson, Chalmers, *The Sorrows of Empire: Militarism, Secrecy and the End of the Republic* (New York, Metropolitan Books, 2004).

Johnson, Robert, 'Misguided Morality: Ethics and the Reagan Doctrine', 103 *Political Science Quarterly* 509 (1988).

Judt, Tony, 'Bush's Useful Idiots', *London Review of Books*, 21 September 2006, 3.

Kagan, Robert, *Paradise and Power* (London, Atlantic Books, 2004).

Kaldor, Mary, *New and Old Wars: Organised Violence in a Global Era* (Cambridge, Polity, 1999).

Kalyvas, Andreas, 'The Sovereign Weaver' in Andrew Norris, ed., *Politics, Metaphysics and Death* (Durham, NC, Duke University Press, 2005).

Kant, Immanuel, *Critique of Judgment* (J.C. Meredith, trans.) (Oxford, Clarendon, 1985).

Kelsen, Hans, *Das Problem des Souveranitat ind die Theorie des Volkerrechts* (Tubingen, Mohr, 1920).

Kelsen, Hans, *The Pure Theory of Law* (Berkeley, CA, University of California Press, 1934).

Kelsen, Hans, *Principles of International Law* (3rd edn) (New York, Holt, Rinehart, Wilson, 1967).

Kennedy, David, 'The Move to Institutions', 8 *Cardozo Law Review* 841 (1987).

Kennedy, David 'A New World Order', 4 *Transnational Law and Contemporary Problems* 329 (1994).

Kennedy, David, 'The Disciplines of International Law and Policy', 12 *Leiden Journal of International Law* 9 (1999).

Kennedy, David ' The International Human Rights Movement. Part of the Problem?', 3 *European Human Rights Law Review* 245 (2001).

Kennedy, David, *The Dark Side of Virtue* (Princeton, NJ, Princeton University Press, 2004).

Kennedy, Duncan, *A Critique of Adjudication* (Cambridge, MA, Harvard University Press, 1977).

Kley, Dale van, ed., *The French Idea of Freedom* (Stanford, CA, Stanford University Press, 1992).

Koh, Harold, 'On American Exceptionalism', 55 *Stanford Law Review*, 1549–1527 (2003).

Koller, David, 'The Moral Imperative: Towards a Human Rights-based Law of War', 46/1 *Harvard International Law Journal* 231 (2005).

Koskenniemi, Martti, *From Apology to Utopia. The Structure of International Legal Argument* (Helsinki, Finnish Lawyers Publishing Company, 1989).

Koskenniemi, Martti, 'Letter to the Editors of the Symposium', 93/2 *American Journal of International Law* 351 (1999).

Koskenniemi, Martti, *The Gentle Civilizer of Nations* (Cambridge, Cambridge University Press, 2002).

Koskenniemi, Martti, 'International Law in Europe: Between Tradition and Renewal', 16 *European Journal of International Law* 113 (2005).

Kosseleck, Reinhart, *Futures Past: On the Semantics of Historical Time* (Cambridge, MA, MIT Press, 1985).

Krug, Francesca, *Values for a Godless Age: the History of the Human Rights Act and its Political and Legal Consequences* (London, Penguin, 2000).

Ku, C. and Diehl, P.F., eds, *International Law: Classic and Contemporary Readings* (Boulder, CO, Lynne Rienner Publishers, 1998).

La Torre, Massimo, 'Global Citizenship? Political Rights under Imperial Conditions', 18/2 *Ratio Juris* 236 (2005).

Lacan, Jacques, 'Kant avec Sade', 51 *October* (Winter 1989).

Lacan, Jaques, *Écrits: A Selection* (Alan Sheridan, trans.) (London, Routledge, 2001).

Laclau, Ernesto and Mouffe, Chantal, *Hegemony and Socialist Strategy: Towards a Radical Democratic Politics* (Winston Moore and Paul Cammack, trans.) (London, Verso 1985).

Lacoue-Labarthe, Philippe and Nancy, Jean-Luc, *Retreating the Political* (Simon Sparks, ed.) (London, Routledge, 1997).

Laertius, Diogenes, *Lives of Eminent Philosophers* (2 vols, H.S. Long, ed.) (Oxford, Oxford University Press, 1961).

Lauren, Paul G., *Power and Prejudice: The Politics and Diplomacy of Racial Discrimination* (2nd edn, Oxford: Westview Press, 1996).

Lefort, Claude, *The Political Forms of Modern Society* (Cambridge, Polity, 1986).

Lefort, Claude, *Democracy and Political Theory* (David Macey, trans.) (Minneapolis, MN, University of Minnesota Press, 1988).

Levy, Erns, 'Natural Law in Roman Thought', 15 *Studia et Documenta Historiae et Juris* 7 (1949).

Lieven, Anatol, *America Right or Wrong: an Anatomy of American Nationalism* (London, HarperCollins, 2004).

Lindqvist, Sven, *A History of Bombing* (London, Granta, 2001).

Loughlin, Martin, *Public Law and the Constitution* (Oxford, Oxford University Press, 1992).

Lyotard, Jean-François, *Heidegger and the 'Jews'* (A. Michel and M. Roberts, trans.) (Minneapolis, MN, University of Minnesota Press, 1990).

Lyotard, Jean-François, 'A l'Insy (Unbeknownst) in Miami Theory Collective, ed. *Community at Loose Ends* (Minneapolis, MN, University of Minnesota Press, 1991), 42–8.

Lyotard, Jean-François, *The Differend* (Georges Van Den Abbeele, trans.) (Manchester, Manchester University Press, 1998).

McCann and others v. *UK*, ECHR, Series A, No. 324, Judgment of 27 September 1995.

McIntyre, Alasdair, *After Virtue* (London, Duckworth, 1981).

McPherson, C.B. *The Life and Times of Liberal Democracy* (Oxford, Oxford University Press, 1991).

Maine, Henry, *Popular Government* (London, John Murray, 1885).

Manderson, Desmond, ed., *Courting Death* (London, Pluto Press, 1999).

Mann, Michael, *Incoherent Empire* (London, Verso, 2005).

Mann, Michael, *The Dark Side of Democracy: Explaining Ethnic Cleansing* (Cambridge, Cambridge University Press, 2005).

Marcus, Greil, *The Shape of Things to Come: Prophecy and the American Voice* (London, Faber, 2006).

Marks, Susan, *The Riddle of all Constitutions* (Oxford, Oxford University Press, 2000).

Marx, Karl, 'On the Jewish Question' in *Early Texts* (D. McLellan, trans.) (Oxford, Blackwell, 1971).

Massumi, Brian, ed., *The Politics of Everyday Fear* (Minneapolis, MN, University of Minnesota Press, 1993).

Morss, John, 'Saving Human Rights from its Friends: a Critique of the Imaginary Justice of Costas Douzinas', 27 *Melbourne University Law Review* 890 (2003).

Motha, Stewart and Zartaloudis, Thanos, 'Law, Ethics and the Utopian End of Human Rights', 12 *Social Legal Studies,* 243–68 (2003).

Mouffe, Chantal, *On the Political* (London, Routledge, 2005).

Mullender, Richard, 'Hegel. Human Rights and Particularism', 30 *Journal of Law and Society* 554 (2003).

Mutua, Makau, 'Savages, Victims Saviours', 42/1 *Harvard International Law Journal* 201, 207 (2001).

Nancy, Jean-Luc, *The Inoperative Community* (Peter Connor, ed.) (Minneapolis, MN, University of Minnesota Press, 1991).

Nancy, Jean-Luc, *The Birth to Presence* (Brian Holmes, trans.) (Stanford, CA, Stanford University Press, 1993).

Nancy, Jean-Luc, *The Sense of the World* (Jeffrey Librett, trans.) (Minneapolis, MN, University of Minnesota Press, 1997).

Nancy, Jean-Luc, *Being Singular Plural* (Stanford, CA, Stanford University Press, 2000).

Navari, Cornelia, *Internationalism and State in the Twentieth Century* (London, Routledge, 2000).

Negri, Antonio, 'Postmodern Global Governance and the Critical Legal Project', 16/1 *Law and Critique* 27 (2005).

Nicaragua v. *USA*, 184 *International Court of Justice Reports* (1986).

Norrie, Alan, *Crime, Reason and History* (London, Weidenfeld & Nicolson, 1993).

Norris, Andrew, 'The Exemplary Exception', 119 *Radical Philosophy* 9 (2003).

Norris, Andrew (ed.), *Politics, Metaphysics and Death* (Durham, NC, Duke University Press, 2005).

Nussbaum, Martha, *Cultivating Humanity: a Classical Defence of Reform in Liberal Education* (Cambridge, MA, Harvard University Press, 1997).

Open Door Counselling Ltd v. *Ireland*, ECHR, Series A, No 246, Judgment of 29 October 1992.

Orford, Anne, 'Locating the Internationals: Military and Monetary Interventions after the Cold War', 38/2 *Harvard International Law Journal* 465 (1997).

Orford, Anne, *Reading Humanitarian Intervention* (Cambridge, Cambridge University Press, 2003).

Orford, Anne, 'The Gift of Formalism', 15 *European Journal of International Law* 179 (2004).

Orford, Anne, 'Beyond Harmonisation: Trade, Human Rights and the Economy of Sacrifice' 18 *Leiden Journal of International Law*, 2005, 179–213.

Osborne, Tom, 'What is Neo-Enlightenment', 2/4 *Journal of Human Rights* 523–30 (2003).

Pahuja, Sundhya, 'The Postcoloniality of International Law', 46/2 *Harvard International Law Journal* 459 (2005).

Panitch, Leo and Leys, Colin, eds, *Socialist Register 2000: Necessary and Unnecessary Utopias* (London, Merlin Press, 1999).

Paxman, Jeremy, *The English* (London, Penguin, 1999).

Perle, Richard, 'Thank God for the Death of the UN', *The Guardian*, 21 March 2003.

Pfeiffer, Peter, ed., *Text and Nation* (New York, Camden House, 1996).

Plutarch, 'On the Fortune or Virtue of Alexander' in *Moralia,* vol. IV (A de Selincourt trans.) (London, Heinemann, 1957).

Porter, Bernard, *Empire and Superempire* (New Haven, CT, Yale University Press, 2006).

Porter, Henry, 'This ID Project is Even More Sinister Than We First Thought', *The Observer*, 19 March 2006, 37.

R. v. *Ministry of Defence, ex parte Smith* [1996] 1 All ER 257 CA.

Rancière, Jacques, *On the Shores of Politics* (Liz Heron, trans.) (London, Verso, 1995).

Rancière, Jacques, *Disagreement: Politics and Philosophy* (Julie Rose, trans.) (Minneapolis, MN, University of Minnesota Press, 1998).

Rancière, Jacques, 'Who is the Subject of the Rights of Man?' in Ian Nalpur and Eduardo Cadavo, *And Justice for All?*, 103: 2/3 *South Atlantic Quarterly* 297 (2004).

Rasch, William, *Sovereignty and its Discontents* (London, Birkbeck Law Press, 2005).

Rasul and Odah v. *Bush* 215 F Supp 2d 55 (DDS 2002).

Rawls, John, *The Law of the Peoples* (Cambridge, MA, Harvard University Press, 2001).

Rawls, John, *Political Liberalism* (Chicago, IL, University of Chicago Press, 2005).

Reiss, H, ed., *Kant: Political Writings* (Cambridge, Cambridge University Press, 1986).

Ricoeur, Paul, *Time and Narrative* (Chicago, IL, University of Chicago Press, 1988).

Rieff, David, *A Bed for the Night* (London, Vintage, 2002).

Rieff, David, 'On the Wishful Thinking of Eminent Persons: the Independent Commission's Kosovo Report', 1/1 *Journal of Human Rights* 115 (2002).

Robin, Corey, 'Protocols of Machismo', *London Review of Books*, 19 May 2005, 12.

Rorty, Richard, *Contingency, Irony and Solidarity* (Cambridge, Cambridge University Press, 1989).

Rorty, Richard, *Philosophical Papers* (Cambridge, Cambridge University Press, 1991).

Rorty, Richard, *Philosophy and Social Hope* (London, Penguin, 1999).

Rousseau, Jean-Jacques, *The First and Second Discourse* (R. and J. Masters, trans.) (New York, St Martin's Press, 1964).

Salecl, Renata, *The Spoils of Freedom* (London, Routledge, 1994).

Sands, Philippe, 'Lawless World: International Law after 9/11 and Iraq', University of Melbourne Law School Alumni Lecture, 15 June 2005 (on file with author).

Sands, Philippe, *Lawless World* (London, Allen Lane, 2005).

Schmitt, Carl, *Der Nomos der Erde in Volkerrecht des Jus Publicum Europaeum*, (Berlin, Ducker & Humblot, 1997) (1950); *Nomos of the Earth in the International Law of the Jus Publicum Europaeum* (New York, Telos, 2003).

Schmitt, Carl, *Political Theology: Four Chapters on the Concept of Sovereignty* (Cambridge, MA, MIT Press, 1985).

Schmitt, Carl, *The Concept of the Political* (G. Schwab, trans.) (Chicago, IL, University of Chicago Press, 1996).

Schofield, Malcolm, *The Stoic Idea of the City* (Cambridge, Cambridge University Press, 1999).

Sellars, Kirsten, *The Rise and Rise of Human Rights* (Stroud, Sutton, 2000).

Shroeder, Jeanne, *The Vestal and the Fasces* (Berkeley, CA, University of California Press, 1998).

Shute, Stephen and Hurley, Susan, eds, *On Human Rights* (New York, Basic Books, 1993).

Simma, Bruno, 'NATO, the UN and the Use of Force: Legal Aspects', 10 *European Journal of International Law* 1 (1999).

Simma, Bruno, ed., *The Charter of the United Nations: a Commentary* (2nd edn, Oxford, Oxford University Press, 2002).

Singer, Peter, 'Great Apes Deserve Life, Liberty and the Prohibition of Torture', *The Guardian*, 27 May 2006, 32.

Slaughter, Anne-Marie, 'Law Among Liberal States: Liberal Internationalism and the Act of State Doctrine', 92 *Columbia Law Review* 1909 (1992).

Slaughter, Anne-Marie, 'International Law in a World of Liberal States', 6 *European Journal of International Law* 504 (1995).

Slaughter, Anne-Marie, 'Good Reasons for Going Around the UN', *New York Times,* 18 March 2003, A33.

Smiel, Kenneth, 'The Emergence of Human Rights in the United States', 86 *Journal of American History* 1248 (1999).

Smith v. *Grady* v. *UK*, ECHR Application No. 33985 and 33986/96, Judgment of 27 September 1999.

Smith, Adam, *The Theory of Moral Sentiments* (Knud Haakonssen, ed.) (Cambridge, Cambridge University Press, 2002).

Soering v. *United Kingdom* Series A, No. 161, 11 EHRR 439, Judgment of 7 July 1989.

Sprinkler, Michael, ed., *Ghostly Demarcations,* (London, Verso 1999).

Stamp, Patricia, 'Foucault and the New Imperial Order', *Arena Journal* 11 (1994).

Strauss, Leo, *Natural Law and History* (Chicago, IL, University of Chicago Press, 1965).

Taylor, Charles, *Hegel* (Cambridge, Cambridge University Press, 1997).

Teitel, Ruti, ' "Humanity" Law: Rule of Law for the New Global Politics', 35 *Cornell International Law Journal* 355 (2002).

Teson, Fernando, *Humanitarian Intervention: an Inquiry into Law and Morality* (2nd edn, Dobbs Ferry NY, Transnational Publishers, 1997).

Todd, Olivier, *Après l'empire* (Paris, Gallimard, 2002).

Tomasevski, Katarina, *Responding to Human Rights Violations: 1946–1999* (The Hague, Martinus Nijhoff, 2000).

Villey, Michel, *Histoire de la Philosophie du Droit* (Paris, PUF, 4th edn, 1975).

Villey, Michel, *Le droit et les droits de l'homme* (Paris, PUF, 1983).

Voegelin, Eric, 'World-Empire and the Unity of Mankind', 38/2 *International Affairs* 171, (April 1966).

de Waal, Alex, 'The Moral Solipsism of Global Ethnics Inc'., *London Review of Books*, 23 August 2001, 15.

de Waal, Alex, *Famine Crimes. Politics and the Disaster Relief Industry in Africa* (Oxford, James Currey, 2002).

Wallerstein, Immanuel, 'The Insurmountable Contradictions of Liberalism', 94 *Southern Atlantic Quarterly* 176 (1995).

Wallerstein, Immanuel, *Utopistics* (New York, The New Press, 1998).

Wallerstein, Immanuel, *European Universalism: The Rhetoric of Power* (New York, The New Press, 2006).

Waltz, Kenneth, *Man, the State and War* (New York, Columbia University Press, 1959).

Walzer, Michael, *Just and Unjust Wars* (New York, Basic Books, 1977).

Walzer, Michael, *Arguing About War* (New Haven, CT, Yale University Press, 2004).

Weissman, Fabrice, ed., *In the Shadow of 'Just Wars'* (London, Hurst & Co, 2004).

Wilby, Peter, 'Tony Blair and His Values' *The Guardian*, 4 August 2006.

World Bank, *Governance and Development* (Washington, DC, 1992).

Young, Iris Marion, *Justice and the Politics of Difference* (Princeton, NJ, Princeton University Press, 1990).

Yunker, James, *World Union on the Horizon* (Lanham, MD, University Press of America, 1993).

Zizek, Slavoj, *Tarrying with the Negative: Kant, Hegel and the Critique of Ideology* (Durham, NC, Duke University Press, 1993).

Zizek, Slavoj, 'Against Human Rights' *New Left Review*, 34, July–August 2005.

Zizek, Slavoj, *The Parallax View* (Cambridge, MA, MIT Press, 2006).

Zolo, Danilo, 'Hans Kelsen: International Peace Through International Law', 9/2 *European Journal of International Law*, 306 (1998).

Zolo, Danilo, *Invoking Humanity* (Federico and Gordon Poole, trans.) (London, Continuum, 2002).

Index

9/11 terrorist attacks 4, 6, 60–1, 139, 257–8, 261

absence of meaning 291–2
Abu Ghraib 78, 117–20, 196, 213
academics 6, 187, 198–9, 207, 225n82, 226; international lawyers 234; universities vi-viii
Ackerman, Bruce 5
activism, human rights 78–9
administrative law 123
aerial bombardment 261, 264
Afghanistan 6, 61–3, 178, 206, 264
Agamben, Giorgio 6, 115–17, 122, 126; policing 243; power 101; state of exception 5n8, 255–6, 281; victims 69
aggressive imperialism 135–8; see also imperialism
Albright, Madeleine 146
Alexander the Great 154, 155n14, 156
aliens 98–9
ambiguity of human rights 10, 188–9
American Bill of Rights 20, 251–2
American Constitution 137, 228
American Critical Legal Studies movement 219–20
American Declaration of Independence 20, 36, 251
American War of Independence 15, 242, 252
Amish 128
amity line 229, 241
Amnesty International 31n34, 58, 61
ancient cosmopolitanism 151–9; see also cosmopolitanism
Anderson, Fred 141, 146

Anderson, Kenneth 259
Anghie, Anthony 173, 241
animal rights 51, 118
Annan, Kofi 254
antagonism 103, 105
anti-communism 29
anti-formalism 219–20
Antigone 16–17
anti-politics 79, 84
anti-terrorist legislation 121
Appiah, Kwame Antony 135, 175
Aquinas, Thomas 18
Arendt, Hannah 23, 99, 118, 121, 179, 187
Aristotle 152n2
Armstrong, David 265–6
Athens 133, 273; see also Greece
auctoritas (legitimate authority) 104, 116
Augustine 18, 159, 237
Aurelius, Marcus 157–8, 175
Authentica Habita vii, x
autonomy 127, 284–5

Bachevich, Andrew 192, 254
Bacon, Francis 241
Badiou, Alain 88, 91–2, 103
Bagehot, Walter 282–3
Baker, Keith 97
Balakrishnan, Gopal 145
Balibar, Etienne 90
Bancovic and others v. Belgium and others 263–4
Bankowski, Zen 86
bare sovereignty 271–4, 279, 283–5, 288–9, 296; see also sovereignty
Barr, Bill 235

Barret-Kriegel, Blandine 152
Bartolus 238
Bauman, Zygmunt 93
Baxi, Upendra 83–4
Beauvoir, Simone de 120
Beck, Ulrich 83, 184, 249;
    cosmopolitanism 135, 151, 160, 167,
    169, 174–5
Bederman, David 205
Benison, Audrey 187
Benjamin, Walter 243, 251, 259, 297
Bentham, Jeremy 10, 20, 96
Berger, Samuel 259
Bernstein, Robert 31
bilateral treaties 231
Bill of Rights 20, 251–2
biopolitical power 114–15, 119, 122n31
bio-power 113, 121, 125–6
bios 116–17
Blair, Tony 184, 209, 211, 216, 222,
    245–6, 264
Bloch, Ernst 13, 152, 156
'blue' rights 22
Bolivia 196
Bologna vi–viii, x
Bolton, John 212–13, 235
Bono 66
Bosnia 74; *see also* Kosovo; Kosovo
    war
bourgeois society 101–2
Bourke, Joanna 119
Bowie, David 225
Bowring, Bill 177n3
Bradol, Jean-Hervé 261
Brehier, E. 156
Bremer, Paul 186
Brennan, Rony 70
Bricker amendment 29
Brown, Gordon 67
Brown, Wendy 78, 93–4, 129
Buber, Martin 128
Buchanan, Ruth 230
Burke, Edmund 77
Bush, George H. W. 3, 32, 143
Bush, George W. 32, 61, 143, 170,
    195–6, 264; American ideology 146,
    185–6; empire 138; international law
    211–13; terrorism 3, 258, 261
Bybee, Jay 119, 212, 234

Campbell, David 188
capitalism 101–2, 129, 186, 292–3;
    emergence of early 193; and

imperialism 143–5; and nation-states
    231–2
capital punishment 252
Carter, Jimmy 30–1
Cassesse, Antonio 202–3, 253, 255–6
Cayton, Andrew 141, 146
charities 58
Charlesworth, Hilary 66, 177n3
Charter of the United Nations 15,
    226–8, 244, 255
Cheney, Dick 31n34, 265
Chesterman, Simon 246
China 81
Chinkin, Christine 225
choice 128–9
Chomsky, Noam 223
Chow, Rey 81
Christianity 32, 52, 69, 90–1, 94, 172;
    history of human rights 17–19; just
    war 237–8
Chryssipus 156
Cicero, Marcus Tullius 17, 157,
    237
cities 152–5, 157; see also *polis*
citizenship 40–1, 98–9, 127, 171–4
civilian deaths 33, 206, 240, 260
civil liberties 6
civil rights 97
civil strife 241
civitas 157
Clark, Wesley 64, 258
classical world 15–17, 34, 51–2, 90,
    105, 172; and ancient
    cosmopolitanism 152–9; jurisdiction
    273–4; just war 236–7
Clausewitz, Karl von 242
Clement of Alexandria 155
Clinton, Bill 32, 143, 192, 223, 254
Cmiel, Kenneth 30, 76
Coetzee, J.M. 149–50
Cohen, Eliot 260
Coker, Christopher 262
Colas, Alex 158–9
cold war, ideological 22, 28, 30
collateral damage 33, 206, 240, 260
Collins, Tim 63
colonialism 29, 83
communism 81, 145–6
communitarians 54–5
community 55, 272–4, 276, 279, 283–4,
    287–8; international 221–2, 245
constitutional theory 282–3
constitution-making 274–6

constitutions: American 137, 228;
emergency 5; world 162, 170, 189,
226–33
constructivism 11
contracts 39–40
control, society of 113
conveyancing 39
Cooper, Robert 136, 190
cosmologies 16–18, 152
cosmopolis (city of gods and men) 174,
294, 298
cosmopolitan communism 145–6
cosmopolitanism 17, 57, 134–5, 141–3,
148–9; ancient 151–9; to come
291–8; modern 159–64; and
sovereignty 270; *see also* postmodern
cosmopolitanism
cosmopolitan justice 291, 293–4; *see
also* justice
cosmopolitan sovereignty 288–90
cosmopolites (citizen of the world) 17,
151, 154
cosmos (ideal order of the world) 152,
154, 159, 174, 292, 294, 298
counter-force 268
Crates 154
Craven, Matthew 234
crimes against humanity 21, 68, 74, 88,
164, 258
critical legal studies 219–20
Cuba 117–18
custom 16
Cynics 153–4, 159

Dark Side of Virtue, The (Kennedy)
217
Darmosch, Lari 226
death 35, 47
Declaration of Independence 20, 36,
251
Declaration of the Rights of Man and
Citizen 10, 12, 20, 92, 96–8, 251,
275
decolonisation 231
De Jure Belli ac Pacis (Grotius) 239,
252
democracy 32–3, 59, 75, 105, 197, 273;
atrocities committed by 161n35; to
come 296–8; global 142; restrictions
on 191; and sovereignty 282–3
democratic norm 196
demos 105, 174, 273
Derian, James Der 223

Derrida, Jacques viii, 70, 248, 252, 292;
democracy to come 296–8; discourse
on human rights 197, 293;
sovereignty 269–71, 280, 282, 295
Dershowitz, Alan 5
desire 7, 12, 34–7, 87, 292; and law 35,
298; and rights 45–50, 285
détente 30
Dicey, A.V. 282–3
differences 44
dignity 40
Diogenes Laertius 154, 156, 298
disciplinary societies 112–14
discourse on human rights 179, 197,
293; *see also* rhetoric
domination 96, 104; see also *potestas*
Douzinas, Costas 13, 208
droit d'ingérance humanitaire 61
Dubois, W.E.B. 28
Dunant, Jean-Henri 58
Duns Scotus, John 18–19
Durkheim, Emile 20
Dworkin, Ronald 115, 213

economic exploitation 41
economic policies, neo-liberal 192, 194,
247, 293
economic rights 41, 97, 185
economic sanctions 177
economy, global 190–1
ego 46–7
Elbe, Joachim von 238–9
electorate 282–3
emergency constitutions 5
empire 117–18, 134, 138; constitution
of 226–33; 'lite' 139–41; and NGOs
62; Roman 158–9; synonyms with
148; *see also* imperialism
Empire (Hardt and Negri) 145, 226,
232
end of history 4, 33, 108, 144, 178,
201, 291
enemies within 241
England 282–3; *see also* United
Kingdom
England, Lynndie 120–1
Enlightenment philosophy 94
entitlements 19, 38
enunciation 275–6, 283
equality 18, 52, 92, 156
eros 153
eroticisation of pain 77–8
ethics *see* morality

ethics, species 53n5, 54
Europe: international law 210, 214, 217,
    220; just war 241; law 229–30;
    suffering 72–4; universities vi–viii, x
European Convention on Human Rights
    (ECHR) 25, 60, 121, 188n37, 189
European Court of Human Rights
    31n34, 56n9, 263–4
European Court of Justice 229
events 103
evil 69–70, 87–8, 121
exceptions see state of exception
exclusion 96–101, 105–8, 111
expansionism 137, 139
experiences of human rights violations
    14

factor X 43, 53–4
Falk, Richard 138, 142–3, 184, 218,
    227
Farer, Tom 32–3, 185
Ferguson, Euan 67
Ferguson, Niall 136
feudal society 101
Fine, Bob 169
finitude 279
Finkielkraut, Alain 82
Finley, M.I. 153
Fitzpatrick, Peter 137, 185
force 251; see also violence
foreign policy 30
Foucault, Michel 111–13, 116, 122n31,
    123
France 98, 161; see also French
    Declaration of the Rights of Man and
    Citizen; French Revolution
France, Anatole 40
Franciscan nominalists 18–19
Frederick I vi-vii
freedom 13, 127–9, 137, 185–6
free will 35–6
French Declaration of the Rights of
    Man and Citizen 10, 12, 20, 92,
    96–8, 251, 275
French Revolution 15, 105, 160–1, 242,
    251
Freud, Sigmund 45, 78, 127
Friedman, Thomas 192, 247
Fukuyama, Francis 43, 53–4

G8 67, 71, 79
Garido, Francisco 56
Gates, Bill 80–1

gays and lesbians 56–7
Gearey, Adam 12
Gearty, Connor 70
genealogy of human rights 26–33;
    see also intellectual history of human
    rights
genetic engineering 53
Geneva Convention 58–9, 117n15,
    195–6, 212
German philosophy 159
Gibbon, Edward vii
Giddens, Anthony 162
Glennon, Michael 202–3, 212, 255
global democracy 142
global economy, imperialism of 190–1
globalisation 6, 83, 136; imperialism of
    143–5; vs. universalisation 181; and
    worldlessness 292
God 17–19, 52, 146, 276
Goldstone, Richard 203
good 35, 69, 88
Gouges, Olympe de 105
governmental rhetoric and policies 60
Grassama, Ibarahim 200
Gray, John 5
Great Britain see United Kingdom
Greece 133; and ancient
    cosmopolitanism 152–9; classical
    15–17, 34, 51–2, 105, 172, 236–7;
    jurisdiction 273–4
Green, Peter 155
'green' rights 22
Grotius 239–40, 252
Guantánamo Bay 59, 117–18, 196,
    212
Guehenno, Jean-Marie 124
Gunther, Klaus 71–5

Habermas, Jurgen 8, 124, 162, 219;
    Kosovo war 207–8; nihilism 291–2;
    postmodern cosmopolitanism 164–8,
    170–1; species ethics 53–4; world
    constitutions 226–7
Hadas, Moses 154
Halttunen, Karen 77, 118
Hamdan v. Rumsfeld 117n15
Hamdi v. Rumsfeld 117n15
Hardt, Michael 62, 113, 115, 183, 190;
    empire 145–6; freedom and
    expansion 137n8, 185; international
    law 225, 235; state of exception 232;
    world constitutions 226, 228–9
Al-Harith, Jamal 118

Harvey, David 145, 231
hate speech 38
Hathaway, Oona 181
Hazlitt, William 77
Hegel, Georg 93, 245, 248, 251, 277–8, 285; Napoleon 81, 100; recognition 37, 40, 44n14, 80
hegemony 148
Heidegger, Martin 53, 109
Held, David 175–6
Henkin, Louis 182
Hipples, Jochen 191
Hirsch, David 169
historicism, defects of 26
history 297; *see also* end of history
history of human rights *see* genealogy of human rights; intellectual history of human rights
Hobbes, Thomas 19–20, 34–5, 277
Hobsbawm, Eric 138
Hoffman, Lord 5
Holbrooke, Richard 254
Holocaust 15, 23, 72, 74, 82, 88
homo sacer 116–17
hospitality 298
Howerd, Michael 136, 253
human 55–6; *see also* humanity
humane war 63; *see also* just war, concepts of
humanism 7, 51–7
humanitarian imperialists 138–41
humanitarian interventions 183, 203, 213n43
humanitarianism 7, 26, 57; and images of suffering 76–8; and liberal theory 71–5; and Live8 66–8; military 58–66, 245; and the other 84–9; politics of 77–84; and victims 69–70; *see also* radical humanitarians
humanitarian law 240
humanitas 51–2
humanity: concept of 51–7; crimes against 21, 68, 74, 88, 164, 258; metaphysics of 289–90; wars in the name of 172
humanity's law 182–4, 202, 230, 232
human nature 51–2
human rights 8–13; activism 78–9; and desire 45–50; distinct from morality 165–6; expression of modern nihilism 285; first reference to 15; genealogy of 26–33; and identity

37–45; movement 15, 22, 74; treaties 30, 181; *see also* intellectual history of human rights; politics of human rights; right
Human Rights Act 6
Human Rights Commission 24, 28–9, 31n34
Human Rights Watch 31
Hussein, Saddam 210, 257

identity 7, 37–45, 279; and psychoanalytical theory 45–6, 48; *see also* self
identity cards law 114
ideological cold war 22, 28, 30
ideologies 11–12, 81, 146, 185–6, 223, 268
Ignatieff, Michael 4–5, 11–12, 52, 68, 73, 258; human rights activism 78–9; imperialism 138–41, 255; Kosovo war 206–7, 208–9, 260; military humanitarianism 62–4; wars 247, 250, 262
images of suffering and violence 76–8, 265–6; *see also* pornography
imaginary identification 266–7
imaginary otherness 85
imperialism 255; aggressive 135–8; humanitarian 138–41; of globalisation 143–5; *see also* empire
individuality 18–19, 34, 270, 277, 295; *see also* identity
individual particularity 44n14
injustice 87
integrity 53n5
intellectual history of human rights: Christianity 17–18; classical Greece 15–17; human rights revolution 22–5; liberal political philosophers 18–20; Nuremberg trials 21–2; *see also* genealogy of human rights
intentions 36
International Committee of the Red Cross 58, 61–2
international community 221–2, 245; *see also* community
International Covenant of Civil and Political Rights 15, 25, 29–30
International Covenant of Economic, Social and Cultural Rights 15, 29–30
International Criminal Court (ICC) 22, 211–12

international economic law 125
international human rights law 23–5
international law 22–4, 58, 60, 149,
    160, 162–4; and end of history 201;
    Europe 217, 220; Iraq war 198–9,
    209–16, 234–5, 259; *Jus Publicum
    Europaeum* 239; and just war 246;
    Kosovo war 202–9, 234–5, 259; and
    pragmatism 222, 224; and terrorism
    258; theory 200–2; United States
    170, 217, 225; and violence 252–3,
    256; *see also* constitutions, world
international lawyers 233–5
International Monetary Fund 226
international rule of law 200, 203–4,
    209, 211, 215–16, 218, 253
internationals 64, 140
international trade 231
Iran 196
Iraq war 6, 33, 178, 186; civilians
    killed in 206; imperialism 136, 141;
    insurgents 195, 268; international law
    170, 198–9, 209–16, 222–3, 234–5,
    256, 259; military humanitarianism
    61–3
Israel 254

Jackson, Robert 21
Jaures, Jean 12
Jewish tradition 128, 156
jouissance 47
judicial proceedings 168
jurisdiction 273–8, 283, 287–8, 290
jurisprudence 10–11, 14, 115–16
jus 17–18, 52, 156, 158, 237–8, 274
jus ad bellum 238, 242–4, 250
jus in bello 58, 238, 240–2, 250
justa causa 178, 237, 239, 245, 250
justice 87, 274, 284–9, 291, 293–4
just war, concepts of 201, 248–50, 259;
    ancient 236–7; early Church 237–8;
    early modern 239–41; modern 242–4;
    postmodern 245–7

Kagan, Robert 169–70, 210, 214,
    216–17, 219
Kalyvas, Andreas 122n31
Kant, Immanuel viii, 27, 79, 91, 94,
    127; cosmopolitanism 160–4; just
    war 240, 245; *nomophilia* 285;
    sublime 265
Keats, John 77
Kelsen, Hans 162–3, 200, 228

Kennedy, David 183, 253; international
    law 199, 201, 217–20, 222–4;
    military humanitarianism 60–5;
    world constitutions 227–8
Kennedy, Paul 145
Kirkpatrick, Jeanne 146
Kissinger, Henry 144
Koller, David 187
Koselleck, Reinhart 172
Koskenniemi, Martti 187–9, 201, 219,
    223–4
Kosovo 54
Kosovo war 74, 166–7, 170, 178;
    international law 202–9, 214–15,
    234–5, 256, 259; military
    humanitarianism 61, 63–4;
    technology 260; violence 254–5
Kouchner, Bernard 61
Krauthammer, Charles 213
Kyoto climate control agreement
    211–12

Lacan, Jacques 45, 46n17, 47, 127
lack 45, 47–9, 87
Lacoue-Labarthe, Philippe 102
language of human rights and
    democracy 32, 59
La Torre, Massimo 174
law: and bio-power 125–6;
    Christianisation of Roman 18;
    cosmopolitan 162–3; and desire 35,
    298; European 229–30;
    indeterminacy of 189; inner voice
    of 90–1; and jurisdiction 273–6;
    and justice 286, 291; *nomos* 152,
    157; and politics 219, 222, 272;
    and right 278; and violence 251–4,
    256, 268, 288; *see also* international
    law; legality; legal positivism;
    nomos
Lawless World (Sands) 213
League of Nations 243, 252
Lebanon 254
Lefort, Claude 108, 282
legality 167, 204–5, 207–8, 215, 217,
    221, 251–2
legal pacifism 163–4
legal personality 53
legal persons 40–1, 93, 284–7, 292
legal positivism 19–20
legal rights 9, 38–41
legitimacy 167
Legnano, Johannes de 238

Lenin, Vladimir 143
Levinas, Emmanuel 73n51, 128
Lewis, Norman 179
Lewis, Wyndam 236
liberal culture, American 72
liberal democratic order 177
liberal political philosophers,
    seventeenth- and eighteenth-century
    18–20, 52
liberal theory 22, 53, 71–5
liberty 146, 185; *see also* freedom
Lindqvist, Sven 265
little object 47–9
Live8 66–8, 71, 75, 79
Live Aid 58–9
local level, protection and violation of
    human rights at 14, 26
Locke, John 19–20
logos (reason) 152, 157–8
London 60, 133
love 38, 48–9
Lyotard, Jean-Francois 87–8, 98

McIntyre, Alasdair 79, 90
McKinley, William 137
Maine, Henry 283
Maistre, Joseph de 93
man, concept of 52, 93
Mann, Michael 75, 149, 161n35
Marks, Susan 196, 234
Martin, Chris 66
Martino vii–viii
Marx, Karl 20, 34, 93, 101–2, 106
master and slave dialectic 37, 80
meaning, absence of 291–2
Médecins Sans Frontières 61, 70
metaphysics 90–6, 271, 274–6,
    288–91
military, gays and lesbians in 56–7
military humanism 7
military humanitarianism 58–66, 245
military technology 259–63
Milosevic, Slobodan 23, 194, 257
minorities 97
modern cosmopolitanism 159–64
modernity 34, 43, 53, 91–5, 98, 271
monarchs 277–8; *see also* sovereigns;
    sovereignty
mondialisation 292
moralisation of international relations
    182
morality 9–10, 27–8, 79, 82, 165–7;
    just war 244, 259; relationship with

legality 204–5, 207–8, 215, 217;
    and violence 251, 268
Morss, John 8
Moses 278
Motha, Stewart 8, 178n3
motives 36
Mouffe, Chantal 102–3
Mullender, Richard 44n14
Mussolini, Benito 248
Mutua, Makau 86
myth 286

name-giving 147–8
Nancy, Jean-Luc 276–9, 286, 291, 294;
    community 272; politics of human
    rights 102, 109; technology of war
    263
Napoleon 81, 100
National Association for the
    Advancement of Colored People
    (NAACP) 28
national interest 246–7
nationalism 98–9, 223n71
national sovereignty 28, 97–8, 178–9,
    229–32, 295; *see also* sovereigns;
    sovereignty
nation-building 140
nation-states 92–3, 97–8, 116, 230–2,
    270, 292
natural cosmology 16–17
natural laws 12, 15, 18–19, 21
natural rights 12–13, 17–18, 20, 33, 93,
    101–2
nature 16, 158–9
Navari, Cornelia 182
Nazis 81, 122; *see also* Holocaust
Nazi war criminals, trial of 21–2;
    see also Nuremberg trials
Negri, Antonio 62, 113, 115, 145–6,
    183, 190; freedom and expansion
    137n8, 185; international law 225,
    235; state of exception 232; world
    constitutions 226, 228–9
neo-humanism 168n54
neo-liberal economic policies 192, 194,
    247, 293
neutrality 58–9
new times 148
new world order 147–8
Nicaragua 213n43
Nietzsche, Friedrich 26–7, 165, 217,
    286
nihilism 285–6, 290–2

nominalists, Franciscan 18–19
nomophilia (love of the law) 91, 159, 226, 285
nomos (law) 152, 157; see also law
non-governmental organisations (NGOs) 26, 30, 58–9, 61–2
non-intervention 179, 244–5
normalisation 125
normality 281
normative positivism 221
normativity 124–5, 251, 268
Norrie, Alan 36
Norris, Andrew 122n31, 280
North Atlantic Treaty Organization (NATO) 167, 188, 202–3, 255, 260, 263–4
Nuremberg trials 21–2, 68, 164, 214, 243
Nussbaum, Martha 175

Ogilvie, Bernard 69, 100
openness 192
oppression 41, 96
Orford, Anne 125, 191–2, 225, 226n87, 253
orthos logos (right reason) 158
Osborne, Tom 168n54
other, the 45, 47–8, 70, 84–9, 293–4, 296
Oxfam 61

pacifism 65, 163–4; see also peace
Pahuja, Sundhya 221, 230
Paine, Thomas 19–20
Pakistan 196
Pal, Radhabinod 29
Palestine 196
paradox of human rights 8, 50
parliament 282–3
particular, the 92–5, 97, 195, 275, 278
Passavant, Paul 115
peace 160, 163, 190, 243–4, 245n17
Perle, Richard 255
petit objet a (the little other object) 47–9
phallus 46–7
Philippines 137–8
pity 75, 80, 82
Plato 16, 153, 236–7, 297
Plutarch 154–5
policing 241–3, 257–9

polis (city) 16, 34, 174, 292; ancient cosmopolitanism 152–5, 159; community 272, 274
political theology, medieval 238
politicians 11, 15
politics: and bare sovereignty 271–4; of humanitarianism 77–84; human rights 76; and law 219, 222, 272; la politique vs. le politique 102–6, 108–9; see also politics of human rights
politics of human rights: and exclusion 96–101; Marx 101–2; and metaphysics 90–6; la politique vs. le politique 102–6, 108–9
politique, la (politics) 102–6, 108–9
politique, le (the political) 102–6, 108–9
pornography 77–8, 120
Porter, Bernard 138–9, 185
Porter, Henry 114
positivism 20–1, 251
postmodern cosmopolitanism 164–70; and citizenship 171–4; proponents of 174–6
potestas (domination) 104, 116; see also domination
poverty 40
Powell, Colin 61, 223
power 17–18, 96, 100–1, 104, 112; bio- 113, 121; biopolitical 114–15, 119, 122n31
pragmatism 72, 222, 224
pre-emptive self-defence 210
pre-emptive wars 265
prisoners 58–9; see also Abu Ghraib; Guantánamo Bay
proletariats 106
property rights 9, 38–40
protest, public 67
psychoanalytical theory 45–9, 55n7, 87

racial minorities 31
radical humanitarians 60, 62, 65–6, 89
Rancière, Jacques 103, 105–8, 273
Rasch, William 103, 169, 173, 256, 269
Rasul and Odah v. Bush 117n15
Rawls, John 53, 94, 115, 167–8, 173, 208, 285
Reagan, Ronald 31
Real 47–8, 86

reason 16–17, 19–20
recognition 37–43, 44n14, 48, 80
recta ratio 158
Red Cross 58, 61–2
'red' rights 22
refugees 99–100, 171
regime change 210
relativists 54
Republic (Plato) 236, 297
Republic (Zeno) 153–5, 297–8
rescuers 68, 71, 73, 84
resistance viii–x, 12–13, 16–17, 293,
    295, 298
revolutions 12–13, 20, 275; American
    15, 242, 252; French 15, 105, 160–1,
    242, 251
rhetoric 32–3, 36, 59–60, 62–3, 197
Rice, Condoleezza 146
Ricoeur, Paul 82–3
Rieff, David 83, 209, 221–2, 246
right 89, 110, 183, 277–8
rights *see* human rights
rights culture 50
Rights of Man, The (Paine) 20
Rimbaud, Arthur 47
Robertson, Geoffrey 258
Robinson, Mary 206
Roed-Larsen, Terje 254
rogue states 3, 136, 139, 141, 218, 229,
    235
Roman law, Christianisation of 18
Rome, classical 17–18, 34, 51–2,
    157–9, 237, 274
Roosevelt, Eleanor 28
Roosevelt, Franklin Delano 29
Rorty, Richard 72–3, 78, 84
Rousseau, Jean-Jacques 19–20, 127
rule of law 124, 227, 282; *see also*
    international rule of law
Rumsfeld, Donald 117n15, 138
rumspringa 128
Russia 15, 61n16

sacredness of human rights 95
Saint Paul 17–18, 52, 91, 103
Salecl, Renata 47, 49
salus populi 6
Sands, Philippe 209, 211–15, 218, 228,
    234
Sané, Andre 31n34
Saro-Wiwa, Ken 81
Saudi Arabia 196
saviours *see* rescuers

Schmitt, Carl 6, 44n14, 171–3, 207;
    cosmopolitanism 161, 165, 167;
    politics of human rights 103–4, 109;
    state of exception 117, 256
Schofield, Malcolm 153, 155
scholarship *see* academics
second world war 23, 74, 243, 249;
    see also Holocaust; Nuremberg
    trials
secular society 96
security: after 9/11 3–4, 184; Hobbes'
    view of 35; human nature's greatest
    need 20; trumps human rights 6, 60
self 37, 46, 279, 281; *see also* identity
self-constitution 281–2
self-determination 96–7
semantic flexibility of the term 'human
    rights' 8–9, 56
sense 292
sentimental education 72, 79
Shamir, Yitzhak 248
Al-Sheikh, Ameen Sa'eed 119
Shell 81
'shock and awe' 265–6
Short, Michael 206
signifiers 46, 55–7
Simma, Bruno 202–3, 226–7
Slaughter, Anne-Marie 177, 203, 208
Slaughter, Joseph 81
Smith, Adam 76–7
social contract 19
socialism 20
social rights 41
sociology 20
Socrates 16
Soros, George 80
South African Constitution 275
sovereigns 35, 117, 171, 232, 256–7;
    see also national sovereignty;
    sovereignty
sovereignty 229–32, 242–4, 250,
    269–70; bare 271–4, 296;
    cosmopolitan 288–90; and justice
    284–8; questioning of 294–5;
    theological 276–83, 289; *see also*
    sovereigns; national sovereignty
Soviet Union 22, 28, 32
space 261, 264
species ethics 53n5, 54
speech, freedom of 188
Stalinists 81
state authoritarianism 19
stateless persons 99

state of exception 5n8, 6, 255–6; and
sovereign power 117, 171, 232,
269; and theological sovereignty
279–82
Stoics 17, 51, 152–8
subjectivity 7, 39, 53, 93, 99, 284,
287
sublime 265
suffering 69, 72–4, 76–8
supranational right 183
surveillance 114–15
symbolic otherness 85–6
sympathy 75, 77

Taylor, Charles 43
technology of war 259–63
Teitel, Ruti 182–3
ten commandments 18, 278
terror, war on 3, 258, 288–9
terrorist attacks 4, 6, 60–1, 257–8,
261
Teson, Fernando 245
theological sovereignty 276–83, 289
theory of human rights 14
Tokyo war crime tribunals 22, 28
Tomasevski, Katarina 189
torture 4–5, 119–20, 212, 234
totalitarianism 282
trade 231
treaties 30, 181, 211–12, 231

Uncle Tom's Cabin (Stowe) 78
uniqueness 44n14, 57
United Kingdom 30n28, 60, 114; anti-
terrorist legislation 121; empire 134;
English constitutional theory 282–3;
Iraq war 209, 215; just war 249
United Nations 15, 23, 25, 27;
compound in Iraq 62;
cosmopolitanism 142, 163; Human
Rights Commission 24, 28–9, 31n34;
just war 244; Kosovo war 202–3;
Security Council 180, 199, 201,
210–11; violence 252–5; world
constitutions 226–8
United States 27–32; Abu Ghraib 78,
117–20, 196, 213; Afghanistan 63;
Agency of International Development
(USAID) 61; cosmopolitan
communism 146; Guantánamo Bay
59, 117–18, 196, 212; humanitarian
imperialists 138–41; ideology 146,
185–6, 223; imaginary identification

267; imperialism 135–8, 143–4, 255;
international law 217, 225;
interpretation of Geneva Convention
195–6; Iraq war 170, 211–13, 224;
Kosovo war 206, 254–5; military
superiority 259–61, 265–6; neo-
liberal economic policies 192;
Nicaragua 213n43; sovereignty 230,
232, 257; War of Independence 15,
242, 252; see also American Bill of
Rights; American Constitution;
American Declaration of
Independence
universal, the 92–5, 97–8, 195, 275,
278
Universal Declaration of Human Rights
10, 15, 28, 75, 96, 180
universalisation 181
universalist exceptionalism 195
universalists 54, 208
universal jurisdiction 22
universities, history of vi–viii, x
utilitarianism 205
utopias 148, 160, 174, 286, 296–8

values 184, 186–7, 221, 246, 285,
289–93
Venezuela 196
victims 69–70, 84, 88
violations of human rights, experiences
of 14
violence 250–7, 265–8, 287–8, 290;
see also wars
visual politics of humanitarianism 76–8;
see also images of suffering and
violence; pornography
Vitoria, Francisco de 239, 241
Vogelin, Eric 158
voyeurism 77–8

Waal, Alex de 66
Waiting for the Barbarians (Coetzee)
149
Wallerstein, Immanuel 83, 99, 194
Walzer, Michael 63, 65, 245
war crimes 21–2, 28, 258, 260
war on terror 3, 114, 212, 255, 258,
288–9
war prisoners 58–9; see also Abu
Ghraib; Guantánamo Bay
wars 163, 172, 252–3; of aggression
214; and cosmopolitan sovereignty
288–9; laws of 58; and policing

241–3, 257–9; pre-emptive 265; and technology 259–63; *see also* Iraq war; just war, concepts of; Kosovo war; military humanitarianism; violence; war crimes; war prisoners; war on terror
weapons of mass destruction 211
Weber, Max 20, 167, 221
William of Ockham 18
Wilson, Woodrow 137, 141
Wolff, Christian 239
Wolfowitz, Paul 265
women's rights 105–6
Wood, Ellen Meiksins 232, 267
Woolf, Greg 159

World Bank 124–5, 190, 226
world constitutions 162, 170,189, 226–33
worldlessness 292
World Trade Organization (WTO) 190–1, 226, 231

Al-Yasseri, Nori Samir Gunbar 118
Yugoslavia *see* Kosovo War

Zartaloudis, Thanos 8, 178n3
Zeno 153–5, 297–8
Zizek, Slavoj 86, 104–5, 128, 292
zoe 116
Zolo, Danilo 164